THE SHOOTING

All Nutty and Rick wanted to do was get away from that table without getting shot. Bill Matiyek showed them the gun.

"Nobody moves from this table!"

Neither Sauvé nor Comeau saw the gunman approaching from Matiyek's left, everything happened so fast. Rick's gaze was riveted to Bill's as the three shots rang out, deafening at so close a range, and Matiyek's head seemed to come apart before Rick's horrified gaze. It wasn't like seeing somebody get shot on TV. He couldn't take his eyes off Matiyek, who looked pained and then slumped over to his right. It all happened in a split second, but it seemed like slow motion, an instant replay that would rerun itself endlessly inside Rick's head.

Nutty knew right away that he'd been shot, too; he could feel it, high in his left arm. He forced himself to stop, to see if the stray bullet had hit any vital organs, but it didn't seem to have gone into his chest. He felt relieved. And then, like almost everyone else in the Queen's Hotel that night, Nutty Comeau started to run like hell.

ALSO BY MICK LOWE

One Woman Army: The Life of Claire Culhane, 1992
Premature Bonanza: Standoff at Voisey's Bay, 1998.

CONSPIRACY
OF
BROTHERS

A TRUE STORY OF BIKERS, MURDER, AND THE LAW

MICK LOWE

VINTAGE CANADA

VINTAGE CANADA EDITION, 2013

Published in Canada by Vintage Canada, a division of Random House of Canada Limited, Toronto, in 2013. Originally published in hardcover by Macmillan of Canada in 1988, and paperback in Canada by Seal Books, a division of Random House of Canada Limited, in 1989. Distributed by Random House of Canada Limited.

Unless otherwise noted, photographs are from the collection of Bill Lavoie.

Lyrics on pp. 61–63 from "We've Got Tonight" reprinted with kind permission of Gear Publishing Company, a division of Hideout Records and Distributors, Inc. Lyrics on p. 321 are Copyright 1966 by Dwarf Music. All rights reserved. International copyright secured. Reprinted by permission.

Vintage Canada with colophon is a registered trademark.

www.randomhouse.ca

Library and Archives Canada Cataloguing in Publication

Lowe, Mick, 1947–
    Conspiracy of brothers : a true story of bikers, murder and the law / Mick Lowe.

Issued also in electronic format.

ISBN 978-0-345-81316-9

    1. Satan's Choice Motorcycle Club. 2. Matiyek, Bill. 3. Murder—Ontario—Port Hope.
4. Trials (Murder)—Ontario—London. I. Title.

HV6535.C33P65 2013   364.152'30971356   C2012-908024-1

Book design by Andrew Roberts
Image credits: Claydowling Harley / Easy Vectors, human skull model / Lotophagl / Dreamstime.com

Printed and bound in the United States of America

2 4 6 8 9 7 5 3 1

for Ruth Reyno, after all

CONTENTS

THE BROTHERHOODS

THE BIKERS

SATAN'S CHOICE MOTORCYCLE CLUB, TORONTO CHAPTER:

GARY *"Nutty"* COMEAU

JEFF McLEOD

LARRY *"Beaver"* HURREN

ARMAND SANGUIGNI

LORNE CAMPBELL

SATAN'S CHOICE MOTORCYCLE CLUB, PETERBOROUGH CHAPTER:

RICHARD *"Rick"* SAUVÉ

MURRAY (MERV) *"Indian"* BLAKER

GORDON *"Dogmap"* VAN HAARLEM

SATAN'S CHOICE MOTORCYCLE CLUB, KITCHENER CHAPTER:

DAVID *"Tee Hee"* HOFFMAN

CLAUDE *"Gootch"* MORIN

NEIL *"Porker"* STEWART

GOLDEN HAWK RIDERS MOTORCYCLE CLUB, PORT HOPE CHAPTER:

LAWRENCE LEON
BILL *"Heavy"* MATIYEK

THE OUTLAWS MOTORCYCLE CLUB:

FRED JONES
SONNY BRONSON

THE COPPERS

SERGEANT SAMUEL McREELIS,
Port Hope Police Department, Ontario
INSPECTOR COLIN COUSENS, *Criminal Investigations Branch (Homicide), Ontario Provincial Police, Toronto*
CORPORAL TERRY HALL, *Commanding Officer, Special (Biker) Squad, Intelligence Branch, Ontario Provincial Police, Toronto*
CONSTABLE DONALD DENIS,
Special (Biker) Squad, Ontario Provincial Police, Toronto

THE LAWYERS

AT TRIAL:

HOWARD KERBEL, *Toronto, for Gary Comeau*
BRUCE AFFLECK, *Oshawa, for Jeff McLeod*
DAVID NEWMAN, *Toronto, for Larry Hurren*
BERNARD *"Bernie"* CUGELMAN, *Peterborough, for Armand Sanguigni*

JOHN ROSEN, *Toronto, for Lorne Campbell*
JACK GROSSMAN, *Toronto, for Rick Sauvé*
TERENCE *"Terry"* O'HARA, *Kingston, for Merv Blaker*
DONALD EBBS, *Peterborough, for Gordon van Haarlem*
EDWARD MARTIN, *Toronto, for David Hoffman*
CHRIS MEINHARDT, *Lindsay, Senior Crown Attorney*
ROLAND HARRIS, *Cobourg, Junior Crown Attorney*

ON APPEAL:

ROSS MCKAY, *Toronto, for Gary Comeau*
EDWARD *"Eddie"* GREENSPAN, *Toronto, for Jeff McLeod*
CLAYTON RUBY, *Toronto, for Lary Hurren*
ALAN GOLD, *Toronto, for Rick Sauvé*
TERRY O'HARA, *Kingston, for Merv Blaker*
BRIAN GREENSPAN, *Toronto, for David Hoffman*

THE JUDGES

AT TRIAL:

THE HONOURABLE MR. JUSTICE COULTER OSBORNE,
Cambridge, Ontario, Supreme Court, Trial Division

ON APPEAL:

THE HONOURABLE JUSTICES JESSUP, ARNUP, AND MORDEN,
Ontario Supreme Court, Appeals Division

BOOK ONE

THE NIGHT

"The seed of our destruction will blossom in the desert, the alexin of our cure grows by a mountain rock, and our lives are haunted by a Georgia slattern, because a London cutpurse went unhung. Each moment is the fruit of forty thousand years. The minute-winning days, like flies, buzz home to death, and every moment is a window on all time."

—THOMAS WOLFE, *Look Homeward, Angel*

I

CATHY COTGRAVE STIFLED A YAWN as her eyes swept over the deserted taproom of the Queen's Hotel for perhaps the hundredth time that day. It wasn't shaping up to be a particularly memorable night. The big, L-shaped room, licensed to seat 220, held at most a dozen patrons. It was early yet, the end of the supper hour, when most of the ten thousand residents of Port Hope, Ontario, were at home finishing dinner with their families, the time when only the most earnest of drinkers would forgo a meal in favour of alcohol. But there was none of the promise of a busy night to come that Cathy sometimes sensed during the slack period of the dinner hour.

Though only nineteen, Cotgrave was already an experienced barmaid—cocky, bright, and alert. Like any good waitress, she was constantly aware of her customers, their drinks, and her surroundings—such as they were. She noted automatically, without really seeing, the bar's dingy interior—the tacky red velvet wallpaper, darkened by a decade of smoke and grime, the round Formica-topped tables, each one surrounded by four wooden captain's chairs, their seats and backs upholstered in dull black leatherette.

Her gaze settled, finally, on a table at the far corner of the room, the only table that was providing a brisk business. There were three rough-looking men at the table, and an equally tough-looking woman, and Cathy knew them all: Bill Matiyek, Fred Jones, Sonny Bronson, and the woman, Jamie Hanna. Though she barely knew the latter three, Cathy considered Bill a good friend. In fact, she'd eaten breakfast with him at Turck's Restaurant earlier in the day. Afterwards they'd gone to her apartment and smoked a joint of Bill's grass, dropped into the hotel briefly, and then driven over to Newcastle to see a friend of Bill's. Matiyek had brought her back to Port Hope in his truck in time to start her three-o'clock swing shift at the hotel.

Cathy liked Bill a lot, a sentiment that was not shared by everyone in Port Hope, where many people considered him the town bully. At the age of twenty-three Bill Matiyek was a veritable grizzly of a man, standing six foot three, weighing nearly three hundred pounds. His massive torso and great belly seemed to overflow the wraparound wooden arms of his chair, and its legs creaked precariously whenever Bill shifted his weight or roared in gales of laughter at something Fred or Sonny said. That was Bill, Cathy thought, with a giant's appetite for living, laughing, fighting, or drinking. He was just as expansive with money. He earned big money at his job on the pipeline, and he wasn't afraid to spend it, especially on his women friends. However mean Bill might be around some people, he was always a perfect gentleman around most women and all children—warm, sensitive, gentle, and generous. Too bad Bill wasn't buying his own drinks tonight, Cathy caught herself thinking. He was a good tipper. He'd bought the first round, but Fred seemed to do all the buying after that, and he wasn't nearly as open-handed. Maybe Fred was repaying Bill for the bennies—the little white diet pills—that the big man was sharing with his friends. As Cathy watched, Lawrence Leon joined the foursome at Bill's table.

Bill was delighted to see Lawrence. They shook hands warmly, biker-style, thumbs up, forearms almost touching. With Lawrence here, Bill's day was now complete, and this was a day he'd looked forward to for months—the first day of his winter-long layoff from the pipeline. All summer he'd labored in the deep, endless trench, throwing heavy wooden pallets out of the muck and over his head with no more apparent effort than a normal man might show heaving a piece of stove wood. Now, a long, lazy winter stretched ahead: partying, drawing pogey, maybe augmenting that income with the odd dope deal.

Besides being best friends, Bill and Lawrence were also brothers of sorts, because they were both officers in the same motorcycle club—the Golden Hawk Riders. Lawrence was President and Bill was the second-in-command, the Sergeant-at-Arms. It was true the Hawks had only seven members, but they were genuine "one-percenters" nonetheless, true out-laws. Bill was pleased to have Lawrence see him here with Fred and Sonny, because they were members of *the* Outlaws, the second most powerful club on the continent. Headquartered in Chicago, the Outlaws were the biggest club in Detroit, west to the Mississippi, south through Dayton, Ohio, and Atlanta, and right into Florida. They'd spread north into Ontario just eighteen months before by taking over several chapters of the Satan's Choice, which had been Canada's largest club. Sonny and Fred were former Choice, and the fact they'd come to see him was a great honour. That thought, plus the tingling rush of the bennies, the countless double ryes, and the expectation of the winter ahead, filled Bill with a warm glow of satisfaction.

The four men fell into the easy, obscene banter common among bikers. The conversation was mundane—Harleys, parties, drug deals and busts, who was in prison, who was at war with whom. Bill and Lawrence regaled the more senior bikers with tales of their trip last April to Daytona, Florida, to the annual Daytona Splash, the largest gathering of outlaw bikers in the world. Thousands of clubbers from across the continent converge on the east Florida beach town each spring, and the ear-splitting roar of Harley engines fills the streets and echoes off the tawdry storefronts from noon each day until long after dark. Bill and Lawrence described in coarse detail the beautiful American broads in their skimpy bikinis who lined Main Street Avenue to watch the non-stop, wheel-to-wheel procession of men and their metal. It had been Bill's first trip to Bike Week, though Lawrence had gone many times. One year, Lawrence never tired of boasting, he'd even had his picture printed up in *Easyriders*, the glossy American biker magazine. Jamie Hanna was studiously ignored by the four men at her table, and this, too, was typical.

Bill truly loved the world of outlaw motorcycle clubs. The no-nonsense way that one biker had with another true brother, the total and absolute freedom. Bill was not one to be pushed around, and he loved to fight—he'd probably started more than his share—but with his size he was the match of any two or three normal-sized men. The club was a way out for Bill—a way to get off his parents' farm in the hills north of Port Hope, a way to be somebody and to escape the drudgery of life on the pipeline.

But the Life had its darker side, too. For this was a world of hair-trigger tempers and hair-triggers, period. Bill was ready for that. He was, in fact, a walking, talking one-man arsenal. His favourite weapon was his .410 double-barrelled, sawed-off shotgun. With its shiny nickel-plated barrels it was a lovely, illegal, and, at close range, highly lethal piece. It looked like something a riverboat gambler might have carried, fitting quite nicely up Bill's sleeve or down the top of one of his black, hand-tooled cowboy boots. Lately he'd even taken to packing another chunk, a little .32-calibre pistol he'd borrowed from his friend Neil Caplan, a part owner of the Queen's. It nestled now in the left-hand pocket of his red-and-black-checked lumberjack shirt.

Bill loved to flash the .410. Sometimes, riding his bike on the country roads north of town, he'd pull it from his boot and, for the sheer joy of it, blast a farmer's fencepost with both barrels, watching the sturdy wooden post atomize before his eyes. But the .32 was his little secret, and he carried it even now, surrounded as he was by friends. For beneath his daunting exterior, running like a disquieting river under the warm flow of the speed and the rye and the grass, Bill Matiyek harbored a deep and abiding fear, mingled with hatred: he lived in utter terror of Satan's Choice, the motorcycle club that Sonny and Fred had betrayed, and that he and Lawrence, by reviving the Golden Hawks, had defied. But tonight, among friends and with his fears at bay, Bill Matiyek downed another round of double rye.

Outside the eternal gloom of the Queen's the autumn sun was setting, the shadows lengthening along Walton Street and its row of three-storey Victorian buildings—some of the finest Main Street "Heritage Architecture" in all of Canada. Across Walton from the Queen's Hotel the proprietors of Cortesis Jewellers and Guardian Drugs had rolled up their awnings, emptied their tills, and gone home to dinner. Later they might spend a quiet evening with their families watching television. *Mork and Mindy* was the smash new sitcom of the season and two John Wayne movies were listed in the TV guide for that night.

But inside the Queen's a true-life Canadian drama was about to unfold, unexpected and unscripted. It was 6:30 p.m., Wednesday, October 18, 1978.

Tee Hee and Porker arrived at the clubhouse of the Kitchener-Waterloo Chapter of the Satan's Choice Motorcycle Club shortly before seven. They were planning to meet Gootch—Tee Hee had planned the whole thing in detail—and it was typical of David "Tee Hee" Hoffman that he would arrive a few minutes early for an appointment. Porker wheeled his old Biscayne into the paint-store parking lot beside the clubhouse and the two men ambled across the empty lot to the clubhouse door. But the heavy steel door opened from the inside as they approached and two strangers stepped out to meet them. Coppers.

"Fellas, there's a little investigation going on in here, and you can't come in till we're through. Would you mind waiting outside?"

Tee Hee looked at Porker, then back at the cops. He shrugged, and the two bikers returned to the Chevy. Another raid was no big deal, especially to Tee Hee, who was, at the age of thirty, a veteran member of the Satan's Choice. Both men had a pretty good idea what it was all about—a woman had claimed she was raped in the clubhouse a few nights earlier, and whoever the police were after, Tee Hee and Porker knew it wasn't them. The two men sat idly in the car for a half-hour or so. It struck them as funny—or highly incompetent—because while the cops were inside, doing their thing, several members whom Tee Hee reckoned the police might have wanted to question about the skin beef also came into the parking lot, saw him and Porker sitting in the car, figured out something was wrong, and quickly took off again. Tee Hee smiled inwardly.

Had he known who was inside the ramshackle two-storey clubhouse, the big biker might have been more concerned. There were, in all, a dozen officers, representing four different police forces. The Waterloo Regional Police, who had the local jurisdiction, were there in force, with both plainclothes and uniformed officers. The Ontario Provincial Police were represented by Corporal Terry Hall, the commander of the OPP's Special Squad, Intelligence Branch, better known within motorcycle circles as the "biker squad," and Constable Donald Denis, who was also assigned to the squad. A member of the Metro Toronto Police biker squad was present. Even the Royal Canadian Mounted Police had a man there. It was an imposing array of elite law-enforcement specialists for such a routine investigation.

At last one of the officers signalled to Tee Hee and Porker. The police were beginning to leave the clubhouse, their business apparently finished, and one of them, a plainclothes dick from Kitchener, told Tee Hee he could go inside, to make sure that everything was in order and that nothing had been damaged. Porker was told to wait outside.

Tee Hee's selection to make the inspection was not accidental. He was widely known and respected by the police present, who also considered him something of an enigma. And Tee Hee was an unusual character, even by Choice standards. Outwardly every inch a biker, with his long ponytail and Fu Manchu moustache, vaguely menacing by his very size—almost as wide as he was tall—Tee Hee Hoffman was much more than a stereotypical biker. There were two clues to his nature in his external appearance: his glasses and his choice of footwear. Hoffman wore horn-rimmed spectacles, a rarity in club circles, but a necessity for a man who spent eight hours a day doing close work; and he almost never wore the heavy leather boots that were a mandatory and practical part of biker apparel. Boots were essential for kicking the heavy kickstart pedal on a balky Harley, and useful for just plain stomping whenever the need arose. But Tee Hee preferred running shoes, and he wore them as long as the weather would permit.

Hoffman coolly appraised the six rooms of his clubhouse: on the main floor, the large clubroom with its bar at one end, a juke box, and an air conditioner that never seemed to work, the floor tiles cracked and chipped by hard use; upstairs, the smaller rooms, one of which contained a grubby mattress lying on the floor. Everything appeared to be copacetic. He had also noticed Terry Hall leaving the building, and Hall had noticed him. Tee Hee had glowered; the cocksure Hall had smiled back.

The burly biker shrugged his approval, and the rest of the coppers began to leave, some of the younger, uniformed ones stealing a last curious glance at Hoffman. He was a tough one to figure out. Here was a guy who'd been a Choice for over ten years and yet he had virtually no criminal record. He held a steady job, in fact he'd had only one job in his whole working life, as a bookkeeper for B. F. Goodrich, where he'd worked since he was nineteen. Despite his club affiliation he was a model employee, respected and trusted by his supervisors, who were gradually promoting him to more responsible positions within the company hierarchy.

To the police, all of this meant only one thing: Hoffman had been very smart so far and his greatest value to the club lay in his ability to handle the ever-increasing cash flow that was pouring into club coffers, the police were certain, from a wide range of criminal activities that included stolen goods, prostitution, and drug-trafficking.

Tee Hee stood at the front door of the clubhouse as the last of the cops departed. The lock, he noticed, had been badly damaged when the coppers had busted in. Porker entered finally, and by then Tee Hee knew exactly what he would do, for his mind, as befitted a man who worked with numbers, was orderly, precise, logical.

Porker would go to buy a new lock—the clubhouse could not remain unlocked overnight. Then Tee Hee would call Claude "Gootch" Morin, the chapter president, to tell him about the raid and that the coast was clear. Finally, he'd have to phone Stratford, where he and Porker and Gootch had been heading before the raid. All their plans were ruined now, anyway.

Tee Hee, so nicknamed by his club brothers because of his high-pitched, tittering laugh, possessed a keen sense of humor. He might have paused, then, to savor the rich irony of the moment. Here he was, treasurer of the

K-W Chapter of the Satan's Choice, an organization that had, only eighteen months before, been compared to the Mafia by police officials quoted in the local newspaper. His sinister plans for this particular evening had been to drive to Stratford, to a shop called "Costumes by Colleen," to rent Halloween outfits for the annual Vagabonds Halloween party in Toronto, slated for one week from Friday.

But Hoffman didn't pause. He reached for the clubhouse phone and dialled Gootch's number. As he did so, a tape recorder clicked on in a building adjacent to the clubhouse. As he talked to Gootch, the reels on the machine turned slowly, in total silence, faithfully recording every word of their conversation. It was exactly 7:36 p.m.

While Tee Hee Hoffman was making his inspection of the Kitchener clubhouse, another waitress, Gayle Thompson, was beginning her shift at the Queen's Hotel. She usually worked through until the one-o'clock closing, and, if necessary, Cathy would work through her usual quitting-time of 11 p.m. It sometimes got quite busy in the bar then, as the afternoon-shift workers from Eldorado Nuclear, Wire and Cable, and Davidson Rubber got off work. Often they'd drop into the Queen's to ogle the strippers and have a few beers, but tonight there was no live entertainment and Gayle could see right away that it looked to be a long, dull evening. When it was quiet like this she and Cathy would both work the whole room, sharing the tips, and Gayle, too, began to serve Bill Matiyek's table.

In many ways, Gayle Thompson and Cathy Cotgrave were remarkably similar. Both were mature for their years, and both felt at home in the tough environment of the Queen's. Like Cathy, Gayle considered Bill Matiyek a good friend, he drank so often at the hotel. He sure knew how to party. Sometimes Bill would get so drunk that he'd start to throw people out of the hotel himself after closing-time, just for the fun of it. It was a standing joke among hotel employees that they should watch Bill closely at the end of a long day's drinking. If he passed out, he weighed so much that all of the staff together couldn't lift him. They'd have to lock him in, and just leave him there until morning.

At about 7:30 Lawrence Leon rose to leave the group at Bill's table. They all urged him to stay, but Lawrence had promised his wife that he'd be home after just one drink, and for once he meant to keep his word. Actually, he'd had three or four drinks in the space of an hour as Fred Jones kept ordering more rounds. The president of the Golden Hawk Riders could see that the others were already half-pissed as he departed.

The evening began to sour a little for the remaining foursome at the corner table after eight o'clock with the arrival of Brian Brideau. Brideau was known to all the Queen's regulars as a speeder, a real street freak, who never seemed to have enough money to support his habit.

Brideau flitted from table to table in the barroom, all twitchy and hyper, hustling drinks or money or both, and no one paid much attention until he got to Bill's table. Matiyek strongly disliked Brideau, considering him a real bug, and the little speed freak's tendency to hang out with the Satan's Choice did nothing to endear him to Matiyek.

Brideau had been bugging Matiyek for money, or for some of Bill's bennies, and an argument started. Bill hooked Brideau, and before anyone knew what was happening both Bill and Fred Jones were on top of Brideau, Matiyek holding him down on the floor while Fred kicked him in the head. It made quite a commotion in the almost empty bar, and Gayle Thompson moved quickly to Matiyek's table and ordered the three of them to take it outside, which they did. Bill and Fred beat Brideau thoroughly before returning to their table. They'd just gotten settled back in when Brideau ran into the barroom, still breathless and shaking. He pointed a finger at Bill. "The next time I see you," he screamed, so loud Cathy Cotgrave could hear him halfway across the room, "your head will be at the end of a shotgun!" With that, Brideau stormed out of the bar, but not the hotel. He stopped at a bank of pay phones in the lobby, lifted the receiver, took a deep breath, and began to make good his threat against Bill Matiyek.

II

RICK SAUVÉ HAD JUST FINISHED putting his four-year-old daughter, Angie to bed when the phone rang. The caller was Brian Brideau. He told Sauvé he'd just been at the Queen's, that Bill Matiyek was in there drinking with two Outlaws, Fred Jones and Sonny Bronson. They had started talking about the Choice, and they told Brideau they wanted to have a meeting with an officer from the Peterborough Chapter. Brideau just thought Rick should know. Sauvé thanked him and hung up.

Rick Sauvé had been a member of the Satan's Choice Peterborough Chapter for less than a year, and he wasn't sure what he should do about Brideau's call. He knew that most of the club's Peterborough Chapter officers were in jail, awaiting trial on a rape charge. Two members were up in Peterborough, probably in a hotel bar somewhere, but Sauvé doubted he'd be able to find either of them. It was a half-hour drive from his house on the outskirts of Port Hope to Peterborough, and besides, since his wife Sharon was at work he couldn't leave Angie alone.

Of course, there was always Merv. He was a real old-timer in the club and he should be at home. Rick remembered Merv had had a number of teeth pulled on Monday and was off work all week. Sauvé called Merv Blaker's number and told him about the call from Brideau. Did Merv know where any of the other Peterborough Chapter guys might be? He didn't. Rick said he'd try to find some other members, he'd call Merv back, and they could all go down to the Queen's and check out what was going on. Merv said that was fine by him.

So there were two of them now, at least, Rick thought. But he wasn't about to walk into that bar with just Merv to back the play. Merv's club nickname was "Indian," because he was an Ojibway. Merv was the quietest, most easygoing guy you'd ever want to meet, at least until he started drinking. Even though he had been in the club since 1967, Merv wasn't much of a scrapper. In fact, he came about as close to being a non-violent outlaw biker as anybody in the whole club. No, Rick would need more brothers than just Merv.

He wondered what was going down at the Queen's. Sauvé knew Matiyek fairly well: he was more than a passing acquaintance but less than a friend. Rick knew that Bill was a close friend of his older brother, Larry, and that the two families, the Sauvés and the Matiyeks, were related by marriage. Sauvé himself had had several run-ins with Bill Matiyek, as had others in the Peterborough Chapter. Most of the hassles had been started by one Choice member, though—Tommy "Retard" Horner. Retard's nickname said it all—he'd fight anybody, any time, anywhere, for no reason at all, and he and Matiyek couldn't spend ten minutes in the same room together without going at each other. But Horner was in jail now, too.

Sauvé was on less certain ground when it came to the two Outlaws. He knew who they were, knew that they'd switched patch from Choice to Outlaws before he'd joined the club, and that a state of near war had existed between the two clubs for a time. And now, here they were not five minutes' drive from his house, and they wanted a sit-down with an officer from the Choice. Sauvé considered all these things before making his next move. It was 9:19 p.m. when he finally reached for the phone and placed a long-distance call to the Satan's Choice clubhouse in Toronto. As he did so, Sauvé had no way of knowing that Brian Brideau had failed to impart two vital pieces of information: first, that he had just been beaten up by Matiyek and Jones, and second, and more important, that Bill Matiyek was carrying a gun.

Nutty Comeau happened to answer the clubhouse phone. Sauvé told him briefly what the situation was: that Matiyek and two Outlaws were drinking down at the Queen's, that they said they wanted a meeting with an officer from the Peterborough Chapter, that Rick couldn't locate any officers, just Merv.

Nutty looked around the clubhouse. There were a fair number of guys around because the weekly chapter meeting had just ended, but he doubted that any of them wanted to make the hour's drive to Port Hope. "Can't you guys down there handle this? Try again to find some of your own guys," he told Sauvé. "If you still can't find anybody, call us back."

Comeau knew that Rick Sauvé was a greenhorn, but everybody had just gotten comfortable at the Markham Road clubhouse, drinking beer, watching the Maple Leafs play one of their first home games of the season on TV. Mike Palmateer was in goal against the Sabres and the teams had played to a scoreless tie in the first period. It was a good hockey game and what the hell, maybe the Leafs were even going to have a decent season for a change. Comeau cracked open another beer and went to join the other guys in front of the TV.

Nutty Comeau was no greenhorn. His real name was Gary, but his nickname suited him perfectly. He was full of nervous energy, always in motion, always mouthing off, playing practical jokes, scheming, and always in trouble. He'd joined the Satan's Choice back in 1970, when he was just eighteen. Now twenty-six, Nutty was a veteran biker with a long criminal record.

His first criminal conviction had been for a minor offence, a $100 fine for possession of hashish; and the second beef was just plain bad luck. He'd gotten pinched for driving while impaired, but he was using false ID. He was released on his own recognizance, but the radio stations reported the charge, under the assumed name. It turned out that the hot ID had belonged to a former copper, whose mother heard about it on the radio and called the police. He was convicted twice: for driving while impaired, and for "acknowledging bail," a rare charge based on the fact that he'd signed out on his own recognizance under a false name.

A year later he'd copped a plea on indecent assault after a clubhouse party. Gary always claimed it was a bullshit charge—the broad had pulled the train before, but this time someone at the clubhouse had stolen her ring and her money, which was stupid. When she got home her mother, who was on welfare, had started hassling her for the rent money. The woman was just a splasher, the type that was forever beating down the clubhouse door, but when she realized her money was gone she decided to lay charges. Some of the Vagabonds had pulled pen time on a similar skin beef only a few months before, and Nutty's lawyer worked out a plea bargain for some of the Choice members. Comeau served six months in the bucket, the only time he'd ever done. Now he was surviving on a pogey rip-off, running a few broads on the street, running errands for some of the other club guys, whatever was going down at the time.

It was just after 9:30 when Rick Sauvé called back. Once again Nutty took the call, and once again Rick said he couldn't find any of the Peterborough Chapter members. Comeau said he'd see what he could do, hung up the phone, and hollered around the clubhouse to see who wanted to go down to Port Hope. No one really did, but late in the second period Sittler put the Leafs two goals ahead and that sort of decided the issue. With Salming and Turnbull on defence and Palmateer in net it didn't look as if the Sabres would be able to come back. About a dozen guys drained their beers and headed for the door. Nutty grabbed a couple of travelers, to drink on the way down.

No one was entirely sure exactly why they were all driving to Port Hope. Some thought that Rick Sauvé himself was in trouble with the Outlaws and Matiyek. Some expected trouble with Matiyek, while others figured the hassle was with Jones and Bronson. Maybe they were trying to recruit Matiyek, to start a new Outlaw chapter in Port Hope, which was Choice territory. Others had never heard of Matiyek but sure didn't mind the chance to settle old scores with Jones and Bronson. A barroom brawl was as good a way to celebrate a Leafs victory as any.

As far as Jeff McLeod was concerned, he was going to Port Hope to render whatever assistance might be necessary. At six feet, 320 pounds, McLeod was certainly the right man for the job. With his full beard and long hair, which he often wore in a ponytail that stretched halfway down his back, Jeff was the very archetype of a big, dumb biker, truly frightening in demeanour and appearance. He was also best friends with Nutty, which was how it happened that they were in the same car. Nutty and Jeff were inseparable—both had grown up in Scarborough within a few miles of each other, though they hadn't really become friends until Jeff joined the club, five years after Comeau, in 1975. McLeod's police record was a lot shorter, too.

Lorne Campbell and Larry Hurren shared a second car. Dark, dangerous, and deceptively soft-spoken, Lorne was an iron-worker—a high-steel man—who supplemented his income by collecting bad debts, usually with a baseball bat and a partner to back his play. Although Lorne was, at thirty, just four years older than Larry, he still regarded Hurren as a kind of godson. He had, after all, given Larry his first ride on a Harley when Hurren was only sixteen, and then sponsored him into the club a few years later. Larry still possessed a certain boyish charm, especially when he smiled.

Armand Sanguigni was in a third car. Of all the members of the Satan's Choice who were speeding through the darkness towards Port Hope, Armand was far and away the scariest. He'd been a suspect in several murders—but there was never enough evidence to convict him. The police also considered him to be one of four members of the Satan's Choice with direct ties to the Mafia. (One of the others was Cecil Kirby, who had left the club two years earlier to become a professional mob hit man before turning police informer and, later, something of a media celebrity, to the everlasting shame of the Choice faithful.) Clean-shaven and not overly large, Sanguigni was also the straightest-looking of the Choice members barrelling down Highway 401 that night. With his handsome looks, Armand Sanguigni could have been mistaken for a college boy. He stood out from the others like a Honda on a club run.

Taken together, they would be twelve of the meanest, roughest tickets ever to darken the doors of the Queen's Hotel and that was a source of great pride and satisfaction to each of them. It gave them a sense of belonging, somehow.

III

THINGS WERE DEFINITELY BEGINNING to drag at Bill Matiyek's table. Just before ten o'clock Fred Jones and Jamie Hanna had gotten into an argument and Jones had slapped her. Neither Cathy nor Gayle was close enough to hear what the argument was about and neither actually saw Fred hit Jamie, but it was a quick, hard slap, and they both heard the "smack" of flesh on flesh.

Jamie left Bill's table then, and took a seat at another table near the bar. There was already an old man sitting there, pretty drunk, whom nobody knew. After a few minutes Bill came over to Jamie's new table to talk things over. He moved back and forth several times, and then Fred came over and sat down to apologize. He even ordered Jamie another beer as a peace offering.

A few more people drifted into the hotel. Sue Foote arrived around 10:30. She noticed the guys at Bill's table, Jamie Hanna at hers, and Rod Stewart at the bar, as she walked through the main lounge and into the shuffleboard room, a partitioned area in one corner of the larger room. Sue ordered a beer and started watching *McClintock*, just killing time until Cathy got off work at eleven. Like Bill and Jamie, Sue Foote was a regular at the Queen's, and she and Cathy had become roommates at the beginning of the month. They had planned to meet Cathy's boyfriend, Doug Peart, and a friend of his, Dave Gillispie, and then go to the Ganaraska, Port Hope's other hotel, for a few drinks. Doug and Dave arrived at around a quarter to eleven, and the three of them played shuffleboard for a while.

Rod Stewart had been in the Queen's, perched on a bar stool, since 8:30, but he hadn't really come there to drink. Stewart was a small-time Port Hope contractor and a member of the Town Council, and he had bid successfully on the job of renovating the gloomy interior of the hotel lounge. Stewart had come in to make some estimates and talk to one of the co-owners of the hotel, Leo Powell. He'd been joined by two friends who were drinking beer. Stewart was drinking Coke.

Neither Rod Stewart nor anyone else noticed the first of the Choice arrivals. Lorne Campbell and Larry Hurren reached the hotel before the others, because the rest had gone to Sauvé's house first, to get directions. Larry knew his way around Port Hope and had guided Lorne to the hotel. Hurren went up to the bar to get a drink and Lorne sat down quietly at a table and started to check things out. He spotted Matiyek right away—it was hard to miss him—and Bronson and Jones. The main Choice contingent, meanwhile, had arrived at Sauvé's. Merv was already there. Before leaving for the hotel they assigned the task of babysitting Angie to two strikers, or trial members.

As Lorne surveyed the peaceful barroom the house telephone rang. The call was for Bill Matiyek, and the big man left his table to take the call on the phone, which was mounted on a wooden post at the bar near Rod Stewart and his friends. Stewart was facing the telephone as Matiyek approached, and he noticed Matiyek stagger slightly as he neared the bar—the result, Stewart decided, of too much drink.

Bill was on the phone when the rest of the Choice members arrived. Sue Foote, who was still in the shuffleboard room, noticed Rick Sauvé and Merv Blaker come in the back door, as part of a larger group. They acknowledged her with a nod, and she smiled back. She knew both men fairly well, and had had dinner at Merv's house in the past.

Another group of Choice members entered the bar through the front door. None of them were flying colours; some were wearing green Hydro parkas, but almost everyone in the room knew Blaker and Sauvé and assumed that the men with them were Satan's Choice. Their arrival together had an enormous impact in the almost empty room. Suddenly a chill was on the evening and the air was heavy with apprehension.

Gayle Thompson felt a clutch of fear at her throat. She hated the Choice. Months before, Retard Horner had pinned her against the bar and threatened to kidnap her if the bartender didn't turn up the jukebox. She'd had no doubt he would have done it, too, if it hadn't been for the timely arrival of Merv Blaker, who'd managed to get Horner settled down. All members of the Satan's Choice had since been barred from the hotel; there was a notice to that effect pinned up behind the bar beside the ice bucket. Gayle went over to speak with Leo Powell, her boss, who was behind the bar. She told him she was certain that the new arrivals were members of the Satan's Choice, that they'd been barred by his own order, and that someone should get the police right away.

Cathy came over and agreed with Gayle. But Leo, to Gayle's immense disgust, seemed to hesitate. It dawned on Gayle that all Leo could see was dollar signs, sudden business on a slow night. He actually wanted them to serve these animals! It was almost eleven o'clock and time for Cathy to go off shift.

"Cash your float," Gayle told Cathy.

"No, no, Cathy, I want you to stay on and help Gayle," Leo insisted.

Rod Stewart was still watching Matiyek. Suddenly Bill seemed nervous, apprehensive. "It feels kind of lonely here," Stewart heard Matiyek say on the telephone. Finally Bill hung up and made his way back to his table.

To Cathy, there seemed to be great confusion as the Choice arrived. They milled around at first, making sure that everyone noticed them. Sauvé and Blaker took a table together not far from the corner of the bar where Rod Stewart was sitting. In the pinball room—another partitioned area at the opposite end of the barroom from the shuffleboard area—a group of the Choice led by a man whom she didn't then know but would later identify as Armand Sanguigni, were talking with Fred Jones. Jones looked kind of hysterical; he was waving his arms around. Cathy went over to Sauvé and Blaker's table and told them they were barred and weren't going to be served. The two bikers just looked up at her and shrugged.

Gary Comeau had arrived with the group that entered through the back door. He immediately noticed a woman sitting at a table with an old man in front of the service area of the bar. She looked kind of interesting and she obviously couldn't be with the old man . . . maybe this wouldn't be such a wasted evening after all. Comeau pulled out a chair at the table and ordered a "50" from one of the waitresses standing behind the bar only a few feet away.

Merv Blaker went up to the bar to get a book of matches and talk to the bartender, Rick Galbraith. Galbraith was a biker too, but not a clubber, and he'd known Merv for years. The Indian looked funny with half his teeth missing, and Rick kidded Merv about it. Larry Hurren was still at the bar and Galbraith, who had been off work all summer and didn't know the Choice were barred, had served him.

Gayle Thompson was waiting for the trouble to start when Leo, along with Julie Joncas, his girlfriend and the head waitress, left the hotel. They said they were going for the cops—the Port Hope police station was across a small park just behind the hotel—but Gayle never forgave the hotel owner for leaving when he did. Wasn't a captain supposed to be the last man off a sinking ship?

Rod Stewart and his friends were still in their stools at the bar. Stewart's back was turned to most of the Choice, which made him distinctly uneasy. With his voice lowered, Stewart asked his friends whether they all shouldn't leave. They decided against it—they didn't want to draw attention to themselves.

Dave Gillispie emerged from the shuffleboard room and walked across the lounge to chat with Sauvé and Blaker. Gary Galbraith, the bartender's younger brother, was a Choice striker and he'd cracked up his bike the day before. Gillispie had heard about Gary's accident and he squatted between Sauvé and Blaker to ask how Galbraith was doing and whether his bike was totalled—maybe he'd want to sell some parts off it?

Gary Comeau tried to strike up a conversation with the broad. She asked him if he was in a bike club. Gary said he was—Satan's Choice.

"Oooooh." She seemed impressed. "What's your name?"

"Nutty's my nickname." But after that there was a lull in the conversation, and Gary began to grow impatient. And he still hadn't gotten his beer. What was going on here, anyway?

Finally Sauvé decided to approach Matiyek. He at least knew the guy, and was from the local chapter. He sat down directly across the table from Matiyek. Right away he could see that Bill was drunk.

"What's happenin'?" Sauvé demanded. "What's the trip goin' on here? You guys wanted to see us?"

To Rick's surprise, Matiyek didn't seem to know what he was talking about. "No," the big man answered, "but I'm impressed."

"You're impressed?"

"Yeah, you got so many friends here. But I got nine friends here, too. Anybody comes toward me, you're gettin' it."

"Whaddaya mean, I'm gettin' it?" Sauvé leaned warily back in his chair. Matiyek, too, leaned away from the table, enough so that Sauvé could see the gun pointing at him from inside Bill's pocket, with the big man's left hand on the butt.

Rick Sauvé was completely unnerved. He'd never had a gun pointed at him before, and he could see that Matiyek was very frightened, and very drunk. He tried to soothe Bill, calm him down, by speaking softly and not making any threatening gestures. Sauvé also shifted around in his chair, trying to inconspicuously squeeze himself out of Matiyek's line of fire, but it was impossible at such close range.

After a minute or so Jamie Hanna appeared at the table. She sat down in a chair to Bill's right. Rick was scared and he wanted her to get away. He leaned across the table towards Matiyek. "Bill, this broad shouldn't be sittin' here. We got somethin' we gotta discuss."

"Yeah, you're right," Matiyek agreed. "Jamie, you'd better leave."

Then Nutty came up, and sat down in the chair Jamie had just left. "What's happenin'?"

"You make one move and your bro's gettin' it," Matiyek warned, showing Comeau the top of the gun. "You got a lot of fuckin' bros here tonight, eh? I'm fed up with your fuckin' bullshit, you guys buggin' me. . . . I'll tell you somethin' right now. You got a lotta guys here, but if I go to the hospital, nine of youse are comin' with me."

Another Choice member approached the table.

"You get the fuck outta here," Matiyek growled, "or you're gettin' it, too." The man backed off.

All Nutty and Rick wanted to do was get away from that table without getting shot. "What the fuck you doin', man? We're splittin'."

"No! Nobody moves from this table!"

Nutty looked nervously across the room to see if his beer had come yet, but Sauvé never took his eyes off Matiyek's, as if to hold him motionless. He would never forget the look in those eyes—so drunk and so scared, so very, very scared.

Neither Sauvé nor Comeau saw the gunman approaching from Matiyek's left, everything happened so fast. Sauvé knew this much—the last thing Matiyek saw in this life was Rick's own face. Rick's gaze was still riveted to Bill's as the three shots rang out, deafening at so close a range, and Matiyek's head seemed to come apart before Rick's horrified gaze. It wasn't like seeing somebody get shot on TV. He couldn't take his eyes off Matiyek, who looked pained and then slumped over to his right. It all happened in a split second, but it seemed like slow motion, an instant replay that would rerun itself endlessly inside Rick's head.

Nutty knew right away that he'd been shot, too; he could feel it, high in his left arm. He and Rick jumped up, panic-stricken. The hard, menacing exteriors of the members of the Satan's Choice evaporated in an instant, and each of them bolted like frightened rabbits for the doors. Comeau forced himself to stop, to see if the stray bullet had hit any vital organs, but it didn't seem to have gone into his chest. He felt relieved. And then, like almost everyone else in the Queen's Hotel that night, Nutty Comeau started to run like hell.

BOOK TWO
THE FLIGHT

"A man's sins and virtues are like his shadow which, though not always apparent, follows him everywhere."

—TIBETAN PROVERB

IV

RICK GALBRAITH WAS REACHING into one of the big beer coolers behind the bar when the first shot was fired. He whirled around towards Bill's table as the loud report of the second and third shots exploded through the room. Then the screaming started. Galbraith felt rather than saw Bill go down—the impact literally shook the floor. The bartender saw a plume of blood gushing from Bill's head as he ran out of the bar and into the lobby to call for help.

Rod Stewart was on his feet, rushing towards Bill before Nutty was even out the door. Stewart knocked over a table and several chairs in his haste to cross the room. It was a terrible sight. Matiyek was still in his chair, but the chair was lying sideways on the floor. Bill's eyes were open and he was breathing, and for a minute Stewart, who was trained in first aid, thought he might be able to do something. He moved Matiyek's table out of the way and struggled to get Bill out of his chair and into a prone position on the floor. By then he had seen the extent of the wound in Bill's head and Stewart knew there wasn't much he could do.

Gayle Thompson saw Bill slump in his chair after the first shot ripped into him. She turned away and ran for the one refuge she could think of— the women's washroom. Jamie Hanna, Cathy Cotgrave, and Sue Foote arrived in the washroom just after Gayle. They were all in tears and tried to comfort one another.

Rick Galbraith was fumbling with a pay phone in the lobby when he spotted a cruiser from the Port Hope Police Department through a lobby window. He slammed the receiver back into its cradle and ran out onto the street, waving his arms. "Bill Matiyek's been shot," he yelled at the two officers in the squad car. "Get an ambulance!" Both policemen jumped out of their car and sprinted through the lobby into the bar.

Gayle was the first of the women to leave the washroom. Almost everyone in the lounge had left, she noticed, except Rod Stewart, who was at Bill's side. She grabbed a handful of towels from the bar and gave them to Stewart.

It was 11:08 when Constables Kenneth Wilson and David MacDonald entered the bar. Wilson noticed several women crying. They were being consoled by a couple of men. There was a small knot of people in one corner.

Wilson found Matiyek sprawled on the floor in a pool of blood. Someone had wrapped a towel around the top of his head. MacDonald called for an ambulance as Wilson checked Bill's vital signs. There were none. It was just six minutes after Wilson and MacDonald arrived when Bill Matiyek—what was left of him—was carried out of the Queen's Hotel.

In their helter-skelter flight out of the Queen's Hotel the members of the Satan's Choice ran through any exit they could find, towards any car they knew belonged to a fellow member. Jeff McLeod ran through the John Street exit beside Bill's table and piled into a car with five or six other guys, one of whom was Armand Sanguigni. It wasn't the same car that Jeff had driven down in, but that didn't matter. The only thing that mattered was to get out of Port Hope as fast as possible. It was pandemonium inside the darkened car; everybody was screaming at each other, and Jeff's heart was pounding in his chest.

"Go, go, go!"

"Let's get the fuck outta here!"

The car raced off up the steep Walton Street hill and within a few seconds they were doing 80 or 100 kilometres an hour up the main street of the sleepy town.

"What the fuck happened . . . ?"

"Just get us to the 401, man!"

"Slow down, for fuck sakes, we'll get pinched for fuckin' speeding!"

They made it onto the 401 and were hurtling through the night at 160 kilometres an hour before someone again told the driver to slow the fuck down. As the lights of Port Hope fell away behind them, and in the relative anonymity of the four-lane highway, the men in the car began to relax a little and to sort out what had gone wrong. Jeff hadn't *seen* the shooting—he'd turned his head to speak to someone when the first shot was fired. Like some of the others, Jeff wasn't even sure who'd done the shooting, and when he found out who it was he shook his head in disgust.

Armand was hopping mad. "They're comin', man! The fuckin' coppers are comin'! There was a fuck of a lot of us there and I just hope the guy's able to take his own beef."

As the miles sped past and the adrenalin began to wear off, Jeff McLeod slumped back against the car seat. One thought kept running through his mind over and over: "I didn't do nothin'. I didn't *do* nothin'. *I* didn't do nothin'."

Like Jeff McLeod, Merv Blaker and Rick Sauvé fled the hotel through the John Street exit. They jumped into Merv's car, which was parked on John Street, and sped away.

"Holy fuck man, what happened?" Rick's throat was dry and his ears were still ringing from the gunfire. They decided to head for the Toronto clubhouse. They talked, briefly, about what had happened and why, and then lapsed into silence. The Indian never had been much of a talker. One thing Rick was sure of, though, and he would remain convinced of it forever: the man who pulled the trigger on Matiyek had just saved his life.

Nutty Comeau had run for only a short distance. He'd been shot! He made himself slow down and walked quickly through the rear door of the Queen's and jumped into the nearest club car. The scene inside was as crazy as it was inside Jeff's car. As the car screamed away he checked himself over once again. His arm was barely bleeding, but it was stinging like a bad toothache. He moved his left arm gingerly, to see if he could feel the bullet. Again, he was relieved that it hadn't struck any vital organs. "Well, at least they can't say *I* did it," Comeau told the other guys in the car. "I got shot, too."

Comeau, Sauvé, and Blaker met at the Markham Road clubhouse to decide what to do next. It didn't take Dick Tracy to figure out that half the people in the Queen's had probably already identified Rick and Merv to the police. The priority seemed to be to get the bullet out of Nutty, and to lie low. But where to go! They decided on Kitchener, Tee Hee's place. He was smart and level-headed; he might know what to do about the bullet, and, besides, his was the only apartment any of them knew how to find. It was well after midnight when they climbed into Merv's car and headed west again on Highway 401.

The pounding at the back door was like a dream at first but it was urgent, and insistent. Tee Hee shook himself awake and checked the alarm clock. It was 2 a.m. Tee Hee rolled out of bed and stumbled to the back door to find Rick, Nutty, and Merv standing there, and he could see right away that something was wrong. Nutty was white as a ghost, and Rick and Indian were clearly upset. The story tumbled out—that Nutty was shot, that some guy named Matiyek in Port Hope had been shot too, only worse. Rick was a hundred percent sure that Matiyek was dead. Tee Hee had never even heard of Bill Matiyek, or that Peterborough Chapter was beefing with him. Hoffman helped Gary take off his leather jacket and after they got it off he noticed the bloody bandage wrapped around Nutty's shoulder. This was crazy. They'd blown some guy away in a public place, a *bar* for God's sake, in front of a roomful of people. It would mean, Tee Hee knew, trouble for the whole club. Big trouble. He called a couple of Kitchener Chapter guys and told them to come right over.

Everybody sat down in the kitchen, and while they waited for the others to arrive Rick asked if he could use Tee Hee's phone. Rick was worried about his job—he was due in at work in just a few hours; and Merv wanted his wife to know he was okay. Rick didn't want to call Sharon—she'd ask too many questions—so he decided to call Roger Davey, an old friend in Port Hope.

Rick went into the living-room to place the call and the others stayed in the kitchen, each man absorbed in his own thoughts. You could have heard a pin drop.

Roger's wife Diane answered, half asleep. Rick asked her to call Sharon first thing in the morning and to get Sharon to call in sick for him. Also to call Merv's wife Karen. They'd both be away for a few days. Diane agreed, and that was it. The whole conversation lasted less than a minute.

"Did you get him?" Merv asked as Rick returned to the kitchen.

"I got Diane. She'll do it."

Merv nodded.

When the other chapter members arrived they talked strategy. One guy said he knew somebody in Windsor who could get the bullet out. The Choice's own Windsor Chapter had gone Outlaws in the big switch, but there was another club down there they were on pretty good terms with, and their guys were solid. It was decided that Nutty, Rick, and Merv would leave for Windsor at first light under cover of the morning rush-hour traffic. Rick and Merv were agreeable—it would put more miles between them and Port Hope.

It was after 3 a.m. when the Kitchener guys went home. Tee Hee bedded Nutty, Merv, and Rick down on couches in the living-room and went back to bed. Each of them drifted off, finally, into an exhausted but fitful sleep.

Bill Matiyek was still on the floor when Sam McReelis arrived at the hotel. A twelve-year veteran with the Port Hope Police Department, Sergeant

McReelis was tall, and with his military bearing he seemed to have been born to wear a uniform. He looked at Matiyek and the scene, quickly noted the presence of Cathy Cotgrave, Rod Stewart, Julie Joncas, Leo Powell, and Gayle Thompson, and issued instructions to Constables MacDonald and Wilson. He ordered both men to secure the hotel and to write down the names of the witnesses who had been present when the shooting occurred. Powell and Joncas had returned to the hotel from the police station just after the shooting, and Powell, McReelis learned, had unfortunately asked most of the patrons and potential eyewitnesses to leave.

After the ambulance attendants had removed Matiyek, McReelis conferred briefly with Wilson and MacDonald. They told him that several witnesses put Merv Blaker and Rick Sauvé in the hotel at the time of the shooting. All three of the Port Hope policemen knew who Sauvé and Blaker were, and McReelis concluded at once that Matiyek's shooting had something to do with the bikers' rivalry.

Like so many of the men he would spend the next three months pursuing, Sergeant McReelis also had a nickname. It stemmed from an incident that had occurred some years before, though local accounts varied slightly. McReelis, in the line of duty, had pulled a shotgun on a carload of local teenagers, one of whom happened to be the daughter of a respected Port Hope family. Word of McReelis's action spread quickly through the small town and he was known forever after—if not actually to his face—as "Shotgun Sam." The imposing police officer was the subject of strongly mixed public opinion. A goodly number of the Port Hope citizenry rested easier on the nights when Sam was on duty. But others wondered privately if Sergeant McReelis was not a touch overzealous in the pursuit of his duties.

The Sergeant returned to the police station and made several telephone calls. First, he called the Ontario Provincial Police to inform them of the shooting and to ask whether they had stopped any vehicles between Port Hope and Toronto that contained members of any motorcycle gangs. They had not. Then McReelis called the Port Hope and District Hospital to check on Matiyek's condition. He had been declared dead-on-arrival.

At 11:45 Cathy Cotgrave arrived at the police station and McReelis spoke to her for a few minutes. She didn't appear to be in any condition to make a formal statement, and the Sergeant told her that the police would take official statements the following day.

Two other eyewitnesses, Doug Peart and Dave Gillispie, consented to give statements to the police that night, however. Sergeant McReelis interviewed Peart himself, and Gillispie spoke to Constable Wilson. Of the two written statements that resulted, Gillispie's would loom especially large. The two men began their discussion at 2:05 a.m., just three hours after the shooting. Gillispie told the Constable that he had arrived at the hotel with Doug Peart at about twenty minutes to eleven. Rick Sauvé, Merv Blaker, and a few other biker types including Fred Jones were in the hotel. He and Doug had met Sue Foote and then played shuffleboard. Afterward, he decided to walk through the main lounge and he'd had a brief conversation with Rick Sauvé and Merv Blaker about Gary Galbraith's motorcycle. While he was talking to Sauvé and Blaker, Gillispie recalled, "the fat guy who did the shooting said to Rick and Merv, 'Are we going to do it with this fat fucker, or what?' I didn't catch any response from Merv or Rick."

Gillispie said he'd gone to talk with Doug Peart then, before telling Gayle Thompson that "something is going down." He had observed to Rick Galbraith that "there was a real sociable crowd in tonight," and the bartender had responded that "he regretted the thought of coming in to work tonight."

"I heard three shots, bang, bang, bang. Just before the shots there were three guys sitting with Matiyek and they were still there and just getting up when I heard the shots."

Gillispie then offered detailed descriptions of two of the men at Matiyek's table. One was of average height with light, curly, almost kinky hair that was fairly long, but not shoulder length. He was heavyset, 190 to 200 pounds. "He was wearing blue jeans and I think a black-leather jacket, but I'm not sure about the jacket." He had a short, light-coloured beard and a moustache. His hairline was receding, he was twenty-seven or twenty-eight years old, and his voice was fairly deep with no accent. "He was the first out the door after the shooting and I have never seen him before. He was the guy who talked to Blaker and Sauvé . . ."

The other man at Matiyek's table weighed about 170, was five foot ten or eleven, and had dark brown hair with a moustache and goatee. His hair was longer than shoulder length, he was about twenty-five, and, Gillispie said, "I have seen him in the Queen's once before."

Wilson asked Gillispie about the third man and the witness decided that, on second thought, only two men had been sitting at Matiyek's table. "You said earlier that 'the fat guy who did the shooting' [was at Matiyek's table]. How did you know he did the shooting?" Wilson asked.

"Okay, I didn't really see the shooting but I felt that that guy did it because he was sitting right next to Bill and he was first out the door. Also, I think I have seen the other guy with him and I don't think he has the guts to do it."

Could Gillispie identify anyone?

"Yes, Fred Jones, Sauvé, Blaker, the big blond guy, and I think the other guy at the table."

It was 3:35 a.m. when Wilson finished his interview with Gillispie, and it was seven in the morning before Sam McReelis finished his written report to the Chief of Police.

Just eight hours after the shooting of Bill Matiyek a considerable number of facts had already emerged in what was now a murder investigation: Matiyek had been killed by three bullets fired at his head at close range; two well-known local members of the Satan's Choice Motorcycle Club had fled the hotel immediately after the shooting, along with a number of other suspects who were also presumably members of the Satan's Choice; the crime had been brazenly committed in a public place, before several dozen potential eyewitnesses; and at least one of the suspects, possibly the gunman himself, had been overheard making a statement to Blaker and Sauvé that suggested that all of them knew what was about to happen.

Matiyek's shooting was clearly intentional, apparently planned and deliberate, and carried out in an incredibly audacious manner, even for a motorcycle gang. It all added up to first-degree murder in a gangland-style execution. Murder was a rare occurrence in Sam McReelis's peaceful town, and a first-degree murder of this type was unprecedented. Sergeant Sam McReelis was sure of one thing: this would be one of the biggest cases in his entire career; maybe *the* biggest.

It was growing light when Sam McReelis dropped his report on the Chief's desk and left for home and a few hours' sleep. Although the police already knew a lot about the case, there was still one big question: who had actually shot Bill Matiyek?

When he had returned from Port Hope, Lorne Campbell had asked to be dropped off at the Cadillac, his favourite Oshawa hotel. It was almost midnight, and he had a lot of drinking to catch up on. Unlike most of the others who'd gone down to the Queen's, Campbell and Hurren had only had about one beer apiece before they left for Port Hope. Campbell closed the Caddy and went home, but he couldn't sleep.

Lorne was a firm believer in facing up to his problems. If he heard that someone was after him, he wouldn't rest until he'd found that person and confronted him face to face. It was a philosophy that Lorne always tried to live by. It was the same way with fear. As long as he could remember he'd had a totally irrational but terribly real fear of spiders. To cure himself, he'd gone to a pet shop and bought a tarantula. Every day he had forced himself to reach into the spider's cage, take it out, and let it crawl up and down his arm. He got bitten three times, and twice he had to go to emergency for treatment. But tarantula bites are rarely fatal, Lorne had learned. Finally he got really sick of the goddamned thing, so he stopped giving it food and water. The spider survived for almost two months without food or a drop of water before it finally died. The experiment, Lorne decided, was a partial success: he was still deathly afraid of spiders, but at least he'd never again fear a tarantula.

It was the same with breaking bones with a baseball bat to supplement his income. He'd always been thoughtful, even philosophical, about the whole deal. Lorne didn't enjoy inflicting pain, he was no sadist. But the way he saw it, if somebody got mixed up with a loan shark or they were fronted drugs and then nothing was delivered, well, if you were going to play, then you had to pay.

Wasn't it the same way with Bill Matiyek? He asked himself that question again and again during those restless pre-dawn hours. He'd had nothing against Bill personally. He felt bad about Bill's death. But somebody in that bar had been going to die. If not Bill, it would have been Rick or Nutty, or Lorne himself—he was sure that Matiyek had been reaching for his gun as he approached the table. Bill was living the Life, and that was that. He'd backed himself into a corner, and he should have known better. Lorne believed that. But he still couldn't get to sleep.

V

DIANE DAVEY KEPT HER word to Rick and phoned Sharon Sauvé first thing Thursday morning. Sharon wasn't surprised to learn her husband wouldn't be home for a few days, because it wasn't that unusual. Things had been pretty rough in their marriage lately. Sharon had been more surprised the night before when she'd gotten home from work and found two strangers—they were obviously bikers—in the house, babysitting Angie. But they were polite enough, and they'd left finally.

Sharon had learned about the shooting while she was at work the night before. She worked at Easton's Texaco, a large truck stop at the intersection of Highway 28 and the 401, just north of Port Hope. Somebody had come in and told them about events in the hotel, but he'd said it had something to do with the Mafia. Sharon didn't even know anybody in the Mafia, and she hadn't given the Matiyek shooting a second thought until she got Rick's message from Diane.

When she finished her phoning, Sharon Sauvé resolved once again to leave her husband. She and a girlfriend had already discussed getting their own apartment, and she'd already told Rick about it. It wasn't the first time she'd told Rick she was moving out, but this time she really meant it. It wasn't that he was a lousy father—Rick was a great father, there wasn't anything he wouldn't do for Angie. Just the month before, when Angie had started school, Rick had gone with her and spent a whole half-day in the pre-kindergarten class, with the other parents. But he was the only father who had shown up, and he'd sat there, with all the mums—this biker, with his scraggly beard and long hair and tattoos. Sharon heard later from some of her friends that the mothers had been very impressed with Rick, and had gone home and asked their husbands why *they* didn't show more interest in their children's education.

No, their family life was great. It was in the man-and-wife department that their marriage was falling apart. She didn't love Rick. She liked him, but she didn't love him any longer. Sometimes she wondered if she'd ever really loved Rick at all. They had met when she was in Grade 10. Rick was twenty-one, he had a steady job at Davidson Rubber, his own car, and his own apartment. They started hanging around together, doing what kids did in those days in Port Hope and Cobourg—driving around, getting high. In the summer they'd drive over to Cobourg beach in Rick's car, which was just an old rattle-trap really, but it was wheels. Rick would hook big home stereo speakers up to the car radio, and they'd put the speakers on top of the car and let the Stones and Led Zeppelin and Neil Young blast out over the waters of Lake Ontario. In the fall Sharon and her friends would sign Rick and his friends into the high school dances, and over the Christmas holidays in 1972 Rick had invited her home to meet his family.

Sharon decided she was in love with Rick. He was older, he had a car— and he was *very* good-looking, all her friends agreed on that, with his long, long hair, strong, clean jawline, and cool, steady gaze. Rick was really skinny then, and looked and acted like a hippie—he liked to wear long India-print shirts with little mirrors sewn in them. He was just a cool, easygoing guy who liked to have fun. After Christmas they started getting serious, but Sharon still wouldn't sleep with him. Then she'd caught him sleeping around on her. Their relationship soured, but Sharon came to understand that, being older, Rick had to get it somewhere.

Finally, in the spring, she gave in, and what should have been the beginning of something turned out instead to be the end. She got pregnant the very first time. She panicked. Her sister wanted her to have an abortion, but she'd been so young, so naive . . . Sharon didn't want to hurt her folks or cause them any more embarrassment than she already had. She figured that if they got married, nobody would get hurt. The wedding took place in October of 1973 at the United Church in Port Hope. She was five months pregnant and seven months past her sixteenth birthday.

They moved in with Rick's folks for the first few weeks after they were married, and Sharon cried every night. She hated being pregnant, hated being married, hated being cooped up. They got their own apartment and Rick was in his glory. He got to go to work and party all the time while she sat home and got huge. She had finished Grade 10, but didn't go back in the fall—at that time not too many people were going to school while they were pregnant, and she was embarrassed by the whole situation.

Angie was born in January of 1974. Rick loved being a father. At first they'd socialized more with married couples, people like Roger and Diane Davey, though they were all a deal older than Sharon. They did a lot of things together, family outings, shopping trips, walks. But as man and wife they just didn't get along. Sharon didn't love Rick, at least not enough to be his wife, and Rick knew it. They fought. Not a lot, it was more like playing mind games on each other—she'd go out with her friends, he'd go out with his friends, and they saw less and less of the other married couples. Sharon's friends were all younger and single, and she and Rick started going separate ways when it came to their social lives. There were times when she wished she could have loved him more. But it was hard, going out with her friends, who always seemed so young and so free to party and have a good time.

They really started going downhill in 1975, when Sharon got her job waitressing at Easton's. The job gave her more independence and her own money, and Rick disliked that. At first he'd wanted her to work, but when he learned that working forty hours a week on all kinds of crazy shifts meant that she wouldn't always be there to do the cooking and the housework, he begged her to quit. But Sharon wasn't about to give up her new freedom, and she'd never been much of a cook, anyways.

Rick, meanwhile, had been fired from Davidson Rubber and had found a new job at Chemtron. Like his dad and most of his brothers, Rick was a strong union man and before long he'd been elected president of his Steelworkers local. He even got sent down to Pittsburgh for special training.

They moved a couple of times during that period, from their first apartment on Bramley to a rented house just around the corner on Sullivan Street. It was about that time that Rick first told Sharon he wanted to join the Satan's Choice. Rick had always loved motorcycles—it was another passion he shared with his father and brothers—and Sharon knew he was friends with Merv Blaker, who'd been in the Choice for years. But she'd pleaded with him not to join. She'd heard so many bad stories, and she believed what she'd heard. Motorcycle clubs were bad news. She wanted nothing to do with them. And Rick hadn't joined then, he just said, "Okay."

In 1977 they'd moved once more, into the house where Sharon was sitting now, on Jocelyn Street. It didn't look like much from the outside, they always called it "the little shack," or "the little house on the prairie," because it was on the northwestern outskirts of Port Hope, surrounded by farmers' fields. But it wasn't bad on the inside, and the rent was certainly right—$85 a month. The Satan's Choice clubhouse was just down the road, though, and Rick told her again he wanted to join the club. This time she'd just told him, "Do what you want. I don't care. You wanna join it, go ahead." And he had.

Being in the Satan's Choice changed Rick. He'd never been a really rough guy, but he seemed different, somehow. He was still a very good father, but he just wasn't his old loving self. It was as if Rick was saying, "I'll just do my own thing. Too bad—too bad about you. I won't cater to you any longer." In one way, Rick's club affiliation was well suited to their lifestyle, because she had her friends, he had his, and they didn't interfere too much in each other's social affairs. It just drove the wedge between them deeper and deeper.

Rick rarely brought his new social life home, but when he did, Sharon—to her own surprise—found herself overcoming some of her old prejudices about bikers. After she met a few of Rick's new "brothers" she discovered that some of them were good people. Like Gordy van Haarlem. He was a member of Peterborough Chapter, and he took to crashing at Rick and Sharon's fairly often. Gordy came across as a really rough, tough guy, and he was in fact a true street fighter, unlike either Rick or Merv. He wasn't that big, but he loved a good fistfight, no matter what the odds against him. His nose had been broken so many times in so many different places that it meandered across his face like a mountain highway, which was how he'd got his club nickname—"Dogmap."

Sharon was amazed at Gordy. He was such a rough and mean guy, but she'd come home from work and he'd have her housework completely done. He'd even have done her laundry. Some of the club guys had their good points, she had to admit.

Sharon sighed and looked up at the kitchen clock over the sink. It was almost eight. Even now, in the harsh light of early morning, in her house-coat with no makeup, slightly dishevelled from too little sleep, and with a lot on her mind, Sharon Sauvé was an unmistakably attractive woman. Her eyes, set off by her dark brown hair, were large and warm. Her face was heart-shaped, with high cheekbones beneath smooth skin, and her figure was firm, yet supple. Sharon's voice was also distinctive, surprisingly husky, with a pleasant, smoky resonance. She took good care of herself, and always dressed well. Sharon would turn heads on any main street and could easily have passed for a photographer's model. But here she was, twenty-one going on thirty-five, with a daughter to get ready for school, a husband who was out God knows where and who was probably in trouble, a sinkful of dirty dishes, and a steady job as a waitress at a truck stop. Yes, this time she was definitely moving out.

Inspector Colin Cousens arrived in Port Hope at 10:15 in the morning to assume overall command of the Matiyek murder investigation. Cousens was tall and raw-boned with prominent ears and a deeply lined face that gave him an aura of dogged persistence. He was nearing fifty, but his greying hair made him seem older, an illusion that was reinforced by a look of perpetual worry or weariness. His appearance gave the impression that there wasn't much he hadn't seen, and indeed, during his twenty-eight years with the Ontario Provincial Police, the past six in Homicide, there wasn't.

As always in these investigations, Cousens was interested first of all in meeting the local officers with whom he'd be working. It could be a delicate matter. Although the crime had been committed, strictly speaking, within the jurisdiction of the Port Hope Police Department, Cousens would be the senior investigating officer of record. Small-town police forces were rarely equipped to handle the intricacies of murder investigation and so the provincial force would provide back-up: forensics, identification, records, as well as, in this case at least, invaluable information from the OPP's own biker intelligence squad. Most small-town cops had had little experience with homicide, and Cousens had learned long ago that the quality of small-town forces, with their scant resources, uneven hiring policies, and lower pay scales, could vary enormously.

It was 11:15 before Sam McReelis returned to the century-old building that housed Port Hope's municipal administration, as well as its police force. Cousens was favourably impressed with McReelis. The younger man struck him as a good cop, as someone who could withstand the sudden public, political, and media pressure that invariably accompanied murder in a small town. Certainly McReelis would play a key role in the investigation because Cousens and his men from the OPP's Criminal Investigations Branch and biker squad simply couldn't be in Port Hope twenty-four hours a day. The local force, led by McReelis, would be indispensable, because it knew the community, and the characters in it. Cousens made a mental note to see that McReelis was brushed up on his interviewing and statement-taking skills, and then both men began to work on the investigation. The first step was obvious: to interview the eyewitnesses.

As the day wore on, many of the most important witnesses drifted by ones and twos into the Ganaraska Hotel: Gayle Thompson was there, along with Cathy, Sue, Rick Galbraith, Doug Peart, Dave Gillispie, and Randy Koehler, who was Gayle's boyfriend and a part-time bouncer at the Queen's. The Queen's was closed on Thursday pending the completion of the police investigation, and none of them really wanted to go back into the place so soon, anyway. Of course, everyone else in the Ganny that afternoon kept coming up to the table, wanting to know what had happened. None of them really wanted to discuss it with outsiders, but in doing so they learned that each of them had seen the shooting from a slightly different point of view, and that no two of them had seen exactly the same thing.

Later in the afternoon a police officer arrived, and one by one they were summoned to the police station. Cathy Cotgrave gave a statement to police, and so did Gayle. She told Cousens that Blaker and Sauvé had been in the bar at the time of the shooting and that she had recognized several others because they were members of the Satan's Choice. She didn't know their names but had heard they were from Kitchener and Toronto.

Thompson also remembered seeing "this person walking towards Bill's table. This person was light blond [with] a beard, he had a hat on but his [hair] stuck out from under his hat. He was average size. He had a green parka. He was about five foot, ten inches . . . the hat was down close to his eyes. It did not have a peak. I saw him after one shot had been fired at Bill . . ."

The police must have been somewhat reassured at the similarities between Gayle Thompson's description of the presumed gunman and Dave Gillispie's description of the night before. Both witnesses saw a blond, bearded man of average height. There *were* discrepancies—Gillispie thought he remembered a black-leather jacket, while Thompson described a green parka on the man she thought was the gunman. But eyewitness evidence is notoriously subjective, and to have two witnesses offer such similar descriptions so soon after the murder seemed a promising lead. The fact that most of the crucial eyewitnesses were sitting together at the Ganaraska, discussing among themselves what they'd seen even before most of them talked to the police, and then returning to the bar afterwards to discuss what they had said, was not, evidently, considered.

Of all the people around the table at the Ganny that afternoon, Rick Galbraith found himself in the toughest spot. The bartender was, after all, a biker. He'd known and ridden with Rick Sauvé and Merv Blaker for years, and his brother Gary was striking for the Choice. On the other hand, the Queen's was his home bar and the people with him in the Ganny were also some of his best friends. Even though he had never joined an outlaw club himself, Rick had owned a Harley long enough to know club attitudes towards Crown witnesses, especially if that witness was himself a biker. After seeing what the choice had done to Bill, right before their eyes, he felt frightened and intimidated. The others seemed willing enough to co-operate with the police, but Rick dreaded the thought of some day having to testify against Rick or Merv, or even Larry Hurren.

And so, when his turn came to visit the police station, the young bartender did the only thing he could—he developed a sudden case of total amnesia. He told the police he hadn't seen anything and couldn't identify anybody. The police, especially Sam McReelis, were frankly sceptical. Rick Galbraith, with his black leathers and equally black beard and longish hair, was a common sight on Walton Street during riding season—he was, in fact, one of the town's best-known bikers.

"Come on, Rick, you know everybody who was in that hotel," McReelis pressed him.

But Galbraith stuck stubbornly to his story and even refused to sign the meager statement that the police wrote down from his interview.

"I ain't signin' nothin'." The brotherhood of the Harley, even at one remove, ran deep.

VI

NUTTY, RICK, AND MERV reached Windsor in mid-morning. By noon they'd contacted their Windsor friends and within a few hours Nutty was taken to have the bullet removed. It was one of the strangest experiences in a life that was getting stranger by the minute.

Whoever the guy was, he was no doctor. He rooted around in Nutty's arm for about an hour while the Windsor guys stood around and watched. The pain was worse than when he was shot. The trauma of being cut open without an anesthetic was so great that blood began to gush from Nutty's nose and mouth.

The other guys were drinking beer and cracking jokes. It was pretty gory. They shouted things like, "Aw, sew it up with a shoelace, Nutty." Nutty didn't think it was very funny. Finally the amateur surgeon gave up. He couldn't find the bullet.

Then one of the Windsor guys said *he* knew a clubber from Detroit whose club had a doctor, a real doctor. Gunshot wounds were nothing over there, nobody would ask any questions. But how would they get Nutty across the river? The Windsor club had a friend—he looked like a real straightjohn—who went to Detroit all the time.

The friend agreed to smuggle Nutty across the border.

"How?" Nutty demanded.

"No problem," the guy answered. "We'll just put you in the trunk of my car."

"You crazy, man? The coppers check your trunk at the border, I'm dead."

"No problem. Really. I'm just gonna call my wife."

The guy made a phone call. "Hello, honey? How ya doin'? Good, fine. Listen, how'd ya like to go over to Detroit for dinner tonight? Great. I'll pick you up in fifteen minutes."

They put Nutty in the trunk and the guy started the car. Huddled in the darkness of the trunk and scared to death, Nutty felt the car driving for a while and then stop. The wife got in and they started driving again.

"Hey Nutty, you okay back there?"

Comeau didn't answer, but he heard the wife, could almost see her looking in the back seat of the car, and then at her husband: "Who *are* you talking to?"

"Hey Nutty, you okay?"

The wife still didn't have a clue.

"Yeah, I'm all right."

At the border Nutty could hear the conversation with the crossing guard.

"Good evening, sir, how are you tonight?"

"Just fine. My wife and I are going out to dinner."

"All right, sir, have a good time."

They dropped him off at a friendly clubhouse where Nutty was told it might take a day or two to connect with the doctor.

Rick and Merv spent all day Friday in a Windsor safe house where they'd agreed to wait until Nutty got back from Detroit. Rick only ventured out long enough to buy some newspapers, hoping to find a story on Matiyek.

He wanted to know if Bill was dead. But there weren't any stories on the shooting at all. Maybe no news was good news—but he doubted it.

The enforced idleness gave Rick a lot of time to think. His own troubles with Bill had started almost a year ago, before Rick had actually joined the Choice. One night, while he was away at work, someone had taken a shot at his house while Sharon and Angie were home alone. Sharon had been very frightened, naturally, and she phoned the Choice clubhouse looking for Rick. Rick found out from a friend of Bill's that it was Matiyek who'd done the shooting. Rick was enraged, and he went looking for Matiyek with a baseball bat. His first stop was his brother Larry's.

Larry had met his kid brother, aluminum bat in hand, at the front door. He'd never seen Ricky so steamed.

"Where is he?" Rick demanded. "Where is that fat fucker? I wanna know where he is right now!"

Larry just had to laugh at Ricky, standing on tiptoes, peering over his older brother's shoulders, going after a man twice his size with a baseball bat. He told Ricky to come in, reasoned with him, and got him settled down. Sure it was crazy, shooting at someone's house, but Bill hadn't hurt anyone, had only hit the mailbox or the side of the house, or something. No self-respecting biker would seriously threaten another man's wife or children. It was just Bill being crazy.

Rick let it ride then, and it was six or seven months before he actually encountered Bill face to face. Rick was with another Choice member, Brian Babcock, when they met Matiyek in a bar. Bill came up to them like nothing had happened, and Rick couldn't stand it. He told Matiyek he wanted to fight, and they agreed to drive outside of town, near Rick's house. Babs offered to come along, to give Rick a hand with the big man, but Rick refused. As far as he was concerned, this was a question of personal honour, to be settled by single combat. They got to Rick's and squared off, and it became apparent, to Rick's surprise and immense relief—after all, Bill really was a giant of a man—that Matiyek didn't want to fight.

"I'd never hurt anyone in your family, Rick. I was drunk and I just wanted to scare you. C'mon, let's shake hands and go have a beer."

But Rick wouldn't shake and he didn't want to drink with Bill. He told the big goof to fuck off, his honour satisfied. Still, Rick thought, he'd respected Bill.

Late that Friday afternoon there was another raid on the Kitchener Choice clubhouse, the second in forty-eight hours. Some of the police busied themselves upstairs, cutting swatches out of the second-floor mattress. But the most important work was going on downstairs in the clubroom, where a tiny room probe was being installed in the air conditioner. The bug was a miniature microphone and transmitting device that relayed a signal to a nearby receiver. For the rest of the fall and winter of 1978–79 the police would be able to record and transcribe not only every telephone conversation to and from the clubhouse, but every word spoken in the main meeting-room of the Kitchener clubhouse.

Once again club members carefully inspected their building after the raid was over. They spotted the missing pieces from the mattress right away, but not the tiny object nestling in the old air conditioner. They pulled the mattress down into the parking lot, doused it with gasoline, and set it afire. Nobody'd be using *that* mattress as evidence in some phony skin beef.

Ontario Provincial Police Constable Donald Denis had taken part in the first Kitchener clubhouse raid and might have been there for the second but for the murder of Bill Matiyek. The morning after the shooting he'd been summoned by his commanding officer, Corporal Terry Hall, and ordered to collect all the photographs he could find of members of both the Satan's Choice and the Outlaws and to proceed to Port Hope to conduct photo line-ups with eyewitnesses.

Denis's selection for the assignment would prove almost fatal to the fledgling investigation. While he was a fifteen-year veteran of the force, Denis had spent most of that time in uniform, transferring to plainclothes in August 1975 and to Hall's biker squad only in January 1978. Part of Denis's responsibilities with Hall's unit was to shoot pictures of bikers, mainly on club runs when it was relatively easy to maintain close surveillance. But when it came to showing those pictures to prospective witnesses, Denis had no training and less experience.

Identification procedures are a scientific part of police work and are absolutely critical for successful prosecutions. Yet the only training Denis received was a quick briefing from another member of the biker squad before he left for Port Hope. And the officer doing the briefing, Denis would be forced to admit ruefully on the witness stand months later, had had no formal training in photo ID procedures, either.

Denis arrived in Port Hope on Thursday afternoon and set up shop in the town hall. In all, he'd been able to locate nearly two hundred photos of Choice and Outlaws members, most of them mug shots culled from OPP Central Records or biker-squad files. The pictures were spread out on a large table and numbered in a particular sequence to facilitate Constable Denis's note-taking. No names were visible. Each witness was asked the same question: Could he or she point out anyone who had been in the Queen's Hotel on the night of the shooting?

The first two witnesses to view the photo array were Gayle Thompson and Sue Foote, on the afternoon of Thursday the nineteenth. Who, if anyone, they identified in the line-up remains a mystery. Denis gave his notes from the viewings to either Inspector Cousens or Sam McReelis, and they were never seen again. Both men later testified they'd simply been misplaced.

On Friday, about the time the second Kitchener clubhouse raid was getting under way, Rod Stewart viewed the line-up. He pointed to pictures of Bernard Baland, Joe Hatos, and Dwayne Wemp, but he seemed so uncertain about any of his identifications that Denis noted Stewart's ID's as "vague." Several other witnesses were shown the array on Friday, but they failed to identify anyone at all, much less the gunman.

But on Saturday afternoon Denis hit pay dirt. Cathy Cotgrave began to point to one photograph after another. She indicated pictures of Larry Hurren, Jeff McLeod, Merv Blaker, Fred Jones, Sonny Bronson, Armand Sanguigni, and Rick Sauvé as individuals who had been in the hotel that night. She told Denis that Brian Brideau had been there, too, but she didn't see his picture. (There was none.) Also, Cotgrave told Denis, she was certain a man named "Tee Hee" had been among the Choice group the night of the shooting, though she was unable to identify either picture of Hoffman in the line-up. Most important, she pointed at two pictures and said one of them could be the gunman. Denis could have kissed her, but he just thanked the young waitress and ushered her out of the room. He returned to the table and flipped both photos to get the names and file numbers, as noted by Central Records. The first was Rae Snyder, a Satan's Choice from the Kitchener Chapter. Cotgrave had pointed to Snyder and said that, with a hat on, he would look just like the gunman, Denis noted. The second photo, numbered 2–6, was one Gary Joseph Comeau.

It was Saturday afternoon before Nutty finally got to see a doctor. He was taken to a clinic and it was a nurse who looked him over first. The nurse hardly noticed the bullet hole. Instead she took one look at his arm and burst out laughing.

"Who did *that* to you?" She was pointing to the roughly sutured wound left by the ersatz operation. The nurse went out and got several other nurses who stood around laughing and marvelling at the three-inch gash in Gary's left shoulder. It was starting to get infected.

Finally the doctor came in. After examining Nutty he ordered an X-ray of his arm. A while later he returned with the X-rays. "There's no bullet in your arm," he told Nutty.

Comeau was relieved, but baffled. He *knew* he'd been shot because there was a hole clean through his black-leather jacket, and a hole in his arm. Could if be that the slug had been traveling so slowly it passed through the jacket, broke the skin, and then glanced off, maybe rolling down his sleeve?

The nurses cleaned up the incision on his shoulder and gave him some pills for the infection. They charged him forty dollars American and told him to have a nice day. Nutty returned to Windsor that same afternoon, as a passenger this time. Merv and Rick were still waiting for him, and the three of them caught rides back home.

Merv Blaker journeyed to Port Hope ahead of Rick because he had to appear in court in Cobourg on Monday. He was facing a speeding charge and he was already low on points, so he badly wanted to beat the charge. He half expected to get arrested for Bill's shooting right there in the courthouse.

An appearance at the Cobourg County Courthouse was not an altogether novel experience for Merv, though, considering that he'd been in the Choice since 1967, he didn't have much of a criminal record: one car theft and several fines for simple possession of marijuana. He'd done thirty days in the local bucket once, for unpaid fines, but that was the only time he'd ever served.

Most of Merv's other legal hassles had stemmed from two of his favourite pastimes—hard drinking and fast driving, and he was famous in the club for both. Whenever anyone asked Merv why he'd joined the Choice in the first place, he would answer that he liked motorcycles and parties. It was cheaper to drink in the clubhouse, and more relaxing being around people he could trust. But people who knew Blaker well suspected the reasons went a lot deeper than that.

Merv was a full-blooded Ojibway Indian and his family came from the Alderville Reserve north of Cobourg. In 1942, three years before Merv was born, his father decided to move the family off the reserve forever, to the white community of Baltimore, just a few miles from Alderville. There didn't seem to be much of a future in being an Indian in Canada at the time. Though thousands of native men were fighting and dying for their country in the Second World War, as they had in the First, Indians didn't even have the right to vote. The only way an Indian could gain first-class citizenship in Canada was to cease being an Indian, and that was what Merv's father did. In a process known as "enfranchisement," Gordon Blaker signed a piece of paper declaring that he was no longer an Indian and would never again lay claim to Indian status, nor would any of his children, or their children.

Outside his family, Merv grew up in the all-white world of Baltimore. He attended the local public school, but he dropped out after completing Grade 8. He picked tobacco, worked in a local garage, and, when he was eighteen, bought his first motorcycle, a 500-cc Royal Enfield. His schoolmates remember Merv as a quiet, painfully shy boy, and, in a white society where verbal skills are highly valued, Blaker's reticence was often mistaken for stupidity.

Merv sold his Royal Enfield and bought a 1956 Triumph 650 and then traded the Triumph in on a brand-new '67 BSA, which was the bike he had when he joined the Satan's Choice Peterborough Chapter in 1967. He started striking around Thanksgiving, just a few months before Tee Hee Hoffman joined the Kitchener Chapter. In hindsight, perhaps it wasn't surprising that Merv would be welcomed into an organization that was widely perceived as being composed of losers, rejects, and misfits. It was unusual for an outlaw bike club to allow a non-white to become a member, for they are notoriously lily-white, especially in the United States. It may have helped that Merv didn't look Indian—his complexion was relatively fair and he always sported a luxuriant black beard. Only his nickname and his prominent classical Roman nose betrayed Merv's racial origins. But to his brothers in the Satan's Choice it didn't seem to matter. Merv Blaker had finally found a home.

The Beezer turned out to be one of the worst bikes he'd ever owned—it was forever plagued with valve and crank problems—so Merv sold it and bought his first Harley, an old '46 Knucklehead chopper. It soon became apparent that Merv had found a place not only to belong, but even to excel. He possessed several skills that were widely admired and highly respected in any outlaw club. The shy, backward Indian kid from Baltimore became an absolute angel on the seat of a Harley. He rode like the wind, popped wheelies like no one else could, planted one boot and manoeuvred a 500-pound monster chopper in a dizzying, ever-tightening donut, engine whining, gravel flying, until the rider was lost, dervish-like, in a cloud of blue smoke and deafening noise. When Merv finally walked away from his machine he'd have this sweet, stoned smile on his face as if he'd just been told some cosmic, inner joke that no one else could hear. Merv Blaker, everyone agreed, was born to ride a Harley. He was one of the best riders anywhere, and it made them all proud that he was one of them.

Merv also proved himself an adept motorcycle mechanic. Unlike many club members, he always did all his own work. One year, on a long club run, he blew a piston on his Sportster. He tore the engine right down to the crankshaft, replaced the piston, and had his bike running the same night.

But if Indian as rider and mechanic was part of Merv's enduring club image, then so was Indian at parties. Though he wasn't a mean drunk, Merv had a drinking problem for sure, and he was a familiar sight at club parties, staggering around, a beer in each hand, more bottles in each pocket, grinning and babbling.

But it was a cold-sober Merv who appeared at the Cobourg courthouse on the Monday after Matiyek's death. He was shy and self-effacing, still missing half his teeth; his heart skipped a beat every time he saw a uniform in the old courthouse. But to Merv's surprise nothing happened—except that he got convicted for speeding, and lost more points off his licence after all.

VII

FRIDAY, OCTOBER 27, was destined to be an important date in the Matiyek murder investigation. Inspector Colin Cousens, Constable Don Denis, and biker-squad head Terry Hall all returned to Port Hope that morning. Denis drove down with a new photo array to show the eye-witnesses, some of whom would be viewing the line-up for the second time. Friday, the OPP officers decided, would also be the day for their first direct contact with any of the suspects, which was how Terry Hall found himself staking out Rick and Sharon Sauvé's house on the edge of Port Hope.

Although he was virtually unknown to the general public, Corporal Terry Hall was a black legend among Canadian bikers. If some men—like Merv Blaker—were born to ride a Harley, and others were destined to live their lives outside the law, then Terry Hall had been fore-ordained to become a policeman, though a most unusual one. He'd first put on a uniform at a precocious age: he was just seventeen when he joined the Metropolitan Toronto Police Force as a cadet. Three years later he was promoted to constable, and a year after that he transferred to the Ontario Provincial Police. Five and a half years later he joined the special squad of the OPP intelligence branch—the biker squad—just as it was being formed.

Since 1973 Hall had inhabited a strange nether region on the fringes of Canadian law enforcement. In appearance and demeanour he was every inch an outlaw biker—tall and beefy with long, curly black hair and a beard to match, a sizeable beer gut hanging over the top of his blue jeans. He lived, breathed, and slept bike clubs, reading all the biker magazines, moving through the strip joints and sleazy bars, mingling with bikers on all the club runs. His assignment was to bust as many bikers as possible. Failing that, the clubbers knew, Hall and his men would simply bust heads. The public didn't seem to care, and besides, what were the bikers going to do—call the cops?

Hall began his stake-out at the Sauvés' at eleven o'clock Friday morning, while Rick was still sleeping off the night shift. Inspector Cousens wanted to have a little chat with Richard Sauvé. Hall's orders were to wait until Sauvé left the house, and then tail him before making his move. That way, Cousens reckoned, Sauvé would be more tractable, and Hall would be less likely to get a door slammed in his face.

Van Haarlem had crashed at Rick and Sharon's the night before, and it was three in the afternoon before Rick and Gordy left the house. Their plan for the day was simple enough. That night was the date of the Vagabonds' big Halloween party in Toronto, an important date on the social calendar. Hundreds of bikers and their old ladies from across southern Ontario would be there. The Vags were one of the big Toronto clubs, along with the Iron

Hawgs and the Para-Dice Riders or PDR's, that, with the Satan's Choice, ran the bike scene in Canada's largest city. The Vags, Hawgs, and PDR's operated in the city of Toronto proper, the Choice mainly in the sprawling eastern suburb of Scarborough. All four organizations were bona fide Canadian independents, and in the fall of 1978 that was terribly important, in the face of recent incursions into Canada by the two most powerful American motorcycle clubs, the Outlaws and their rivals, the Hell's Angels. The California-based Angels were still consolidating their power in Quebec after taking over the Popeyes in Montreal. The Outlaws, by persuading Choice chapters in Windsor, St. Catharines, Ottawa, and Montreal to switch patch, had established a significant foothold in Canada's most populous province. The Toronto independents now found themselves caught in a pincer movement by the Outlaws, from Ottawa and Montreal on the east, and from Windsor and St. Catharines to the south and west.

In strategic terms, the last two remaining Choice chapters outside Toronto—Kitchener and Peterborough—were all that protected the city's flanks. Toronto, should it fall to one of the American clubs, would be a rich prize. The city dominated English-speaking Canada, and its population of well over two million made it one of the larger metropolitan areas on the continent. The four independent Toronto clubs were acutely aware of all this and had evolved a rough working relationship to stave off the American threat. There were occasional flare-ups within the loose alliance, but each club knew that an all-out war within Metro could be fatal to them all. Social affairs like the Vags' Halloween party were therefore important politically as well as socially.

Hall finally got into action as Rick and Gordy left the house shortly after three. They were going to pick up Sharon after work at Easton's, then they'd swing by for van Haarlem's girlfriend Patty, before heading to Toronto. Hall caught up with them just outside the entrance to the big truck stop. He parked and sauntered over to Rick's car. He'd caught Sauvé completely off guard, and he looked in the driver's-side window and leaned against the car, savoring the moment.

"Hi there, Rick." Hall's tone was low, cordial, even confidential. "I think it's time we had a little talk."

"About what?" Sauvé struggled to regain his composure and put on his club face.

"Oh, I think you know."

"No I don't."

"It'd be in your best interest, let's put it that way."

"Am I under arrest?"

"No, but if you don't talk to us I think you might be."

Rick went in to get Sharon, and Hall drifted around to the passenger side.

"Hiya, Gordy."

Van Haarlem greeted Hall with a grunt.

"Tell me somethin', Gordy. How'd you manage to miss that night?"

Van Haarlem gave Hall a malicious look. "Just lucky, I guess." The implied "Fuck off, copper" was obvious.

Rick and Sharon returned to the car. Hall agreed to follow them back to Sauvé's, where Gordy and Sharon would get off. Rick would take his own car down to the police station. Hall followed him all the way. Before he dropped Gordy off, Rick asked Dogmap to call him a lawyer.

Hall escorted Sauvé to the police chief's office. Inspector Cousens and Sam McReelis were there. Terry Hall left the room.

Cousens explained that he was in town to investigate the murder of Bill Matiyek, that Sauvé was not under arrest, that they just wanted to talk to him. Cousens was preparing to write everything down.

"Where were you on the night of October 18 last?"

Rick told them he'd worked until 3 p.m. that day, and then babysat at home until 11 p.m. He'd gone to the Queen's Hotel after for a drink, but he was denied service.

"Who else was at the hotel?"

Rick didn't answer.

"Did anything unusual happen while you were there?"

Again, no answer.

The Inspector kept probing the young biker about events in the hotel that night—who else was there, what happened, what he had seen—while Sauvé sat in stony silence. The intervals between questions grew longer and longer, and the three men just sat there, around the chief's desk. Outside the closed office door there were sounds of a telephone ringing, the steady clatter of a typewriter, the murmur of official conversation. Inside the chief's office was the pregnant, awful silence of a stalking. The hunter and the hunted.

Both Cousens and McReelis watched Sauvé closely. To the Inspector's practised eye the young biker appeared uncomfortable, unhappy, dejected. That was the word—dejected. Cousens decided to try another tack.

"Look Richard, you're a—a quiet type of guy. We just want to know what happened. We're sure you just got caught up in this thing."

Sauvé's eyes met Cousens's with a level, penetrating stare that was at once coolly angry, defiant, and contemptuous.

"I got nothin' to say to youse people."

Cousens wrote out a "statement." It was just seven lines long, and Sauvé refused to sign it. Not much to show for an interview that had lasted nearly an hour.

It was almost 4:30 when McReelis opened the office door. Hall took Sauvé into another small room, just the two of them.

"Listen," Hall told Sauvé, "I want you to realize you could be in very serious trouble here. If you help us out, we'll help you out. We can move you and your wife and daughter out west, we'll give you money, a whole new identity . . ."

"I didn't do nothin' wrong. I got nothin' to say."

It was nearing eleven o'clock by the time they got to the Halloween party. After booking into a motel, they drove to the dance. Once they finally got there it was a great party, even Sharon had to admit that. The band was topnotch, and the place was packed—there must have been three or four hundred people there. Rick went as Frankenstein, Sharon as a pygmy.

Sharon was nervous to be around so many bikers in one place. She just sat at their table and kept her mouth shut and didn't make a move. Gordy's girlfriend Patty was quite straight, too—a Jehovah's Witness, in fact. So they stayed together and Sharon told Rick not to leave her side, which he didn't, except to circulate a little, quietly, telling a few of the Choice guys about his interview with Cousens.

She could take some of Rick's "brothers" now, when she met them individually or in small groups, but in large numbers Sharon still found them intimidating. And their women—they were so tough, so hard. They often seemed as scrappy as the men, or scrappier.

Still, the party itself was fun—everybody just danced and had a good time. There was a costume competition where everybody walked around in a circle and got judged, just like at a Halloween party back home at the Legion, Sharon decided. It wasn't that wild, really.

After the party ended, neither Rick nor Gordy noticed a car pull out after them and ride their tail, at a discreet distance, all the way across Toronto and Scarborough on the 401 through the light 2 a.m. traffic. It must have been three or four in the morning before they finally went to bed. The last thing Sharon remembered was thinking that she'd really had a good time. Maybe they should try going out like this, as a couple, more often . . .

Constable Don Denis spent all day Friday and most of Saturday afternoon watching witnesses pore over his photo arrays in the Port Hope police station. For this, the second major viewing session, Denis had added photographs to his original line-up. Recalling Cathy Cotgrave's tentative identification of the gunman, Denis was careful to include more pictures of Gary Comeau.

The OPP constable followed the same routine he had established the week before. Each eyewitness was asked to indicate the photograph of anyone he or she had seen in the Queen's Hotel on the night of the shooting. After each witness had finished and left the room, Denis would check the reference number of any photos identified and then jot down the names in his notebook, also noting any relevant comments that the witness might have made while making the ID. At the start of each viewing Denis noted the time, but—and here he was unwittingly committing his first major blunder—he failed to note their exit, or finishing, times. His notes would reveal that fifty minutes or so elapsed between viewings. But had it taken Cathy Cotgrave five minutes, or fifty, to make what appeared to be a number of definite, positive ID's? No one would ever know.

Sue Foote was the third witness of the morning to view the line-up. The first two weren't particularly helpful, but Gayle Thompson's roommate, who was examining the array for a second time, pointed to a number of photographs. She identified Fred Jones and Sonny Bronson from the Outlaws, and Larry Hurren, Rick Sauvé, Tee Hee Hoffman, Merv Blaker, and Gary Comeau from the Satan's Choice. She also told Denis that a big guy with long blond hair tied in a ponytail that stretched down to the small of his back had also been present. She thought his name was Jeff. Foote added that they were all wearing ponytails, except for Hurren. Even Rick Sauvé, who never wore his hair in a ponytail, had had one that night.

Rod Stewart saw the pictures for the second time early in the afternoon. The contractors ID's, which Denis had recorded as being "vague" the first time around, became even more confusing. He pointed to pictures of Sonny Bronson, Dennis Crossfield, Frank Martin, David Flood, Michael Anderson, and Walter High. Apart from Bronson, the ID's didn't jibe with any of the other witnesses'. Moreover, Stewart had failed to identify a single one of the photographs he'd selected just a week earlier.

As the day wore on, more and more witnesses, including Stewart's two drinking partners, turned up blanks. They just couldn't identify anyone.

But the trail grew warmer the next afternoon. At 1:30 on Saturday Denis varied his routine: he permitted two witnesses, Cathy Cotgrave and Gayle Thompson, to view the array at the same time, a decision that violated all precepts of scientific identification procedures. Denis instructed the two waitresses not to talk to one another while viewing the pictures, but there was little doubt that each could see which photos the other was selecting.

Perhaps not surprisingly, both made a number of positive ID's that afternoon. Cotgrave once again selected pictures of Merv Blaker, Rick Sauvé, Fred Jones, Armand Sanguigni, Larry Hurren, and Sonny Bronson. This time she identified two pictures of Tee Hee Hoffman, whom she'd failed to recognize before, even though the young barmaid was certain he'd been in the hotel. Sanguigni, she told Denis, had been in the pinball room. She pointed to a picture of Jeff McLeod, whom she'd identified before, as well as two new faces: Michael Gallaway and Randy Gobo. She paused at a picture of Gary Comeau and then pointed. "Could be trigger man," Denis recorded in his notes, though those weren't necessarily Cotgrave's exact words. She came back to the same picture of Comeau a second time. "Thought to be the trigger man," Denis noted. This time she made no mention of Snyder's picture.

Gayle Thompson meanwhile was pointing to pictures of Fred Jones, Sonny Bronson, Merv Blaker, Rick Sauvé, Larry Hurren, and Michael Everett. She selected Tee Hee Hoffman from two different photographs and, like Cotgrave, identified Gary Comeau as the possible gunman.

While Denis was busy with Cotgrave and Thompson at the police station that Saturday afternoon, Terry Hall was also in the neighborhood. Like Denis, Hall too had decided to pursue the investigation with somewhat unorthodox methods. The procedures followed by both men were unlikely ever to be written up in OPP "how-to" instructional manuals, but to them it was results that mattered.

Early that afternoon both Rick Sauvé and Merv Blaker got calls from Bobby Cousins, a long-time member and former officer in Peterborough Chapter. Cousins was, in fact, one of the more senior Choice members that Sauvé had tried to locate before calling the Toronto clubhouse the night of the shooting.

Terry Hall, Cousins told Sauvé and Blaker, was drinking at the Plaza Hotel in Cobourg and he wanted to speak to both of them. Would they come down to the hotel? It was an unusual request, and it should have set off alarm bells. What was their trusted brother Bobby Cousins doing sitting in a hotel drinking beer with the most hated copper in biker chapters from Thunder Bay to Cornwall? And why was Cousins making calls for Terry Hall?

Both Sauvé and Blaker agreed to meet with Hall. To this day, neither man can offer a satisfactory explanation for his behavior, but it was characteristic of most of the Choice members in the days and weeks that followed the shooting of Bill Matiyek. They all returned to their homes and resumed their daily lives with a sweet indifference that can be ascribed only to colossal gall, incredible naivete, or absolute conviction as to their innocence. It was inexplicable behavior for a group of supposedly hardened criminals suspected of a cold-blooded gangland-style execution.

Merv rode his Sportster the five miles from Port Hope to Cobourg, but carefully folded his ancient denim cut-off with its precious patch and put it in his helmet before entering the Plaza Hotel, in observance of the hotel's "no colours" policy. Terry Hall, Bobby Cousins, and a third man—Hall introduced him as Roger, a guard at Warkworth, a medium-security federal prison not far from Cobourg—were sitting together at a table covered with beer glasses and empty bottles. It was only 1:30 in the afternoon and the hotel had opened at noon—pretty heavy drinking, Merv couldn't help thinking, even by his own standards.

Though, like everyone else, Merv had heard innumerable Terry Hall stories, he'd never actually spoken to the man. Yet Hall greeted him like a long-lost brother. Hey Merv, how ya doin', lemme buy ya a beer, let's see, they call ya Indian, right? Right. Merv's guard went up sky-high, but he let Hall buy him a beer.

Rick arrived about twenty minutes later and the five of them spent the rest of the afternoon and part of the evening swilling beer, at Hall's expense. The whole thing was pure Terry Hall; a master at work. Step into my parlor, said the spider to the fly. Hall rarely spoke outright about the Matiyek investigation. He'd just sideswipe the subject, laughing, watching their faces, and then circle around and bring it up again, hours later. In between he'd dodge and feint, bob and weave, almost one of them, but sowing the seeds of doubt, the seeds of discord. Let's see now, had it been this or that Choice member (he knew all their nicknames too) who'd told him this or that during one interrogation, or was it over a beer at a club run to Wasaga?

His job, after all, was special *intelligence* squad, and Hall had learned the subtle arts of paranoid mind games and the value of disinformation as well as any spy-master from the CIA—or so he fancied.

It was eight hours of pure bullshit poker with Terry Hall as dealer. Finally, around eight, as they all got drunker, Hall began overplaying his hand. He made a joke of the fact that he'd tailed them all the way to and from the party, and the natural enmities began to spill over. Hall and Sauvé got into an argument over which of them was the fittest. Rick was really into fitness, and he started yapping about whether he or Hall could run the fastest or throw the farthest or bench-press the most. "Aw, fuck, I could go up one side of ya and down the other," Sauvé told Hall, only half joking.

"Oh yeah?" They decided to fight it out on Tuesday.

Meanwhile, Cousins and the prison guard, Roger, started arguing over something or other, and they decided to go outside and settle it right then. When they came back in, the biker's shirt was ripped and he was sporting a few bruises. Then Hall and Cousins got into it—Bobby always was that stupid. *They* decided to step outside, and when they came back it was obvious that Bobby had gotten another pounding. The whole thing was too embarrassing, too weird, and Blaker and Sauvé finally left the Plaza.

VIII

FROM THE POLICE POINT OF VIEW, the investigation into the murder of Bill Matiyek was reaching a difficult phase. Most of the potential Crown witnesses had now seen the photo line-up at least once, and most had been peculiarly unhelpful—they either couldn't or wouldn't identify any of the members of the Satan's Choice who had been in the Queen's on October 18. Blaker and Sauvé were exceptions. They were so well known and had been identified so often, it was obvious they had been there. Most of the witnesses had not merely identified the two bikers—they *knew* them. Sauvé, moreover, had admitted he was there.

But many of the Queen's patrons were themselves barflies and rounders, with little use for the police. They were no more helpful in interviews with Cousens and McReelis than they had been in the photo sessions with Denis. At one point, after a particularly long day in Port Hope, Inspector Cousens returned to Toronto headquarters, and Terry Hall watched him collapse wearily into a chair. "I've never been told to 'fuck off' so many times during one investigation in my life," Cousens told the head of the biker squad.

On the other hand, Denis's work with the photos had turned up important evidence from three witnesses—Cathy Cotgrave, Gayle Thompson, and Sue Foote. The three women had now viewed the line-up twice each. Besides Blaker and Sauvé, and Fred Jones and Sonny Bronson from the Outlaws, they had each identified Tee Hee Hoffman, Larry Hurren, and Gary Comeau as being in the hotel. Cotgrave and Thompson agreed that Comeau could be the gunman. The identifications of Sanguigni and McLeod were shakier, but they were certainly secondary suspects.

In the absence of any stronger, fresher leads, the police continued to interview the prime suspects in the first week of November. On Thursday, November 2, Cousens and McReelis drove to Kitchener to talk with Tee Hee Hoffman. They met with Waterloo Regional Police Detective Colquhoun, and the three men drove to the offices of the B. F. Goodrich company. Hoffman agreed to talk with them at the police station.

Hoffman denied any knowledge of the shooting, except for what he'd read in the newspapers. He reminded his interrogators of the police raid, adding that he'd stayed at the clubhouse to help repair the battered door and to make a few phone calls. Several other members, including Neil Stewart, Joe and Tom Ertel, and Drago Salajko had seen him at the clubhouse after the raid. Shortly before eleven, Hoffman added, he'd gotten a lift home, where he'd watched the eleven o'clock news before going to bed. He said nothing about the late-night visit from Comeau, Blaker, and Sauvé.

It was obvious to the investigators that, for the early part of the evening at least, Hoffman had an air-tight alibi. Colquhoun, among others, remembered Hoffman at the clubhouse during the raid. Assuming that the last of the police had left at 7:30 or 8 p.m., though, Hoffman would still have had time to make the two-hour drive to Port Hope. The only people he'd been with during the latter half of the evening were other members of the Satan's Choice, not the most believable of alibi witnesses, whereas the three witnesses who put Hoffman in the hotel during the shooting were credible.

Although Inspector Cousens, Sergeant McReelis, and Corporal Hall were doing most of the leg work on the investigation, Constable Don Denis had really become the point man, and it was his efforts that would lead most directly to the laying of charges. Denis returned to Port Hope to show more photo line-ups five days after Cousens's interrogation of Hoffman, on Tuesday, November 7. Denis had continued to add photographs to his array, and at some point he noticed that several witnesses were having problems with the ever-increasing mass of pictures. It may have been a coincidence, but Denis seemed to locate additional photographs mainly of the individuals who had now become prime suspects. By early December he would have no fewer than seven photographs of Gary Comeau in the line-up. Perhaps because he was having trouble finding a table big enough to spread out all the pictures on, Denis began to stack the photos when he had a multiple array of a single individual.

Sometimes, Denis noted as he watched the witnesses peer at the photographs, the viewer would fail to notice that there were additional pictures underneath the one on top of a stack, especially when the visible photo was larger than the ones underneath. To call the witnesses' attention to the fact that there were pictures underneath, Denis took a red magic marker and placed a red dot on the pictures of certain individuals. Six of the eight individuals who would eventually be charged with the murder of Bill Matiyek had their pictures so marked. Just when this was done and just which pictures were seen on which date by which potential Crown witness, it was impossible to say—Denis failed to record the exact dates when he added to the array.

Although his rogues' gallery of Satan's Choice members was fairly comprehensive from the outset (it included pictures of some people who had ceased to be members months, even years, before), there was no picture of

Lorne Campbell in the very first photo array shown. At some point a single picture of Campbell was added, but it was perhaps not surprising that it would be overlooked by every viewer, especially as the stacks of pictures of certain individuals grew with every viewing, some with a red dot on the top just so that the witnesses wouldn't miss anything. Constable Denis was only trying to be helpful.

By the second week in November, life had pretty well returned to normal for Nutty Comeau. His wounds were healing nicely, there didn't seem to be too much heat on, and life was, as it had always been for Nutty, once again almost without a care. There was one tiny cloud, largely hidden beneath the horizon, and Nutty couldn't see its exact dimensions. Maybe it was the shooting of Bill Matiyek or, more immediately, getting shot himself, but as he approached his twenty-seventh birthday Gary Comeau was becoming, for the first time in his life, introspective.

It was the Life he wondered about, and his own life. He was still interested in the club—the club and his brothers were the only life he knew outside his family. But after eight years in the club, maybe it was the routine that was getting him down. It was the same thing over and over. Sleep until mid-afternoon, maybe have supper at home, go down to the clubhouse for a few beers, then over to one of the Scarborough hotels—the White Castle or Knob Hill, usually—to check out the strippers and do a little business, drink until one o'clock, then back to the clubhouse to party until he puked or passed out. Sleep most of the day, then get up and do it all over again. Maybe he needed to find a steady broad, and slow down a bit . . .

On November 9, Inspector Cousens contacted Nutty and Jeff McLeod. Nutty wasted no time in calling his lawyer, Howard Kerbel. A downtown Toronto criminal lawyer, Kerbel had represented Comeau before, in addition to a number of other Toronto Chapter members of the Satan's Choice. Kerbel agreed to act as a go-between and arranged for a meeting involving Cousens, Comeau, and McLeod at his office the following afternoon. Kerbel himself couldn't be there, but he'd arrange for a student to sit in on both interrogations.

Cousens commented immediately on the resemblance between Nutty and Jeff. They really did look like brothers. Both were about six feet,

Comeau's hair just a shade more auburn than McLeod's and with more of a curl, and, even though he was fifty pounds lighter than McLeod, Comeau, at 270, was no lightweight. Big, big boys.

Cousens questioned Comeau first, but both men were pretty much just going through the motions. The greying inspector asked Comeau if he was a member of the Satan's Choice. Nutty said he was, since 1970.

"Did you know a William Matiyek?"

"No."

"Did you know any members of the Golden Hawks Motorcycle Club in Oshawa?"

"No."

"Did you ever know anyone by the name 'Heavy'?"

"No. There's a 'Heavy' in the Last Chance Motorcycle Club."

"When was the last time you were in Port Hope?"

"It would have to be about eight months ago, or June of '78."

"Where were you on October 18 of 1978?"

"At this time I have nothin' to say."

"Would you consent to a line-up for purposes of identification?"

"No."

"What do you know about the murder in the Queen's Hotel in Port Hope on October 18 last?" .

"I know that a person was killed, I read it in the *Sun*. It mentioned my club."

"Do you know or have you heard of any of your members being in Port Hope at the Queen's Hotel when the murder took place?"

"I don't know nothin' about that."

Cousens showed Comeau the statement. The big biker didn't bother to read it, much less sign it. The whole thing took fifteen minutes, and Cousens fared no better with McLeod.

The even bigger biker denied knowing Bill Matiyek, or any other members of the Golden Hawk Riders. He'd last been to Port Hope in June or July of 1978, to the clubhouse there.

"Do you know where you were on October 18 last?"

"I don't know."

All McLeod knew about Matiyek was what he read in the newspapers. No, he wouldn't consent to a line-up, and no, McLeod didn't know anyone else who'd been at the Queen's Hotel on October 18.

On his way back uptown, Cousens thought about Comeau and McLeod. Strange, maybe, but the Inspector didn't have quite the same feelings about bikers that many of his younger colleagues did. They viewed these motorcycle gang members with a mixture of contempt and outright hatred. Cousens had spent almost thirty years of his life working among men and he was the father of three boys, each of whom would become cops. Cousens felt he knew men, the character of men. He had no use for bikers, but he always had the feeling that if the country were ever at war, many of these characters would make good soldiers. Combat infantrymen. They were tough, they were mean, and they were loyal to the point of suicide, the very best of these bikers. Cousens thought again about his encounters with Comeau and McLeod and Sauvé. Good soldiers, yes. And lousy liars.

Constable Don Denis, meanwhile, soldiered on with his photo arrays. On Saturday, November 18, he showed them for the first time to David Gillispie, the first person to give police a statement after the shooting, and the only witness to have overhead the "fat fucker" statement to Blaker and Sauvé. Gillispie had little difficulty picking out photos of Blaker and Sauvé and Fred Jones. He paused at picture 3–2. It was, Denis knew, Gary Comeau. He might've been with Jones, but Gillispie wasn't sure. Gillispie pointed to a second picture, 2–6. Gary Comeau, again. He might have been the gunman. Then Gillispie came back to 2–6. The gunman sure looked like him. Most of them were tall and slim, except for the guy who pulled the trigger. Denis reported his results immediately, as he always did, to either Inspector Cousens or Sergeant McReelis.

On Friday, November 24, Gillispie viewed the line-up a second time. This time he selected only one photograph, a picture of someone named Seguin. He looked like the gunman. One step forward, two steps back. That was the problem, the investigators knew, with eyewitness ID, but it was all they had.

The same night Sue Foote saw the line-up for her third time, and it looked like two steps forward again. Except for one new photo, her ID's jibed exactly with the ones she'd made back on October 28. And this time she was positive on McLeod. Gayle Thompson, during her third viewing, told Denis that, with a hat on, Comeau would look like the killer.

Cathy Cotgrave came in for her third, and final, viewing on Monday, December 4. She picked Larry Hurren, Armand Sanguigni, Tee Hee

Hoffman, Gary Comeau, Merv Blaker, Rick Sauvé, Sonny Bronson, Rae Snyder, Jeff McLeod, and Fred Jones. Snyder was possibly the gunman. Then she looked at Comeau's picture. No, on second thought, if it was anybody, it was probably Comeau.

After Cathy left the police station Denis reviewed his notes. Like Sue Foote and Gayle Thompson, Cotgrave's ID's had been remarkably consistent, right from day one. It had been a long haul. A total of twenty-two potential Crown witnesses had viewed the line-up over a period of seven weeks. The majority had been unable to identify anyone at all. Most of the others had identified either Blaker, Sauvé, Jones, or Bronson. Only a handful had identified anyone else. Foote, Cotgrave, and Thompson were good. Gillispie was shaky. Rod Stewart picked faces no one else had seen at all, and his selections had been completely inconsistent from one viewing to the next. Don Denis packed up his photo collection for the last time, and returned to Toronto.

IX

THE FIRST WEEK OF DECEMBER was a time of taking stock. The police investigators reviewed their evidence. Was it sufficient to lay a charge? Far and away the best evidence appeared to be the eyewitness ID's of Sue Foote, Cathy Cotgrave, and Gayle Thompson. Their identifications were solid and consistent, and should stand up in court. There was certainly a paucity of physical evidence. They had Matiyek's blood-soaked clothing, and one of the slugs that had lodged in his brain and fragments of a second. They had David Gillispie's "fat fucker" statement, which had been given to police within hours of the shooting, a statement that had now been signed and sworn by the witness. That certainly seemed to indicate knowledge of intent, even conspiracy. Murder weapon? Nothing, except that no spent casings were found anywhere in the hotel. The suspects' exit after the shooting had been so hasty, everyone agreed, that they hadn't stopped to clean up evidence. Conclusion: the murder weapon was a revolver. Triggerman? Gary Comeau, if Cotgrave and Thompson were right, but the ID's weren't quite positive enough. Comeau as prime suspect, anyway. Motive? Enmity between the Satan's Choice and the Golden Hawk Riders, maybe. Gang warfare, and a gangland-style execution.

But there were some nagging loose ends. One of Terry Hall's informants, apparently in Port Hope, had confided that someone else besides Matiyek had been shot that night. Hall had reported this intelligence to his superior, but Cousens, as he would testify later, considered it very vague. There was also the matter of the missing third slug. All of the witnesses agreed they heard three shots, but, try as they might, the investigators had only found enough fragments in Matiyek and the wall behind his body to equal one bullet. A second was found in his brain. Where was the third one? And where was the murder weapon?

On Tuesday, December 5, the day after Cathy Cotgrave had completed her third viewing of the photo array, the police obtained arrest warrants for seven members of the Satan's Choice: David George Hoffman, Gary Joseph Comeau, Murray Blaker, Armand J. Sanguigni, Jeffrey A. McLeod, Richard Michael Sauvé, and Larry J. Hurren. The charge: conspiracy to commit murder on one William J. Matiyek. The police also obtained search warrants for the premises of each of the accused, as well as the Satan's Choice Toronto clubhouse, 1860 Markham Road. Maybe that would shake out the murder weapon. By the night of the fifth, all of the elaborate planning had been completed for a major police operation the following day.

On Wednesday, at 11:05 a.m., the police, led by Colin Cousens, arrested Tee Hee Hoffman at his place of employment, the B. F. Goodrich Co., in Kitchener. The suspect—now an accused—was placed under arrest, informed of the charges against him, cautioned that anything he said might be used against him, and taken to his residence, an apartment at 20 Blucher Street. A search was commenced in his presence. Certain items of clothing, most notably Hoffman's club colours, were seized. No handgun was discovered, but the police impounded one item that would have great significance to the life of the long-time Kitchener biker—his telephone bills.

Jeff McLeod learned of Tee Hee's arrest later that afternoon, when Nutty came to pick him up at the Scarborough Mid-Centre Youth Arena, where Jeff had just finished playing hockey. It was always quite a sight, a 320-pound biker on skates, carrying the puck down the right wing and across the blue line, his long hair cascading from under his helmet, all the way down to the small of his back. But Jeff moved with surprising grace for such a big man and he looked like what he'd once been—a fairly talented junior hockey player.

"Hey, man, didja hear the news?"

"No, what?"

"They busted Tee Hee this morning."

"What for?"

"Port Hope."

"Whaaat?"

"Conspiracy to commit murder."

Neither of them could quite believe it. Had the coppers learned of Nutty, Rick, and Merv's visit to Tee Hee's the night of the shooting? They must have. But it was kind of ironic, too. After all this time, the coppers finally bust somebody for Matiyek and get a guy who wasn't even there. Typical coppers—big investigation and they get the wrong guy. Tee Hee was innocent—he should be able to beat it, they agreed. They both laughed.

Nutty and Jeff went to the clubhouse and were relaxing over a beer, their guards totally down, still marvelling over the ineptitude of the police, when the guard dog started barking. He was a great junkyard dog, a mean Dobe that scared most of the members too, and nobody thought much about the racket until there was a terrific crash on the clubhouse door and one whole wall of the building began to sway slightly, threatening to come crashing down on their heads.

"What the f—?"

There were about a dozen people in the clubhouse, a couple of them broads, and it took everyone a second or two to figure out what was going down. Then, pandemonium.

"Coppers, man!"

"It's a raid!"

Everybody was on their feet.

"If ya got anything on ya, get rid of it!"

Everyone was running now. Nutty and Jeff sprinted upstairs to the second floor, to see what was going on. Fuckin' coppers, Nutty thought to himself. It burned him, the way they always came bustin' through doors, like they'd seen one too many episodes of Eliot Ness and *The Untouchables*. Hadn't they ever heard of doorknobs, for fuck sakes?

They peered out the upstairs window.

Outside, the street was blood-red with the light of cherry tops. Cruisers and paddy wagons were everywhere. They'd actually locked off the street, the whole of Highway 48, and they were about to go at the clubhouse door again with a tow truck that had been converted into a battering-ram. But the cops had failed to reckon with the fact that the heavily reinforced door had also been reinforced to the surrounding wall. One more shot with that sucker and the whole damned clubhouse might collapse around them. Nutty and Jeff looked at each other in disbelief.

Nutty stuck his head out the window and instantly wished he hadn't. He heard the metallic "click" of about twenty guns—safeties being released, semi-automatics being cocked. There were police sharpshooters poised, ready, behind every cop car.

Oh well, he was already there, now. "Go to the back door," Nutty screamed, "and we'll let youse in."

The SWAT team with M-16s swarmed through the clubhouse like flies on fresh meat. "Everybody on the floor," one of them bellowed. It was strictly paramilitary style: gun barrels to the head, combat boots heavy on the back as they were lying there on the floor. Jeff noticed they even had little mirrors attached to their gun barrels, so they could see around corners. Just like the movies.

Inspector Cousens was in overall charge, but he let the Divisional Commanders supervise their individual units. They did an extensive search of the clubhouse, looking for illicit drugs, illegal weapons (a .38 Colt revolver, on a .45 frame, perhaps?), any form of contraband. Cousens was pleasantly surprised to see McLeod, Comeau, and Hurren all lying on the floor. Four down, three to go.

"Jeffrey McLeod, Gary Comeau, Larry Hurren, you are all under arrest for conspiracy to commit murder on the person of William J. Matiyek," Cousens read them the charge.

Terry Hall escorted Jeff into the front room. "You're under arrest. You can't talk, you can't do nothin'."

Sam McReelis was with Nutty. "Hey, man, it's cold out there. Lemme get my jacket."

"Sure. Which one's yours?"

Without even thinking, Nutty pointed at his black-leather jacket, hanging up with a bunch of others in the hallway.

"Get movin', Comeau. Where you're goin' you won't need a jacket."

They were driven to 42 Division Headquarters, where Metro Police officers filled out their arrest records.

At 11:46 p.m. Gary Comeau was ushered into an interrogation room. Colin Cousens was waiting for him, and he proceeded to make minute observations about Nutty's left arm, very minute for an investigator who would testify under oath, ten months later, that he had disregarded Terry Hall's intelligence that someone besides Bill Matiyek had been shot in the Queen's Hotel. He noted what appeared to be a rough-looking incision on the under part of the upper portion of the accused's left arm, and a second round scar, about one-quarter of an inch in diameter. It looked like an entrance wound.

"What happened to your arm?"

Gary Comeau had nothing to say.

"What'm *I* here for?" Jeff McLeod asked his guards, still playing the role, all wide-eyed and innocent, just a big dumb biker.

"Believe me, it ain't for unpaid parking tickets. Shut up!"

They were led out of 42 Division Headquarters then, put into cruisers, and driven to the Downsview headquarters of the OPP, a two-storey red-brick box just off the 401 at Keele Street. The driver got out of the car and left Jeff and Larry alone in the back seat. It was after midnight now, and it was the first peace and quiet, the first solitude almost, that Jeff had experienced for several hours. His head was still reeling from everything that had happened. They sat, bathed in the orange-sodium glare of the streetlights suspended over the OPP parking lot and shining down off the 401, the muffled whine of tires at 100 kilometres per—the thinning, late-night freeway traffic, the whisper of the heater fan, the low idle of the cruiser engine. *The idle of the engine!* Jeff's attention was suddenly drawn to the steering-column of the cruiser. Their guard had left the keys in the ignition and the motor running! The same thought, he could see, had suddenly occurred to Beaver. They both looked down at their waists. They were handcuffed, but the cuffs had just been put through their belts. They could easily bust the leather, free their hands, and . . .

"They want us to make a move for it," Jeff said dully. "They're just waitin' in there, and then they're gonna kill us. . . ." Unh-uh. No fuckin' way. After all, what did he really have to worry about? He hadn't done nothin', and besides, this was Canada. They didn't go around convicting innocent men for murder.

Jeff and Larry sat in the idling police car for ten or fifteen minutes until finally several policemen came down the steps with Tee Hee.

Don Denis opened the car door and slid into the driver's seat He turned around and smiled at them. "I got a chunk," he said, "so don't get any ideas, because I'll dust both of ya's." He didn't say it in a derogatory way, merely a statement of fact.

Tee Hee and Nutty were in a second cruiser, and the two cars pulled onto the 401, heading east towards Port Hope. Nutty's mind was spinning like a knobby on a hill climb. They couldn't convict him on a murder beef. Christ, he'd been shot himself. For the first time he thought about his leather jacket with its bullet hole. Slowly he came to realize that it was the only physical evidence he had to prove that he'd been shot. During the days and weeks to come, Nutty would lie awake nights in the Cobourg County bucket, thinking about that jacket. He called the clubhouse, he got his lawyer to call, the guys would look all over the place for it. But the jacket had vanished, as if it never existed. Almost as if he'd never been shot. But he *had* been shot. Hadn't he?

Rick Sauvé heard about the Toronto clubhouse raid on his car radio that night on the way to work. Graveyard shift again. "War games tonight on Markham Road," the announcer boomed out, "as police raided the clubhouse of the Satan's Choice. Three members of the motorcycle gang were charged with conspiracy to commit murder and another member was charged earlier in the day in Kitchener. Police say more arrests are pending. . . ."

The net, Rick knew, was closing around him. He went to work anyway.

They came for Merv Blaker at 2:30 the next afternoon. Merv was in bed when he heard a knock on the door. He looked out the window and saw Cousens and McReelis and a half-dozen other members of the Port Hope Police Department. He went back to bed. The cops walked right in.

Cousens told him to get up, that he was under arrest for conspiracy to commit murder. They searched the house and seized his colours. Karen was at work, but his mother-in-law was home. She started to cry as they led Merv from the house.

"Don't worry about me," he told her. "I'll make bail and be home by tomorrow night."

Friday night Rick Sauvé was still at large. He and Sharon were going to a rock concert, so they dropped Angie off for the weekend at Sharon's mother's. As far as Sharon was concerned, it was mainly for the concert, but Rick knew better. He wanted his daughter out of the house.

They drove to Toronto as planned. The concert was Bob Seger and the Silver Bullet Band. Both Rick and Sharon were big fans, and Maple Leaf Gardens was a sell-out. It was a great concert, until about halfway through. Then Seger told the audience he wanted to perform a new song, a song that he and his band had never before performed in public. A hush fell over the audience and the lights dimmed until the singer was bathed only in the blue and violet and orange wash of the big follow-spots that cut through the reefer haze from the back of the huge building, knifing over the heads of the assembled thousands.

I know it's late,
I know you're weary,
I know your plans
Don't include me.

Still, here we are,
Both of us lonely,
Longing for shelter
From all that we see.

Rick felt the hairs on the back of his neck begin to prickle. A great concert had become unutterably special, as if the singer had written, was singing, a song just for him, to him, about him and Sharon. It was the kind of moment that everyone went to concerts to experience, but seldom did.

Why should we worry?
No one will care, girl,
Look at the stars now,
So far away.

We've got tonight,
Who needs tomorrow?
We've got tonight, girl,
Why don't you stay?

Sharon shivered too. The ache in Seger's voice was telling her life's story:

Deep in my soul
I feel so lonely,
All of my hopes
Fadin' away.

I hoped for love,
Like everyone else does.
Ya know I keep searchin'
After today.

The love song echoed, resonated, through both of them on the drive back to Port Hope, as Sharon curled up beside Rick in the cozy, dark warmth of the car:

So there it is, girl,
We've got it all now,
And here we are, babe.
What do you say?

It was with them still as they tumbled into bed in their little house on the prairie, and everything was almost as it had been so many summers before, when they had made love in the sand of Cobourg beach, before Angie, before Easton's, and before Rick had watched Bill Matiyek's head explode before his disbelieving eyes.

We've got tonight,
Who needs tomorrow?
Let's make it last,
Let's find a way.

Turn out the light,
Come take my hand now,
We've got tonight, babe,
Why don't we stay?

We've got tonight, babe,
Why don't we stay . . .

The mood lasted through Saturday, just the two of them in the house, and Rick drove to Peterborough to do some Christmas shopping. Sharon wrapped the presents on Saturday night and put them under the tree.

The police came for Rick on Sunday morning, at 9:30. It was the first arrest that Colin Cousens wasn't in charge of, and Sam McReelis had a field day. Sharon asked them to please take their boots off at the front door, but they ignored her as they tossed the house. Sharon had been through raids before, and she hated them. It made her feel so helpless, so insignificant.

They seized Rick's colours out of the closet, and then started in on the presents under the tree.

"Hey, whaddaya doin'," Sharon screamed, starting to get hysterical. "I spent all night wrappin' those presents! Here, let me do it."

But they wouldn't. Rick watched as Sam McReelis, like some kind of reverse, malevolent Santa Claus, picked up each present and shook it, listening for a rattle, before ripping it open. Finally he came to one marked for Rick's uncle Albert. It was heavy, and it made a metallic rattling noise. McReelis looked up at Rick with a big grin.

"What's this, Rick? You sure Uncle Albert isn't gettin' a handgun for Christmas?"

He tore it open and found, as Rick knew he would, an electric drill.

Finally, they told Rick he was under arrest. "You, Richard Sauvé, are charged that between the 1st day of January, 1978, and the 18th day of October, 1978, at the Town of Port Hope and in the said County of Northumberland and elsewhere in the Province of Ontario, unlawfully did conspire with others, and with persons unknown, to cause William John Matiyek to be murdered, contrary to Section 423 subsection 1, subsection (a) of the Criminal Code of Canada. You are not obliged to say anything unless you wish to do so, but whatever you do say may be considered as evidence."

Rick still had nothing to say.

They started to take him away when Sharon, with tears in her eyes, asked if they wouldn't wait long enough for her to go and get Angie, so Rick could say good-bye to his daughter.

"Now, Mrs. Sauvé, do you really think that's such a good idea? For her to see him like this?"

Sharon decided it wasn't such a good idea, and they took Rick to a waiting squad car. He had no way of knowing that he would never see his home again. As it was, he never looked back.

They took him to the Port Hope cop shop for booking, fingerprints, and a mug shot, and then threw him into the drunk tank, a black hole without a light or a window, for a few hours, before they drove him over to the Cobourg County bucket. Nutty, Jeff, Larry, Merv, and Tee Hee were already there.

That night, December 10, 1978, was the first night Rick Sauvé, age twenty-six, had ever spent in jail. He never dreamed that he would spend the next twenty-five years of his life there.

BOOK THREE

THE LIFE

"I'd just like to spit in society's face. Because I'm doing what I want and they're doing what everybody else wants—that's the whole thing. I just feel fantastic when they spit in my face, because all it is is, they're jealous of me . . ."

—EARLY CLUB MEMBER IN NFB FILM
Satan's Choice, 1966

"What are you rebelling against?"
"Whaddaya got?"

—MARLON BRANDO AS MOTORCYCLE GANG LEADER TO
COFFEE-SHOP WAITRESS IN *The Wild One*, 1954

X

THE VOLKSWAGEN VAN LABORED NORTHBOUND through Ontario's cottage country on a bright summer day in 1959. It carried a typical Canadian family on their annual vacation—father, mother, eight-year-old daughter, seven-year-old son, and a newborn baby. They weren't rich, but, as the mother would recall many years later, the family always managed to take a summer holiday together, even if it meant cramming all five of them into an undersized tent pitched in a public campground somewhere north of Toronto.

The children were bored by the endless expanse of trees and rocks surrounding the narrow ribbon of asphalt. Suddenly the air quivered with thunder, impossible on such a cloudless day. The boy and the girl scrambled to the window of the old bus, eager to see what was creating such a noise. They were greeted by a scene of incredible speed and power and splendor, or so it seemed to the lad, as hundreds of motorcyclists riding two abreast streamed past the van, heading south. The roar of engines, the gleam of chrome, the easy indifference with which the men occupied the deep-dish saddles of their Nortons and Indians and Harleys bespoke an unimaginable sense of freedom. The boy, his heart racing, hung over the front seat so that he could look through the windshield as if to discover the origin of these magnificent, wind-whipped furies.

Finally, when the procession had passed, Gary Comeau turned to his mother.

"Who was that, Mum?" he asked, still wide-eyed.

"Bad men, son. Bad men," was all she answered.

The memory of his first, fleeting encounter with a motorcycle club never left Gary Comeau. He thought of it often as the gloomy winter of 1978–79 descended over the Cobourg county jail. Sometimes, he wondered if Bernie might not have been on that run. Now wouldn't that have been something?

The Satan's Choice Motorcycle Club was born, as one man's vision long before it became a reality, on a bloody summer afternoon outside Oshawa at the Battle of Pebblestone. Bernie Guindon's club, the Golden Hawk Riders, was hosting a field meet, next to the old Pebblestone Golf Course, for all of the southern Ontario motorcycle clubs, including the Black Diamond Riders and their leader, Johnny Sombrero. Based on Steeles Avenue in Toronto, the BDR's were the undisputed kingpins of Ontario motorcycle clubs in the late fifties and early sixties. Through a series of often heavy-handed manoeuvres, Sombrero and his members had succeeded in shutting down most would-be rival organizations across the city of Toronto.

But in the summer of 1959 a feud started when a newly formed club, the Para-Dice Riders, announced its existence square in the middle of Sombrero's fiefdom. Matters came to a head the day of the Hawks' field meet. There were a lot of clubs there, but Bernie noticed that the Black Diamonds all stayed at one end of the field—they'd brought their own booze and food—and they were going out into the woods a lot and coming back with logs.

Bernie, a talented boxer who had won Golden Gloves Championships in the United States, slipped over to some of the older Hawks. "Hey, there's gonna be a fight. I can see it comin'. Let's get ourselves fuckin' armed here. We're gonna take a beatin' if we don't do somethin'."

But the older guys, some of whom were Second World War and Korean vets, just passed it off. "Aw, nothin's gonna happen here, it's a field meet." There were a lot of other clubs there besides the Black Diamonds and the Hawks. The Para-Dice were there, the Canadian Lancers, the Vagabonds, and several smaller clubs.

The fight started at the end of the day between Bernie and the Sergeant-at-Arms for the BDR's. The immediate cause of the fight has long since been forgotten, but Bernie figured the BDR's wanted it, and he was just the excuse.

The young Hawk had been in another serious fight just the weekend before when he'd had to take on three guys in Grant Pit. He'd gotten a real beating and two shiners, so he'd decided to wear his helmet when he could see trouble brewing at the field meet. He dropped the Sergeant-at-Arms from the Black Diamonds and fell to his knees to drive a shot deep into the guy's belly. He heard a long grunt and the air rushing out of his adversary's midsection, but then more Black Diamonds were on him. They hurt his nose a little bit, but the helmet protected him from any real damage. He managed to free himself somehow and looked around. Fists and clubs were flying everywhere—there were forty, maybe fifty guys flailing away all around him.

He saw two of his fellow Hawks get smashed in the head with clubs, so Bernie grabbed a post of his own, and started beating any Black Diamond in sight. Suddenly a BDR named Tom Bird and Johnny Sombrero himself loomed up in front of him. Bird was a big man, six feet, maybe 220.

"Drop it," Sombrero ordered Guindon, pointing at Bernie's club. Bernie looked at Bird and Sombrero. Bird had a club in his hand, Sombrero had one in his hand, and finally Bernie did drop his club and turned and started running up the hill. The hill was terraced into about three tiers and at the top of the second step Bernie whirled and threw a blow at Bird with all he had, his best knockout punch. Bird went down, out cold, and Sombrero disappeared. Later Bernie heard that some of the Black Diamonds picked up the unconscious Bird and threw him in a van before leaving the battleground. Bird didn't wake up until he got to Pickering, that's how hard Bernie had hit him.

Bernie helped a Hawk who had been smashed full in the throat off the field, to a house that belonged to a friend of his across the street. When he returned to the battle he could see that the Hawks had taken a complete shellacking. Some of the younger guys had fought pretty well, but a lot of the older guys had simply run away. A few Black Diamonds were still lingering around the field; Bernie caught up with one of them.

"Are you a Black Diamond?" Bernie asked.

The guy said, "Yeah," and Bernie suckered him so hard he was knocked right through a fence and down into the gravel pit that adjoined the Hawk clubhouse. One of the Oshawa guys picked up a post from the broken fence and went into the pit and started beating him. Bernie couldn't see the Black Diamond, he was on the ground, but he could hear the Hawk telling him not to move every time he hit him, and the kid kept moving of course, every time he got hit. Finally somebody stopped the Hawk from hitting the guy any more, but Wiggy, Bernie's friend, wanted to drop him down the well and drown him. They managed to talk Wiggy out of that idea.

Bernie was still seething because he had wanted to jump into Wiggy's five-ton truck, which was parked at the top of a hill, and use it to run the Diamonds down, bikes and all, but the Hawks wouldn't let him.

It had been a bloody, bitter afternoon. More than one guy had a bootful of blood, Ab Everest had gotten a broken leg, and Russ Millburn, another Hawk, was hospitalized with a blood clot in the brain.

Worst of all, the Black Diamonds and Johnny Sombrero had carried the day. But it wasn't the licking they'd taken as a club that most bothered Bernie—there was no disgrace in losing a fight. What rankled was that the older guys, who should have been the Hawk leaders, had let themselves be taken by surprise despite Bernie's warning, and had then run away. He lost a lot of respect for the Hawks that day, and he was no longer sure it was the kind of club he wanted to belong to. Bernie wanted a club full of members who would never back down from a fight, no matter how long the odds, that would never let itself be taken by surprise, that would be big enough and powerful enough to beat Johnny Sombrero at his own game.

The Battle of Pebblestone sent a chill through all of the Toronto-area clubs. The Golden Hawks were, after all, a well-established, well-feared club in their own right. If the BDR's could wipe them out right in front of their own clubhouse—and as far as Bernie and a lot of others were concerned, that was what had happened—then none of the smaller clubs were secure.

Gradually Bernie drifted away from the Golden Hawks. After Pebblestone he started to think of them as the "Chicken Hawks," and he wasn't afraid to say so. His personal life was in a state of flux, too. He'd landed a steady job at General Motors' South Plant in Oshawa, but his first marriage was breaking up. And there was his boxing career to think of. Finally Bernie quit the club. He kept his bike, though. In late 1963 or early 1964 he, a friend named Al Sparks, and some other guys they worked with decided to start a new Oshawa club. They called themselves the Phantom Riders. Bernie himself drew up the club crest, which was supposed to depict a phantom riding a motorcycle. Everybody thought that when they took the rough sketch in to the crest factory on Queen Street in Toronto, somebody there would polish the design. But they reproduced the patch exactly as it had been drawn and the Phantom Riders were saddled with the worst-looking crest in Ontario.

Still, the Phantom Riders did a lot of club runs and had a good time. Most people had British bikes—BSA's, Triumphs, and Nortons—with a few Harleys and Japanese bikes thrown in. They weren't as big as the bikes that would come later and they were forever breaking down on the highway, so the runs weren't very long, maybe 190 or 200 kilometres.

Bernie and his two most trusted confederates, Reggie Hawk and Carmen Neil, had succeeded in molding the Phantom Riders into a successful local club by early 1965, but Bernie wasn't satisfied. He longed for something more, something bigger, and the President of the Phantom Riders acted on his ambitions in the spring and summer of 1965.

Perhaps remembering that several clubs had formed a short-lived union called the Amalgamated Riders Association in the early 1960s, Guindon got in touch with three other well-established clubs in southern Ontario— the east-Toronto-based Canadian Lancers, the Wild Ones from the west Toronto–Port Credit–Burlington-Mississauga area, and the Throttle Twisters from Preston, a small town east of Kitchener-Waterloo.

Bernie's proposal was simple but audacious: the Lancers, Wild Ones, and Twisters should join with his own Phantom Riders to create a new super-club. With its broad geographic base and superior numbers, such a club would overnight become the most powerful force in Ontario, Guindon argued. The proposal was unprecedented because it took the organizational level a step further than the Amalgamated Riders had done. The new formation would actually function as a club, with each of the former organizations transformed into chapters of the new organization.

But what to call the new club? Somebody remembered reading a feature article about Johnny Sombrero and the BDR's in the Toronto *Star Weekly* where Sombrero had specifically mentioned the Satan's Choice as one of the clubs he had wiped out. The Satan's Choice, Sombrero had boasted, would never rise again. Everybody liked the idea of calling the new super-club by that name and showing up Johnny Sombrero.

Which raised the problem of colours. Why not use the old Choice crest, too? Even though the old club had been dead since 1958, someone had an old Choice patch lying around somewhere, and it looked good, certainly a lot better than the Phantoms' funky motorcyclist or the Twisters' gloved hand on a throttle, or the Lancers' somewhat unimaginative helmeted knight's head. The Choice crest looked positively mean, with its fanged red devil's head breathing fire on a field of white, the words "Satan's Choice" ablaze above and below the wicked-looking devil. It would, they decided, do nicely. And so, over a period of months, the organization that would evolve into the most famous club in the history of Canadian outlaw biking was born.

XI

SOME TIME IN THE FALL OF 1964, an unknown young film director named Don Shebib persuaded the National Film Board of Canada to let him make a movie about motorcycle clubs in Canada. Shebib selected Martin Duckworth, a young Montreal cinematographer, as his camera-man. Both men would go on to distinguished careers in the Canadian film industry—Shebib as the director of a number of celebrated feature films and Duckworth as a maker of documentaries. But the 30-minute black-and-white film that resulted from the months that Shebib and Duckworth spent with the Canadian Lancers in the late summer and early fall of 1965 is still a classic in its genre, an insightful profile of the status of Canadian motor-cycle clubs in the mid-sixties. They titled their movie *Satan's Choice*.

The portrait that emerges is one of youthful rebellion, of a group of young men who have "rejected the traditional middle-class values of mate-rial goods, security, and conformity," as the narrator intones early in the film. We see the young rebels drinking beer and singing club songs accompanied by someone playing the guitar, in a clubhouse meeting, on a club run. It is a mild, benign picture of apparently harmless youthful alienation with no hint of the violence that preceded the founding of the Satan's Choice, no inkling of the still greater blood-letting yet to come. What had caused this new social phenomenon? Shebib and Duckworth record two Lancers waxing philosophical over a few beers.

"I'd say the majority of society today does absolutely nothing. All they depend on is they go to work in the morning and they come home at night. They sit down, they have supper, they watch television, they worry about whether they've got a new car in the driveway, whether their house is the best-looking house on the street, that's what the average person worries about. This doesn't enter my mind at all. I figure the most important thing is a person's way of thinking, what goes on inside their mind."

A second Lancer agrees. "They're all making good money so they can buy a newer car than the people next door. As long as they're in line and they're as big and as fat as the next carrot, what's the difference? The whole idea I think of life, really, is being happy and the way I'm happy is to do what I want."

Nearly a generation later, they seem impossibly young, fresh-faced, and clean-cut, these Toronto youths who are rebels maybe, but not yet outlaws. They are the very face of post-war North America, the first flower of the baby boom. South of the border their photographed portraits graced a million working-class homes, smiling, well-fed, complacent, beneath the bill of a U.S. Marine Corps dress-uniform cap, or the forage cap of a private first class in the United States Army. Those boys would learn about the real world soon enough.

But in Canada the luxury of prolonged mass adolescence would last longer. Not for them the life of the nine-to-five carrot, the three-bedroom bungalow, the mind-numbing monotony of the suburbs. Surely there had to be more to life than *that*.

It had not always been so, as their parents, who survived the Great Depression and the Second World War, knew all too well. To them, the ownership of a tract home, a new car, a television set, represented the tangible fulfilment of the North American Dream. Any blue-collar worker with a steady job could have these things, along with something even more valuable: if a man was lucky and didn't drink or gamble or get hurt on the job, he could afford to send his son or daughter to college, or even university, thus providing his progeny with a meal ticket to the white-collar world, a passport out of the assembly line or construction site or steel mill or hard-rock mine. The great North American promise of upward mobility had finally, it seemed, arrived.

It was not only the working-class kids who were in rebellion, of course. So were the children of the middle class, for whom a university education and entry into a profession were a simple birthright. They, too, rejected what they regarded as the materialism and conformity of their parents' generation, but their rebellion took a much different form.

Where the sons of the working class were drawn to the power and speed of the internal-combustion engine slung between two wheels, the middle-class kids had a far grander vision: they would remake a competitive, aggressive society, in their own image through peace, love, and good vibes. If the lingua franca of the working-class rebels was grease, booze, and violence, the currency in the middle-class world was flowers, drugs, and pacifism.

The privileged descendants of the middle class had been given to understand, almost from birth, that they would one day inherit ownership and control of society—on their parents' terms, of course. But the working-class kids had no such illusions. As individuals, they feared they would grow up to be as powerless as their fathers and mothers, their parents' dreams of upward mobility notwithstanding. Perhaps because of this inherently divergent starting point, the two great youth rebellions of the mid-sixties would follow increasingly divergent paths over the next two decades.

Since they were powerless as individuals, working-class young men gravitated almost instinctively towards organization. Only by banding together could they create an enclave against an overwhelmingly powerful mainstream society. The feel for organization was deeply ingrained. It was their fathers' generation that had organized the great industrial unions of the 1930s and '40s. But the working-class rebels of the sixties would create organizations that elevated the notion of union "brotherhood" to a much higher plane. For all their boorish, bullying, and often brutal behavior towards outsiders, the bikers were not necessarily, as they were so often represented, moral or physical cowards as individuals. And for all the prattling of their ideology—and a kind of ideology it would become—about absolute freedom of the individual from the constraints of society, they would remain, at heart, highly collective individuals. They combined into organizations that were self-disciplined and self-regulating, with strict codes of conduct concerning honesty, loyalty, and trust. Ultimately, it was understood, the individual might be called upon to sacrifice all for the good of the collective, even life itself. And on rare occasions, that was exactly what happened.

The organizations founded by the middle-class rebels—the student radicals and hippie counterculture—were, by contrast, far looser, far more individualistic and voluntary. Beards and long hair, after all, were easily shorn when a scion of the middle class decided to regain his rightful place on Bay Street. The devil's-head tattoo on one's arm—which marked a full member of the Satan's Choice—branded a man for life.

But in 1965, when these two parallel movements were just beginning, they shared at least one icon in common. It was the first "personality poster" ever printed, a blow-up of a black-and-white publicity still from the movie *The Wild One*. This picture of a surly young Marlon Brando, dressed in a studded black-leather jacket, was a familiar sight on the walls of every hippie "head shop," just as it was a commonplace on the wall of every bike shop. Its popularity was remarkable, not least because the young people who were toking up or fiddling with carburetors beneath it had been in grammar school when the photograph was actually taken in 1954. There was something about the impudent, heavy-lidded arrogance of Brando, it seemed, that appealed deeply to both classes of rebellious youth.

The film from which the poster had been made was a genuine case of art imitating life, for the movie's story line was loosely based on a true incident. On the July 4 weekend of 1947, hundreds—some reports said thousands—of motorcyclists descended without warning on the unsuspecting town of Hollister, California. They quickly disarmed the village's tiny police force and indulged in a riotous weekend of drinking, mayhem, and destruction, terrorizing the citizens of this hitherto obscure southern California community. The whole thing was a police officer's nightmare—and a biker's dream—and it made headlines across North America. Still, sensational as the episode was, it would probably have been forgotten but for the movie it inspired.

In a piece of sheer casting genius, director Laslo Benedek chose Marlon Brando to play Johnny, the taciturn, bullying gang leader who terrorized the small California town. Lee Marvin was selected as the head of a second, rival, gang. The film was a critical and a modest box-office success when it was released in 1954, but it proved to be eleven or twelve years ahead of its time. When it was rediscovered by a new generation of young rebels in the mid-sixties it assumed the importance of Holy Writ, manifesto, and mythology, all rolled into one 97-minute package.

To its middle-class viewers, *The Wild One* was a metaphor, Brando's antiheroic character representing a repellent yet fascinating symbol of iconoclasm, of what might happen when the sacred cows of their parents—the sanctity of private property and womanhood, the rule of law—were utterly swept away.

Bikers, however, took it literally—and still do. Brando and Marvin were positive role models. Brando's macho, swaggering indifference seemed particularly heroic and it would set a tone, a standard, for an entire generation. The idea of taking over an entire town, of totally disarming a police force, was particularly appealing, and *The Wild One* contributed mightily to the mythology of the club run, where hundreds of lawless freebooters would take to the open road, their secret destination known only to a few. Were they headed *here*? Were they headed *there*? Hundreds of police would mobilize, scurrying to set up roadblocks in advance of the avenging hordes, valiantly protecting some innocent local populace from anarchy, pillage, and a fate worse than death.

To this day it's a rare biker who has not seen *The Wild One* at least once, and police harassment and surveillance of all club runs in Canada is a game played in deadly earnest. To the middle-class kids it was, after all, just a poster, only a movie. To their working-class counterparts, *The Wild One* would forever after define an aspect of life, The Life. And so the circle was closed. Life imitated art imitating life.

XII

IN 1966, AS HE STOOD POISED on the verge of outlaw history, Bernie Guindon, then only twenty-four years old, was already a veteran in Toronto club circles. He was widely respected for his self-discipline, and his athleticism, but he was admired in other ways, too. The Choice founder combined courage with a quick intelligence and a keen sense of diplomacy. Bernie always seemed to know how to get things done without ever appearing manipulative. He was a dreamer who would prove time and again his ability to act on and achieve his visions. The young Oshawa biker radiated energy and confidence. To be around Bernie Guindon was to feel utterly and irrepressibly alive, living for the moment, and yet moving towards some grand and glorious future.

Bernie Guindon was also a man whose time had most decidedly come. The youth rebellion was gaining momentum everywhere, creating whole new worlds in music, politics, morality, culture, fashion, and lifestyle, and the trickle of young working-class men featured in Shebib's documentary was about to become a torrent.

What motivated the young men who flocked to the Satan's Choice during the club's great period of expansion? One member, Bill Lavoie, suggested they were like soldiers without a war.

"We were the generation that never had a war to go to. Both generations before us had the First and Second World Wars to fight. Korea. We had fuck-all. The fuckin' government wouldn't let us go over to Vietnam. We didn't have nothin' to do. And I think that was the reason why some of the people came to the club, was it gave some kind of an outlet to their—"

"Aggression?" an interviewer asks.

Bill scowls. "Well, some highly educated people might call it 'aggressive tendencies' but I just call it ordinary lightheartedness, somethin' to do. The conquering of boredom, if you know what I mean.

"Like, you could sit in the hotel, with the rest of the morons in this world, and fill your face full of beer, which was what they were all doin', or you could go out and do somethin', like join a club, which I did, and a lot of other people did. And drink with them, and have a good time with friends. That was more or less the choices ya had back in those days, ya know."

In the spring of 1967, Bernie began to add new chapters to the Choice: in Guelph, Ottawa, Montreal, Kingston, and Peterborough.

David Hoffman joined the club that spring, striking for the Preston Chapter, a few months after Merv Blaker had been accepted in Peterborough. Tee Hee, as he would soon be known, had just turned nineteen. David Hoffman had grown up on a small family farm between New Dundee and Plattsville, sixteen kilometres southwest of Kitchener. Unlike many other Choice members, Hoffman was a successful student, and in the winter of 1965–66 he was attending Grade 13 at Waterloo Oxford Secondary School, a rural high school not far from New Hamburg. A few of his friends owned motorcycles and one day Hoffman went for a ride on one. He drove it two blocks, and he was hooked. He bought his own bike, a '61 Norton, just a week later.

Some time that winter a friend of Hoffman's showed up at the arena in New Hamburg wearing Choice colours. Hoffman was intrigued. He liked the idea of hanging out around other guys who owned bikes, and he was invited to a few club parties. After finishing school that spring, he found himself a steady job at B. F. Goodrich in Kitchener, bought a brand-new bike, and began to strike for the Preston Chapter. After six weeks he was given his full club colours, just in time for the annual May 24 club run to Wasaga Beach, up on Georgian Bay.

Merv Blaker found the beer, parties, and club runs a powerful inducement to club membership. Indeed, the years of the late sixties would later be recalled as "the beer drinkin' days," a kind of Golden Age when all motorcycle clubs, but especially the Choice, were undergoing a period of tremendous growth, and when living the Life was a far more simple and carefree proposition than it would later become.

The years from 1967 to 1969 were also crucial in an organizational sense. As Bernie watched club membership explode and new chapters mushroom across Ontario and Quebec, it became apparent that an entirely new organizational structure was needed. His response was to be the capstone of his career as leader of the Satan's Choice and would provide an organizational legacy that survives, largely unchanged, to this day.

A National Constitution was developed that would govern all of the club's far-flung chapters. Each chapter would elect its own executive officers: a president, vice-president, and treasurer, as well as a road captain who would be responsible for organizing and co-ordinating club runs. Certain chapter executives would, in turn, sit on a national executive headed by a national chairman and a national secretary-treasurer. The two national officers were elected by the membership as a whole. The first national chairman was Bernie himself.

It was a tricky and time-consuming business, not least because each article of the new document had to be ratified by every chapter. It was also a daunting organizational challenge to strike an acceptable balance between the interests of the individual chapters and the good of the club as a whole. The central leadership also found itself confronting an age-old Canadian problem: the sheer size of the country. At the height of its power the Satan's Choice Motorcycle Club would have thirteen chapters, as far west as Thunder Bay, Ontario, and as far east as Montreal—a road distance of some 2,000 kilometres. (There was even, briefly, a chapter in Campbell River, British Columbia, on Vancouver Island. It was known, somewhat grandiosely, as "VanIsle One," but here even Bernie Guindon's organizational genius and reach exceeded his grasp, and the chapter was disbanded after a few months—the distances were simply too great.)

It was only natural that each member would feel the greatest allegiance to the chapter in his own community, and the individual chapters would remain the key building-blocks in the overall organization. Dues were paid to the chapter treasury, and a portion of the money was to be forwarded to the national organization. Which "wannabees" were selected to strike and which strikers were allowed to become full members was left up to the chapters, but the whole club was given a loose veto power if a member became unruly or was found to be unable to live up to the high standards upon which the organization always prided itself. Chapter meetings were held weekly and attendance was strictly mandatory. Meetings of the national officers were less frequent.

To counterbalance the power accorded each chapter, the full club expected certain things in return. Each chapter was expected to host at least one club run or field day every riding season. In this way each chapter would visit the city and clubhouse of every other, and every member would get to know all of his brothers, at least casually.

Club regalia was codified, too. Strikers were to wear a small diamond-shaped club crest, full members the much larger back patch sewn to a denim or leather "cut-off," or sleeveless jacket. Patch and jacket together constituted a set of full colours, which were accorded the greatest reverence. A member was strictly forbidden to loan his colours to a non-member, or to surrender them to anyone, under any circumstances. Any non-member caught wearing even the smallest reproduction of the club colours would be lucky to escape with his or her life. A number of ancillary insignia were also allowed. A small patch, or "side flasher," denoted a member's chapter affiliation, a shoulder patch club office, if any. Tiny diamond-shaped patches bearing the number 13 were always popular with regular dope-smokers. (The letter "M" was the thirteenth letter of the alphabet, and it stood for marijuana. Sometimes the letters "FTW" would appear beneath the 13, which meant "Fuck the World.")

Anyone could wear the FTW patch, but the wings patch, another small badge, shaped to resemble a pair of wings, had to be earned. The wings came in three colours—red, green, and black. Red wings were awarded to a member who publicly performed cunnilingus on a woman who was having her period, black was for performing oral sex on a Negress, and green was for "eating out" a woman who had a dose of the clap. The wing patches were always a special favourite of Crown prosecutors during any biker trial. They would, understandably, bend over backwards to get the significance of the wings into the evidence, to persuade jurors just what kind of animals the men in the prisoner's dock really were.

The "one-percenter" patch was another common insignia. It stemmed from a remark made by the president of the American Motorcycle Association in the mid-sixties. In an effort to distance his organization from the bike clubs that were springing up across the continent, he declared that outlaw clubs represented only "one percent" of the legitimate motorcycle-riding public. Outlaw bikers seized on the remark as a back-handed compliment, and a one-percenter would forever after refer to the one percent of society who dared to live outside the law. As club colours represented the indelible line between the elite and simple "citizens," so, too, did the one-percenter patch denote the difference between conventional and outlaw motorcycle clubs.

But even outlaws, the framers of the Choice constitution realized, needed rules, and so a strict code of discipline, complete with penalties, was developed. The code governed all aspects of club life. Hard-drug (heroin and speed) use was severely frowned upon and needle use was absolutely forbidden: it made a member too unreliable. Homosexuality was prohibited, excessive drunkenness proscribed, and that most insidious of sins in any volunteer organization—indifference—was considered a punishable offence.

Penalties varied from small fines, payable to the club treasury, for minor offences, to demotion from full member back to striker in serious cases, to outright expulsion, a punishment usually reserved for the most severe and incorrigible offenders.

All of this varied in practice, of course, and the disciplinary level often depended on the mood and customs of the individual chapter. Preston Chapter (later Kitchener-Waterloo) was famous throughout the club for its tight discipline. Perhaps because it was one of the two charter chapters and contained an inordinately high number of long-time members, Preston prided itself on its strict standards. A member who arrived even five minutes late for a chapter meeting was subject to a fine, no matter who the member was. If his excuse happened to be that he'd been stopped by a copper and hassled over a faulty left-turn signal on the way to the clubhouse, the response could be swift and unyielding: Tough shit, you're supposed to keep your bike in good running order and it wouldn'ta happened, or you shoulda left sooner for the meeting. Fifty cents to the beer kitty.

Sometimes there was a certain irony to outlaw law, and the club would successfully "rehabilitate" an offender who was impervious to all the police and courts in the world. Club rules carefully defined "riding season"— usually May 1 through October 15—though the time frame altered by a week or two over the years and could vary with the latitude of the chapter. To remain a member in good standing, each brother was required to have his bike on the road promptly at the beginning of the season. Suppose a member failed to get his bike street legal because he owed too much in unpaid speeding or traffic tickets. His pleas would fall on deaf ears and his membership could be temporarily suspended pending the payment of his fines. The club often prevailed where society had failed, not because the Satan's Choice sanctioned the social rule of law, but because *not* obeying a particular law could disrupt the good order of the club itself. The club's interest, it went without saying, came first.

A similar attitude was often evident towards members who became "problem children." If an individual was, say, drinking too heavily and picking fights with other members or with citizens in a way likely to bring embarrassment or disrepute on the club, he might receive a serious temperance lecture or, if the chapter members agreed, he might be ordered to go on the wagon at all club functions. Sometimes it happened that a member proved to be a thoroughgoing bad actor, unable to function within the club's legal framework, much less society's. Often such a member would be "babysat" by his brothers, who would display a surprising degree of patience and sensitivity in an attempt to get the individual back on the straight and narrow.

Although many club rules were honoured more in the breach than in the observance, a few infractions were simply and absolutely intolerable. Lying to, stealing from, or cheating a brother would almost invariably earn a member the ultimate epithet: he would be branded as "NG"—no good—and summarily expelled.

And above and around all the other rules, permeating every other aspect of club life, there was the Rule of Rules, whether written or unwritten: a member never ever complained to or co-operated with the police. If a Choice happened to be waylaid by three members of another club and beaten within an inch of his life, he would never dream of filing charges against his assailants. The club would exact revenge at its own time and place. If a member happened to witness an illegal act, even if it involved citizens and had nothing to do with the club, it was unthinkable that he would take the witness stand or give evidence in any way. And most important, of course, a member would never agree to give evidence against a brother.

There were rare and specific circumstances where a member might be allowed to cut a deal with police, a procedure known as "working a patch." If a member was pinched in the commission of a crime and he was offered a lighter sentence for a minimal degree of co-operation, the "patch" would be carefully considered by his chapter. Throughout the early part of the 1970s the deal often involved the surrender of illegal firearms (usually handguns) in return for a plea bargain. If the chapter, after full discussion, determined that the quid pro quo was sufficient, a few guns would be coughed up out of the club stash. But as the seventies wore on and the police war against bikers intensified, the ante was upped to an unacceptably high degree: the police began to demand bodies, not guns—they insisted on help in prosecuting other bikers. A member was expected to rat or "put it on" his club brothers, or the members of another, rival club, and this, for the most part, the members of the Satan's Choice steadfastly refused to do. In this regard, the trial for the murder of Bill Matiyek was to prove the ultimate test.

Besides the written rules governing club organization and discipline, an informal code of behavior quickly evolved that became a form of social custom. One of the principal tenets in the code was to provoke, outrage, and shock conventional society at every possible opportunity. Thus the profusion of Nazi symbols—huge flags, the double lightning bolts of the ss, swastikas, the Iron Cross, and Second World War German army helmets. While the ill-defined politics of motorcycle clubs in the sixties could in no way be described as liberal, and while club members did indeed view themselves as an elite body of supermen who dared to transcend and flout the laws and conventions of lesser mortals, it is doubtful that Canadian club members, at least, ever considered themselves fascists. The Nazi insignia, members insist now, as they did twenty years ago, was displayed for its shock value, and nothing more.

Another favoured means of offending "straight" society was the concept of the "class act." In its more modest form a class act might be nothing more than members holding hands in public or kissing one another on the lips. Just refusing to shave, bathe, or get a haircut was a kind of passive class act, guaranteed to insult a society that often seemed to elevate personal hygiene to the level of tight-assed sterility. The acknowledged king of the class act was Howard "Pig Pen" Berry, a member of the Peterborough Chapter. Pig Pen was far and away the filthiest, foulest member the Satan's Choice ever had, which was no mean accomplishment in itself, and there was nothing he wouldn't do for a class act: eat a live bird, human shit, dog shit—even most members considered *that* kind of gross.

In this way the biker code of the sixties was not so different from their hippie cousins'. Much hippie behavior, after all, was calculated to shock a materialist society out of its mind-numbing complacency. But after that similarity the two groups pretty much parted ways. Bikers had nothing but scorn for hippies, whom they saw as wimpy peacemongers. They were the perfect objects for biker violence: they were weak and disorganized and they didn't know how to fight back. Best of all, there was little fear of police reprisal for such actions, for the police hated hippies, too. "When things got dull we could always go stuff a few hippies into trash cans," a Choice veteran would recall many years later. "How do you think we got our boots?"

As the Life evolved, the need to shock society gradually diminished in importance, but another touchstone of the biker code that had always deeply troubled non-bikers would remain essentially unchanged: the members' collectives attitude towards women. Like few other areas in society, motorcycle clubs were to remain a man's world, the growing influence of the women's movement notwithstanding. Club membership was strictly limited to men, and to say that women were treated like even second-class citizens would be generous in the extreme. "We treat our women with respect," a clubber would likely answer when challenged on the point, and, in a strictly limited sense this was true. The wives, girlfriends, mothers, and sisters of *members* were generally accorded great respect. But they were respected as a kind of adjunct to, if not the outright property of, a brother. Respect for a brother, and a brother's property, was a cardinal club rule. The notion that as a gender women should be treated with respect because they were the *equals* of men simply did not compute. In a way, of course, it might be argued that club members were at least consistent here; all males who were not one-percenters were less deserving of respect, too.

But the view that women were nothing more than chattels, property like a brother's chopper or the clubhouse dog, had profound implications. Women as property came in one of two forms: private, belonging to one member, or social, the property of the club as a whole. It was not an altogether novel concept. The female sex was divided into two groups: wives and old ladies, virgins and good girls on the one hand, and broads and sluts, hambones, douche bags, cunts and whores, on the other.

From women as property it was but a short jump to women as sexual object, a thing to be used, and abused, however and whenever a member or chapter saw fit. It came with the territory. One aspect of club behavior that most scandalized society, from the mid-sixties on, was the biker penchant for gang sex, known variously as training, pulling a train, or splashing. It was sensational, titillating stuff to a society that was essentially monogamous and straitlaced, and stories about orgiastic group sex among bikers added to their aura as lusty, pillaging Huns. The important question was: when did gang sex become gang rape?

In truth, there was rarely a shortage of female volunteers for such rough trade, and many club members will occasionally cite the availability of women as one of the reasons they joined the Choice. Women, sex, and parties were simply an integral part of the biker lifestyle, and the Life exercised a powerful attraction to a surprising number of young women. In their defiance of society, their no-bullshit attitude, bikers were powerful and attractive in their way.

Every girl had her limits, and it was when that line was reached, ignored, and crossed that gang fucking became gang rape. A woman might take on seven guys and then decide that number eight was too much. That was her limit, but by that time everybody was too horny to care. And besides, what was she going to say? That when she fucked the first seven guys the act was between consenting adults, and therefore legal, but with the eighth guy she was raped? Try selling that to a judge and jury.

In fact, indecent assault charges—the legal term for rape or skin beefs— were among the most common charges laid against bikers, but convictions often proved more difficult to obtain. The police complained that the plaintiffs in such cases were intimidated into changing their testimony or dropping charges altogether, which undoubtedly happened. But if women were property, and if the broad *asked* for it, then you beat the charge any way you could, no real harm done.

Women had another use, too—as meal tickets. Even in the beer-drinking days a kind of natural kinship was formed between strippers and bikers. The bond deepened throughout the seventies and eighties as more and more hotels offered stripping and its more explicit offshoot, table dancing, as a feature attraction. In their own way dancers were outlaws, too, beyond the pale of polite society. A symbiotic relationship resulted. A single dancer or a whole stableful might become the property of a club member, or of an entire chapter. The bikers offered physical protection and companionship, sometimes functioning as managers and booking agents, and the dancer split her income with the club, or with a member. Many dancers quite simply preferred the company of bikers to the pallid, repressed business goofs who came to watch them perform. Club members were straightforward guys. With them, you knew where you stood. Dancers, in turn, became increasingly important sources of club revenue. The money was lucrative and it was legal. In many cities clubs came to control the stripping, table-dancing trade, and the surest way to find members of the local outlaw club in any community even today is to follow the dancers.

But for all the outrageous behavior and outlandish dress and sexual mores, it was a far more bizarre incident that first drew the attention of the news media to the Satan's Choice Motorcycle Club and turned their activities into a cause célèbre. The 1967 episode would always be remembered by club old-timers as the Great Chicken Race controversy.

It all started with the field meet that was an integral part of any club run. Half the fun was definitely in getting there. Across southern Ontario outlaw bikers and their girlfriends would gather at designated rendezvous points on Saturday morning and begin the long run to the meet. Once assembled, the pack would pull out, riding two abreast, the road captain and the chapter president at the fore. It was an awesome spectacle as the pack spread out, a long chain of monster machines, everyone proudly flying his full colours, the finest moment of the year for many. *This* was what it was all about: to be free, on the open road, surrounded by fellow members whose brotherhood went deeper than blood, to be truly, at last, "in the wind."

"Have you ever been on the road running in a pack with a couple of hundred Harleys?" a woman who loved the Life once asked. "Then you've never lived. There's nothing else like it. It's the *power* I love. You walk into a restaurant or gas station in some jerked-off little town in your black leathers and Harley gear and the looks you get—the fear and respect in people's faces—is amazing."

The arrival at the campground was an important moment, too. Other chapters, other clubs, would be carefully watching, counting machines at the entrance, gauging who had lost and who had gained strength over the winter. And then the overheated engines would be turned off and the scooters carefully mounted on their kickstands, and everyone would greet everyone else, bear-hugging, rabbit-punching, rolling around on the ground, wind-burned and thirsty, high from the excitement of the day's run and the partying yet to come.

Everybody got hellishly drunk on Saturday nights and it would be at least noon on Sunday before people were sober enough to get the field meet itself under way. In the early days, citizens were allowed to attend the field-day events, usually for a nominal fee, a dollar a head, and they'd turn out by the hundreds to watch the fun, and sometimes reporters and photographers from the local newspapers would come out, too.

The events varied from straight-out racing and jumping bikes for distance off a specially built staging to more exotic contests like the balloon, wiener-hang, and shit races. In the balloon race the contestants would pair off into two-man teams. A balloon was tied around the drivers' necks and each passenger was armed with a rolled-up newspaper. The object was to break everyone else's balloon while defending your own. The team with the last balloon intact wins.

The shit race was a lot of fun, too. Three bags of pig manure—human feces would do in a pinch—were placed on the field and inside one of them was a rubber ball. Whoever located the ball and crossed the finish line with it first won a prize.

As a grand finale, somebody dreamed up the idea of the Great Chicken Race. The plan was to put a live chicken at one end of the field with the two-man teams lined up on the starting-line at the other end, maybe a quarter-mile away. At the starting signal everybody would tear off towards the chicken, riding flat out. The guy on the back would jump off, catch the chicken, get back on the bike, and return to the starting-line. Whoever brought the chicken back won the Chicken Race. Unfortunately for the bird, when you had thirty-five bikers after one chicken, it didn't often get across the finish line in one piece. The rules were changed slightly: whoever brought the single biggest *piece* of chicken back won the race. The Chicken Race was an immense success the first year it was tried, but evidently some citizen complained to the police. The following year the Ontario Humane Society turned out in force, complete with a police escort, to stop the race. As the Humane Society official cited the appropriate section of the Criminal Code which forbade such atrocities against animals, somebody threw an axe at him. It landed in the ground about two inches behind his feet, and he beat a hasty retreat, as did the police. The Chicken Race went on as scheduled, but the Humane Society was not to be so easily deterred.

The next day the *Oshawa Times* carried a story about the controversy, beneath the headline "CHICKEN GAME RESULTS IN CHARGES AGAINST SATAN'S CHOICE." Thomas Hughes, the general manager of the Ontario Humane Society, told the newspaper that charges would shortly be laid against club members under Section 387 of the Criminal Code of Canada which made it an offence to, "in any manner, encourage, aid or assist at the fighting or baiting of animals or birds." Section 387 was an admittedly obscure provision of the Code, Hughes told a reporter, and the forthcoming charges would be used "for probably the first time in Canada."

To the bikers' consternation, the media kept harping on the Chicken Race every time the club had a field day. How did citizens' minds work anyhow? When you thought of all the lousy chickens killed every day. Humane? How did they think a hawk killed a chicken?

Finally the club decided to compromise, just to keep their field days from being raided over a stupid chicken. They switched to a *turkey* race, and they cut the bird's head off just before the start of the race. A turkey race was better in one way—since it was a bigger bird, everybody had a better chance of getting a piece of it, but a headless turkey just didn't offer the sport of a live chicken, and eventually the race was discontinued.

The *Oshawa Times* gave the last word on the subject to a Humane Society official, who elected to remain anonymous: "There should be something done about these people. . . . They are pretty brave when they are in their groups all together, but when they are alone, they are just as scared as that chicken."

XIII

WHILE THE LIFE EVOLVED and Bernie Guindon and his motorcycle club established their hegemony over the Canadian biking world, the young boy who had thrilled at the sight of a bike run from the back of a vw van in 1959 was entering adolescence.

As he grew older, Gary Comeau's problems in school increased. His mother was convinced that her oldest son wasn't a bad boy, just foolish, and often, she believed, his teachers picked on him. She never did forgive the teacher who made fun of him once, in front of the whole class, about his teeth. Gary had always had a fair overbite, and his two front teeth were particularly prominent. The teacher told him "to put his teeth back in his mouth"—or so Gary told his mother and his stepfather, Gene King.

Even as a youngster Gary Comeau was always bigger than most of the other children in his classes at Precious Blood School, a Roman Catholic elementary school just two blocks down Hexham Avenue from his home in Scarborough. Gary was poor at his studies, but he displayed a positive genius for mischief that placed him on a collision course with school authorities early and often. "Gary has a tendency to bully the other children," Sister Bertha noted typically on his Grade 2 report card. Gary hated school and his happiest moments were tearing around the neighborhood, playing baseball or street hockey with the other kids, although even with his size advantage he never particularly excelled at either sport. His family remembers him as a sturdy, cocky little he-man, impervious to both caution and discipline: always getting into trouble, and then running to others for help. At Betty's insistence they took the boy to an orthodontist, who told them it would cost $1,200 to correct Gary's buck teeth with braces. The family, to Betty's everlasting regret, just didn't have the money.

Gary's first real trouble with the law came when he was eleven or twelve. He and a school chum decided to break into Precious Blood one night, looking for things to steal. They hadn't had the foresight to bring a flashlight, but they were devious enough to realize they didn't dare turn on the lights without giving themselves away. One of them hit on the bright idea of using matches to see their way, and they started burning pieces of paper. Somehow a wrestling-mat in the gym caught fire, which in turn started part of the school ablaze. Gary and his friend were questioned soon after the incident, and they confessed. Betty King was pleased that her son didn't deny his guilt, and she was satisfied that the whole thing wasn't done intentionally, as Gary would always swear later. Gary might have had his problems over the years, but he never denied what he had done and he would never lie, especially to her—of that she was certain.

Since Gary was still a juvenile, no criminal charges were laid over the incident, but he was ordered to see a child psychologist, who decided that a change in schools might be in order. Gary transferred to Annunciation, another Scarborough separate elementary school, for Grade 8. The good sisters of Precious Blood, one suspects, were not at all unhappy to see the back of Gary Comeau, and the feeling was strictly mutual.

Although no one else in his family would even remember the incident, that first glimpse of a motorcycle club from the back of the family van would remain, for Gary, one of his clearest boyhood memories. That moment, preserved forever in his mind with an almost mystical clarity, marked a turning-point in his life. Who *were* those men? Where had they come and where had they gone? He *had* to see them again.

Gary's mother would be the indirect and unwitting agent of the contact. It was Betty who always insisted that the family take a summer holiday together. She was determined that her children, who were growing up in an urban environment, should commune with nature and fill their lungs with fresh country air at least two weeks out of the year. Often they went to Wasaga Beach.

It was there that Gary got his second, closer look at a bike club. He was fifteen the year they came rolling in on their bikes one day, noisy and magnificent, with wild-looking women riding on the back. Gary finally summoned the courage to actually talk to them. He'd seen them around, not far from the family's rented cottage, whipping up and down the street on their bikes, drag-racing, and one of them was waving a huge Nazi flag from the back of a bike. The next day, donning sunglasses, a cut-off blue-jean jacket, and his toughest swaggering air, Gary ventured into a restaurant where he knew they had gathered. He was terrified as he ordered a pack of smokes from the counterman, and once the bikers spotted him, an overgrown punk kid playing his ridiculous role, they began to hoot and holler and razz him unmercifully. But Gary hung tough and as he left the restaurant one of the bikers relented slightly. "Hey, take it easy, kid."

"Okay," Gary answered with an indifference that he surely did not feel. He was thrilled, and more fascinated than ever. He was certain now—the Life was in his blood, had always been in his blood. There was no doubt about it.

That fall Gary entered Porter Collegiate to begin Grade 9, but his heart just wasn't in it. As he was still under sixteen and required by law to attend school, Gary was forced to confer with Board of Education authorities before he could drop out. They offered him a deal: he would be allowed to quit Grade 9, provided he found a job within thirty days.

Gary found a job the very first day. He was a big kid and looked a lot older than he really was. He drifted from one laboring job to another for the next few years. When he was sixteen, Gary was hired on as a nut-mixer in a Scarborough candy factory—the place where Poppycock, a sweet confection of peanuts and popcorn, was made. Often, to relieve the monotony, Gary and his co-workers would engage in nut fights, throwing chunks of peanuts and popcorn at each other. One day Gary missed his target and hit an older woman in the eye with a piece of candy. She reported him, and he was fired, but the job provided Gary with one lingering legacy—a nickname. A lot of people had thought he was crazy anyway, after the school fire, and working in a nut factory was just too perfect. If he wasn't nuts, he sure did do some nutty things. Although he would always remain Gary to his family, almost everyone else would from then on call him Nutty.

A friend of Gary's bragged to him one day that he was a good friend of a member of the Satan's Choice, and asked Gary if he wanted to come to a really big club party in Richmond Hill. Gary said sure, not knowing that the night would be a rite of passage from which there was no turning back.

The joint was already jumping by the time Gary and his friend got there, and the young Grade 9 dropout couldn't believe his eyes. He had never seen anything like it. The party was at the Blue Bird Inn, a dance hall that the Choice had rented for the evening. The walls of the place were throbbing with the beat of rock-and-roll, and hundreds of bikers and their women were dancing, their heads bobbing, the floor shaking. Nutty noticed that some of the women were half nude, their breasts jiggling and swaying to the music. It was like Sodom and Gomorrah, raw lust. Now this, Gary decided, was living.

He'd bought a lid of dope for the party and after a few hours he and a couple of his friends decided to sneak outside and blow a few joints. They got into a friend's car and were cruising some of the back roads around the dance hall, smoking grass, when they drove right past about thirty police cruisers, with their lights out, parked on the side of the road.

"Holy Christ! That's for the party!"

"Yeah, we better go back and tell somebody."

They never made it. They got pulled over themselves and were told to get out of the car. The police held them in a quarry for a while, and then they were put in the back of a paddy wagon, and that was how Gary Comeau got in on his first raid. He watched the whole thing go down from the little window in the back door of the paddy wagon.

The police drove up to the Blue Bird Inn and surrounded the place. A bunch of coppers kicked the door in and the building exploded in noise: screaming and swearing, the sound of breaking glass, bodies hitting the floor and the walls, bikers diving out through windows and coppers diving in. The owner of the Blue Bird was there, watching his whole place being smashed up.

Eventually the back door of the paddy wagon swung open and the coppers starting throwing bikers in. Sometimes they would beat a guy with their billies first. They squeezed in as many bodies as they could before the door slammed closed and the paddy pulled away. Gary was surrounded by a milling throng of huge, hairy, stinking, swearing bikers, and he thought it was just great until he suddenly remembered the ounce of pot that was still stuffed into the top of his boot. Holy shit.

"Uh, listen somebody," Gary said timorously. "Uh, I've got a lid of dope on me . . ." his voice trailed off.

"Fuck, kid," one of the bikers bellowed, "where do ya think y'are? We ain't goin' fer a fuckin' pizza. Here. Give it to me."

Gary complied, and the biker opened up the baggy and dumped its contents on the floor. They all stomped on it, grinding the powder and the seeds and stems into the accumulated filth and grime of the paddy floor, and somebody pissed on it. Problem solved.

Then, to Gary's utter amazement, one of the bikers began to sing.

Three Satan's Choice they crossed the Rhine,
   ta-boo, ta-boo,
Three Satan's Choice they crossed the Rhine,
   ta-boo, ta-boo,
Three Satan's Choice they crossed the Rhine,
They fucked their women and drank their wine,
   ta-boo, ta-boo,
   ta-boooola-ka boolaka boo.

More of Gary's fellow prisoners started singing, too. Gary had learned the melody in school, but the song had been called "When Johnny Comes Marching Home."

They came upon a wayside inn,
  ta-boo, ta-boo,
They came upon a wayside inn,
  ta-boo, ta-boo,
They came upon a wayside inn,
The dirty fuckers they marched right in,
  ta-boo, ta-boo,
ta-booooola-ka boolaka boo.

The innkeeper had a daughter fair,
  ta-boo, ta-boo,
The innkeeper had a daughter fair,
  ta-boo, ta-boo,
The innkeeper had a daughter fair,
With lily-white tits and golden hair,
  ta-boo, ta-boo,
  ta-booooola-ka boolaka boo.

Everybody but Gary seemed to know all the words, and as more and more of the bikers joined in, they started to sway back and forth, rocking the paddy wagon from side to side on its springs.

They laid her on a feather bed,
  ta-boo, ta-boo,
They laid her on a feather bed,
  ta-boo, ta-boo,
They laid her on a feather bed,
They fucked her and fucked her until she was dead,
  ta-boo, ta-boo,
  ta-booooola-ka boolaka boo.

They lowered their voices for the next verse, as if it was a funeral dirge, and the gyrations of the paddy wagon, which had been getting wilder, diminished momentarily.

> They took her down a shady lane,
>   ta-boo, ta-boo,
> They took her down a shady lane,
>   ta-boo, ta-boo,
> They took her down a shady . . .

Suddenly everyone shouted the next lines and the following verse, and threw themselves from side to side until Gary was sure that the vehicle would tip and roll over.

> AND FUCKED HER BACK TO LIFE AGAIN!
>   ta-boo, ta-boo,
>   ta-boola-ka boolaka boo.
>
> And when they died they went to hell,
>   ta-boo, ta-boo,
> And when they died they went to hell,
>   ta-boo, ta-boo,
> And when they died they went to hell
> And fucked the devil and his wife as well . . .

Gary felt the paddy wagon, which was now careening wildly down the road, speed up, and then the police driver, who had obviously been through this kind of thing before, stepped hard on the brakes, screeching to a halt. In the back of the paddy Gary and everyone else was lifted off his feet and sent flying towards the front of their cage, smashing into the wall and each other, until they were just one big mass of hopelessly tangled arms and legs, one huge biker sandwich.

At the cop shop Gary protested his innocence. "Hey, I'm not a Satan's Choice. I was just drivin' down the road!"

A police sergeant eyed him sceptically. "Yeah, but you were there. How old are you, anyway?"

"I'm only sixteen," Gary answered eagerly, truthfully.

They cut him loose then, and for the life of him Gary could never remember how he got home that night. That didn't matter. What he always did remember was the excitement of that night, how it caused him to fall in love with the whole scene. The fun of the raid outweighed the heat. Much later, as he found himself watching more and more of life from the back end of a paddy wagon, Nutty Comeau came to realize that it was the other way around. Like the faceless driver of the police van who had stomped on the brakes at exactly the right moment, the heat always managed, by fair means or foul, to get the upper hand. And then it wasn't nearly so much fun.

As the 1960s drew to a close the Satan's Choice Motorcycle Club had reached the height of its power. Because of its broad geographic base, the strength of its membership, and its multiple-chapter organization unified under a central executive and constitution, the Choice had become far and away the most formidable outlaw bike club in Canada.

At its peak the club had strong, ongoing chapters in ten cities in two provinces: Oshawa, Toronto, Kitchener-Waterloo, Peterborough, St. Catharines, Windsor, Kingston, Ottawa, and Hamilton in Ontario, and Montreal in Quebec. Smaller, short-lived chapters had also been established at various times in Sudbury, Thunder Bay, Cornwall, Guelph, Hull, Quebec, and Campbell River, B.C.

As the reputation and notoriety of the Satan's Choice grew, it must have seemed to the public that the club had many hundreds, even thousands, of members. Today, even club veterans are uncertain of what the total Choice membership was at its highest point—estimates range from 250 to 400.

In some of its locations the Choice enjoyed a monopoly position as the only club in town, but in most, especially the larger centres, it coexisted, albeit sometimes uneasily, with other outlaw clubs. In Toronto the Para-Dice Riders and Vagabonds also flourished, along with the Iron Hawgs and the Last Chance Motorcycle Club. Kitchener-Waterloo was shared with the Henchmen, Windsor with the Lobos, Oshawa with Bernie's old club, the Golden Hawks. In Montreal the Choice had powerful rivals—the Sundowners and the Popeyes—and an all-out, but inconclusive, war broke out between the Choice and the Popeyes in the early seventies.

There were occasional local challenges to Choice supremacy, but even where they might be heavily outnumbered in a particular locale, the Satan's Choice were respected as a force to be reckoned with because it was understood that an affront to one club chapter was an injury to all. They were heady days. "You couldn't go nowhere without running into the Choice," a club veteran recalls. "We were the first club to move into the modern era. Other clubs might still be using bike chains. Well, we were using something else."

The last real challenge to Choice supremacy occurred in the fall of 1969, at a field day just outside Hamilton. The steel city was deemed to be joint Wild Ones–Choice territory, and there were rumors that members of the Wild Ones, which had been one of the four founding Choice chapters before reverting to their own patch, had been mouthing off about "takin' care of the Satan's Choice once and for all."

The Satan's Choice decided on a unique show of force to quell this incipient rebellion. The club mustered every member and every bike it could: as many as two hundred machines passed through the gate for the field meet as if to say, "Here we are. Either make your goddamned play or shut up."

Much like the Black Diamonds a decade before, the Choice occupied their own end of the field. They were sitting in little circles on the ground, like a bunch of Indians, cleaning and checking their weapons when a senior member of the Vagabonds wandered over to get a look at what they were doing, and he could see they weren't getting ready to play ping-pong. The rumored challenge was not forthcoming, and the day passed without incident.

The field-day events went ahead as scheduled, but to show their utter disdain, the Choice contingent didn't even bother to participate. Everyone else walked lightly and stayed away from them. As they rode off the field it was a proud moment, for some of them the proudest, happiest moment of their entire lives. How far they'd come in ten years! From nothing more than a dream, a grand vision in the mind of one man, to the most powerful club in the country. They rode with slow majesty down Hamilton Mountain, west down King Street, and on to the four-lane 403 leading to the Queen Elizabeth Way.

As the long line of bikes rounded the sweeping curve beneath the stubby Gothic towers of the Cathedral of Christ the King, it was impossible to see the beginning or the end of the procession from the middle of the pack. The chrome had never gleamed as brightly, the growl of Harley thunder had never sounded sweeter than it did on that day. Had a bigger group of tougher, meaner, more lawless motherfuckers ever ridden down this or any other Canadian pike? It was exhilarating to be young and in the middle of the pack, face in the wind, surrounded by bikes as far as the eye could see, knowing you were immune from the puny conventions of society, exempt from the laws that governed mere citizens, protected by true club brothers who were just as tough, just as mean, just as solid, as you. Where else could the son of a cook or a farmer's boy have gained such power, such *respect*, while still in his early twenties?

An onlooker could have stood on the side of the road that day and watched for many minutes as the long row of bikes snaked around the curve before the road captain kicked his machine into fourth gear and the pack began to run flat out, the bikes whipping past two by two, in a dizzying display of power and speed. They topped a small rise then, and were gone, like a mirage shimmering off a highway in the simmering summer heat, riding hell-bent towards some stirring, mysterious destiny, they were sure.

But it was not to be. The Smoky Seventies lay dead ahead.

BOOK FOUR
THE HEAT

"Bikers don't play by the Queensberry rules and I don't think we should have to, either."

—ONTARIO PROVINCIAL POLICE SERGEANT,
FEBRUARY 1986

XIV

ALTHOUGH NONE OF THEM KNEW IT, the seeds of self-destruction were already riding with the Satan's Choice, even on the day of their triumphal procession through the streets of Hamilton. The 1970s, which had opened with such promise, were to prove an unmitigated disaster for the club. In the first place, Bernie Guindon was no longer in his rightful place at the head of the pack. On May 15, 1969, the charismatic Choice founder was sentenced to five years in prison for rape, and his leadership would be sorely missed. A number of successors would hold Guindon's position of National Chairman, but none of them would ever be as widely acknowledged and respected, and as decisive, as Bernie Guindon.

Increasingly, as the decade progressed, the Satan's Choice would find itself embattled on two fronts: on the one hand the club was endangered by the expansionist designs of American outlaw organizations, and on the other it faced ever more severe police repression.

By late 1966 and early 1967 Bernie Guindon and his Oshawa Chapter of the Satan's Choice had become the target of a crackdown by city police. It seems trouble had a way of following Bernie and his gang into the local pubs. More than one Oshawa saloon was trashed in bloody melees between the Choice and bar patrons, usually started by some local punk or would-be rounder who decided to prove his toughness by taking on a member of the Satan's Choice.

Oshawa police began a campaign of systematic surveillance and harassment of the Oshawa Chapter. Police cruisers were stationed outside Bernie's house almost around the clock, and visitors were often stopped and questioned. The newspapers were littered with stories about the results of the crackdown—club members were in the courts more and more often, usually on petty charges ranging from dangerous driving to making unnecessary noise on their motorcycles at all hours of the night to lacking mudflaps and failing to make turn signals.

But the first incident that really catapulted the Satan's Choice and its challenge to law enforcement into the public eye was a police raid on a club party early on the morning of Sunday, September 24, 1967. The party, held in a ramshackle farmhouse in Markham Township north of Toronto, was billed as "The First Annual National Convention" of the Satan's Choice, and the *Toronto Star* reported that more than 300 "delegates" from eleven chapters were in attendance.

The whole affair was a police misadventure from beginning to end and proved a public relations bonanza for the Satan's Choice. There had been, in fact, two raids that night, but the first had ended in disaster when twenty-three policemen attempted to bust up the party. "It was the old story," a club veteran recalled nearly two decades later, "about thirty coppers trying to surround three hundred of *us*." The first raiding party was forced to retreat "under a barrage of beer bottles shortly before midnight after grabbing a case of beer and $5 from the cash box at the bar," according to the *Star*. To make matters worse, and this was not reported, the raiders had not thought to guard their squad cars. A few club members left the farmhouse while the ill-fated raid was in progress, broke into the cruisers, and ripped out their radio microphones. When the beleaguered police returned to their cars to radio for back-up they found themselves cut off and forced to give up the raid entirely.

They retreated to the Markham police station and hastily assembled reinforcements from the OPP Downsview detachment and the police forces of Stouffville, Markham Village, Whitchurch, Vaughan, East Gwillimbury, Richmond Hill, and Metro Toronto. It was 4 a.m. before the second raiding party, armed with riot guns and tear gas and totalling eighty-four policemen, made their second, and this time successful, charge. To avenge the damage done to their squad cars some of the police piled up all the bikes they could find and drove a heavy truck back and forth over them.

By Sunday afternoon the farmhouse looked like a combat zone. "Not a window or door was left intact," the *Star*'s man on the scene reported. "Furniture had been torn apart. Every breakable thing was broken. Police found one hand-gun and one shotgun.

"Twenty motorcycles, belonging to arrested members, were strewn all over. Their gas tanks, spark-plugs, distributors and headlights were smashed. Cables were cut. Sand had been poured into many of the fuel tanks. One machine, a custom-built showpiece valued at $4,000 and trimmed in red paint, had its 3-foot long front forks twisted like a pretzel. There were tire marks on it."

In a lame cover-up that now seems as thin as the yellowing newsprint on which it was printed, one police spokesman suggested that a rival club had shown up after the raid "to tear the place apart." The whole affair was clearly a triumph for the social order.

Considering the variety of illegal, anti-social acts that were presumably taking place to warrant such a display of police force in the first place, there was an embarrassing dearth of actual criminal convictions, and even they were not achieved before the Satan's Choice had a field day, both literal and figurative, in the warm glow of the media spotlight.

The newspapers and television newscasts were full of pictures of black-jacketed motorcycle miscreants cutting up as they were led into the Don Jail, strutting and blowing kisses at their captors. On Sunday afternoon the members of the Satan's Choice and the Vagabonds who had prudently deserted the party before the second police raid showed up on their bikes outside the Don Jail for a game of football.

All day Monday, members of the Satan's Choice were paraded in front of a magistrate inside the tiny Richmond Hill courthouse while hundreds of bikers, reporters, police, and onlookers milled about outside. The court-house grounds, the Toronto *Globe and Mail* reported, had become "a tourist attraction" as local high school students came to watch the motorcyclists, who swaggered and romped outside the courthouse, even joining the Reverend A. B. Arnott, of the Richmond Hill Baptist Church, in an a capella rendition of "What a Friend We Have in Jesus." In the end, about $1,000 in fines was levied against the Satan's Choice, the vast majority of it in the form of $10 individual fines for being a found-in at a public place where liquor was illegally on sale, and $3.50 for court costs. The affair left a bad taste in the mouths of many police officials. It also escalated the stakes in the battle between the police and the bike clubs. And there was certainly no indication that the police had succeeded in beating a sense of respect into the thick skulls of their biker adversaries. "We'll get even," the *Toronto Star* quoted a biker as saying. "When the guys that own these machines get out, you're going to see a lot of cops with scars."

A second incident that significantly hardened police attitudes towards bikers took place at a Choice field day outside St. Catharines. Apart from the organized mayhem of the meet events, the field day was an entirely peace-ful affair, and club organizers had selected a site miles from anywhere to ensure that their activities wouldn't bother anybody. Between two and three hundred Choice members and their women were watching the usual Sunday afternoon events when a long line of Ontario Provincial Police cruisers and vans drove to a stop on a road bordering the farmer's field where the field day was being held. The police emerged from their cars, and some began to put on riot gear: special helmets with visors, padded uniforms, shields, and over-sized nightsticks. Police appearances at field days weren't unusual, but normally there would be some kind of parley with police officials who checked it out and then left. No one in the club had ever seen the new OPP riot equipment, and the police made no effort to talk to or hail the field-day participants. Instead, seventy to one hundred OPP crossed the fence between the road and the field, assembled in a flying wedge, and began to move slowly, in unison, towards the bikers. Bernie grabbed the microphone on the sound truck that was being used for the field-day events and boomed out instructions.

"Okay everybody get your fuckin' helmets on. . . . Do whatcha can. . . . Get the chains off yer bikes. . . . Take that fuckin' jump apart, pick up anything ya can. . . . These fuckin' assholes are spoilin' fer a fight. . . . Everybody stay where ya are. . . . Everybody stay where ya are. . . ."

The phalanx continued to advance, the coppers stutter-stepping, banging their nightsticks on their shields, in classical anti-riot formation. In a crowded city street, or in front of a strike-bound factory where they were attempting to escort strike-breakers across a picket line, this slow, menacing progress might have had its desired effect—to strike terror into the hearts of their adversaries. But in an open field, against a group that loved nothing more than a good scrap, it proved a monumental tactical error: it gave the Choice time to get organized.

"Be cool, be cool, let 'em come," Bernie's voice echoed. Everyone stood his ground, and as the tip of the wedge reached the crowd of bikers the mass split open and gave ground.

"Okay, close," Bernie ordered, and the bikers closed ranks again, completely encircling the phalanx. The police were surrounded and outnumbered three or four to one by bikers armed with bike chains, boards, rocks, fists, whatever anybody could get his hands on. And that wasn't counting the women, who could get awfully mean when something like this broke out.

The members of the phalanx, who had been contemplating their situation and were perhaps feeling like Custer surrounded by the Indians, used their wedge to make a wide turn and then back off the field of battle. The Choice let them go until they were halfway to the road before letting out a few war whoops and starting to chase the retreating coppers. The flying wedge broke apart and the police ran headlong for their cars, slipping in the mud, burdened by all their riot gear. They took off their equipment, put it back into their vehicles, climbed into their cars, and drove away.

It was a rout. But what nobody could figure out was why the police had come in the first place. Had some of the guys who left the field meet early gone into town and committed some crime? The whole thing was unreal. The cops had risked a bloodbath over sweet dick-all. It didn't figure.

XV

IN THE SPRING OF 1970 Nutty Comeau attended his first club chapter meeting. He was one of four prospective strikers present. The chapter president looked each of them over carefully, asking them in turn why they wanted to be members of Satan's Choice, and how old they were. Nutty was fourth in line and he dreaded the question about his age. Club rules said that you had to be twenty-one to join, and he was only eighteen, but for some reason the president never asked his age, and he was accepted as a striker.

The police, once they began their all-out media offensive against the club, always claimed that strikers had to commit one or more illegal acts to become a full-fledged member, which just wasn't so. In fact, as Nutty learned, it was against club rules for a sponsoring member to order a striker to do anything illegal. But they sure kept you running. Nutty lost fifteen pounds during one two-week stretch of his striking period, but he survived the six weeks, and in May of 1970 Nutty Comeau was awarded his club crest as a full member of the Satan's Choice. It was, without doubt, the proudest day of his life.

Gary didn't tell his parents that he'd become a member of a bike club, but Betty could see that he was changing. Gary had always been a very clean boy, but now he'd leave the house and be gone a couple of days at a time without telling anyone; and when he came home he'd be practically in rags, the knees torn out of his pants, filthy dirty, and he didn't seem to care. Betty King spent many nights waiting up late for him, crying when she realized he wasn't coming home. But she came to understand that when children get to be a certain age and they want to go out, you can't follow them. Gradually she got over it.

As the 1970s progressed, the Life continued to evolve, and not always in the most pleasant directions. People were getting older, for one thing. Gary Comeau later estimated that when he joined the Choice in the spring of 1970 the average age of the members was twenty-three or so. By 1978, he reckoned, the average age was twenty-eight. As they neared their thirties, the more senior members of the Satan's Choice bore little resemblance to the teenagers who had descried and rejected the "materialism" of their parents when they first formed the club back in 1965. The novelty of poverty had long since worn off—it cost money to keep a six- or seven-thousand-dollar Harley-Davidson on the road, to pay club dues, to pay club bar bills. Many members, like Merv and Tee Hee and, later, Rick Sauvé, supported themselves by working, usually as skilled tradesmen, factory workers, or laborers. But others, including Nutty, Jeff, and Armand Sanguigni, managed to survive without holding down a steady job. The fact that you could live without working became an undeniable attraction of life as a club member.

There were all sorts of ways to make a buck if you were a patch-holder in good standing. There were women: getting your old lady to become a dancer or to turn a few tricks. There was motorcycle theft, which involved stealing the machines and stripping them down, selling the hot parts to local cycle-shop owners who didn't ask too many questions. (Many Harley dealerships or parts stores were owned by bikers, anyway.) Owning a patch opened up other possibilities, too. Increasingly the Choice and other major outlaw clubs were becoming a law unto themselves. Their fearsome reputation, their unpredictability, and their willingness to use violence gave club members great "respect" on the street among gamblers, rounders, and drug-dealers. Even the Mafia, it was said, were reluctant to challenge the well-established club.

But it was drugs—marijuana, hashish, speed, and, much later, cocaine— that would prove most lucrative and most ruinous to the biker way of life. The drugs themselves were merely a commodity, a means to an end. But because they were illegal and because some club members were uniquely placed to engage in trafficking, the drug trade was a rich source of money, and therefore of power. With the money, however, came a spiralling cycle of greed, suspicion, betrayal, and violent reprisal. The problem with living *outside* the law was that you couldn't go *to* law when someone got ripped off. Taking care of business became an ever more paranoid and dangerous pastime. Veteran club members today—and there were some old-timers who had no use for drug-taking and were deeply suspicious of drug-dealing—estimate that ninety percent of the murder and mayhem that became the most notorious hallmark of motorcycle clubs was directly related to drug deals and the struggle for money and power. "Drugs," as Bernie Guindon would remark sadly, "were the ruin of many a good club member, and many a good club." The beer-drinking days were definitely over.

In 1973 senior law-enforcement officials in Ontario decided to take specific action against what they defined as an entirely new breed of criminal, the outlaw bike clubs. They formed the Special Squad, or SS, under the Intelligence Branch of the Ontario Provincial Police. The mandate of the new unit was to gather intelligence on outlaw clubs across Ontario and to disseminate it to local, regional, and national police forces anywhere in Canada or the United States. The biker squad would monitor club activities by technical surveillance, physical surveillance, infiltration, and informants. Its members would conduct criminal investigations or assist with them, take part in clubhouse raids, study club documents and paraphernalia seized in raids, read books and magazines related to biker life, and generally immerse themselves in the biker subculture. More importantly, Ontario law-enforcement officials decided, outlaw motorcycle clubs would henceforth be considered as "organized crime," on a par with the Mafia as a clear and present danger to the Canadian way of life.

One of the first officers appointed to the new intelligence unit was OPP Constable Terry Hall. Then just twenty-five, Hall pursued his new assignment with vigor, relish, and characteristic good humor. Flamboyant and fearless, Hall would come to typify the OPP biker squad more than any other individual in its history. Certainly in 1973 assignment to the squad must have seemed like a policeman's dream. No more uniform detail, no more Highway Traffic Act violations, no more nickel-and-dime. Now they were on the track of hardened criminals, organized crime, with the full panoply of police power at their disposal, and full political backing. Bikers had suddenly become a priority law-enforcement target, and it was understood that if a few of the legal niceties went unobserved, if the odd civil right was violated, the politicians were prepared to wink and look the other way. Few votes would be gained by defending the civil rights of a group who had shown themselves to be only too willing to violate the rights of just about everyone else.

From 1973 on, Terry Hall and the biker squad seemed to be everywhere. Every club run, every field day, would inevitably be met by dozens of police officers, squad cars, and roadblocks. ID's and driver's licences would be examined, every bike would be scrutinized down to the most minute detail, while biker squad members with telephoto lenses and video cameras took pictures of everyone in sight. And always, always, Terry Hall would be there, strolling up and down the line of bikes, chatting and smiling, putting names and nicknames to faces, faces to characters, characters to the hundreds of photos and videotapes that were accumulating in special squad files. He even had T-shirts made up to wear at roadblocks, to give the occasion his own special touch. If the event was a Choice club run, Hall would wear a T-shirt bearing the name and club crest of a rival organization that said SUPPORT YOUR LOCAL OUTLAWS. If he was harassing the Outlaws, his T-shirt would, of course, read SUPPORT YOUR LOCAL SATAN'S CHOICE. It was doubly infuriating. Not only was Hall flaunting the colours of an enemy organization in their faces, he was violating all outlaw club protocol by wearing a crest without permission. And there wasn't a damn thing any of them could do about it.

If anybody ever got too threatening with him, Hall would jab a finger into his chest, abruptly lose his friendly, smiling demeanour, and adopt an icy, menacing tone. "Just remember one thing, punk—*my* gang's bigger than *your* gang."

Long after his years on the biker squad were over, Terry Hall would admit that the police had themselves waged a campaign of "reverse intimidation" against bikers. It made sense. Who understood the tactics of muscle, hardware, and brotherhood better than bikers? But over the long haul the strategy of pitting one "gang" against another would yield distinctly mixed and not-altogether happy results.

So far as Jeff McLeod was concerned, the idea that motorcycle clubs were organized crime and that, by definition, those who belonged to one, including himself, were therefore "organized criminals" was a load of police bullshit, pure media hype. They certainly weren't angels, but to compare the Satan's Choice to the Mafia always seemed to him to be laying it on a little thick. While there were some members who held steady jobs, had families, and came around only on the weekends, others were just bums—Jeff put himself in this category—who didn't really work *or* hustle. They'd just hang out, always looking for a party or a free meal, often crashing at the clubhouse, or at their parents', too poor to afford their own apartments. Sometimes they'd do odd jobs for some of the heavier guys, middling drugs or hot goods, and they'd get a few dollars for their trouble, but that was about it.

Jeff estimated that only ten percent of the Choice were into really heavy, big-time drug-dealing by the latter half of the seventies, but it definitely was not an organized activity involving the whole club. The reason was simple: there was just too much money involved. The really successful dealers, the professionals, were extremely guarded about their business, jealous of both their sources and their customers. As for himself, Jeff had few illusions about ever becoming one of the big-time dealers. With his massive bulk, full beard, and long ponytail he was far too conspicuous to ever deal dope successfully.

In that, as in so much else, Jeff's size and appearance seemed to be the major determinant in his whole life. It had even, in a sense, led him to join the Satan's Choice in the first place. "Where else," he'd ask rhetorically, "could a 320-pound man go to get laid?" Jeff's childhood had been happy, if somewhat solitary. He got good marks at Scarborough's Warden Avenue Public School and at Corvette Junior Public School, at least until he was in Grade 6. It was at about that time that his father and mother separated and his grades deteriorated, although like all of the other young men whose lives were forever altered by events in the Queen's Hotel, Jeff would never blame his parents or family for what happened to him. His parents' break-up was amicable enough, and although Jeff lived with his mother, who soon remarried, he also spent considerable time with his father, who also remarried when Jeff was eleven.

Father and son shared a mutual passion for sports, particularly baseball and hockey. With his father as mentor and coach, Jeff blossomed into a first-rate hockey player. Like thousands of other ten-year-olds who played shinny on the neighborhood rinks across Scarborough, Jeff dreamed of playing in the National Hockey League, but in his case, for a time at least, it seemed that the dream might actually come true. He had natural ability and a decided size advantage; by the time he was twelve Jeff was five foot eleven and weighed almost two hundred pounds. He played Peewee for Shopsy's and one year he led the Metro Toronto Hockey League in scoring. The scouts began to show up to watch him play, and Jeff was invited to several try-out camps of the Toronto Marlies, the major junior "A" team in the Maple Leafs organization. He continued to grow—not up, just out—and his weight soared to well over two hundred pounds before he was fifteen. He survived several of the cuts one year at the Marlies' camp, and then one day, after practice, the coach called him into his office. He told the young winger that he wanted him to play in the Scarborough Hockey Association, and to lose weight, and promised the Marlies would keep in touch.

That was the beginning of the end for Jeff's hockey career. He simply could not stop eating junk food. Players whom he once could have simply knocked over in a rush across the blue line had caught up in their growth, and Jeff was now so fat and so slow that they could blow right past him. When he was fifteen he quit organized hockey for good.

Jeff had completed Grade 10, but when he was sixteen he dropped out of school just before taking his Grade 11 finals. He landed a job as a loader in the garage of the *Toronto Star* down at the foot of Yonge Street, a job he would hold for the next four years. He was an amiable, above-average employee, but both at work and at home he remained a loner.

When he was nineteen or so, Jeff started hanging around in some of the Scarborough hotels, and that was where he first met members of the Satan's Choice. Unlike most other members of the club, Jeff had no particular interest in motorcycles, but he liked the scene. The parties were good, there was lots of booze, lots of women, and, in an organization made up of many inordinately large men, his size was no longer an issue. He felt accepted among bikers, and found a strong sense of camaraderie for perhaps the first time in his life.

Jeff bought himself a bike and began to strike for the Choice. Despite his size, there is no indication that he'd ever been particularly aggressive, but once he got his patch Jeff became a lot more cocky. He started riding to work with his colours on, and blowing shifts at the *Star* the morning after parties. In truth, there was very little future in heaving bundles of newspapers around on the *Star* loading-dock, because for insurance reasons the company laid a loader off when he turned twenty-one, and you had to be twenty-five to become a driver. In July 1976, just before his twenty-first birthday, Jeff found himself out of a job. He went on pogey and began to hang out at the clubhouse more and more, though he kept his room at his mom's and paid her room and board out of his unemployment cheque every two weeks. His mother and stepfather didn't like his involvement in the club, but were unable to change his mind.

Before he joined the Choice, Jeff had had almost no criminal record, just an absolute discharge for marijuana possession. Despite that, Jeff was never much of a drug-user. He might smoke up or take chemicals once a month or so, and he'd never smoked tobacco. The greatest vice in Jeff's life was food. He was always known as an eater, in the way that other members were known for being boozers or dopers. Although he continued to play baseball and pick-up hockey, Jeff gained still more weight, perhaps because he was no longer working regularly. From the time he was laid off until he was arrested for the Matiyek shooting in December 1978, Jeff consistently carried 320 pounds on his six-foot frame.

If Jeff's size tended to shape the way he saw the world, it also influenced the way everyone else saw him, a fact that he could never fully comprehend. It was all too easy for people both inside the club and out to dismiss Jeff McLeod as big, dumb, and slow, but there was much more beneath his hulking, intimidating exterior. He was keenly observant, highly analytical, and sometimes judgemental to a fault, all faculties that were never much in vogue around the clubhouse, and he kept them well hidden. The only external clue to Jeff's mental abilities was the parallel lines that furrowed his fairly high forehead. Then, as now, one of his characteristic habits was to unconsciously wrinkle or knit his brow as he struggled to precisely frame a phrase or think a problem through. But even this trait was open to misinterpretation, seeming to confirm that he lacked intelligence, when it was really facile glibness that he was seeking to avoid.

His first run-in with the law came on the streets of Scarborough when he was riding his bike alone and wearing his colours. A copper pulled him over for what he expected would be a routine ID check. To Jeff's utter astonishment the cop began to write ticket after ticket for things that were supposedly wrong with his bike. When he finished writing, the copper handed him a thick sheaf of tickets. "Here, asshole," he said as he placed three hundred dollars' worth of tickets in Jeff's hand.

"Yeah, I'll see *you* later," Jeff glared.

"What did you say?" The copper went wild. He grabbed Jeff, put him in an arm-lock, and started screaming, the spittle flying into Jeff's face. "You asshole, you punk, you fuckin' punk kid!"

Jeff was charged with and convicted of threatening a police officer, ordered to post a $1,000 peace bond, and told to stay away from the Choice clubhouse.

He was genuinely shocked by the incident. He'd always heard the club guys sitting around talking about police harassment, raids, battles with the cops, but Jeff always tended to dismiss them as war stories—like a bunch of veterans sitting around the Legion drinking beer and bragging about battles they'd probably never even been in. He certainly never thought something like this would ever happen to him. He was a nice guy. They didn't understand.

That his very size, demeanour, appearance, and choice of friends and associates could themselves be threatening to a great many people never really occurred to Jeff. In this he exercised a remarkable capacity for self-delusion, a characteristic he would retain long after he was in serious trouble with the law.

A few months later Jeff spent one night in jail after he was picked up on an indecent-assault beef (he was acquitted), and that was, until he was charged with conspiring to murder Bill Matiyek, the only time he'd ever been locked up.

XVI

FROM THE START, members of Canada's foremost motorcycle club had distinctly ambivalent feelings towards their counterparts in the United States. As early as 1968, an emissary of the Hell's Angels arrived in Toronto to discuss an amalgamation of the two clubs. He was met at the airport, according to club lore, his proposals were summarily rejected, and he was put back on a plane to California.

Many Choice members insist that the American clubbers were a different breed of biker altogether, although the comparison seems as difficult to pin down as does a comparison of the American and Canadian national characters or identities.

Certainly there were some obvious differences. Perhaps the most obvious was in jargon: Americans called their strikers "prospects," and club brothers were "bros." But American members also styled themselves as super-patriots. Angels president Ralph "Sonny" Barger had volunteered to send his whole club to serve as "a guerilla band" in Vietnam back in 1967. Even their bike of choice, the Harley-Davidson, was imbued with patriotic significance: the Milwaukee-based Harley-Davidson Motor Company was the sole American motorcycle manufacturer to survive the flood of Japanese motor-cycle imports of the sixties and seventies. The Japanese products were lighter, quicker, cheaper, and better-engineered. They were also, as the hard-core American biker magazines never tired of telling their readers even in the 1980s, "brought to you by the folks who bombed Pearl Harbor." Increasingly H-D was equated with the embattled American way of life. Two of the most popular corporate logos became the number "1" draped in the red, white, and blue of the American flag, and a ferocious bald eagle, wings outstretched, about to pounce on some unsuspecting prey. This patriotic pandering was, one suspects, as appealing to the company's second-largest market—American police departments—as it was to the largest, American bikers themselves.

Canadian clubbers, on the other hand, rode Harleys because "they were the best road bikes for the money," or, if the truth be told, because they were loud, powerful, heavy, and often dirty. There was simply something about a Harley that the sleek, quiet Japanese bikes lacked. It had history, tradition, it was what Lee Marvin rode in *The Wild One*, but few Canadians rode them because it was the righteous patriotic thing to do. The virulent jingoism of the American biker lifestyle left most of the Canadian bikers with the same vague sense of unease that American patriotism tended to inspire in Canadians generally, and Canadian clubbers became convinced, in their own quiet way, that they and their country were superior, and there was no need to flaunt the fact.

Still, they were in bed with the elephant, like everyone else in Canada, and it was a part of Bernie Guindon's enduring legacy that the American clubs should always be regarded with a healthy, respectful mistrust. While the Choice, even at its peak, could not match the two big American clubs chapter for chapter or member for member, it nevertheless enjoyed unchal-lenged supremacy and outsized authority on its side of the border. Given the difference in size between the two countries, the Choice was, in its way, even *more* powerful.

The Age of Association between the Satan's Choice and the Outlaws

Motorcycle Club began innocently enough around 1974. It started with reciprocal visits between the so-called border chapters of the Choice, Windsor and St. Catharines, and Outlaw chapters in Detroit and Buffalo who partied and did business together.

As time passed, the relationship between the Choice, under Bernie's successor, Garnet "Mother" McEwen, and the Outlaws warmed and deepened, and in 1976 Mother and the Outlaw leadership formalized an association between the Outlaws and the Choice. A special patch was drawn up to commemorate the undying friendship: the "association patch," which had a devil's pitchfork crossing an Outlaw piston to symbolize this unprecedented trans-border bond. It meant that a Choice in the States or an Outlaw in Canada was considered an equal, in every way, by the host club. The ties were a great deal more than just fraternal. They also meant that a club member wanted in one country could expect to find refuge in the form of false ID and a place to hide out in the other country. There were decided dividends for the more business-minded Choice members, too. With its lax handgun laws the States provided a seemingly endless supply of chunks and heavier artillery, and, according to police reports, the Outlaws were only too happy to sell Canadian chemicals, especially speed, in the much larger and more lucrative American markets. It was truly, in the parlance of a later generation, free trade, Americans and Canadians doing business on a level playing-field. Something for everyone.

The association bylaw to the Choice constitution was passed into law by each chapter, with scarcely a demurral. There was, however, one still and almost silent voice crying in the wilderness, and that was Merv Blaker. Even after it became a club rule, he never sewed the association patch on to his colours, and people noticed, too. Of course Indian, being Indian, never actually *said* anything, and everybody had too much respect for him to force him to comply. By 1976, after all, Merv was almost a ten-year member, and there weren't many of those guys left. Besides, Merv was about the only club guy anyone could think of who'd never gotten a tattoo, either. Weird.

Much later, after what was about to go down had gone down, everybody was lining up with insights into the American club mentality and how they should have seen the whole thing coming. A Peterborough Chapter veteran recalled how he'd partied with the Outlaws down in the Carolinas somewhere and been freaked out when he realized that about half of them were

Vietnam vets and they were crazy when it came to killing. They *liked* it. Even when it came to your average *heavy duty* Canadian biker, he didn't kill for the fun of it. For money or territory or to make a point maybe, but not because he took pleasure in it. If the Yankee clubs ever took over in Canada, he added with perfect 20-20 hindsight, there'd be a lot more killing.

And it probably was true that the association helped to nudge the Choice a little further into the fast lane than they would normally have gone, made them a little greedier, a little more firepower-oriented, than they would otherwise have been. But the sad fact of the matter was that the Satan's Choice were now embroiled in the classic Canadian-American love-hate relationship, a distinctly Canadian malady, since Americans never thought enough about Canada to either love or hate their northern cousins one way or the other. The even sadder fact was that the Satan's Choice, like other Canadians in the past, succumbed to the blandishments of their cousins to the south: more money, more power, the willingness to kill, the winter get-away.

With Bernie back in jail, the club blundered blithely along into the whole con. Terry Hall supplied the bait but it was two Canadian newspaper reporters who unintentionally set the trap.

Early in 1977 two young reporters from the *Kitchener-Waterloo Record* approached the Choice chapter in that city with an idea for a feature story. They said that they wanted to tell the true story about bikers, to set the record straight. The end product, they confided, would be strongly sympathetic to the biker cause. The Kitchener Chapter consented to co-operate with reporters John Kessel and John Schenk. Over a period of weeks the two reporters drank beer and smoked dope with club members, were granted occasional access to the clubhouse, and conducted extensive interviews with a number of members, including chapter president James "Batch" Ostrom, former chapter president Larry Kowtuski, and Tee Hee Hoffman. So convinced were the Kitchener members of Schenk and Kessel's sincerity that they were extraordinarily candid in their interviews.

It's not hard to imagine their reaction when Schenk and Kessel's story finally appeared on the afternoon of Thursday, March 10, 1977. Nobody in the chapter had to read much further than the front-page headline: "Bike gangs labelled a hotbed of crime—Threat to KW," to know they'd been badly set up.

"Waterloo Region, the home of Mennonites, Oktoberfest and farmer's markets, a breeding ground for organized crime?" the story began. "Impossible! Terry Hall, an OPP intelligence officer who rode undercover with many of Ontario's motorcycle gangs for two years, says it's so." A photograph of the club crest appeared beside a long list of the club's alleged illegal activities, including "the manufacture and sale of illegal drugs, prostitution, gambling, murder and other violence for pay, counterfeit money and bogus-check rings and the fencing of valuable stolen goods." Both the Kitchener Choice and the Henchmen were as much a part of the organized-crime scene as they could make themselves, Hall told the reporters.

"'You've got to treat all bikers like Al Capones . . . they should be prosecuted for every infraction,'" added John Lang, a special drug prosecutor for the Kitchener-Waterloo region.

The story filled an entire page inside the paper with lurid, detailed accounts of criminal activity: how the Choice protected members of the Outlaws wanted in the States, how the club operated "speed labs" in Montreal, Peterborough, and St. Catharines, how Bernie Guindon had been convicted of trafficking in PCP after he was caught with 235 pounds of nearly completed drugs worth between $33 million and $60 million, and how club members used women as prostitutes, bad-cheque pushers, and counterfeit-money circulators. "'We don't need the Mafia in Kitchener,' Dave James, a Waterloo regional detective said, 'We've got the Choice.'"

"Most of the club members have criminal records, but the records only represent the 'tip of the iceberg,' a term police commonly apply to the number of crimes they are able to solve. The reason they are not caught is that a Choice member's involvement is most often on a managerial level. He handles drugs or stolen merchandise as little as possible, and not at all at the stage when they are resold to the public. And if the drug-buyer is caught with the merchandise, it's not likely he'll tell police where he got it because of the Choice reputation for violence, especially against 'snitches' (informants)."

Only far down in the story did its authors include a few quotes that were favourable to the club.

"Ralph Lockhardt, a Maryhill landowner who has let the club use his property for 11 years for the Thanksgiving Day motorcycle competition, said: 'They have been more honest with me than the cops who lied to get on my land once. The cops have done everything possible to convince me not to let them use my field.' Mr. Lockhardt had a rare moment once—he saw club members crying. It was because they had been invited to eat at his dinner table with his family."

Buried still deeper in the story were a few non-prejudicial quotes from several other Kitchener Chapter members. "Seventy-five per cent of the violence bikers get into is provoked by 'citizens' out for a reputation, said Tee Hee, 26, the club's accountant and an accountant at a Kitchener-based company. He said he is even provoked at work. 'I've had guys say things to me—if I was on the street I'd probably tell him to shut his mouth or I'd close it for him. I brush things off there though 'cause I try not to mix business with pleasure.'"

"A former club president emphasized the fraternal aspects of the club. He asked not to be named because he owns his own business. 'There ain't no organization in society with the friendship, or, if you like, the brotherhood of ours.'"

The exposé also included a third story, about Bruce Affleck, a crusading Crown Attorney from Oshawa. "Want to get rid of bikers?" the headline over the story asked. "Call Crown Attorney Affleck." Schenk and Kessel described Affleck as "Ontario's roving bike-gang prosecutor, [who] has a master plan guaranteed to rid your town of outlaw motorcyclists."

Affleck's secret weapon, the reporters explained, was to lay conspiracy charges against outlaw clubs. "Conspiracy, unlike bylaw infractions, Highway Traffic Act offences and even some Criminal Code charges, often carries with it a prison term. 'If they're getting together and holding noisy pot parties, we charge them with conspiracy to violate the anti-noise bylaw. If they are inviting minors, giving them drugs, we charge them with conspiracy to violate the Juvenile Delinquency Act. In other words, we engage in a campaign to accommodate the public outcry.'" This was, of course, precisely what Terry Hall and his OPP biker squad were attempting to do by planting "intelligence" with journalists. The *Record* piece would be the opening salvo in just such a campaign.

"'I think you should operate on the premise,' Affleck said, 'bikers aren't universally bad and do, in some sense, make a contribution. There are kids that go through some phase where belonging to a biker group is very important . . . and for whatever reason, as unacceptable to society as they are, want to become involved in a social organism. . . . But the moment that the public becomes involved and if there is any indignation or public feelings aroused, then I'm going to step in and it's game over.' "

Kessel and Schenk also got some policemen on the record boasting of their illegal activities. "Bill McCart, a Guelph veteran detective, admits the city got rid of the Blood Brothers by 'stepping on them.' 'We raided one place four times a week. It was strictly harrassment [sic], no question about it.'

"A Brantford detective said the city pushed the bikers beyond the city limits through strict enforcement. 'But they are still functioning as a pain in the ass,' the detective said. 'They are dirty filthy animals.' Ken Rae, a former Assistant Crown Attorney in Kitchener, said there have been rumors of not-so-legal ways of getting rid of bikers. 'Take a truck and run down their motorcycles.' "

News of the *Record*'s exposé on the Kitchener Chapter ripped through all of the other Choice chapters like a cannon shot. How could Ratch and Butch have been so stupid? Making the whole club look like a bunch of babyeaters!

Schenk and Kessel didn't know it, but their story had appeared at a critical moment in the history of the Satan's Choice. Mother, the national chairman, was a strong proponent of "Yankeeization." When some of the guys got drunk they were starting to strut around and actually talk like Americans— "Hi bro, how y'all doin'?" as if the guy came from Georgia instead of Oshawa. Some elements, led by Mother, became hypercritical of other chapters, as if people in Toronto or Peterborough or Kingston weren't as heavy or as righteous as they should be.

In the wake of the *Record* article, Mother, backed by a majority in the St. Catharines, Windsor, and Montreal chapters, demanded the expulsion of the entire Kitchener Chapter! Throwing out an individual member had certainly happened before, but expelling an entire chapter was wholly without precedent. Despite their disastrous mistake of talking to reporters and getting sucked in, most of the Kitchener guys were solid; one or two even went back to the days of the Throttletwisters, and they'd been at Bernie's right hand when the whole club was founded. A majority of the members in Toronto, Peterborough, Kingston, and Kitchener, naturally, decided to oppose their National Chairman and his forces. The Satan's Choice was split right down the middle, with bitter accusations flying. In the end Mother and his forces were voted down. Kitchener was saved. But internally the club's once cohesive organization was now a shambles.

A few days later a secret meeting was called for, significantly, Windsor, a border city, but only Choice chapters and individuals loyal to Mother were notified. After the secret meeting, Mother announced that his St. Catharines Chapter and Windsor had both decided to join the Outlaws. Other chapters began to fall like dominoes. Hamilton decided to swap patch, and so did Montreal. Montreal, in turn, influenced Ottawa Chapter to turn Outlaws. Only Toronto, Oshawa, Kitchener and Peterborough remained loyal to the Choice.

Due in no small measure to increased police harassment and surveillance by the OPP biker squad, and because of the aging process among the membership—many guys had gotten married, settled down, and drifted away from the club—the membership levels of the Satan's Choice had already gone into a serious decline. From its peak of three to four hundred members in 1969 to 1973, the ranks had thinned to about one hundred and ten before the Schenk-Kessel exposé. Now the fifty or so Choice loyalists were in a highly precarious position. They were heavily outnumbered, both in locations and in troops, by the new Canadian Outlaws and their American bros. The Choice die-hards braced themselves, awaiting the eventual Outlaw consolidation throughout Ontario. They vowed to go down fighting and made the usual war preparations: fortifying clubhouses, obtaining weapons, stepping up security. Eventually, they reasoned, if the Outlaws wanted to control Ontario, they'd have to have Toronto. They waited grimly, through the spring and summer of 1977, for the other shoe to drop. For some reason, it never did.

In little more than one four-week period in March 1977, Canada's biker-club map was dramatically redrawn. For the first time one of the two big American organizations had gained a serious base north of the border. Using a little guile and playing on the Canadians' own envy, the American club had accomplished what no law-enforcement agency had been able to do in a dozen years: deliver a potentially mortal blow to the most feared motorcycle club in all of Canada—without firing a single shot.

For John Schenk and John Kessel, their scoop on the Kitchener Chapter of the Satan's Choice was an undoubted triumph of investigative journalism. They'd bearded the lion in his den by winning the confidence of the Choice and then betraying it. They had badly burned their sources, it was true, but that was life in the big city. By any standard, their story was an outstanding example of enterprising, audacious reporting.

Terry Hall was pleased by the *Record* coverage, too, and by a *Maclean's* magazine article later that summer that kept the anti-biker momentum going. He'd always think of it later as "our first big break." Lest anyone should miss it, the official police line on bike clubs was printed in italics on the story's first page: *"The outlaw motorcycle gangs are North America's newest and most overlooked form of organized crime."*

And so a flourishing new sub-genre in Canadian journalism was born: bikers as gangsters, bikers as Mafia, bikers as organized crime, "maturing crime organizations." Almost without exception the stories would be written based exclusively on information received from police sources, Crown Attorneys, or bikers-turned-informers. Few, if any, reporters made any serious attempts to get the bikers' side of things. *Was* there another side of the story? Who knew? And, in truth, obtaining the other side of the story in the future would prove exceedingly difficult. Reporters were just like cops; their stories sure read that way.

The police, however, had unintentionally opened Canada up to a whole wave of direct involvement by American motorcycle clubs in Canada—and thereby acquired a new problem for themselves. In retrospect, no one in the Satan's Choice believed that the *Record* article was a decisive factor in the Outlaws split—their takeover of the Choice had long been an objective of the American club. On the other hand, the police anti-biker public relations initiative had definitely facilitated and accelerated the Outlaws' play.

Nor was that the only consequence of the media campaign, for, like one multinational firm seeking to stay even with a competitor in a new market, the incursion of the Outlaws into Canada produced yet another reaction. Not wanting to see themselves outflanked by their only serious rival, the most feared and powerful outlaw club in the world made a move of their own: the Popeyes of Quebec let it be known that they, too, were switching patch: within eight months of the appearance of the *Record*'s exposé, the Hell's Angels had set up shop in Canada.

BOOK FIVE
THE BUCKET

"They call us organized crime. We're not organized at all. We're a bunch of fuckin' beat-offs, man. We ain't got fuck-all organized."

—CLAUDE *"Gootch"* MORIN
DURING KITCHENER CHAPTER MEETING,
OPP TAPE TRANSCRIPT, FEBRUARY 5, 1979

XVII

THE SOUND STARTED LIKE A LOW, steady growl. Oh, no, not again. Nutty rolled over and pulled his blanket over his head. He heard the others beginning to stir, too. The noise gathered strength with a slow, predictable rhythm, until the ragged sound rattled the steel bars and concrete walls of the Cobourg County bucket, echoing down the range like a thousand chain saws.

"Hey! Beaver!" Nutty heard Jeff say. "Wake him up for Chrissakes!"

They were all awake now, except for the snorer, his open mouth emitting that regular ragged sound, the only one of them who had attained the sweet state of absolute indifference. Sleep. That was the only escape that any of them had from the boredom and the unremitting cold of this place. And now they were denied even that.

They heard Larry Hurren punch Tee Hee.

"Tee Hee! Hey, Tee Hee! Wake up, man! You're snoring again."

"Huh?" Tee Hee started awake for an instant, rolled over, and returned to biker heaven. The noise, mercifully, had stopped, but they all knew that in a few minutes the low growl would start again.

"He should have an operation or somethin'. I mean, this is unreal."

"Yeah, I'll give 'im a fuckin' operation."

Someone snickered. That Tee Hee was a snorer of epic proportions was common knowledge throughout the club. People would do just about anything to avoid sharing a tent with Tee Hee on a run, or even the tent next to him. Hell, you could hear him right through the walls in a cheap motel. But here in the cramped confines of the Cobourg bucket, with its four small cells and tiny range, the snoring had become more than just a club in-joke. It definitely constituted cruel and unusual punishment.

They were seven now. Gordy van Haarlem had been picked up and charged with conspiring to kill Bill Matiyek during the second week of December, their first full week in the bucket. Everyone was amazed when Dogmap was brought in, because, like Tee Hee, he hadn't even been in the hotel.

"Dogmap! What the fuck *you* doin' here?"

"Aw, just along for the ride, boys, just along for the ride." It was hard to figure out how serious a case the Crown might have against them since they'd charged two totally innocent members and managed to somehow miss the shooter. There was a warrant out for Armand Sanguigni too, but he was still on the loose, the only one of them who had made the slightest effort to evade capture. Go, Armand.

On Monday, December 18, a bail hearing was held for Gary Comeau, Larry Hurren, and Jeff McLeod at Osgoode Hall in Toronto. Howard Kerbel, the legal wheelhorse for the Toronto Chapter, was chosen to represent all three of them. Only Larry made bail, and then only after his parents signed a $10,000 surety that would be forfeit if he failed to show up in court. He was also restricted from speaking to any witnesses in the Matiyek case and from associating with any member of a motorcycle club, or anyone with a known criminal record. Jeff's bail application was denied, no doubt in part because he refused to accept his parents' offer of help in posting a surety. Gary was denied bail because of his long criminal record and club membership.

The remaining six (Armand was still at large) spent a cheerless Christmas in the Cobourg County jail and then, the day after Boxing Day, bail applications were presented for Rick Sauvé, Merv Blaker, and Tee Hee Hoffman. Howard Kerbel handled Merv's bail application as well as Rick's.

Tee Hee had selected Ed Martin of Kitchener as his lawyer. Like Kerbel in Toronto, Martin had had a long association with the Choice chapter in his city. One of his most spectacular successes had come in a defence of Kitchener Chapter member Drago Salajko on a particularly nasty rape charge. Although three of his co-accused were convicted of indecent assault, Martin won Salajko's acquittal because the victim could not remember actually being raped by Drago, although she recalled seeing him standing there with his pants down. Martin's defence broke new ground in the area of passive acquiescence—the notion that mere presence when a crime is committed does not, in itself, prove guilt—and the "Salajko precedent" became a classic textbook case on the subject, one that was studied by a whole generation of law students. Tee Hee had faith in Martin. He was rather quiet and soft-spoken, a rare trait in a lawyer, and Tee Hee thought he looked to be a thinker.

Sharon Sauvé and Rick's father, Pierre, attended the bail hearing, along with Robert Henry Hoffman, Tee Hee's father, and Merv's wife, Karen. Tee Hee's application was heard first. Martin noted that his client was a native of Ontario, had very little in the way of a criminal record, and had a job to return to at B. F. Goodrich in the event he was granted bail. On the witness stand, Tee Hee's father testified that he and his wife were willing to post a surety—the family farm if necessary—as a guarantee for their son's release.

Pierre Sauvé followed Mr. Hoffman. A diminutive, banty rooster of a man and father of eleven, the elder Sauvé was a loving, loyal father, and, like Robert Hoffman, there was no doubt in his mind that his son was totally innocent of any conspiracy to kill Bill Matiyek. His Ricky had told him that there had never been any kind of plot to kill Bill, and that was enough for Pierre. The Sauvés' family home in Cobourg was mortgage-free, the elder Sauvé testified, and Pierre and Adeline would be willing to post whatever sureties the court might deem necessary to gain their son's release.

Next it was Sharon's turn. She walked nervously to the witness-box, dressed in her Sunday best. She hated this. She took the oath, and as Rick's lawyer Howard Kerbel began asking her questions Sharon felt as if she was in a dream. None of this was real. Yes, she was the wife of Richard Anthony Sauvé. She was twenty-one. Why had she come? None of their family or friends, knowing how rocky the marriage had become, would have blamed her for washing her hands of Rick, for splitting from him once and for all. Was she doing this for their daughter, who missed her father so? "Four," Sharon heard herself say, "Angie will be five next month." Was she doing it for Rick? For herself? She just knew Rick could never commit murder, or even plan it. *Oh Rick, why?* Where did they live? "Rural route number four, Port Hope."

"Could you speak up please," the Judge asked. "I'm having difficulty hearing you."

"Rural route number four, Port Hope," she repeated. It was like a dance, she decided, with this lawyer Kerbel leading. She kept her answers short. Eighty-five dollars a month rent; thirty-seven a month hydro; waitress at Easton's three and a half years, $3.75 an hour; she brought home $129 a week; Rick cleared about $180. Yeah, kinda hard right now getting by, without Rick; there was a bank loan and the Chargex. Yeah, Rick babysits when they worked opposite shifts, which happened two, maybe three times a week.

"Do you feel that you can exercise any control over your husband if he is allowed out of jail?"

"Yes, probably."

"In the past has he ever consulted with you and taken your wishes into consideration in his conduct?"

"Yes he has."

"I take it you were aware that he was a member of the Satan's Choice Motorcycle Club?"

"Yes."

"If he was required to do so, would he sever his relationship with that club while he was on bail?"

"I really don't know."

"Well, if you were to ask him to do that and if it were a condition of the bail, would he obey the condition?"

"If I asked him to he probably would, but I wouldn't ask him to." *Oh mister, you don't know Rick, so proud, so stubborn, not in a mean way but*—a slight edge crept into the lawyer's voice and Sharon sensed she'd missed a step.

"All right, but if it were made a condition of his bail, would he obey the condition?"

"Probably, yes he would." There. Now they were back in step again.

"You are aware that he was convicted of the charge of possession of LSD?"

"Yes." Yes, but Sharon thought everyone knew what had happened: it wasn't Rick's drugs. The acid was Gordy's. The cops were raiding the Little House and Rick told Gordy that he'd say it was his, because Gordy had a record already, and Rick didn't. That was just the kind of man Rick was, to do something like that for a friend. Maybe *that* was why she was here.

"I have no other questions."

The same basic questions were asked of Karen Blaker with regard to Merv: his employment record, their family income, the value of their house, Merv's criminal record, his club membership. Karen said she was certain that if Merv was released on bail and she asked him to quit the Choice he would. She was the last supporting witness for the bail applicants.

Crown Attorney Pearson called Sam McReelis to the witness stand. The Port Hope Police sergeant provided a brief summary of events in the Queen's Hotel on the night of the Matiyek shooting. A group of ten to fifteen men had entered the hotel between 10:55 and 11 o'clock that evening. Eyewitnesses had identified the men as being in the Satan's Choice because of Blaker's and Rick Sauvé's presence. Sauvé had been seen sitting across the table from the victim. One member of the newly arrived group stood near the John Street exit of the hotel, pulled a gun out of his pocket, and fired one shot into the head of Mr. Matiyek. "At this point the group got up in concert and corralled around our victim and the gunman, obscuring the view of the patrons. At this point, two more shots were fired into the victim's head and after this, the gunman escaped through the door followed by the rest of the party that had come in."

The bail applicant David Hoffman was one of the members of the Satan's Choice whom eyewitnesses had later identified as having been in the hotel. There were approximately twenty-five patrons in the hotel at the time of the shooting.

No, the police had not been able to locate the murder weapon.

Then Crown Attorney Pearson dropped a bombshell. "Subsequent to your investigation commencing, do you have any evidence to give to the Court with respect to threats that any witnesses involved in this case may have received?"

"Yes," replied McReelis. "A witness has already been approached and informed that if that witness testifies or speaks to police, then that witness will end up dead like Bill Matiyek."

This revelation, Pearson told the Judge, went straight to the heart of the Crown's opposition to bail for the applicants. The group with which the applicants associated had a practice of threatening and intimidating witnesses. The character and associations of the applicants were a relevant consideration.

"Yes, I am a believer in that," Justice Krever agreed. "Also, if there is in fact evidence that this group systematically behaves in a certain way with respect to charges that are pending against their members . . . "

Then, Kerbel demanded, would the names of the witnesses who claimed to have been intimidated be revealed to the Court "so that the evidence can be tested"? It was, after all, a very serious allegation.

"The Crown has very very serious concerns with respect to revealing the names of any witnesses involved in this case," Pearson replied. He would prefer to simply abandon the line of questioning.

Kerbel began his cross-examination of the witness. When had Sergeant McReelis first become aware of the alleged involvement of Blaker and Sauvé in the offence?

Within two days of the shooting they had been identified by eyewitnesses.

Hoffman's ID had taken a bit longer—perhaps a month or a month and a half.

Had anyone actually been charged with the substantive offence, the murder itself?

No, attempts to identify the gunman had failed.

Then what led police to connect Blaker and Sauvé to the gunman?

Because they had entered the hotel at the same time as the gunman, as part of a group.

"When was Blaker and when was Sauvé arrested?"

"Mr. Blaker was arrested on the seventh of December, Mr. Sauvé on the tenth."

Yet the murder was on the eighteenth of October and Sergeant McReelis knew of Sauvé's and Blaker's alleged involvement by the twentieth?

"Correct."

"Why the delay between the twentieth of October and the seventh of December?"

"There was a lot of witnesses to interview to question, a lot of background to gather up."

"Okay, so I take it that you weren't too concerned about Mr. Sauvé or Mr. Blaker leaving, taking off some place?"

"No, we were not."

"Well, by the twentieth, everybody in Port Hope knew that Blaker and Sauvé had been identified, isn't that true? . . . And if everybody in town knew about it, Sauvé and Blaker would certainly know about it if they were at the hotel, they would know that they would have been identified?"

"Yes."

"As far as you know, they made no attempt to leave the jurisdiction?"

"Not to my knowledge, no sir."

The preliminary hearing was scheduled to begin on February 19, Kerbel informed the Judge, which would preclude a trial during the February assizes. The next sitting of the Supreme Court in the Judicial District of Northumberland would not be until October 1979. Should Hoffman, Sauvé, and Blaker be denied bail, they would be in jail for at least the next nine months. Martin and Kerbel argued that their respective clients had shown themselves to be suitable applicants for bail. They had the support of their families, none of their criminal records contained convictions for any type of violent crime, none had shown the slightest tendency to run away once they realized they were suspects in Matiyek's murder; even Sergeant McReelis had confirmed that.

Crown Attorney Pearson strongly disagreed. "My submission is that there may be a reason why they didn't flee. My submission is that they may not have fled because they were confident that for one reason or the other this trial, or the trial which should follow these charges . . . will never come about. We have had the evidence of Sergeant McReelis that there have been specific threats with relation to this offence. . . . These three applicants . . . are in association with . . . a club which has as its principal purpose, criminal activity. . . . I would submit that this was a public execution, this offence has all the hallmarks of a public execution. It was a very brazen act, it was one that was committed by people who were very confident that they could succeed without any retribution at all."

Mr. Justice Krever thanked the three lawyers. "Seldom have I had such assistance in a bail application." But, the Supreme Court Justice added, he saw a distinction between the case of David Hoffman and the cases of Mr. Sauvé and Mr. Blaker. There seemed to be less evidence against Hoffman, whereas the evidence against Blaker and Sauvé "put them right in the picture.

"Despite the fact that the two other accused have families, a wife and children in each case, I did not discern in the evidence called on their behalf the same kind of scruples. It is not a question of smearing everybody in the group of guilt by association but it is a question of the right attitude and values. . . . I am less satisfied that Messrs. Sauvé and Blaker will be under the same kind of moral persuasion to observe the terms of Recognizance as Mr. Hoffman. I therefore intend to dismiss the applications of Mr. Sauvé and Mr. Blaker. . . ."

Rick and Merv would remain in jail until the fall.

For the five members of the Satan's Choice who now remained in jail, it was a truly terrible time. The winter of 1978–79 was one of the coldest in living memory and they could never get warm. They were deemed too dangerous to be released into the jail yard for exercise with the rest of the prisoners, so they hardly ever got any fresh air. If they did, it cut into everybody else's yard time, which made them extremely unpopular with the other inmates.

For exercise they had a single tennis ball; for entertainment a hazy old black-and-white portable TV, and a Scrabble game.

The cells were tiny, and the range was a mere twenty feet long. The days quickly blurred into a featureless monotony relieved only by visits from family and lawyers and heated exchanges over the Scrabble board. "Hey! That ain't no word!" "Is so! It's in the fuckin' dictionary!" But of course they had no dictionary, so the arguments raged on for hours.

The routine was unvarying: Wake up for breakfast at seven; meals, such as they were, were brought in on a cart. Mop out cells before being locked out on to the range at eight o'clock. The range was a space as blank as their lives, with a picnic table in the middle. For reasons no one could ever understand they weren't allowed to have their TV until after noon, so they'd sit around the picnic table, staring longingly at the lifeless TV set, which stared back at them from just outside the range. The rest of the day they'd watch soaps and try to keep warm. They devised a kind of hockey game, using the tennis ball as a puck. Jeff would wrap towels around his arms and legs and pretend to be Mike Palmateer in net at the Gardens and everyone would take shots at him. The only thing to look forward to, Jeff remembers thinking, was mealtime, but the food wasn't great and just about everyone began to lose weight. Jeff's hair began to fall out in handfuls.

It was hard, under the circumstances, not to get on each other's nerves. They switched cells at one point, and that helped, rearranging themselves according to sports. Jeff was a Leafs fan and Nutty was too, perhaps because of his mother's lifelong love of the team. Rick liked the Canadiens, while Merv and Gordy really didn't care about sports. They picked their new neighbors accordingly.

They talked about their case until they were all thoroughly sick of it, and about whom each of them should select as a lawyer. Nutty decided to stick with Howard Kerbel: he'd been relatively satisfied with the Toronto lawyer's work in earlier cases. Merv remembered another criminal lawyer who had represented him in the past, a young Kingston solicitor named Terry O'Hara, and Merv asked his wife to contact him. O'Hara, only eighteen months out of Queen's University Law School and not yet thirty years old, agreed to take the case.

In hiring O'Hara, Blaker had no inkling that he was making a choice that would prove controversial among his co-defendants. In taking up the cause of Murray Blaker, and that was how O'Hara would eventually come to see the matter—as a cause, far more important than a mere case—the Kingston lawyer had no idea that he was embarking on a decade-long legal and personal struggle, much of which he would conduct free of charge.

Even at the age of twenty-nine and as a rank junior in the halls of criminal justice, Terence George O'Hara cut a startling, unforgettable figure. In his long black solicitor's gown O'Hara seemed a strange anachronism, a character who had somehow taken a wrong turn in time and escaped from the pages of Charles Dickens's *Bleak House*, or Shakespeare's *Henry IV*. Tall, with a luxuriant shock of reddish, sandy-coloured hair and a beard to match, O'Hara seemed born to play the part of Falstaff, the dishevelled, corpulent fool. Like Falstaff, the Kingston lawyer possessed a booming voice and a loud, barking laugh that was always ready to address the evident absurdity of life.

Like the boon companion of Henry IV, O'Hara seemed to fill any room that he was in, not only with his wit and his voice, but also because of his sheer size. For, like Falstaff, O'Hara was immensely overweight, a condition emphasized by his lawyer's gown, which fit snugly over his massive girth and then fell in a myriad of seemingly empty folds almost to the floor. Like Falstaff, it had been many a year since Terry O'Hara, standing erect, had been able to see his own knees. And, like Falstaff's, O'Hara's external appearance was a friendly, concealing sham.

In his spare time O'Hara raced rally cars, and he was a crack shot with both pistols and shotguns. He possessed a first-rate legal mind that was equally at home in the law library and in the extemporaneous cut-and-thrust of the courtroom. O'Hara would come to be regarded as a lawyer's lawyer or, perhaps more correctly, as a criminal's lawyer. There was no case too hopeless, no accused too desperate, for Terry O'Hara. Whatever the outcome, the accused, judges, Crown Attorneys, and even police would agree, Terry O'Hara offered the best criminal defence that Legal Aid could buy.

It wasn't that he lacked ambition, but somehow O'Hara's aspirations lay outside the common quest of being named a Queen's-Counsel or to a patronage judgeship, or buying the finest home in the best part of the city. He was satisfied with his two-storey yellow-brick home and with his offices, which were, like his home, comfortable, if modest. O'Hara's main love was his work, wearying as it was. There was no time of the day or night that his home or office phone might not ring, a beleaguered client calling from the local lock-up to say that he'd just been charged with shoplifting, or a prison official calling with the news that so-and-so at Millhaven had just been charged with Murder One, and wanted Terry to defend him.

But all of that would come later. In January of 1979, all Terry O'Hara knew was that, in agreeing to defend Merv Blaker, he had undertaken his first murder case.

Right from the start Jeff McLeod hadn't liked Howard Kerbel. There was just something about him Jeff didn't trust, even if he had been acting for the club for a long time. If Nutty wanted Kerbel for his lawyer that was fine; Jeff would find somebody else on his own. His eventual choice stemmed from another legal action that Jeff and ten other Choice members were involved in, quite apart from the Matiyek murder. That case was one of two others that the Choice were accused in even as they languished in the Cobourg bucket, and both were indicative of how little the Satan's Choice had come to endear themselves to the residents of the Port Hope–Cobourg–Peterborough area.

In the first case Jeff, Nutty, Beaver, and Dogmap, along with seven others, stood charged with unlawful assembly, the result of a major fracas that had taken place at the Alderville Indian Reserve, Merv Blaker's family's old reserve, just north of Cobourg. The previous June they'd all been on a club run to the Peterborough area and had decided to attend a big dance on the reserve. They crashed the dance hall, colours flying, fights broke out, and a near-riot ensued. In the second case, three members of the Choice had been charged with an alleged October 10 rape, also on the Alderville Reserve, although none of the accused in the Matiyek murder was involved.

There were five lawyers acting for the Choice in the unlawful-assembly case, including Kerbel and Don Ebbs, a Peterborough lawyer who had often acted for members of the chapter, but one in particular had impressed Jeff McLeod. He was from Oshawa and his name was Bruce Affleck, the same Bruce Affleck who had been described as "Ontario's roving bike-gang prosecutor" by reporters Schenk and Kessel in their biker exposé only eighteen months before. In that short time the scourge of the Satan's Choice had become one of their putative legal saviors, a fact that impressed Jeff McLeod, and a lot of other club members, too.

Nineteen seventy-seven had been something of a watershed year in the colourful life of Bruce Affleck. It had opened in a blaze of media glory—the January 15 issue of *The Canadian Magazine* had done a full-colour spread on him, declaring him "one of the three best prosecutors in Canada," as determined by judges, police, defence lawyers, and his prosecutorial peers. It says a great deal about the man that not one but two framed copies of the magazine would still grace the walls of his downtown Oshawa law offices ten years later.

The magazine writer had called him the "winningest crown prosecutor in the country," and Bruce Affleck savored the description. Those were the two things he did best: winning and prosecuting. Indeed, prosecuting was the only thing he'd ever done. Like Bernie Guindon and Lorne Campbell, Affleck had grown up on the streets of working-class Oshawa, the son of a GM worker. He'd worked his way through the University of Toronto as a bouncer in the tough night clubs along the old Yonge Street strip—places like the old Brown Derby. Many a rounder remembered him from those days in the early fifties even after he became a Crown and put some of them away. Whether as a bouncer or a prosecutor, Affleck had a solid image on the street—he was tough but fair. He'd gravitated to the Crown's side of the legal world within a year after graduating from Osgoode Hall Law School. He became an Assistant Crown Attorney in 1959 and was named a Crown Attorney in 1961 at the age of twenty-nine, which made him the youngest full Crown Attorney in Canada at the time.

The appointment was a judicious one and Affleck's rise was little short of meteoric. In addition to being the Crown Attorney for the Judicial District of Durham, he would shortly be named the Chief Crown for the East Central Region for Ontario, and would, in due time, become a Queen's Counsellor and a Bencher in the Law Society of Upper Canada. Bruce Affleck would also, along the way, become something of a legend.

He was bright (IQ: 149, he was fond of telling interviewers), articulate, and eminently quotable, having long ago learned to cultivate reporters, and he was endowed with a truly photographic memory. After spending twenty years in the profession, and in court almost every working day of those years, there was rarely a case or a face or a name that Affleck couldn't recall almost immediately and accurately.

But his greatest gift lay in his genius at cross-examination. The book on

Affleck, whether as a Crown or on defence, was that his research and pre-trial preparation might be thin, and his general working knowledge of the law only average, but that none of this mattered. His ability to get to his feet and simply wing it, whether before a hostile witness or a sceptical jury, was, everyone agreed, simply nonpareil.

During his nearly twenty years as a Crown Attorney, Affleck had prose-cuted forty-five murder cases, and he claimed a ninety-percent conviction rate. The secret of successful trial work, Affleck believed, was brevity. Don't baffle a jury with legal jargon, or bore its members with rambling examina-tions. Keep things simple, direct, and to the point, and respect the common sense of the jurors.

But it was draining, always being the central courtroom actor at major trials, and by 1977 the role of Canada's most flamboyant and successful Crown prosecutor had begun to take its toll. Affleck suffered a series of near-fatal heart attacks which accentuated his haggard, slightly dissipated appearance. He was overweight, he had dark bags under his eyes, and his heavy jowls made him look far older than he really was.

The task of being an active prosecutor was stressful in many ways, as any honest Crown Attorney will admit. How many hundreds of criminals had Affleck prosecuted successfully, sending them to prison for how many thousands of years? It was every Crown's secret nightmare that one day his luck might run out, that he would find himself in the wrong place at the wrong time, suddenly confronting someone he'd helped to convict. Maybe the guy would have had too much to drink, or maybe he cared more about revenge than about staying out on parole. You couldn't be too careful. Bruce still shuddered inwardly whenever he thought about a close encoun-ter he'd once had with two members of the Choice. He and a couple of friends had been eating breakfast in a hotel dining-room when a pair of club members strolled in, wearing their colours and chain-link belts. They sat at a nearby table, and for the next half-hour Affleck couldn't take his eyes off them. Their presence was unsettling to the people he was with, too, because they were aware of their host's reputation as Canada's foremost biker prosecutor. Affleck was positively fixated on the bikers, and on their belts, because the gossip was that they used the chains as weapons, wrapped around their fists. . . . When they had finished eating the two bikers approached his table. One of them had his hands on his belt, and

Affleck was certain that at any moment a titanic struggle was about to break out . . .

"Are you Bruce Affleck?" one of the bikers asked him.

For once, Affleck was speechless. His heart fluttered. He swallowed hard, and nodded.

"I just want to say you're all right. You prosecuted me once, and you're fair."

With that they turned on their boot heels and were gone, leaving Affleck in a cold sweat. No, you just couldn't be too careful.

And there was one other reason that Affleck had ended his long service to the Crown: money. For all his apparent affability. Bruce Affleck was, like most successful lawyers, a highly competitive man. He liked to keep tabs on his law school classmates, plot their course up the curve of the professional pecking-order, compare their progress with his own. Had John been named a QC yet? No, but Richard had been named a provincial court judge just last year. Ah, good for him. Ian's firm had upwards of twenty lawyers on staff now. And what do you suppose, Bruce would ask a visitor slyly, were Ian's billings last year?

It was in the last category that Bruce definitely felt he was falling behind. Despite his celebrity and flair, Bruce had earned only $45,000 as a senior Crown Attorney. Not bad money for 1977, perhaps, but not one-quarter what some of his classmates were earning, even though they might lack his abilities.

And so, on November 1, 1977, a memorable retirement party had been held in honour of Bruce Affleck, attended by no fewer than 112 lawyers and 6 judges—someone, probably Bruce, had counted. At the age of forty-six the Chief Crown Attorney for the Judicial District of Durham was about to become simply Bruce Affleck, Esquire, Solicitor and Queen's Counsel.

The subject of lawyer selection by those accused of conspiring to kill Bill Matiyek was widely discussed not only among the accused, but within the wider ranks of the Satan's Choice as well. With the possible exception of Jeff McLeod, whose father had offered to hire the best lawyer he could find and to pay for it out of his own pocket (an offer Jeff declined) it was understood that none of the accused or their families could afford to mount an effective legal defence from their own resources. Each of the accused would, therefore, retain a lawyer appointed and paid by Legal Aid.

It was also understood that if a really good lawyer should demand more than the going Legal Aid rate, the club would "up" the necessary funds from its own coffers, which made the choice of lawyers a question of more than passing interest to every member. In the clubhouses and bars and on visits to the accused, debates over the merits and liabilities of various lawyers continued for several weeks.

There was, however, unanimous agreement on Jeff's choice of Bruce Affleck to lead the defence team. He was already highly respected by the club because of his solid reputation while a Crown, and because he had prosecuted so many of them so effectively. Anyone who knew so much about putting bikers behind bars should be equally knowledgeable about how to get them off. Also, this was a murder trial, and who had had more experience at murder trials, albeit as a Crown, than Bruce Affleck?

Gordy van Haarlem had decided to retain Dob Ebbs for his defence. Ebbs was well known to members of the Peterborough Chapter and, since van Haarlem would be mounting an alibi defence (he had been drinking in a Peterborough hotel on the evening of the shooting), Ebbs was in the same town as the corroborating witnesses, and conveniently placed for the necessary pre-trial interviews.

Rick Sauvé was never quite sure how he had gotten Jack Grossman as his lawyer, except that he had been assigned to the case by Legal Aid. A Toronto criminal lawyer of middling reputation and experience, Grossman struck Sauvé as a decent sort. He would do. Larry Hurren was assigned David Newman, another Toronto criminal lawyer. He was one of the more inexperienced members of the defence team, especially in murder trials, but Beaver, like most of the other accused, didn't take any of this too seriously. All he'd done was stand at the bar while the whole thing went down. He hadn't really *done* anything. How much trouble could he really be in?

XVIII

EVEN DURING THE BUSIEST of rush hours Hexham Drive in Scarborough is a quiet suburban street, and it was no busier than usual just before four o'clock on the afternoon of Wednesday, January 10, 1979. That was probably why Gene King, Junior, Gary Comeau's younger brother, happened to notice the car parked down the street by Precious Blood School with four men sitting in it, when he got home. Still, he didn't think any more about it until he heard a knock on the door. The four men identified themselves as police officers and presented him with a search warrant for the premises. Gene Junior, age twenty, let them in.

Where, they wanted to know, was Gary's room?

He showed them to the back bedroom at the end of the hall, and the police began to search Gary's closet and chest of drawers. Did his brother keep his possessions in any other room of the house? Did he, by any chance, own a green Hydro parka? Gene replied in the negative to both questions. As he watched, the police seized some of Gary's stuff—an address book, some Choice items, and then they found a green Hydro parka.

Gene told them that the parka was his, which it was—he was using the back bedroom himself while his brother was in jail—but the cops inspected the coat carefully, anyway, especially the upper part of the left sleeve.

The youngest son of Gene and Betty King was starting to get fed up, especially with the tall guy from Port Hope, who struck him as a real power-tripper, a frustrated cowboy, who actually got off on walking into strangers' homes and taking them apart. Gene told them all to shove it, he wasn't going to answer any more questions, and then his mother got home.

Betty was immediately upset to find her home being searched, and they hadn't even shown the courtesy to take off their boots. One of them, the tall one, asked her whether she knew that her son had been shot.

"No," Betty answered truthfully, "I don't know about it."

"Well, we think Gary got shot," he repeated, and that upset her even more. Betty decided to go downstairs to call her sister and tell her what was happening, she had to talk to somebody, but the police officer followed her to the phone.

"Lots of gang fellas do things their parents don't know about. We think he got shot that night. Why don't you ask him when you come down to visit him next time?"

Two days later, at 6:15 on a Friday evening, the police finally caught up with Armand Sanguigni, at a house in Rexdale. He was driven to Cobourg the same night and he joined Gary, Jeff, Merv, Rick, and Gordy in the bucket.

Almost from the time of his arrival the other five could feel the screws tighten several notches. Security was stepped up, and it was apparent to everyone that the police considered Armand highly dangerous. On *this* murder, they seemed to be saying, you're going down, motherfucker.

That weekend, as she always did, Betty King drove to Cobourg to visit her son. She asked Gary whether he'd been shot. He told her that he had, but that he wasn't in any pain and that the wound had healed. The whereabouts of the bullet was still something of a mystery, he whispered, but he believed it was still inside his body. He had been in the hotel when Matiyek was killed, but Gary assured his mother he had had no part in the shooting and no idea that it was about to happen. He was innocent of any conspiracy.

Betty returned to Toronto with a heavy heart, although she believed her son implicitly. It was like the time the school caught fire. She was certain Gary had told her the truth. She knew in her heart that her son couldn't kill anybody, or even plan such a thing. He wasn't a bad boy, just very, very foolish. Betty's only consolation was that at least Gary hadn't lied to his mother.

On Monday, January 15, 1979, a second charge was laid against each of the eight members of the Satan's Choice accused of conspiring to kill Bill Matiyek. After a thorough review of the evidence, Crown Attorney Chris Meinhardt had concluded there were sufficient grounds to charge each of the bikers with first-degree murder. The new charges were a sensational development: one of the largest blanket first-degree murder indictments in the annals of Canadian law. To prove its case, the Crown would have to establish beyond a reasonable doubt that each of the eight co-accused had planned and deliberated the murder of Bill Matiyek. Since no such thing had happened, the six Choice members told one another over and over in the Cobourg bucket, how could the Crown possibly convict them of first-degree murder? It was just more copper bullshit, although the sentence for first-degree murder—twenty-five years, with no parole—was no joke.

Bruce Affleck, for one, took the news quite seriously. He knew Chris Meinhardt. Although based in Lindsay, Ontario, a small town just west of Peterborough, Meinhardt was far more than a simple small-town Crown Attorney. He had succeeded Affleck as the Chief Crown for the East Central Region and he was something of an Affleck protégé. Meinhardt had articled in the Attorney General's office, and had then served as an appellate counsel for the AG. Slender, and with an air of cool, intimidating aloofness, Meinhardt could at times appear—to someone already unsettled by the court surroundings—quite bloodless, even ruthless. This trait had earned him a cruel nickname—Chris Mean Heart—among defence lawyers who had faced him in court. A punishing worker who more than made up in preparation whatever he might lack in native ability, Chris Meinhardt was the kind of Crown who prosecuted to the limit of the law and to the level best of his abilities one hundred percent of the time. He was not to be taken lightly.

There were other worrisome developments in the weeks leading up to the preliminary hearing, tell-tale signs that this was to be no ordinary murder proceeding. For one thing, the Crown was making none of the usual pre-preliminary disclosures as to who its witnesses and what its evidence might be. Even Terry Hall, whom Howard Kerbel always considered genial and who had sometimes been willing to informally share information before other trials involving the Satan's Choice, had stopped talking. Everyone was playing this one extremely close to the vest, ostensibly because of the threat that had already been made against one of the potential Crown witnesses. Which club member had done this to which witness remained a closely guarded secret, and the defence lawyers admonished their clients to get word out any way they could: no member was to approach, talk to, or intimidate any witness in any way, and this order was duly circulated throughout the club.

Some members of the defence team had also heard through the legal grapevine that Ontario Attorney General Roy McMurtry planned to personally prefer indictments even if the case was dismissed at the preliminary hearing for lack of evidence. It was an unusual procedure for the province's top law-enforcement officer to overrule a provincial court judge, but it was well within McMurtry's legal rights and a sign of just how seriously the Crown was taking this case.

As the gravity of the situation began to weigh on the defence lawyers, some of them began to take unusual precautions. Suspecting that their meeting-room at the Cobourg jail might be wired for sound, Affleck communicated with Jeff by written notes during the most sensitive parts of their conversations. Kerbel did the same when interviewing Gary, and he destroyed the notes after he left the jail.

There was also the question of how many of these concerns the lawyers should share with their individual clients. It was a little like being a doctor and knowing that your patient had contracted a fatal disease: how, when, and what should you tell the patient? There was a fine line between candor and cruelty. Affleck struck Jeff as upbeat and optimistic, although he'd always add, "Look, this is major-league stuff. Murder One. We can't screw around." Still, Jeff always came away feeling as if they might just beat this thing at the preliminary—or at least *he* might—and some of the others came away from meeting their lawyers with the same hope.

In the two weeks prior to the opening of the Matiyek murder preliminary, the Satan's Choice could have opened up a new chapter at the Cobourg Court House. In just over a fortnight, nineteen club members were paraded through the local courts on a total of thirty-nine charges, including the Matiyek murder. The alleged offences included unlawful assembly, assault to commit bodily harm, indecent assault (rape), buggery, common assault, conspiracy to commit murder, and first-degree murder.

At a preliminary hearing on Thursday, February 2, three club members were committed to stand trial for rape, buggery, and assault. Two days later a dozen members were present for sentencing on the Alderville Reserve dance melee. One of them was acquitted, and the other eleven, including Jeff McLeod, Gordon van Haarlem, Gary Comeau, and Larry Hurren, were found guilty of unlawful assembly and sentenced to two years' probation.

XIX

MONDAY, FEBRUARY 19, 1979, dawned clear and cold, and early that morning a small cavalcade wound its way down Highway 2 from Cobourg to Port Hope. In the front of the line was a gun truck—an armored cube-van bearing the standard black-and-white colours of Ontario Provincial Police vehicles. Behind the gun truck was a paddy wagon carrying Nutty Comeau, Merv Blaker, Rick Sauvé, Armand Sanguigni, Beaver Hurren, and Dogmap van Haarlem. They were handcuffed and wore manacles around their ankles, and they were chained together in pairs. In the rear vehicle rode a watchful armed guard.

The paddy wagon pulled right up on the snow-covered grass outside the Port Hope police station, which also served as a courthouse, and the six members of the Satan's Choice who had been denied bail lumbered up the town-hall steps, awkward against the unfamiliar restraints.

It was Nutty who first noticed the gun truck, which had been backed up to gain an unobstructed view of the short space between the paddy wagon and the door of the town hall. The rear doors of the gun truck had been thrown open and there was a machine gun, mounted on a tripod, pointed right at them, a policeman at the ready behind it.

"Will ya look at that!" Nutty nodded at the gun truck, as they trudged into the building. "What a fuckin' joke!" What were they expecting? The club had maybe thirty-five or forty members left—the coppers knew that. Did they really think that the guys who were still on the street were going to come swooping down like Spider Man in some desperate attempt to free them?

The police also assumed, as Gordy would reflect later, that they wanted to be busted out. Suppose they did escape? Where were they going to go, and what would they do once they got there? They'd be in some strange town, maybe even in a strange country, walking down the road kicking stones. Rick and Merv were married and they each had a kid. Gordy himself had just learned that Patty was pregnant and that he was going to become a father for the first time. None of them wanted to leave their families. No, far better to get on with it, to prove their innocence, and get this whole thing over with.

Despite the handcuffs and manacles and machine gun, they had lost little of their cocky, club edge that cold February morning. "They got nothin' on us" was the attitude. Whatever worries or self-doubts each might harbor that something might go wrong, could go wrong, they kept it resolutely to themselves. The police show of force even added to their confidence. The whole thing was a joke, too absurd to be taken seriously. They were innocent, they were the Choice, and proud of it. Fuck The World.

The purpose of a preliminary hearing under Canadian law is to determine whether there is sufficient evidence to bring a case to trial. While the burden of proof lies with the prosecution, there is no obligation for the Crown to call all, or even most, of its evidence. The state must establish only that there is a *prima facie* case against the accused and that the matter should be handed over to a judge and/or jury for a full trial. In practice, the preliminary hearing is also an opportunity for the defence to gauge the merits of the case for the prosecution, without necessarily calling any evidence of its own.

Port Hope Crown Attorney Roland C. Harris, acting as junior for Chris Meinhardt, wasted little time in playing one of his evidentiary aces in the case of *Regina v. Richard Sauvé, et al.* As his first witness he called Cathy Cotgrave.

The nineteen-year-old barmaid was nervous at first, but as the day wore on her confidence grew. She began by telling Harris her whereabouts on October 18: how she'd run into Bill Matiyek on the street downtown, gone for lunch with him at Turck's, and accompanied him to Newcastle, and how he'd driven her to work just before four o'clock.

On their way into the Queen's, she and Bill had encountered two men, Sonny Bronson and Fred Jones. Bill had invited them in for a drink. The bar was quiet that evening, until about five to eleven, when about twenty people arrived, seemingly all at once. She recognized Rick Sauvé, Merv Blaker, and Larry Hurren, and she pointed each of them out in the courtroom.

She also identified Armand Sanguigni—he'd been in the pinball room talking to Fred Jones—and she pointed to Gary Comeau and David Hoffman, who, she was certain, had been standing at the bar, although she didn't know their names. Comeau had been wearing a green parka and she'd seen him standing beside the John Street exit, near Bill's table at the time of the shooting.

Gordy van Haarlem shifted uneasily in his seat and made a mental note to himself. *He'd* worn a green Hydro parka into the courthouse that very day—it was the only winter coat he had. He'd have to get rid of that parka, for sure.

The man she identified as Comeau had also been wearing a toque, he had blond hair, and he was big. Cathy pointed out Jeff McLeod among the accused—he'd been there, too, sitting at a table right across from Bill's when the shooting occurred, and Jeff's heart sank, though he tried not to show it.

She'd assumed they were all Choice, because she recognized Sauvé, Blaker, and Hurren, and she hadn't served any of them—all members of the Satan's Choice had been barred for life from the Queen's since May. *Well, maybe she don't know it,* thought Rick, *but I been served in the Queen's lotsa times since May, and so has Merv. Somebody served Beaver too.*

Yes, she had told Merv Blaker that they were all barred and wouldn't be served, and he'd merely shrugged his shoulders. Rick Sauvé had been sitting at Bill's table and Jamie Hanna had been there with them, briefly. Jamie had spoken to Rick and Bill and then left. Rick Sauvé and Jeff McLeod were still at the table when the man she'd identified as Gary Comeau approached the table from the area of the men's washroom. He pulled a gun out of his pocket and shot Bill three times.

Thoughts raced like screams through Nutty's head. *No, she's got it all wrong! I was sitting with Matiyek, not Jeff. She's confused us. And I didn't do the shooting, I was shot myself, for Chrissake. But where's the bullet? And where's my black-leather jacket? God, no. This can't be happening.*

Betty King had driven down from Toronto for the first day of the preliminary, and Cathy Cotgrave's testimony, serious as it was, brought a rush of relief to her. Even as her son was being accused of murder, Betty knew beyond any doubt that it couldn't be true. *A toque!* Twice the waitress had said the gunman was wearing a toque. Ever since she could remember, Betty had never known her son to wear a toque. She'd always put one on him when he went outside to play in the winter, but whenever he came home he'd have lost it or it would be in his pocket. His ears could be frozen blue, but Gary just wouldn't wear anything on his head. She was exactly the same way. So it wasn't Gary. She'd never really doubted, but . . . she couldn't help smiling.

In his opening cross-examination for the defence, Bruce Affleck zeroed in on the police investigation. When had Cathy Cotgrave first been interviewed? How many times? When had she seen photographic line-ups, and who had she identified each time?

The nineteen-year-old fielded each of his questions smoothly, replying with accuracy. Her memory appeared sound, and unshakable. Only in her description of the murder weapon was Cathy Cotgrave's recollection clearly at variance with provable facts. It was bronze-coloured, with some brown in it, she recalled, and, after having the difference between a pistol and a revolver explained to her, she remembered it as having been a pistol. But since no spent casings were found at the scene, the gun was evidently a revolver. That much, at least, was known to the defence, as well as to the Crown.

After the lunch break, Affleck's cross-examination fared a little better. Had the witness known that Bill Matiyek carried a weapon? Yes, a friend had told her later in the evening.

"Prior to the shooting occurring?"

"Yes."

"You knew he was carrying a loaded gun?"

"I was told it wasn't loaded."

Next Affleck wondered about the altercation between Matiyek and Brian Brideau. She had seen the fight, or at least the part that had taken place inside the hotel, Cotgrave replied. Bill had held Brideau down and Fred Jones had kicked him in the head. Brideau had been injured and appeared agitated and upset.

"And Mr. Brideau made a threat at that time, in your presence, to Mr. Matiyek, didn't he?"

"Yes."

"And he indicated he was going to get a gun and kill him, didn't he?"

"Well, not . . . he said, 'The next time,' he said to Bill, 'The next time I see you your head will be at the end of a shotgun.'"

The first hour or so of Howard Kerbel's cross-examination yielded little new information. But after a ten-minute mid-afternoon recess Kerbel returned to the subject of Matiyek's own gun and Cathy Cotgrave abruptly changed part of her earlier testimony: she had discovered that Matiyek was armed only *after* he was killed. Cathy also admitted that Gayle Thompson had been present when she viewed the photo array for the second time the week following the shooting. She'd been able to identify certain photographs—Comeau's, she later learned—as being the gunman because "I was watching the table all along."

"Why?"

"Well, I just thought something was going to happen, so I just kept watching the table."

Court was recessed for the day then, because the room it was occupying on the second floor of the Town Hall was also the City Council chambers, and a meeting was scheduled for that night. The co-accused weren't quite so cocky as they were being led back to their paddy wagon. Gordy was desperately trying to get someone to swap coats with him—Armand, Rick, even

Larry were about the same size—but everybody just laughed at him. "Aw, Dogmap, whatsa matter? Thought you were just along for the ride."

They discussed Cotgrave's testimony at length. She'd been a convincing witness, they had to admit. Still, what she said wasn't all bad: she had, after all, brought out the fact that Bill had had a gun, too, and about the fight with Brideau. It went some way towards confirming their side of the story.

But Brian Brideau would never confirm or deny that part of the story. Because the lawyers for the men who had been there had decided not to call witnesses, they would not get the chance to force Brideau's story out of him.

Kerbel returned to the Brideau connection the next morning, over frequent and strenuous objections from Chris Meinhardt. Cathy Cotgrave confirmed that Brideau was a known drug-user, that he had been barred from the Queen's as a troublemaker, and that he appeared to be drunk the night of his fight with Matiyek and Jones.

What about the witness herself—had she ever used speed?

"Yes, I have."

"And around the month of October 1978 were you using speed?"

"No."

"Have you ever purchased any drugs from Mr. Matiyek?"

"Sometimes."

"Did he administer any drugs or narcotics to you that day?"

"No." A less than truthful answer, since she had smoked up with Bill early that afternoon.

"Where was Jamie Hanna? Where was her table?"

"Directly in front of the bar."

"And who was seated at the table with Jamie Hanna?"

"Just an older man and the fifth from the left."

Kerbel turned towards the prisoner's box. "The fifth from the left—indicating McLeod?"

"Yes."

Nutty's heart soared. *See—she's doing it again. I was hustlin' Jamie Hanna at the table with the old man, not Jeff . . .*

"And did you ever see the man who is fifth from the left sitting at Mr. Matiyek's table?"

"No, he was standing at Mr. Matiyek's table . . . at the time of the shooting."

Kerbel ground away at Cathy Cotgrave for another hour, to the growing exasperation of the Crown, the witness, and even Judge Scullion. Only at the end of his cross-examination, which had now taken up the better part of half a day, did Comeau's lawyer elicit one more bit of new and significant information: Cathy Cotgrave was quite certain that the gunman, whom she had identified as Gary Comeau, had pulled the gun from his pocket and fired it with his left hand. As Betty King, Howard Kerbel, and anyone who had taken the trouble to notice knew, Gary Comeau was right-handed.

Jack Grossman, for Rick Sauvé, questioned Cotgrave closely about his client's movements just before the shooting. She'd seen Sauvé sitting at Bill's table for three or four minutes before the first shot was fired. After some confusion, she decided that Sauvé had been seated on Matiyek's left.

Had the witness discussed her observations of the incident with her friends?

"Yeah, we talked about it."

"Who, specifically, did you talk to?"

"Well, Sue Foote, my friends . . . like Gayle Thompson, people that were there . . . like we just couldn't believe that it happened, wondering why it happened and things like that."

Had they actually compared their observations?

"We could have. I'm not really sure."

"For example, identifying so-and-so was there, or this fellow was there, that guy did this, or someone else did that, that type of discussion?"

"Yeah, I think we did. Yeah."

"How often would you do that?"

"Not very often."

After lunch, Ed Martin cross-examined and underscored the unintentional "collusion" of the witnesses: Cathy again admitted that she and her friends had discussed the names and faces of the accused.

As with each of the accused, Tee Hee's interest naturally intensified when his own lawyer was cross-examining. It seemed to him that Martin had gotten no further in shaking Cotgrave's identification of him than had Sanguigni's lawyer. He'd never seen this broad before in his life. But he had to hand it to her, she was convincing, and she stood up to all these lawyers very, very well. For the first time a most unwelcome thought occurred to David Hoffman, one that would grow throughout the preliminary until it became an awful, unshakable conviction: despite the fact that he'd been two hundred kilometres away when it happened, he was going to go to prison for the shooting of Bill Matiyek.

Cathy Cotgrave's long ordeal in the witness stand was almost over. Only Terry O'Hara remained to cross-examine. Miss Cotgrave knew Murray Blaker? Yes, to see him. And she would agree that he was a well-known, unmistakable figure about town? Yes. The big lawyer's tone was warm, soothing.

Had the witness ever seen Mr. Blaker and Mr. Matiyek together before that night? No. And she had never known them to fight in any way? No.

O'Hara's voice became almost apologetic. "I know you're probably getting tired of it by now . . ." but he just wanted to determine once more whether she'd had anything to drink before she met Bill at midday. No. Any other drugs—prescription, nonprescription, marijuana? No.

"Okay. Now, let's take it up until the time you left the apartment. Did you have anything to drink between lunch and the time you left the apartment?"

"No."

"And did you have any other intoxicant of any kind during that time?"

"Yes."

"What did you have?"

"Marijuana."

"About how much did you smoke?"

"Just one."

Bruce Affleck watched O'Hara's cross-examination with deepening respect. The young lawyer had gotten to a truth that the witness had denied only a few hours earlier when Kerbel had been cross-examining. The witness was the same, but the handling was vastly different. O'Hara seemed to use his very size, which could have easily been intimidating to any witness, to his advantage. "How could anyone so obviously fat and happy be threatening?" he seemed to say. His demeanour was affable, friendly, without ever becoming overly familiar.

Cathy also admitted having "one or two" Southern Comforts during the afternoon, but no other stimulants of any kind after she began work at four o'clock.

It was already late in the afternoon, but the cross-examinations of Cathy Cotgrave had been time-consuming, so the Court decided to proceed with the next Crown witness. Jamie Hanna was sworn. The witness said she was nineteen years old and that she and the deceased had been "going together" for "the last three or four months" prior to the shooting. She recounted sitting with Bill, Sonny, and Fred until, shortly after eleven, "these persons came in slowly and, like, in bunches." The atmosphere in the bar became "suspicious."

There was an old man at her table and another guy had come and sat down. She hadn't talked to the newcomer but the old man did and she overheard the conversation. Yes, this second guy was part of the group she believed to be the Satan's Choice. *That was me*, thought Gary.

"What was the conversation?"

"The old man asked—"

Bruce Affleck interrupted. "No, your Honour, with the greatest efforts, how does this become admissible?"

He could show the relevance of the answer, replied Deputy Crown Attorney Harris.

Now Ross McKay, the lawyer for Armand Sanguigni, was on his feet, too. "It is not its relevance my learned friend Mr. Affleck is complaining of, your Honour, it is—"

"Hearsay," Judge Scullion interjected.

It was a legal argument that would be heard again and again throughout the preliminary hearing and the trial. On the surface, the rule against the admissibility of hearsay evidence is simple enough. It was an ancient concept in British common law—that statements made by someone other than the witness, or statements made to someone else by the witness outside the earshot of the accused, could not be presented as evidence by a witness in court. The purpose of the hearsay rule was to protect any accused from second- or third-hand information, gossip, or innuendo. There is, however, one major exception (and many minor) to the hearsay rule: if the witness claims to have heard a statement *by an accused*, and so long as that accused is present in court to hear the alleged statements and is free to cross-examine the witness and to rebut the statements later on the witness stand, then the evidence is, generally, deemed to be admissible. *Admissible* hearsay evidence would come to have a tremendous bearing on the fate of the accused in *Regina v. Sauvé*.

Was one of the speakers in the conversation one of the accused? Judge Scullion asked the witness.

"Do you see the person . . . in the courtroom and could you look carefully, please?" Harris added.

Before Jamie Hanna could answer, Ross McKay was on his feet again, objecting to Harris's question. The witness had already viewed the accused and, with the exception of Sauvé and Blaker, had been unable to identify them. "I object to her having a second run, as it were."

Judge Scullion decided to reserve judgment on the admissibility of the conversation.

"Miss Hanna," Harris continued, "after this conversation between the two parties who were at your table, what did you do?"

"I turned to the waitress, Cathy Cotgrave, and told her to call the police."

"No, your Honour, with respect—" McKay was on his feet again, and another legal wrangle ensued. It was late in the day, and the texture of the proceeding, which had been fairly smooth, was beginning to fray.

After several minutes of legal sparring Harris resumed his questioning.

"Where did you go [after telling Cathy to call the police]?"

"I went over and I sat with Bill Matiyek."

"And how long were you at that table, just with Bill Matiyek?"

"About a minute and a half."

"Did anyone else come to the table after a minute and a half?"

"Yes."

"And who was that?"

"Rick Sauvé."

"And what did Rick Sauvé do when he came to the table?"

"He whispered in Bill's ear and then he turned to me and he said, 'Chick, get the fuck away from this table.'"

No, thought Rick. *No, no, that wasn't how it had happened, at least not quite. I was already at the table, sitting across from Bill. Yeah, I wanted her to get away from the table, but not because we knew Bill was going to get shot. It was because I thought Bill was about to shoot me. She makes it sound like I was givin' Bill the kiss of death or something.* And that was how they all came to regard the story: "The Kiss-of-Death Statement."

Was anything else said, and by whom?

"Yes, and by Bill. . . . He agreed with him. He said, 'Yes, I think you better leave.'"

"Was there anything further said?"

"Good-bye."

"Who said that?"

"Bill."

"To you?"

"Yes."

"Where was Rick Sauvé when you left?"

"Still at the table."

"Standing or seated?"

"Standing."

She hadn't even reached her own table when "I heard a pop and I turned around and Bill was getting shot." She vaguely saw a man about six feet tall with blond hair, blond beard and moustache, standing at the John Street exit. "He was shooting Bill."

"Why do you say he was shooting him?"

"Because I saw the gun."

"What size of gun was it?"

"It was hand-size. It was a hand revolver."

"Do you know what a 'revolver' means?"

"Only from . . . no, I don't."

"No further questions."

The audience that had packed into the makeshift courtroom sat in stunned silence after Hanna's sensational testimony. The consternation must have been nearly as great along the defence table.

It was Howard Kerbel who finally rose to his feet. "Prior to cross-examination, I wonder if it might be an appropriate time for a recess so we can confer together? I'd like to talk to my friend about this."

"Very well," Judge Scullion agreed.

It was nearing five o'clock when the hearing resumed, and Judge Scullion was still mulling over the admissibility of the hearsay evidence about the conversation with the old man. "Mr. Meinhardt, perhaps you can help me also with this. As I look at the Information [the official police document spelling out the charges] it says, 'unlawfully did conspire together, the one with the other and others of them and with persons unknown.' Is that right?"

"Yes, sir."

"It is the allegation by the Crown that the person who came in was one of the fifteen, sat down at the witnesses' table—that was one of the persons unknown . . ."

"Yes."

But it wasn't "a person unknown," thought Nutty. It was me. And I wasn't talking just to the old man, I was talking to her, too. I told them I was in the club, and I even told them my nickname, which I sure as fuck wouldn't have done if I'd been planning to dust Bill Matiyek two minutes later.

"Your Honour, there is one question I omitted to ask the witness. . . ."

"I think you can ask another question, Mr. Harris."

"Miss Hanna, have you been threatened by anyone since the murder incident—the murder?"

"Yes."

"I would ask if you see that person who threatened you in the courtroom today?"

"Yes, I do."

Every eye in the courtroom was riveted to Jamie Hanna's outstretched hand, the forefinger pointing in the direction of Pierre Sauvé.

Rick's father stood up in highest dudgeon. "Is she pointing at me?" he sputtered. "Because well, sir, if she's pointing at *me* . . ."

All the other guys in the prisoner's box were looking at Rick. *Your old man?* Rick looked out at his dad, all red in the face and indignant, and started to laugh. Some of the others did, too.

"That man that's sitting in the front row," Jamie Hanna pointed, "second from the left . . . *second* from the left."

Pierre Sauvé looked about him and realized he was *third* from the left. Sheepishly, he sat down.

"Are you referring to the fellow smiling at you with the glasses and long blond hair?"

"Yes."

"And do you know his name?"

"Bob Cousins."

Bobby fuckin' Cousins, thought Rick. *The one who called me and Merv down to the Plaza that day to meet with Hall. Jesus, would Bobby be that stupid—to threaten a juror?*

"Do you know if he is affiliated with any club?"

Now the whole courtroom was in chaos. Some people were still laughing about Pierre, everybody was looking at Cousins, who just sat there grinning and looking sick, and about half the lawyers on the defence team were all jumping to their feet at once.

Judge Scullion hastily intervened. "Well, there has been a threat on the witness. She has named the person. Now, leave that up to the authorities. I don't think you should go into that any further."

"I don't think it is appropriate that he should be sitting here if that is the case."

"Again, I will leave that up to the authorities, but in the meantime, sir, would you step outside."

Harris quickly pressed on. "Your Honour, with respect, it is the Crown's position that this is relevant in regards to the common conspiracy involving members of the Satan's Choice, and it is relevant to the preliminary hearing itself, in light of that."

McKay rose. "The logical extension of that is that we bring in all the known members of the Satan's Choice and add them to this indictment. It may sound facetious, but I am not being facetious."

Bruce Affleck supported McKay's arguments, adding that the defence had decided to postpone its cross-examination of Jamie Hanna, pending the Judge's ruling on the admissibility of the overheard conversation. The next morning they got their answer: Jamie Hanna's hearsay evidence was admissible.

XX

A LONE FIGURE TRUDGED up the steps of the Port Hope Town Hall. With his jet-black hair, goatee, and dark hazel eyes he could easily have been mistaken for an Indian, but he was of Scottish extraction, as his surname revealed. He didn't want to see any of the guys, and he didn't want them to see him, didn't want them to know he'd even been there.

He believed that when you had a problem you had to face it head on, and that was why he had come. He located the room reserved for witnesses waiting to testify. It was full of people, and the door was, fortunately, open.

He stood outside in the hallway for as long as he dared, in plain view. He paced back and forth, stopped, pulled a cigarette from its pack and lit it. All of the rote gestures of the heavy smoker were performed with his left hand. He forced himself to wait there until the cigarette had been smoked down to its filter. *Come on, you bastards, look at me.* He had to know this one thing: would they, could they, identify him?

When the ash was down to the nub he dropped the butt to the floor and crushed it beneath his boot. Lorne Campbell slipped out of the Town Hall then, and returned to Oshawa.

Rollie Harris walked his next witness through examination-in-chief. Susan Jean Foote, twenty-three, indicated that she had grown up in Cobourg, and was "a really good friend" of the late Bill Matiyek. She described her meeting with Doug Peart and Dave Gillispie in the TV-shuffleboard room in one corner of the lounge. She then recounted the now-familiar story of the bikers' entrance.

She knew Rick and Merv really well—they had nodded or waved to her when they entered. She knew Tee Hee from parties, too. In all, Sue Foote estimated that fifteen to twenty people had arrived at the bar between ten-fifty and ten-fifty-five, and it made her feel "a little tense . . . the air was a little heavy . . . there was a few problems between Matiyek and the club. . . ."

Affleck, Kerbel, and O'Hara were on their feet in unison.

"You are pretty light on your feet, Mr. O'Hara," the Judge observed with a smile.

"They say sometimes fat men are, your Honour. It seems to me that if you say you know something of your own knowledge, it is not automatically the magic formula to quote hearsay with an aura of admissibility."

"If you want to bring out these questions you will have to make a base," Judge Scullion warned Harris.

Sue then described where four or five of the bikers were just prior to the shooting. "There were a lot of them just kind of staggering around the bar . . . they were walking in and through the tables and just making sure everybody knew they were there, it looked like to me." No, she couldn't say just who was walking around.

After that some of them stood up "and they started heading towards the side door and then there were shots and they were pretty well around the table at the time of the shots—like, trying to get out the side door, and then as soon as the shots they were gone. There was a couple of them ran out the back door."

She heard three shots, but couldn't see Bill for the heavy traffic in front of his table, and when she finally did see her friend, he had already hit the floor. The Choice members were fleeing through the exits.

Under cross-examination by Bruce Affleck, Sue Foote conceded that she might have confused Jeff McLeod with someone else and that she had learned his name only after reading it in the newspapers. During Howard Kerbel's cross-examination the witness admitted that she had discussed her observations with Cathy Cotgrave on several occasions. She also conceded that Comeau's description could have fitted several people in the hotel, including, possibly, the third man at the Matiyek table.

At the conclusion of Foote's evidence, Jamie Hanna was recalled briefly. Unlike Susan Foote, Jamie could not remember seeing anyone standing around the Matiyek table during the shooting, but she agreed with Cathy Cotgrave: the gunman had been left-handed.

David William Gillispie was the next Crown witness. He'd arrived at the Queen's about ten to eleven to meet Cathy Cotgrave. About ten or fifteen minutes later "between ten and fifteen people" arrived in the bar "from all different exits." He recognized two people in the group, Richard Sauvé and Merv Blaker, who were sitting at a table together. Approximately five minutes after they'd come in, Gillispie recalled, he'd gone over to talk with Sauvé and Blaker, kneeling down between them. He'd been wondering about a motorcycle accident involving Satan's Choice striker Gary Galbraith.

"Did anyone further come to the table?"

"Yes."

"Did he make any comment?"

"Yes, he did."

"What did he say?"

"He stated . . . he said, 'Are we going to get on with this fat fucker?' This is a quote."

Rick looked at Merv. *It's true that Gillispie came to our table and squatted down and talked with us about Gary's bike. But I don't remember anyone making a statement like that.* The witness was asked whether he could identify the person who had uttered the "fat fucker" statement. Was he in court?

"I believe it's this guy over here, the third from the left."

"Indicating, for the record, Mr. Comeau."

"All right," Judge Scullion nodded. "I think the statement is admissible. Go ahead."

"Again Mr. Gillispie, if you can, what was the statement made by this gentleman you are facing?"

"He said, 'Are we going to get on with this or are we going to do it to this fat fucker?'"

"And who was he speaking to at the time?"

"Sauvé and Blaker."

"What reaction, if any, did you see on the part of Blaker or Sauvé?"

"I did not see any reaction."

"What did they do? What did you do?"

"I simply got up and left."

"Why?"

"Well, I was just—thought it was not the place for me to be."

"Did you see their faces at the time the comment was made?"

"Yes."

"What can you tell us about their faces at the time?"

"They had a look somewhat of dismayzed why—"

"I'm sorry. Dismayzed?"

"Dismayzed—like they seemed speechless at the moment that the statement was made and then immediately I went back to the back lounge."

After a few minutes, Gillispie said, he had emerged from the shuffleboard room (the south lounge) and gone to stand at the bar. Sauvé and Comeau were now seated at Matiyek's table. Sauvé was on the right-hand side of Bill and Comeau was on the left, from Gillispie's point of view. Approximately five minutes passed before the shots were fired. Between four and eight people were gathered around the Matiyek table; some were sitting and some were standing, and they blocked his view of the table.

"I next heard gunshots and saw people fleeing from the hotel through different exits." The witness could not identify any of the people who were around the Matiyek table.

Affleck had no questions, but under cross-examination by Howard Kerbel,

Gillispie conceded that he wasn't absolutely certain that it had been Comeau sitting at Matiyek's table. None of the other defence lawyers had any questions, and the witness was excused.

Rod Stewart was sworn and proceeded to give his version of events. He described his urge to leave, and his reasons for staying. "I felt if I got up and left it would be . . . it would be an antagonistic gesture. Later I stayed because I tried to give first aid."

"To Bill?"

"To Bill Matiyek."

About three minutes before he was murdered Bill Matiyek was called to the telephone, which was located at the bar, near where Stewart had been sitting. When Matiyek had finished a short conversation he returned to his table and perhaps a dozen of the Satan's Choice followed him. ". . . the group was in a kind of shape like this around the table." Stewart drew a figure in mid-air with his hands.

"You are describing what appears to me—is it fair to say a horseshoe shape?"

"I guess so, yeah."

The next thing the witness remembered was the shots being fired and confusion as a number of people tried to get out the doors all at once. One of them was making a concealing gesture, as if he were trying to hide a gun. He was wearing a green Hydro parka with the hood down. At the close of Harris's examination-in-chief, court was recessed for the day.

There was a great deal for the defendants to discuss in the bucket that night. They were bewildered where Foote, Gillispie, and Stewart had come up with the "horseshoe" angle—the notion that some of them had been intentionally blocking the Matiyek table. It just hadn't happened that way—everything had gone down too fast for that. But it *was* true that everyone had jumped to his feet and headed for the exits just as soon as the shooting started. Maybe that was what the witnesses had thought they'd seen. They noticed the horseshoe only after the first shot was fired, when everyone had jumped up and they assumed they'd been standing there before. This kind of bullshit would never stand up in court. Would it?

Bruce Affleck had contemplated Rod Stewart overnight. Stewart cut an impressive figure on the witness stand—handsome, well-dressed, articulate—

the very model of a credible witness. And his testimony had been so graphic, so damning. There was always, Affleck knew, a danger in cross-examining a witness like Stewart: you were apt to make his testimony even stronger.

The next morning, when Stewart returned to the witness stand, Affleck declined to cross-examine. Howard Kerbel's questioning confirmed Affleck's fears in short order.

Kerbel questioned Stewart closely about the horseshoe, and about the possibility that it was something he'd noticed only after the shooting, and not before.

". . . You have described this as being a horseshoe. Do you make—do you arrive at the conclusion based upon what happened afterwards?"

"Not really. In the description of a horseshoe is—you know there's the Horseshoe Falls, which isn't much of a horseshoe, and then there's the horseshoe you see on a horse—"

"Yes?"

"—and it's quite a horseshoe, and then there's the horseshoe around Julius Caesar, you know."

The reference to one of history's most famous murder conspiracies stopped Kerbel dead in his tracks, totally destroying the tempo of his cross-examination. "That's very good. Where does one go after that? Okay, Mr. Stewart, I am not questioning your powers of observation, as such; what I am trying to determine is whether your description of this group of people being in a form of a horseshoe arises from what occurred immediately after, or what occurred at the time of the hearing of the shots."

"It is certainly confirmed because as a group breaks up, it breaks up in relation to what it had been."

"That's right."

"In other words, my recollection is reconfirmed by what I saw after."

The next-to-last Crown witness was pathologist John Whiteside, who had performed a full autopsy on the body of one William John Matiyek at approximately ten o'clock on the morning after the shooting. The doctor had discovered three bullet wounds, two in the head and one in the lower jaw and neck.

The first bullet had entered the skull just in front of the left ear and passed through the lower part of the brain. The bullet itself had been found lodged in the right side of the brain.

The second bullet had entered the head through the back of the skull and had blown a hole in the skull just behind the right ear. The third had traveled across the shoulder, where it had made a groove, smashing the jaw on the left side before deflecting downward through the neck and hitting the thyroid cartilage, where it deflected once again, exiting on the right side.

The bullet wounds were the cause of death. The first wound was certainly fatal. The second one probably would have been, though not right away, and the third bullet would not have been fatal.

Could the doctor ascertain the order in which the shots were fired? Kerbel asked in cross-examination.

No, he could not.

Had he noticed any powder burns in the area of the entrance wounds?

If there were any, they were very small, and he had not observed them.

What had happened to the bullet found lodged in the brain?

It had been removed, largely intact, and was turned over to the Identification Branch of the police. The second bullet had shattered into fragments, which had also been removed and turned over to the police.

"With respect to this third bullet, did you find any fragments?"

"No."

"To the best of your knowledge, was the bullet itself ever recovered?"

"Not to my knowledge."

The last witness for the Crown at the preliminary hearing was then called to the stand: he was Acting Corporal Terry Hall, of the Ontario Provincial Police. The examination-in-chief was conducted by Chris Meinhardt, who began by asking Corporal Hall to detail his duties with respect to motorcycle clubs.

Hall described the Satan's Choice Motorcycle Club. It had three chapters, located in Toronto, Kitchener, and Peterborough. He estimated the total membership to be about seventy-five members, unified under a national chairman, although each chapter had its own executive. The club's total membership had declined from about a hundred and twenty members in Ontario and Quebec, owing to an internal split involving the Outlaws Motorcycle Club. Hall went on to describe the Choice colours and the ancillary regalia and their significance: the "One Percenter," "69," and "13" patches.

And was the witness familiar with the Golden Hawks Motorcycle Club?

Yes, there were ill feelings, bad blood, between them and the Choice. The Golden Hawks had been told by members of the Satan's Choice to stop wearing their colours in public. The Hawks, which had once been based in the Oshawa area, were a very small club, with approximately ten members. They no longer had a clubhouse. The Choice, on the other hand, were "one of the largest motorcycle clubs of this type."

Once again Bruce Affleck had no questions under cross-examination, but Howard Kerbel did.

During the arrest of his client, Mr. Comeau, had the witness "come in possession of a dark leather jacket that had a tear or hole in the left arm?"

"No sir."

How long had the Corporal known the accused, David Hoffman? asked Ed Martin.

Since 1974.

And had he seen David Hoffman while conducting the October 18 raid on the Kitchener clubhouse?

"Yes sir, I did."

Had the police investigated David Hoffman's whereabouts on the night of the eighteenth?

"To my knowledge, no sir, I wasn't aware of it."

Had the Corporal spoken to other police officers about the raid?

"I am certain we have discussed the fact we were in the clubhouse, the fact that Mr. Hoffman was there."

For the early part of the evening, at least, Tee Hee Hoffman now had an airtight alibi—he'd been seen in the presence of a police raiding-party, by the police themselves, two hundred kilometres away from the scene of the crime.

After a brief cross-examination by Terry O'Hara, Corporal Hall was excused. The case for the Crown had now been concluded.

XXI

THE PRELIMINARY HEARING was moved to the Cobourg County Court and on the morning of Friday, February 23, 1979, the presentation of the case for the defence began with the Clerk of the Court cautioning the accused.

"Richard Sauvé, Murray Blaker, David Hoffman, Gary Comeau, Jeffrey McLeod, Armand Sanguigni, Larry Hurren, Gordon J. van Haarlem, having heard the evidence, do you wish to say anything in answer to the charge? You are not bound to say anything, but whatever you do say will be taken down in writing and may be given in evidence against you at trial. You must clearly understand that you have nothing to hope from any promise of favour and nothing to fear from any threat that may have been held out to you to induce you to make any admission or confession of guilt, but whatever you say now may be given in evidence against you at your trial, notwithstanding the promise or threat. Richard Sauvé, do you wish to say anything yourself or call any witnesses on the charge of murder?"

Jack Grossman rose to his feet. "I am instructed Mr. Sauvé has nothing to say at this time and no witnesses to call at this time."

"Murray Blaker, do you wish . . ." the Clerk repeated the question for each of the accused, his voice flat, emotionless.

One by one the defence lawyers stood to answer the caution for his client. None of the accused wanted to say anything, and only Don Ebbs for van Haarlem, Ed Martin for Hoffman, and Kerbel for Comeau had any witnesses to call.

The caution was repeated on the second charge, conspiracy, and the responses were the same.

The two defence witnesses called by Ebbs on behalf of van Haarlem corroborated the biker's alibi. The first witness said he'd been drinking with van Haarlem from eight o'clock until one-thirty a.m. at the King George Hotel, a downtown Peterborough discotheque. Van Haarlem had been present throughout the evening and had left the table to go to the washroom or to talk to a few people. At most he'd been away for several minutes, nowhere near long enough to make the one-hour return trip to Port Hope.

The second witness was the bouncer from the King George. He specifically remembered van Haarlem being in the hotel on the night of the murder because he'd noticed the biker wearing his club colours, which was against the hotel rules, and he'd asked him to take them off. Van Haarlem did so and spent the whole evening in the bar until well after closing-time. He'd been with another Choice member, Bobby Cousins, the bouncer recalled, and because of their presence and reputation he'd kept a close eye on the van Haarlem table throughout the night. Van Haarlem had not left his table for more than twenty or twenty-five minutes at a stretch, of that the witness was absolutely certain.

Howard Kerbel called his first witness, Julie Joncas, but under cross-examination by Roland Harris, Joncas provided more damaging testimony against the accused.

"Miss Joncas . . . I understand there were occasions upon which you would ride in Mr. Matiyek's truck with him?"

Yes. Many times within a month or so before the murder, he had taken her to work. Bill made a point of driving past the homes of Choice members, particularly Merv Blaker's and Richard Sauvé's, to "see if there were any vehicles parked around the homes that he knew of that belonged to other members of the Satan's Choice, and if so, then he would take me and drop me off and he would leave."

Both Merv and Rick were inclined to scoff at this evidence, then as now. For Matiyek to have driven past Rick's house, in particular, would have meant going many miles out of his way, especially if he was taking Joncas, who lived in central Port Hope, to the Queen's, which was right downtown. Such a lengthy, time-consuming detour made little sense. But Joncas's was just the first in an ever-increasing mass of evidence which suggested that Bill Matiyek was a deeply worried man just before his death, and chief among his worries were the members of the Satan's Choice.

If his first witness only added to the case against his client, with his second witness Howard Kerbel was about to strike pay dirt. Ontario Provincial Police constable Donald Denis was called to the witness stand. Denis told Kerbel that his main role in the Matiyek murder investigation had been to show photos to prospective witnesses. At Kerbel's request, Denis read a complete list of all the witnesses to whom he'd shown the photo array, and when. In an examination-in-chief that would take many hours over several days, Kerbel asked Denis to detail exactly which identifications had been made by which prospective witnesses at which viewing session. Some of the photo arrays were entered as exhibits.

Denis admitted that on October 28 Cathy Cotgrave and Gayle Thompson both viewed the line-up at the same time.

"Was there any particular reason for having Miss Cotgrave and Miss Thompson view the pictures at the same time?"

"I believe it was the only occasion it did take place and for why I don't know; it just happened, I guess."

". . . Were they talking to one another?"

"Yes, I suppose."

The photo arrays had also been expanded over time, Denis testified. There was only one picture of the accused, Comeau, in the first set, but after Cathy Cotgrave had tentatively identified him as one of two men who might have been the gunman at her first viewing on October 21, the number of pictures of Comeau had been increased to seven one week later.

"Is there any reason why Mr. Comeau's picture appears . . . seven times?"

"I have more photographs of Mr. Comeau than anybody else. . . . I used what photos were available to me."

"I think we all appreciate that. What I am asking is: Does anyone else's picture appear seven times?"

"I don't know. I don't believe so."

It was now late Friday afternoon, and Kerbel's examination-in-chief was only just beginning. "It is becoming apparent to me, your Honour, that these pictures are going to form the very core of Mr. Comeau's defence," the Toronto lawyer declared. ". . . I want a list of everyone who is in there [the photo line-ups], the number of times the pictures appear, and the order in which they appear."

Denis agreed to provide such a list. Court was adjourned until the following Thursday morning, when Kerbel resumed his examination-in-chief of Denis, but the officer's testimony—and Kerbel's examination—now began to bog down in a welter of confusion and complexity. First, Denis said, he'd been incorrect in his earlier testimony—there'd been only two photographs of Comeau on the twenty-eighth of October, not seven. Had he a list of exactly which photos were shown? No, he hadn't, but he did take a photograph of the overall array, and this was entered as an exhibit.

Next Kerbel questioned the ID's made by some of the earlier witnesses, notably Rod Stewart. The contractor's ID's had failed to tally with any of the other witnesses', Denis responded, and Stewart had failed to identify pictures of any of the accused, including David Hoffman. Stewart had been the first person to view the array . . . or maybe he hadn't. Court was recessed to allow Denis to study his notes.

No, once again his earlier testimony had been incorrect, Denis apologized when the hearing resumed. Sue Foote and Cathy Cotgrave had been the first two people to view the first line-up the day after the shooting. He wasn't sure which of them had been first. And which, if any, pictures had Sue Foote selected?

"I can't recall, sir," though Blaker and Sauvé were definitely picked out.

"Do you keep any list or any document which would indicate the photographs Miss Foote picked out?"

"I had at the time, sir."

"And I take it from your response you no longer have that."

"No sir, I don't."

"Do you know where it is?"

"No sir, I don't . . . that particular sheet of paper was lost. . . . To the best of my recollection it was given to either Sergeant McReelis or Detective Inspector Cousens."

Who had Miss Cotgrave selected?

On the nineteenth it wasn't Miss Cotgrave who viewed the line-up, but Miss Gayle Thompson. "I may have confused the names."

Very well then, what pictures had Miss Thompson selected?

"I can't recall, sir."

Well, had she selected any photographs at all?

"I can't recall, sir."

On October 21 at 3:20 p.m. Cathy Cotgrave had viewed the line-up for the first time and she selected pictures of Larry Hurren, Jeff McLeod, Merv Blaker, Fred Jones, Sonny Bronson, Armand Sanguigni, Rick Sauvé, Brian Brideau, and Tee Hee Hoffman. Gary Comeau or Rae Snyder could be the gunman; if Snyder had a toque on he would look like the gunman. She had also made a remark about Tee Hee Hoffman.

"What did she say?"

"She stated he was present but she could not ID a picture."

"Did you ask her what she meant by that?"

"No."

Kerbel's examination-in-chief dragged on. Denis recounted which witness had seen pictures on which dates, and who, if anyone, each had identified. It became clear that he was uncertain about exactly which photos had been shown on which dates. The photographs shown had now been returned to individual file folders, and the best he could do was to give the total number of pictures in each folder. There were seven of Comeau, but Constable Denis was uncertain how many of them had actually been used at any one showing—"most of them" probably were.

By mid-afternoon Kerbel had been handling the hundreds of photographs which had comprised the various photo arrays for the better part of a day, and something about them had caught his attention. "Could you tell me what the significance of the red marker is on several of the photographs?"

"It was to indicate there was more than one photograph. I had noticed some of the witnesses were going over them without realizing there was another photograph underneath."

"I see. Okay." And there was a red mark on one of Mr. Blaker's pictures?

Yes.

And on Mr. Hoffman's?

Yes, sir.

And on a picture identified by one witness as Mr. Ertel?

"Correct."

And on a picture of Mr. Comeau?

"Correct."

Mr. Sanguigni's picture had been marked?

"That's correct."

Mr. Snyder's picture, too?

"Right."

A picture of Drago Salajko had been marked? And another of Michael Everett?

"Correct."

But what about the pictures in folder S-9? Someone named Leveque. There were multiple pictures of him and no red marks.

"It is apparent there is more than one."

"But no red marking."

"Correct."

But there was a red mark on one of Mr. McLeod's pictures?

"That's right."

And a mark on one of van Haarlem's pictures?

"That's right."

And pictures of Lorne Pfeffer and someone named Smith had also been marked?

"That's right."

"Okay. Just so that I understand your explanation of these red marks: Would you just tell us again why the red markings were put on?"

"In most of the cases the top photograph was larger than the bottom; some of the witnesses were finding some difficulty in realizing there were more than one photograph. I indicated to them that the red markings showed that there was more than one photograph and it was left at that."

"And there would be no correspondence, I take it, if we go through each one of these, to the red markings of people who have been identified by the various witnesses as being present in the hotel?"

"The only reason the red markings were there was strictly to show them there was more than one photograph of that individual."

Kerbel didn't press the point any further, but it was now abundantly clear that at least six of the eight men eventually accused of the murder of Bill Matiyek had had attention-drawing red marks on their photographs by the latter stages of the police photo line-ups.

After several brief cross-examinations, Constable Denis was excused. Although it was now late in the day, Howard Kerbel was ordered to press on, and he called his third, and final, witness, Sergeant Samuel McReelis.

The Port Hope Police sergeant detailed his role in the murder investigation, which began just minutes after Bill Matiyek had been shot. McReelis confirmed that he'd been told of Sauvé's and Blaker's presence in the hotel within hours of the shooting.

"When, if ever, did you become aware that there was a gun either in that area or on Mr. Matiyek?"

"I—it was the following day, October 19, some time that night, I believe."

McReelis confirmed that he'd been present when several of the accused were arrested and that he'd been one of approximately forty officers who took part in the Toronto clubhouse raid on the night of December 6. Hurren, McLeod, and Comeau had been arrested as a result of that action.

"And did you either personally or anyone under your direction seize anything from [the clubhouse]?"

"No, I didn't seize anything, sir. . . ."

". . . And if anything had been seized, into whose possession would it have come?"

"It would have come into my possession."

At the conclusion of McReelis's testimony Howard Kerbel read a joint statement of both the defence and the Crown counsel into the record. It contained five main points:

First, a gun had been found on the body of Bill Matiyek. It was a .32-calibre semi-automatic pistol. It was loaded, but there was no bullet in the breech.

Second, no jacket or coat was seized by any police officers during the Toronto clubhouse raid.

Third, the third bullet that struck Matiyek was not found at the scene or elsewhere.

Fourth, no physical descriptions or names of persons involved in the shooting of Mr. Matiyek were given to the officers who attended at the scene on the eighteenth of October, 1978.

Fifth, David Gillispie did not give P.C. Wilson a description of the gunman or the others involved in the shooting of Mr. Matiyek.

Strangely, two of the five points were patently false and a third was highly dubious. It was quite clear that both Sauvé and Blaker had been identified to police by bar patrons within minutes of the shooting. It would also become clear that David Gillispie had given police a detailed description of the person he believed to have been the gunman within hours of the shooting. This description matched Gary Comeau and dovetailed neatly with the descriptions of the other witnesses.

Finally, there was the question of Gary Comeau's black-leather jacket, which he had last seen hanging up in the Toronto clubhouse during the police raid. He specifically remembered telling McReelis that it was his, and then the jacket had simply disappeared. The hole in the left shoulder of that jacket was the only tangible evidence Nutty could think of that he'd actually been shot by the third bullet which had never been found.

Two weeks passed from the end of the preliminary until Judge Scullion handed down his judgment as to whether the evidence against the accused merited a trial, and the growing importance of that jacket was not lost on anyone. It was clear from the preliminary evidence that the Crown would finger Gary Comeau as the gunman. But if he'd been shot himself how could he possibly have been the trigger man? And the only evidence that would exonerate him had mysteriously vanished. They waited with a growing sense of foreboding for Scullion's judgment.

The accused returned to Cobourg County Court for the judgment one month to the day after they'd arrived for the opening of the preliminary hearing in such high spirits. After nine days of evidence, their court appearance on March 19 was so brief as to be almost an anticlimax.

Judge Scullion said that he'd written a forty-two-page judgment which he would not bother to read in court. "I am sure everybody is just interested in the bottom line, as far as this matter is concerned."

First, the Judge briefly summarized the evidence—that Matiyek was a member of the Golden Hawks and would take extra precautions when Choice members were in town; the entry of "between 15 and 20" Choice in an apparent attempt to intimidate the hotel's staff and patrons; the "fat fucker" statement; the "kiss of death" statement; the "horseshoe"; the killing.

Most of the rest of the judgment related to the law governing conspiracy. The bottom line, as Scullion described it, was in the final paragraph of the ruling: "I have reviewed all the authorities cited and I have read over my notes extensively. Having considered the principles as I comprehend them and applied them to the evidence . . . it is my opinion that there is sufficient reliable evidence, if believed and uncontradicted, that a properly instructed jury acting judiciously could convict. I am, therefore, committing all the accused to stand trial on both charges."

XXII

THE SPRING OF 1979 found the eight accused dispersed across southern Ontario. Tee Hee, who was still free on bail, had returned to his job at

B. F. Goodrich in Kitchener and was living at his parents' farm near Plattsville. Larry Hurren was staying with his family in Bowmanville, east of Oshawa. Rick Sauvé and Merv Blaker had been transferred to the Lindsay jail, while van Haarlem went to Peterborough and Gary Comeau, Jeff McLeod, and Armand Sanguigni were moved to the jail in Whitby, where they were at least closer to their families.

The distance between them complicated the preparation of a coherent legal strategy for their defence. Although they were to be tried jointly, there was now no opportunity for all eight of the accused to discuss the preliminary evidence among themselves, or with their lawyers en masse. Instead, individual counsel met with individual clients, and the lawyers themselves conferred, usually two at a time, by telephone.

Further confounding matters was the delicate situation in which the accused now found themselves. It was clear to everyone that a number of club members who had also been present in the Queen's the night of the shooting had not been identified or charged. Everyone knew, too, that the police investigation had failed to correctly identify the gunman. Ever loyal to the club above all else, not one of the six who'd actually been at the shooting was about to implicate any more members by naming names, even to their own lawyers.

And so began a kind of cat-and-mouse game between each of the accused and the men assigned to defend them. It was to continue for many months, in some cases for many years. To this day it remains difficult to determine exactly what each of the accused told his own lawyer in the months preceding trial.

It is clear from Howard Kerbel's lines of questioning at the preliminary that Gary Comeau had disclosed most of the true story to his lawyer very early on. Nutty's arrival at the hotel, his conversation with Jamie Hanna and the old man, his presence at the Matiyek table at the time of the shooting, the fact that Matiyek had had a gun himself, the improbable and as yet unprovable fact that Gary had himself been shot, and the disappearance of his black-leather jacket, all of these salient points in Comeau's side of the story had evidently been revealed to Kerbel from the beginning. Any physical record of what Comeau might have told, his lawyer has long since been destroyed, not least because of the extreme caution with which the defence team felt obliged to conduct its affairs—the police investigation was ongoing, after all, and there was still a gunman on the loose. But there was one point that Kerbel could still recall from memory alone many years later: despite the identifications of no fewer than four eyewitnesses, Gary Comeau insisted that Tee Hee Hoffman had not been in the hotel that night, and he told his lawyer that from the outset.

Terry O'Hara worked hard on Merv Blaker's behalf in the months that followed the preliminary. He prepared for a second bail hearing, researched the law for supporting arguments in a change-of-venue application, and visited Merv and his family. Like Kerbel, O'Hara came to believe that Tee Hee Hoffman had been nowhere near the shooting. The big Kitchener biker, O'Hara was convinced, was the victim of a very bad case of mistaken identity. (Kerbel even had a very good idea of which Toronto club member had been mistaken for Tee Hee.) Similarly, there was a growing consensus among the defence counsel that Armand Sanguigni had been present at the murder, even though he'd been identified by only a single eyewitness— Cathy Cotgrave.

Like each of the other accused, Blaker steadfastly maintained his innocence. There had been no conspiracy, no planning and deliberation in the killing of Bill Matiyek, and he'd overheard no "fat fucker" statement uttered by anyone. While other members of the Satan's Choice Peterborough Chapter may have had their run-ins with Bill in the months before his death, Merv had nothing against the man, had never had any trouble with Matiyek himself.

Terry O'Hara weighed each of these facts carefully. He'd known his client before the shooting and there was certainly nothing in Murray Blaker's record or background that exhibited the slightest tendency towards violence. As O'Hara came to know Murray's family, came to better understand their simple but unshakable conviction of his innocence, the Kingston lawyer became convinced that Merv's biggest problem was his membership in the Satan's Choice. O'Hara had known plenty of bikers. So far as he was concerned, they were basically cowards who liked to operate in groups. They certainly weren't above killing, but a public execution in front of so many potential witnesses was just not the biker style. Like all cowards, they preferred to do their business furtively, in dark alleys or on back-country roads, at minimal risk to themselves. Moreover, as he got to know Murray better, Terry O'Hara came to an extraordinary conclusion about his client: Murray

Blaker, he decided, was a totally honest man, one of those rare individuals who is incapable of duplicity. It wasn't something O'Hara could say about many of his friends, much less his clients. But for all his reticence, his apparent lack of self-confidence, and his reluctance to answer questions, Terry O'Hara came to regard Murray Blaker as one of the straightest, truest men he'd ever known.

There was one other external factor to weigh upon the scales, and that was the presence of Armand Sanguigni. Although still a relative novice as a criminal lawyer, O'Hara had been around long enough to know Armand's reputation with the police, and about his criminal record. Merv's lawyer was inclined to believe what was said about Armand. If Armand Sanguigni had killed one man, and O'Hara was quite convinced that he had, then he'd probably killed ten. Sanguigni was capable of it. He was also, and this was the point, a professional. He did his work well, took it seriously, and had never been convicted. Why would any self-respecting button man get himself embroiled in such a messy business as the killing of Bill Matiyek had turned out to be? He wouldn't, O'Hara reasoned, unless he'd had no idea going in what the outcome would be. Had Sanguigni known in advance that he was going to be part of a murder in such a sloppy, unprofessional fashion, he wouldn't have been within a hundred miles of that hotel. Ergo, O'Hara concluded, there had been no conspiracy, no first-degree murder as defined by the Criminal Code, in the first place. The scales came to an overbalanced, lopsided rest, and Terry O'Hara reached a conclusion that would grow into an absolute and unswerving conviction over the years: he was defending an innocent man.

During his months of pre-trial preparation Bruce Affleck, on the other hand, came reluctantly to a completely different conclusion about his own client. Jeff McLeod, the former Crown Attorney decided, was lying through his teeth. He liked Jeff, but McLeod insisted on running this phony alibi past him again and again. It was so patently false that Affleck was embarrassed to present it before the courts: McLeod claimed to have been in Kitchener on the night of the shooting, at the Choice clubhouse there.

He'd even gone so far as to interview a couple of women with whom McLeod claimed to have been partying in Kitchener on October 18. They both struck Affleck as absolute bimbos, their evidence totally unconvincing.

Chris Meinhardt would tear them limb from limb during cross-examination. The whole situation was appalling. Here he was, a Bencher in the Law Society of Upper Canada, a member of that elite group, elected by a vote of his peers to stand as a kind of moral gatekeeper over the ethics of the profession. And he was now supposed to argue an alibi defence that he believed to be absolutely false. He just couldn't do it, and he told McLeod; and so the alibi defence was never used. Jeff, however, stuck stubbornly to his story, a fiction that he was to maintain for many years. And so it happened that the most experienced, and in some ways the most gifted, member of the defence team would conduct a trial without knowing the full truth of what had happened in the Queen's Hotel on the night of the murder of Bill Matiyek.

On May 24, the lawyers for the defence finally won a round. At a day-long change-of-venue hearing in Toronto before a Justice of the Ontario Supreme Court, the defence team presented its arguments for moving the trial out of the Port Hope–Cobourg area. The lawyers presented a detailed analysis of the local news coverage of the Matiyek killing, citing especially the number of times the accused had had their pictures printed in the newspapers. They also argued that feelings in the area were now running so high against the Satan's Choice that their clients could not possibly hope to obtain a fair trial from a jury composed of local residents. In the end, the Court agreed. The trial would be moved to London, Ontario.

Terry O'Hara was less successful at a second bail application for Merv Blaker on June 18. Although Merv's mother, older sister, and two brothers-in-law testified on Blaker's behalf, the bail application was once again denied, primarily because of his membership in the Satan's Choice and because of Bobby Cousins's threat against Jamie Hanna.

Just eight days after Blaker's second bail hearing a new anti-biker offensive was launched in the news media, this time on the pages of Canada's most prestigious newspaper, the Toronto *Globe and Mail*. The Saturday, June 23, 1979, paper featured a flashy front-page story which, however, contained little that hadn't already been reported by John Kessel and John Schenk in their *Kitchener-Waterloo Record* and *Maclean's* exposés two years before. Bikers were "the new form of organized crime," according to police sources. Bikers also controlled "a burgeoning criminal network that police rank next in power to the Mafia." Their criminal activities were now so profitable that bikers "tend to wear suits and go around in Cadillacs, Continentals, and Corvettes," according to a senior Montreal police official.

But the *Globe* story did contain one major new wrinkle: police biker intelligence officers were predicting an imminent all-out war in Ontario between the Hell's Angels and the Outlaws, probably that summer. The prospect of a summer of bloody gang warfare between the Angels and the Outlaws would become an annual staple of biker reportage. Every summer, police intelligence officials would retail the same dire predictions, and every summer the stories would receive page-one treatment in newspapers across the country from editors who evidently failed to remember they'd carried almost the exact same story the year before.

Still, it was clear to everyone that the Life was changing. The Smoky Seventies were definitely ending with a bang on all fronts, and police repression was reaching new heights. In the United States, during the early morning hours of June 13, federal officials launched their most ambitious crackdown ever on the Hell's Angels. More than two hundred members of the new Biker Enforcement Team (BET) conducted a three-state sweep of Angels clubhouses and homes that resulted in twenty-two arrests. Sonny Barger, the leader of the Hell's Angels, was caught in the net and his bail was set at $1 million. BET was a new, ultra-elite unit composed of federal agents from the Drug Enforcement Agency, the Treasury Department, the Federal Bureau of Investigation, and other assorted intelligence operatives, working under a joint command.

Besides the usual police arsenal of automatic rifles, shotguns, and flak jackets (no gunplay was reported during the predawn raid against the Angels, though several federal officers received minor wounds when their own weapons accidentally discharged), the BET members were also armed with a powerful new weapon—the RICO statutes. The Racketeer-Influenced and Corrupt Organization Act gave U.S. police sweeping powers against organized crime while at the same time removing virtually all of the constitutional rights of organized criminals and racketeers. Simply belonging to a "criminal organization"—a Mafia "family" or a motorcycle club—was deemed a criminal act in itself, and a member's personal property could be seized, *in toto*, by the state, whether it could be shown that the gains were ill-gotten or not. The Angels were charged with racketeering and conspiracy.

The trials that followed would prove disastrous for the state. In August 1980, conspiracy charges against Barger and his wife Sharon were dropped, but new racketeering charges were laid. A second trial was scheduled but then something extraordinary happened: Scott Barnes, a member of BET, quit the team and gave a whole new meaning to the term "police informer." Barnes, who had been with U.S. Army Intelligence before becoming a federal agent, charged that BET members had become so zealous in the enforcement of their duties and so intoxicated with their sweeping new powers that they had become virtually indistinguishable from the bikers themselves. On camera, Barnes described "drug set-ups, acts of violence, fire-bombings" committed by federal officers "to get the leadership" of the Hell's Angels. Barnes's videotaped allegations were devastating. He had quit BET, Barnes added, because at the rate things were going, federal agents would themselves soon begin committing murder in the name of the law—if they hadn't already—and he wanted no part of it.

The second Angels trial under the RICO statutes opened in California in the fall of 1980, and it ended in a hung jury.

But all of that would come later. The first story in the Globe's exclusive series appeared just ten days after the raid against the Angels, and it revealed a mounting police frustration with biker prosecutions north of the border, too. Again and again law-enforcement officials complained that bikers were becoming "almost invulnerable in some instances to police prosecution because of their willingness to intimidate witnesses and complainants." But the highly disciplined, almost paramilitary style of the clubs made infiltration almost impossible. Invariably such stories also contained plaintive police calls for more men, more money, more police power to stem the lawless tide.

The first installment of Peter Moon's series had appeared in the Globe and Mail on Saturday morning, and later in the day police moved in strength against Ontario bikers. In Toronto, police had used a truck as a battering-ram to smash in the steel door of the Para-Dice Riders clubhouse after a Friday-night altercation between members of the PDR's and the Iron Hawgs. In Hamilton, sixty members of the Hamilton-Wentworth Regional Police made sixty-three raids on the residences and clubhouses of motorcycle gang members. Police speculated that the PDR–Iron Hawgs incident "could be related to the impending war" between the Angels and the Outlaws.

The *Globe* devoted virtually a full page to the second part of Moon's series, which elaborated on the supposedly pending Angels-Outlaws confrontation. On Monday afternoon, Ontario Attorney General Roy McMurtry called a press conference at the Ontario legislature to respond to the *Globe*'s stories. McMurtry, who was also the province's Solicitor General, said senior police officials had assured him Moon's articles were "quite accurate." Ontario's senior law-enforcement official evidently made this statement with a straight face, though it must have been evident to even the casual reader that the same "senior police officers" that McMurtry had consulted were the sources of much of the information contained in the *Globe* stories in the first place. The upshot was that the Ontario Provincial Police were to be given extra men to combat the growing problem of outlaw clubs, biker trials were to be expedited, "and certainly whenever bikers are convicted we are going to press for very severe sentences whenever that is warranted." Some "additional draconian measures . . . may have to be implemented," McMurtry warned, but he refused to elaborate on just what those measures might be.

It is astonishing to see how differently the *Toronto Star* reporter at the McMurtry news conference saw things. He reported that "senior police officials had assured [McMurtry] that biker gangs were under control. [McMurtry] said senior police officials did not expect a major biker gang war to erupt this summer." Toronto readers of both newspapers might have been forgiven for wondering whether the *Globe* and the *Star* reporters had attended the same news conference.

Ten days later, on the evening of Thursday, July 5, the defence team had its first, and only, major pre-trial meeting to evaluate the evidence from the preliminary hearing and to plot its trial strategy. The defence line-up had changed slightly since the preliminary five months before. Armand Sanguigni had discharged Ross McKay in favour of Bernard Cugelman, a Toronto lawyer with considerable experience representing motorcycle club members.

The eight lawyers met at Howard Kerbel's comfortable North Toronto home to sort out a myriad of legal details. As Kerbel's girlfriend served chilled white wine and hors d'oeuvres, they began to grapple with what would become a vital strategic question: would their clients take the witness stand, and, if so, which ones? It was already apparent that two of the accused—David Hoffman and Gordon van Haarlem—would adopt a totally different defence strategy from that of the other six. They would enter an alibi defence, central to which would be their own testimony. With a single exception, the lawyers for the other six accused were emphatically opposed to putting their clients on the witness stand. The hold-out was Terry O'Hara. The young Kingston lawyer argued forcefully that Murray Blaker, at least, should testify on his own behalf, and that the others should, too. O'Hara was convinced that Blaker, for all his shyness, would make an excellent witness, not least because his client was telling the truth, a fact that would ultimately shine through to the jury.

But Affleck, Kerbel, Grossman, Newman, and Cugelman were strongly opposed to putting Blaker, or any of the others, on the stand. First of all, it was a fact that each of the accused was a member of the Satan's Choice and had a criminal record, however minimal that record might be in some individual cases. They simply weren't credible witnesses. They were, moreover, witnesses who would fall directly into Meinhardt's strength on cross-examination—bikers with records. Few prosecutors were as capable of exploiting such weaknesses as Chris Meinhardt.

Secondly, it was clear that none of the accused was willing to name names on the witness stand. How would they respond when Meinhardt asked them point-blank which other club members were in the hotel that night or, worse, who had actually done the shooting? In the worst case, they might actually be cited for refusing to answer and could face indefinite jail sentences for contempt of court.

Finally, the five lawyers agreed, it would be a mistake to put Blaker alone on the witness stand, not only because he wouldn't be believed but because it would leave the other accused in an untenable position: the jury would surely wonder why he had testified and the others hadn't.

No, far better to adopt a more conservative posture, attempting to exploit deficiencies in the Crown's case through cross-examination. It was apparent from the preliminary that much of the prosecution's evidence against the accused was in the form of eyewitness testimony, and even at the preliminary it was clear that there were inconsistencies and contradictions within this body of evidence. Everyone knew that eyewitness identifications were among the frailest and most tenuous forms of evidence, and the OPP identification procedures had been highly suspect.

Besides, there was still the question of the missing third bullet. If they could somehow get it removed from Comeau's body, that alone would cast strong doubts on the accuracy of the Crown witnesses who had identified Comeau as the gunman.

There was also another possibility, Kerbel told the gathering. He'd been in touch with the Satan's Choice, and it was conceivable that the real gunman would offer to testify for the defence. Surely that would prove highly damaging to the credibility of both the police investigation and the eyewitnesses.

The meeting moved on to points of law that would likely have to be argued at trial. O'Hara had prepared his own list of thirteen controversial questions that would require research and wondered what legal issues the others anticipated. To his surprise and chagrin, no one else had thought of any. O'Hara quickly volunteered to provide most of the legal research for the team—he still had access to some of his old professors at Queen's and he would, in fact, consult with them about Blaker's defence during the trial and long after.

Finally, there was the question of the order in which each of the eight would cross-examine. It was agreed that Affleck, as senior defence counsel, would go first, and O'Hara, as junior, last. By putting Affleck in the lead-off position, the team was opening with its strongest cross-examiner, and by putting O'Hara last, the two men agreed privately, the defence should be well served in the clean-up position, too. O'Hara would clarify, polish, and tie up any loose ends that might have been left by the other seven.

The meeting broke up around a quarter after ten and everyone seemed satisfied, except Terry O'Hara. Although he'd been solidly outvoted on the question of the accused testifying, all of the arguments had left him inwardly unmoved. He resolved to keep urging Murray to take the stand—he really didn't feel Blaker had any other choice.

The call came for Roger Davey while he was at work at the Eldorado uranium refinery in Port Hope. The caller was Sam McReelis. The Port Hope Police sergeant wanted to speak with Roger down at the police station concerning the murder of Bill Matiyek. It was the last thing in the world that Roger Davey wanted to hear.

It was high summer now, and Roger had watched events unfold in the eight or so months since the killing of Bill Matiyek with a keen interest.

As a Port Hope biker himself, Roger had a number of insights and observations into what happened, but he was careful to keep them to himself. Rick Sauvé, after all, had once been one of his closest friends, so close that he'd been best man when Rick and Sharon had gotten married.

But they'd drifted apart, especially after Rick joined the Choice. Roger didn't like the way the club had changed his old friend—it pumped him up, seemed to put him on a real ego trip. Privately, too, Roger was inclined to accept the Crown's version of events in Bill's shooting. He had no use at all for Matiyek—considered him a loud-mouthed, overgrown bully—but he also believed Bill to have been a major thorn in the side of the Choice. By reviving the Golden Hawks as Matiyek, Lawrence Leon, and a handful of others had done, and by daring to wear their patches publicly in Choice territory, Bill had openly defied the power of the Satan's Choice, and he'd paid the price. Personally, Roger believed that the Choice guys had been just cocky enough to think they could walk into the bar, blow their local adversary away, and assume that no one in the place would have the guts to testify against them. If so, Roger knew, they had made a gross miscalculation. Far from giving in to intimidation, the witnesses had rallied, refusing to knuckle under to the threat of further violence in their own town.

In many ways Roger Davey typified the difference between a mere biker and a club member. To the average citizen who might catch a glimpse of Roger or Rick Galbraith riding their bikes down Walton Street, there was no observable difference—Roger, after all, owned a mean-looking Harley, an extensive collection of Nazi memorabilia, and a number of handguns. He wore his hair long and usually dressed in a black-leather jacket. But, in the final analysis, Roger Davey was not an outlaw. He had had invitations from several clubs to become a striker and he'd considered them carefully. But in the end he'd always decided that wasn't quite what he wanted, and so he had remained just a simple, independent biker.

When he arrived at the cop shop, McReelis came right to the point. Wasn't it true that Roger had received a telephone call from either Rick Sauvé or Merv Blaker early in the morning of October 19 last year?

Roger denied it.

McReelis produced a piece of paper, a bill from Bell Canada with Roger's phone number on it. He *had* taken the call, here was the proof.

Well, maybe he had.

Roger knew a lot more about this murder, didn't he? He knew what had happened? The police were looking at a possible charge here—for conspiracy after the fact—unless Roger would make a statement. Murder one, conspiracy after, a very serious charge.

Reluctantly, Roger told them what he knew of the phone call. He left Diane, who had really taken the call, out of it.

The cops wrote out a statement and demanded that Roger sign it. He refused, and once again they threatened him with conspiracy charges. Roger signed the statement. They told him he'd probably be called as a witness at the trial.

Roger Davey returned home that night a frightened, confused, and deeply worried man. Had he been tougher, more streetwise, more, in fact, of the outlaw that his image suggested, Roger Davey might have called the police bluff, demanded to see a lawyer, refused to co-operate. But Roger, like most law-abiding Canadians, found lawyers' offices, police stations, and court-rooms to be highly intimidating places. He tried to sort it all out. He was going to have to testify against the Satan's Choice, and that scared the hell out of him. At least, though, he'd protected his wife. Better him than her. Roger Davey was caught between two groups of men, each of whom wore uniforms, carried guns, and, it turned out, intimidated witnesses. And worst of all, Roger Davey was going to have to tell less than "the whole truth" at the first-degree murder trial of one of his best friends.

On July 26, word reached Gordy van Haarlem that he'd become a father. Patty had given birth to a little girl, and they decided to call her Amber. In some cases, Gordy had learned, jail authorities allowed new fathers to visit their babies and wives at the hospital, under guard of course. Gordy applied for the privilege, and was turned down. His jailers had evidently decided that, as a member of the Satan's Choice who had already been denied bail and who was awaiting trial on the charge of first-degree murder, he was too great a security risk to be granted an escorted pass. More than a month would pass before Gordy got a glimpse of his first-born child.

XXIII

A TRIAL DATE had at last been set, for Tuesday, September 4, and as July slipped into August the pace of pre-trial preparations quickened perceptibly. Lawyers spent more time with their clients, and with each other, ironing out details of their cases. Finally, in the last week of August, the accused were moved to London in advance of the trial. For the six in custody their transfer to London meant they were reunited for the first time since the preliminary hearing six months before.

On August 27, all of the defence counsel met with Chris Meinhardt and his junior, Roland Harris, for a pre-trial conference with Ontario Supreme Court Justice Patrick Hartt in Toronto. The purpose of such conferences is to assist the Court in the anticipation and resolution of problems that might arise during the trial. It is also intended as an opportunity for the Crown and the defence to disclose their respective cases.

The theory of the prosecution was recorded, in writing:

"The deceased was a member of the Golden Hawks Motorcycle Club. Prior to the death there was enmity between the deceased and members of Satan's Choice, as well as enmity between Satan's Choice and the Golden Hawks.

"As a result of this enmity Satan's Choice made a decision to take action against the deceased. On October 18, 1978 a number of them from all three chapters attended at the Queen's Hotel in Port Hope where the deceased was drinking.

"They came in as a group, killed the deceased and left as a group. The total time from arrival to departure being about 10 minutes."

For its part, the defence team disclosed that it would be raising three specific defences—alibi, lack of intent, and self-defence. The estimated length of the trial was put at twelve weeks.

On the eve of the final weekend before the trial, police messengers delivered a heavy parcel to the offices of the lawyers for the eight accused. The parcels contained two thick blue-bound volumes embossed with the gold seal of the Ontario Provincial Police, and their contents were possibly the most sensational Crown disclosures yet. The books contained the transcripts of the telephone wiretaps and the room probe from the Kitchener clubhouse of the Satan's Choice, and their arrival just before the last long weekend of the summer had the impact of a hand grenade thrown into the centre of the defence camp.

While the transcripts contained little definitive evidence against the accused in the Matiyek murder trial, they were, most of the defence lawyers agreed, highly incriminating when it came to the Satan's Choice Motorcycle Club as a whole. Most of the eight hundred pages in the two bulky volumes were devoted to the weekly meetings of the Kitchener Chapter from early November until the end of March. The voice of one of the accused—Tee Hee Hoffman—appears only at the first meeting. After that, in observance of his bail restrictions, Hoffman was forced to forgo his active leadership role in the chapter. But even though none of the other accused were actually in the transcripts, the defence lawyers worried that the introduction of the transcriptions at trial would prove highly prejudicial to their clients.

Even nearly a decade after they were recorded, the two volumes make fascinating reading that is, by turns, chilling, funny, boring, and, ultimately, more than a little sad. The transcripts are also one of the very few objective yardsticks by which one can gauge the veracity of police claims about club activities, which had been so widely reported in the press, and of club counter-claims about police activities, which were never reported.

The overall picture that emerges from a careful reading of "the wires" is one of a motorcycle club in steep decline. Police repression was proving effective in reducing the club's active strength. Indeed, by the winter of 1978–79, the Satan's Choice had exactly twenty-two members on the street in any given week: ten in Kitchener-Waterloo, a like number in Toronto, and two in Peterborough. The Peterborough Chapter was, as the Kitchener Chapter members reluctantly agreed at the meeting of February 26, dead or dying, the result of the arrests and imprisonment for the Matiyek murder, the Alderville Reserve mini-riot, and the pending rape charges, plus an increasingly outraged citizenry in both the Peterborough and the Port Hope–Cobourg areas.

The Matiyek murder had exacted a particularly steep toll on club fortunes, and the killing itself was receiving distinctly mixed reviews inside the Kitchener clubhouse. Chapter president "Gootch" Morin summed up both the upside and the downside in a rambling monologue on February 5:

"If you're goin' to start plannin' big things and doin' all kinds of things, then you gotta have everything figured out ahead of time. It's to the point now—you know yourself—you can walk in a bar and go boom boom boom. . . . Just to show you how stupid we operate we go rah rah rah that happens and the next thing you know eight people are gettin' picked up. Hey, if we had any brains at all, you give some guy ten g's or five g's, he offs the cocksucker, right? Everybody's home. Nobody gets picked up. He gets picked up, 'Hey, call your own lawyer, fucker. We don't know you. We're payin' you for a hit.' That's the way it works, you know, if we had any brains at all. We'd be payin' people to do these things. Five g's. It's costin' us twenty grand in lawyers now."

The cost of paying certain lawyers "under the table" threatened to exhaust the club treasury, and the acute money shortage was a constant source of internal bickering as the winter wore on. The Kitchener treasury contained about three thousand dollars, the national treasury perhaps seventeen thousand, hardly a fortune for part of "a burgeoning criminal network that police rank next in power to the Mafia," as the *Globe* put it. And even those totals were by no means solely the proceeds of heavy criminal activities. Much of the money was derived from monthly dues payments, "fund-raisers," like any other organization. As the preliminary hearing dragged on and the prospect of a lengthy murder trial loomed, several of the lawyers in the Matiyek case demanded more money. In early February there was talk of a two-hundred-and-fifty-dollar per-capita levy, but the amount had increased to five hundred dollars per member by the end of March.

Unlike the media accounts where bikers were being increasingly depicted as wealthy perpetrators of lucrative criminal activity, the Kitchener Choice members appeared to be struggling simply to maintain a subsistence.

The transcripts gave the lie to several other aspects about club life that were gaining widespread currency in the news media, courtesy of police "intelligence" sources. One such assertion was that motorcycle clubs were strictly top-down organizations. ("Each club has a president who is referred to as 'the boss' or 'the boss man,'" the *Globe* informed its readers. "He rules with absolute authority until replaced.") The Kitchener Chapter of the Satan's Choice was, quite by contrast, a highly democratic institution. More often than not, decisions were made by consensus rather than by outright votes, and then only after lengthy discussion. Like many another group attempting to govern itself consensually, this often led to exhaustive debates where a given subject would be talked to death.

On the other hand, Eagle Scouts the Kitchener members most definitely were not. Their discussions might range from waylaying and viciously beating a club adversary to planning a gang rape to intimidating a trial witness with the same casual indifference with which most "citizens" might discuss last night's hockey game or make a grocery list. Traffic in illegal drugs or guns was a commonplace, though there was little indication that drug-dealing was a highly organized club-wide activity.

Still, life was not all beatings, bombings, and insurance-job barn-burnings. On January 23, the Kitchener Chapter had a lengthy debate on their club-sponsored broomball team which played every Sunday night. The informal games had become quite popular among non-members, and there had been a tendency for all seventeen players on the Choice team to take to the ice at once. Perhaps, it was suggested, some rules should be adopted regarding substitutions? The debate was long-winded but inconclusive. Later the same evening discussion touched on another pressing organizational question—outsider access to the clubhouse phone number. This was a semi-serious issue, since the members suspected (rightly) that the telephone was wiretapped and feared that someone might call in and drop some casual but incriminating comment in conversation with a member. The number was already unlisted, but it had a way of circulating among wives, girlfriends, and friends, even though an earlier meeting had resolved that the clubhouse number would remain a closely guarded secret. A compromise was reached: members could give the number out with discretion, but not to "business people."

In the end it's hard for a reader not to come away from the transcripts with a feeling of sadness, not only for the victims of the club, but for the members themselves. They seemed to be living in an ever-tighter, more constricted world, hedged in by suspicion, paranoia, and mistrust. Members moved from the one or two hotels from which they hadn't been barred to the clubhouse and motorcycle shop to the occasional bike show to the courts, jails, and prisons, and back again. The police harassment was unceasing and their every move, every telephone conversation, every clubhouse meeting, was closely monitored and then scrutinized for possible illegal activity. For a group whose members had once prided themselves on "absolute freedom" to do what they wanted, who talked of daring to live "in the wind," their lives were now the most circumscribed of all.

The disclosure in the Kitchener clubhouse wires of paying legal fees "under the table" was greeted with consternation in the defence camp. Under the rules of the Ontario Legal Aid Plan, which was paying the costs for most of the defendants, a lawyer must disclose *all* fees accepted from a client in addition to Legal Aid.

The names of Howard Kerbel and Bruce Affleck arose as lawyers who were being paid directly by the Satan's Choice. Affleck made no bones about it; he frankly admitted having accepted eighteen thousand dollars from the club which had been delivered to his Oshawa office in cash, in a brown paper bag. In Kerbel's case, the OPP transcripts would trigger an investigation by the Ontario Legal Aid Plan which continued long after the trial was over, but no disciplinary action was ever taken.

No one involved in the case read the wires as closely as Tee Hee Hoffman. Tee Hee spent the whole long weekend at his parents' farm outside Kitchener poring over the transcripts, searching in vain for some scrap of evidence that would support his alibi. He noticed that certain telephones had been tapped as well as the clubhouse interior, and while most of the two transcript volumes were devoted to the weekly meetings, there were also transcriptions of a few phone calls. So, the clubhouse phone *was* tapped, as they'd suspected all along. So was the phone at K-W Cycle, the bike shop owned by long-time Kitchener member Larry Kowtuski. Hoffman studied the phone records carefully, especially the calls made on the clubhouse phone. There was a transcription of one telephone conversation from the clubhouse number on October 10, and a couple of others on October 29. But what about the calls *he'd* made on the same phone on the eighteenth, the night of the murder? The calls to Gootch and the Stratford costume shop after the police raid had ended? They were nowhere to be found. How could that be? The coppers, Tee Hee became convinced, were sleazing, purposely withholding evidence that could be crucial for his defence, and he told Ed Martin so. But his lawyer, Hoffman discovered, had reasons for looking at the whole thing quite differently. Even if Hoffman was right, and even if they could somehow obtain the missing tapes, Martin told his client, there would be problems with introducing the evidence at trial. To do so would only call attention to the *rest* of the wiretap evidence, and that would harm all of Tee Hee's co-defendants.

Terry O'Hara had soldiered on, almost as stubborn and obdurate as the taciturn man he was defending. A third bail request in August had been denied. Now, he alone remained unperturbed by the wiretap transcripts. The reason, he told his colleagues, was that the transcripts were, quite simply, inadmissible. The rules of disclosure were clear on the point: the Crown was required to make all evidentiary disclosures at least seven days prior to trial. For whatever reason, Meinhardt had missed the deadline by several days. If he attempted to adduce the transcripts, the defence would object on those grounds, and the trial judge should have little choice but to rule in their favour.

But even as they were scrambling to somehow address the wiretap disclosures, another nasty surprise was brewing for the defence team, unknown to any of them. Back in Port Hope on Sunday, September 2, just two days before the trial was set to begin, Lawrence Leon had, at long last, decided to come in from the cold.

For the President of the Golden Hawk Riders, the ten months since the killing of his best friend had been the most terrifying time of his life. He'd always known they were running a certain risk by reviving the Hawks within Choice territory, but Lawrence had never thought it would lead to murder. Anyway, they'd packed the club in after Bill was killed.

Lawrence had learned of Bill's death on the night of the murder and the news had filled him with stark terror. The Hawk president became convinced that the Choice were coming after him next. An avid gun collector, Lawrence Leon began to sleep with a loaded gun beneath his bed. He told his wife Linda of the various ways the Choice might "do" him—opening up at close range from a passing car while he was driving home, blowing him away while he was riding his bike out on some country road, posing as stranded motorists and then when he stopped to help . . .

Leon knew that Bill had had run-ins with the Choice before, especially with Retard Horner. Sometimes, late at night in the summer before his death, Bill would come over to Lawrence's place, where Linda had heard them talking. Once Lawrence had come to bed after such a meeting and said, "Boy, Bill is really paranoid."

The police had interviewed Lawrence Leon in April, but like the true outlaw biker he had always aspired to be, he had "dummied up," and told the police nothing. He'd spent the rest of the time basically avoiding contact with both the Choice and the police.

But by the last Sunday of the summer, Lawrence had had a change of heart. He agreed to talk to the police in Port Hope, agreed to make a statement, agreed to testify. It was true that he hadn't been in the hotel at the time of the murder, though he had, of course, been there with Bill and Fred Jones and Sonny Bronson earlier in the evening. But Lawrence had a great deal to say about the history of relations between his club and the Choice, and about the often stormy relationship between Bill and the Choice.

The prosecution was delighted by Leon's sudden emergence. He would be perhaps the most compelling witness yet in strengthening the police theory of a gangland-style slaying, and the opening of the trial was now less than forty-eight hours away.

Bill Matiyek. (Port Hope Police)

The Choice, Peterborough Chapter, westbound on the 401 at the height of club power in 1969. Chapter President Bill Lavoie heads column on right.

The Beer Drinkin' Days—a balloon race at St. Catharines Field Day, 1969.

Above: The jumping competition, St Catharines Field Day, 1969. (George Lobb)

Right: Choice founder Bernie Guindon on a run to Preston, Ontario, 1968 (George Lobb)

"In The Wind." Bill Lavoie aboard his chopper, the Black Baron, westbound for Kingston, 1969. (George Lobb)

Club memorabilia on the wall of the Markham, Ontario clubhouse before it was destroyed in a police raid on the night of Wednesday, December 6, 1969.

Above: The Heat. Terry Hall–style harassment of a club run. Hall is shown in centre with his hand in his pocket. His T-shirt reads: "Support Your Local Outlaws." (Gary Comeau)

Left: The first wave of Ontario Provincial Police arriving on the field of a meet near St. Catharines, Ontario. Note consternation on the face of a club member in the foreground. (George Lobb)

The OPP, including some in riot gear, are marched unceremoniously off the field by club-weilding members. (George Lobb)

First police photo-array of Satan's Choice and Outlaws members shown to eyewitnesses shortly after the murder of Bill Matiyek. Lorne Campbell is not included. (Port Hope Police Force)

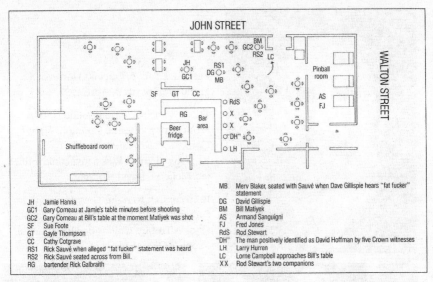

JOHN STREET

WALTON STREET

Pinball room

Shuffleboard room

Beer fridge

Bar area

RG

SF   GT   CC

JH
GC1

RS1
DG
MB

RS2
BM
GC2
LC

RdS
X
X
"DH"
LH

AS
FJ

JH	Jamie Hanna		MB	Merv Blaker, seated with Sauvé when Dave Gillispie hears "fat fucker" statement
GC1	Gary Comeau at Jamie's table minutes before shooting		DG	David Gillispie
GC2	Gary Comeau at Bill's table at the moment Matiyek was shot		BM	Bill Matiyek
SF	Sue Foote		AS	Armand Sanguigni
GT	Gayle Thompson		FJ	Fred Jones
CC	Cathy Cotgrave		RdS	Rod Stewart
RS1	Rick Sauvé when alleged "fat fucker" statement was heard		"DH"	The man positively identified as David Hoffman by five Crown witnesses
RS2	Rick Sauvé seated across from Bill.		LH	Larry Hurren
RG	bartender Rick Galbraith		LC	Lorne Campbell approaches Bill's table
			X X	Rod Stewart's two companions

Interior floorplan of the Queen's Hotel lounge, October 18, 1978, and proximate location of key players, according to eyewitnesses. (Trial transcript)

The Disneyland School of Canadian Prison Architecture. Collins Bay Medium Security Federal Prison, Kingston, Ontario. (Correctional Service Canada)

Collins Bay, cellblock #2. Door at rear leads to "the hole," known euphamistically by the staff as administrative segregation. (Correctional Service Canada)

Left: Rick Sauvé, Queen's University graduation portrait, April 1987.

Middle: The Millhaven Bulldogs, 1981. Front (l. to r.): Bernie Guindon, Gary Comeau, Larry Hurren. Back row (l. to r.): Rick Sauvé, unidentified, Jeff McLeod, David Hoffman.

Bottom: Left to right, Gary Comeau, Rick Sauvé, and Jeff McLeod with the Satan's Choice Trophy, Collins Bay Exceptional People's Olympiad.

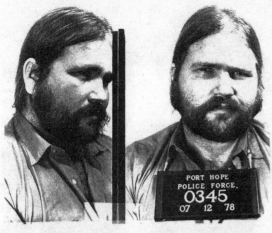

Above: Jeff McLeod, booking shot, December 12, 1978. (Transcript)

Right: Jeff McLeod following his Queen's University commencement ceremony, May 1987. (Ruth Reyno)

Merv "Indian" Baker fooling around during club run, 1969.

Gary at Collins Bay Pen, summer 1987. (Ruth Reyno)

From left, Lorne Campbell, Gary Comeau, and Rick Sauvé with a Satan's Choice patch painted by Gary. Taken in Millhaven Penitentiary Gym, November 1983.

BOOK SIX
THE TRIAL

"The whole thing was a notable failure. Defending the innocent imposes a much greater burden on a lawyer than defending the guilty. My client was innocent, and I have to live with what happened to him. But I don't have to do the time. There isn't a week goes by that I don't think about that."

—TERRY O'HARA, 1985

———

"Where there is judgement, there, there is falsehood."

—OLD RUSSIAN PROVERB

XXIV

THE MIDDLESEX COUNTY COURTHOUSE rises from the corner of Dundas and Ridout streets like a forbidding grey sentinel, guarding the modest, meandering course of the Thames River and the western approaches to the central core of London, Ontario. If form can be said to follow function in modern architecture, the purpose of the courthouse can be learned from a quick glance; the law, it seems to say, is an imposing monolith, intimidating and humbling to the innocent and guilty alike. Almost as an afterthought, and perhaps to soften this severe impression, someone has planted ivy around the base of the building. Although the vines have grown luxuriantly over the massive slabs of pre-stressed concrete at the lower reaches of the fifteen-storey structure, the building's fortress-like appearance remains overwhelming.

The morning of Tuesday, September 4, 1979, was a busy time for the staff of the London courthouse; indeed, the pace of life had quickened throughout the city of 250,000. Although it still felt like summer, the Labour Day weekend was over, the summer holidays had drawn to a close. Schools were reopening, and the merchants along Dundas and York streets were packing away their summer merchandise and already planning their pre-Christmas sales.

The beginning of the Fall Assizes always brought an air of anticipation to the courthouse, but on this morning the excitement was tinged with anxiety, even danger. Since before breakfast members of the Ontario Provincial Police Tactical Rescue Unit, the force's elite SWAT-style team, had been combing the building, searching for bombs, unlocked doors, and any other potential breaches in security. The TRU squad, as it was commonly known, was composed of officers specially trained to deal with hostage-takings, shoot-outs, bombings, and any other form of urban terrorism. They were experts with tear gas and semi-automatic and automatic weapons and the heavier artillery that the OPP, like other North American police forces, was adding to its arsenal. The TRU squad members liked to think of themselves as being extra-tough, and everyone in the courthouse that morning could see they were taking their assignment very, very seriously.

Indeed, the security precautions surrounding the Satan's Choice murder trial were a new wrinkle in Canadian criminal justice, wholly without precedent. The planning had taken several weeks and the operation was a joint effort of the OPP, the London Police Department, and the Middlesex County Sheriff's Department, which had its offices in the courthouse building. The TRU squad had been brought in from across Ontario to secure the building and provide an armed guard for the accused.

Further complicating security headaches that morning was the inordinately large number of prospective jurors that had been impanelled for the trial. A total of two hundred and fifteen citizens of Middlesex County had to be processed by courthouse staff before the jury selection could even begin.

Mac Haig drank in the details of that September morning with all the relish of a sixteen-year courtroom veteran: the sober, slightly worried looks on the beefy faces of the TRU squad members, the bantering of the lawyers in their black robes and wing collars, the milling confusion of the jury panel. Even that very first morning he could see that this trial was going to be something special—right up there with Demeter.

Haig had covered the Demeter trial for the *London Free Press* right here on the fourteenth floor of the courthouse building exactly five years before, and he had always considered it the high point of his career. Peter Demeter, a self-made Mississauga millionaire, had been charged with conspiring in the bloody murder of his wife Christine, a beautiful fashion model. The trial had everything—it turned out that Demeter had had a gorgeous mistress in Vienna, had insured Christine's life for a million dollars, and had sometimes spoken of ways to get rid of his wife. The mistress testified, as did a number of Toronto underworld figures with nicknames like "The Duck," "The Tractor," and "Foxy." There was even an honest-to-God mystery witness, a police informer dubbed "Mr. X," who was permitted to testify with a paper bag over his head.

It was a London, Ontario, court reporter's dream. All the big-time Toronto media covered the story daily and the combination of money, murder, and sex proved irresistible to the public. There had been no need for Mac to hassle with the editor for space during that run—he was practically guaranteed front-page play for as long as the trial lasted, which turned out to be ten weeks, the longest murder trial in Canadian legal history. Demeter was convicted of non-capital murder, and sentenced to at least ten years in prison.

Almost without thinking, Mac Haig began to make mental notes, comparing this biker trial to Demeter's. Demeter had been tried in Courtroom 22, while the Choice would be in Courtroom 21. You turned right off the elevator for Demeter, left for the bikers, though the courtrooms themselves were identical or, more correctly, mirror images of one another. In some ways this trial already promised to outstrip Demeter, even though it hadn't started yet. Haig was astounded at the security on the fourteenth floor— he'd never seen anything remotely resembling it in all his years covering court. And the jury panel here was far larger: Demeter had had seventy-six potential jurors, compared to two hundred and fifteen for the bikers.

Some of Haig's instincts about the Choice trial would prove correct—it would turn out to be superior to Demeter's on several counts. But, disappointingly for him, it would never garner the notoriety of the earlier proceeding. None of the accused were millionaires, after all; Bill Matiyek was hardly a luscious fashion model; and there was no sex at all in the story that anyone could see. There would be few front-page bylines for Mac Haig, or anyone else.

Even that first morning the story seemed to fizzle. The jurors were sent home shortly after noon, and the preliminary motions and legal arguments that had been scheduled for that afternoon before the jury selection had to be cancelled because of, as Mac would put it in his story that night, "behind-the-scenes developments."

His story the following day, headlined "Tight security cloaks murder trial—'Like an armed camp,'" did not fully convey the import of what was happening at the Middlesex County courthouse. It was as if the law, even in the fourteenth-floor fastness of its own fortress, was somehow under siege, as if the ghosts of Bernie Guindon and his minions were going to come blasting their way into the London courthouse to set their brothers free. It was a farcical prospect, but the truth was even more absurd: the police, after staging elaborate security measures in and around the courthouse, had also put up cordons around the city of London to intercept the in-riding hordes. The net had proved successful, resulting in the "behind-the-scenes developments" that had disrupted the first day of the trial. On the way to his own trial for first-degree murder, Larry Hurren had been spotted by the ever-alert provincial police, searched, arrested, and charged. While hundreds of prospective jurors milled about, while dozens of trigger-ready police patrolled the courthouse, while the Crown Attorneys fumed, and while Mac Haig groped for a first-day lead, Beaver Hurren was once again languishing in jail. The charge against him: possession of an ounce of marijuana.

The defence lawyers couldn't help chortling discreetly up the sleeves of their gowns, seeing the police hoisted on the petard of their own security paranoia. The situation was far less amusing to the Crown and the senior police officials, and the phone lines burned hot to the Attorney General's office and back to the local constabulary where Hurren had been detained. The instructions were simple: release the suspect and make damned sure he gets to London by morning.

It was not every senior Ontario judge who would have appreciated the full absurdity of the situation: the cost to the taxpayer for security alone at the trial was enormous, especially in the first few days, and unforeseen delays simply compounded the expense. But Coulter Arthur Anthony Osborne was no ordinary Ontario Supreme Court Justice. There is every reason to believe that he simply retired to his chambers and had a quiet laugh to himself over a glass of good Scotch. Years later he would recall the Hurren incident with a broad grin, and recount the story with some gusto, how zealous police had managed to stop a man from attending his own murder trial. It was a bit like delaying a hanging because the condemned man had been caught with a stolen package of Lifesavers on his way to the gallows.

But on that first Tuesday in September Mr. Justice Coulter Osborne was still something of a closed book to most of the lawyers at the Matiyek murder trial, because he was a very recent appointment to the bench. Osborne had been named to Ontario's most senior court by Pierre Trudeau's government, just eleven months before, at the youthful age of forty-four. A product of private schools, Osborne had graduated from the University of Western Ontario in London in 1955 and from Toronto's Osgoode Hall Law School in 1959.

Although his background appeared traditional, the new Supreme Court judge was in fact a far cry from the staid scions of Ontario's WASP establishment who had, for generations, graced the province's senior bench. A talented basketball player, Osborne had starred for the varsity during his school days at Western and played on the Canadian Olympic team at the 1956 Games in Melbourne, Australia. He alternated between point guard and short forward (at six foot one, by modern standards *very* short), before the term "swingman" was invented. Even twenty years after his competitive career was over, there was still an athletic mien to Coulter Osborne, a slender, easy grace that women found attractive and that put men at their ease. It may have been this athleticism that caused him to look considerably younger than his age, a somewhat disarming trait in a Supreme Court Justice.

It was hard to square him with his predecessors, many of whose life-sized oil portraits stared sombrely down from the walls of Toronto's Osgoode Hall. Here was no fusty, three-piece-suit and pinstripes man, but someone who preferred more casual attire—grey flannel slacks, sports jacket, and school tie, worn more as a concession than as a statement. His style was, in a word, preppy, a legacy perhaps of his years at Hamilton's Hillfield School and St. Andrew's College outside Toronto.

There was something undeniably appealing in his informality, his apparent refusal to take himself too seriously, despite his exalted position. His authority, when he was required to exercise it, lay in his rich and perfectly modulated baritone voice, which seemed to rise mysteriously from within his spare frame. The thoughts and opinions it uttered were invariably well-reasoned and expressed in impeccably rounded sentences which were, more often than not, punctuated with a quick wit and a smile.

During the long proceeding over which he was about to preside, Mr. Justice Coulter Osborne would reveal himself to be judicious, open-minded, and assiduously fair. No defendant, no defence counsel, indeed, no prosecutor, could ever have asked for more. And yet, in the end, as far as the accused were concerned, Coulter Osborne's very competence as a trial judge would prove both a blessing and a curse.

Larry Hurren arrived in London in time for the resumption of court on Wednesday morning and shortly before noon the eight accused were arraigned. After reading out the charge against them the Court Registrar asked each of the accused how he pleaded. Each rose to his feet and answered, "Not guilty." With the exception of Tee Hee Hoffman and Gordy van Haarlem, those would be the only words ever spoken by the accused in court.

It took a full day to select the jury. One hundred and fifty-eight members of the jury panel were asked two basic questions—had they seen any media accounts of the Matiyek murder case, and did they have any personal bias against members of motorcycle clubs—before twelve jurors satisfactory to both the Crown and the defence were selected. The jury was composed of seven men and five women. They included a pensioner (who would be elected jury foreman), a travel agent, a teacher, four housewives, a paint store manager, a laborer, a stock clerk, an electrical worker, and the owner of a clothing store. Taken as a whole, the jury was a reasonable reflection of Middlesex County: white, middle-aged, middle-class, and probably somewhat to the right of centre politically. Southwestern Ontario might not have been the ideal venue for eight bikers charged with murder to stand trial—the defence would have preferred a more cosmopolitan centre like Toronto—but a London jury would, at the very least, be more impartial than one from the Port Hope area.

On Thursday afternoon Judge Osborne dismissed the newly selected jury until the following Monday. The rest of the week would be devoted to the discussion and resolution of a number of pre-trial motions, two of which were absolutely critical to the defence.

The first concerned the admissibility of evidence regarding the defendants' membership in the Satan's Choice. Ideally, the defence wanted to prevent any reference to club affiliation on the grounds that even the most impartial of jurors might be tempted to judge the defendants guilty by association. On the other hand, this objective had already been undercut by the defence itself. The defence team had earlier argued for, and been granted by Judge Osborne, the right to challenge prospective jurors on the grounds that they might be prejudiced against bikers, thereby telegraphing to the twelve jurors actually selected that motorcycle club activities were somehow involved in the case. Moreover, it had already been widely reported in the London news media that the accused were members of the Satan's Choice. It is also difficult, in hindsight, to see how the jury could have made any sense at all out of the murder of Bill Matiyek without mention of the club affiliations of both the deceased and the accused. In the end, the defence attorneys admitted membership on behalf of their clients to avoid having the issue worked to death by Meinhardt.

The question raised a panoply of legal issues: motive, enmity, evidence of bad character, guilt by association. The Crown would also, left to its own devices, attempt to adduce evidence concerning the club itself: history, organization, the significance and meaning of colours—how many times had Bruce Affleck himself, while a Crown, explained the significance of the black, green, and red wing patches to a disgusted jury?

In his preliminary ruling on the admissibility of club membership, Coulter Osborne stated that while evidence of bad character was not admissible, some forms of evidence could not be ruled inadmissible merely because the jury might infer bad character from it. "Here we have a set of circumstances where it is asserted that eight people are within reasonably narrow confines (i.e., the Queen's Hotel). If it is a fact that those eight persons are connected with one another, in my view, that is a relevant fact and it makes little difference that their connection bears with it a connotation that I think justifiably concerns defence counsel."

Round one, therefore, went to the Crown, and one of the most celebrated trial lawyers in Canada would stubbornly insist years later that from this moment forward it was impossible for the accused to receive a fair trial—that their interests were hopelessly prejudged in the eyes of the jury before a single witness was ever called.

In his second crucial pre-trial ruling, Osborne conceded a point to the defence. It concerned that linchpin of the case for the defence: the elusive third bullet. The quest for that bullet would loom ever larger for Gary Comeau and his lawyer, and Coulter Osborne's ruling on the matter would ricochet through the trial with all the unpredictability of the slug itself on that fatal night in the Queen's Hotel.

"I will issue an order directing that Mr. Comeau be taken to some radiologist," intoned Justice Coulter. The defence, in fact, had little more to go on than the Crown: two visible but by now well-healed scars, the negative results of the X-rays taken in Detroit, and the unshakable conviction of Gary Comeau himself that the bullet was still somewhere inside his body. It was an exceedingly slender reed upon which to rest so much of the defence's case. But Osborne instructed Kerbel and Meinhardt to arrange a convenient time for a radiologist to make the necessary examination.

With that, court was adjourned until the following Monday.

XXV

THE TRIAL OPENED WITH Chris Meinhardt's opening address to the jury. The evidence would show that a number of the accused had entered the Queen's Hotel through various entrances just ten minutes before Bill Matiyek was shot, the veteran Crown Attorney promised. A number of people in the group moved towards Matiyek's table just before the shooting. After the shots were fired, the members of the group left the bar hurriedly through various exits.

The first Crown witness was Constable Kenneth Wilson of the Port Hope Police Department. He described how he and his partner had been flagged down by bartender Rick Galbraith at 11:08 p.m. They found Bill Matiyek lying on the floor in a pool of blood, and Constable Wilson was unable to find any visible signs of life in the big man. Wilson said he left the hotel shortly after 1 a.m. and returned to the police station, where he took a written statement from David Gillispie at 2:05 a.m.

Next, pathologist John Whiteside was called to the witness stand. He repeated his testimony from the preliminary hearing: that the deceased had received three gunshot wounds from his left side, but that only one bullet had been recovered from the body intact. Forensic analysis revealed the slug to have been "a jacketed nine millimetre soft point projectile, fired from a revolver rifled to Colt specifications." A weapon had also been found in the clothing of the deceased. A test for alcohol had revealed Matiyek's blood contained 149 milligrams of alcohol per 100 millilitres of blood. The legal definition of intoxication for driving was 80 milligrams of alcohol, Whiteside told the jury.

Meinhardt's next witness was Corporal James Moore, an identification officer with the Ontario Provincial Police. Corporal Moore had been present when Constable Wakely of the Port Hope Police Department had removed a weapon from the clothing of Bill Matiyek. The gun, which had been concealed in the left breast pocket of the deceased's red-and-black-checked bush jacket, was a .32-calibre automatic pistol. It had been loaded, with eight rounds in the clip but none in the breech. The gun would hold a total of nine bullets fully loaded.

This testimony would forever mystify both Gary Comeau and Rick Sauvé. Both men vividly recalled Matiyek's threat that he had "nine friends" as he showed them the top of his gun. *Nine*, not eight. And the pistol had been in the lower left pocket of his bush jacket, not in the breast pocket. What had become of the ninth bullet? Had Matiyek himself simply miscalculated, or had someone purposely removed the round from the chamber? And how had the pistol moved from one pocket to another on the body of a dead man? It was one of the minor mysteries of the case, one that would remain forever, tantalizingly, unresolved.

Constable William Wakely, an identification officer for the Port Hope Police Department, followed Moore on the witness stand. Meinhardt produced a brown paper bag which the constable identified as containing Matiyek's clothing. The Crown Attorney reached into the sack and pulled out Matiyek's bush jacket and blue work shirt. The accused watched in horror—they were stiff as cardboard with ten-month-old dried blood. Bruce Affleck rose to object but he was too late—the blood-encrusted shirts had already been entered as evidence and seen by the jury.

Chris Meinhardt then called OPP constable Donald Denis to the witness stand. Denis told the Crown Attorney that the special police squad to which he was assigned "deals in investigating outlaw motorcycle gangs."

David Newman, Larry Hurren's lawyer, rose to object, and the jury was excused from the courtroom while legal arguments ensued. Newman objected to the use of the term "outlaw motorcycle gangs," and applied for a mistrial, an application supported by all of the defence counsel; the application was denied. It was now late in the afternoon of Tuesday, September 11. The trial had been under way for a full week, and the jury had only just begun to hear the evidence. There had, in fact, been so many legal wrangles among the lawyers that the jury had spent nearly as much time outside the courtroom as in it, and the situation was about to get worse.

The jurors returned to the courtroom and Meinhardt resumed his direct examination of Constable Denis. The identification officer explained how he had gathered up pictures of members of the Satan's Choice and Outlaws Motorcycle clubs and proceeded to Port Hope, and how he had shown various photo line-ups to various witnesses over the next few weeks.

Once again David Newman objected and applied for a mistrial, again with the support of all defence counsel, and once again the jury was asked to leave the courtroom. In the absence of the jury Newman argued that the very presence of his client's picture in police files could be taken as evidence of bad character and evidence of a previous criminal record. Once again Coulter Osborne rejected the mistrial application, but he cautioned Meinhardt to be careful not to associate simple membership in the Satan's Choice with criminal activities and evidence of bad character. The jury returned to the courtroom.

Denis then explained the different file folders marked "scmc" and "omc" containing the pictures that were used for the photo arrays, and each folder was entered as an exhibit. He also explained the significance of the red markings on some of the photos before court was adjourned for the day.

The next morning Bruce Affleck presented yet another mistrial application because of the photographs that had been accepted as evidence through Constable Denis. The legal arguments on the application took the entire morning, and once again the jury was excluded. Affleck argued once more that the photographs were prejudicial to the accused: many of them were obviously mug shots containing police identification numbers—clear evidence of bad character or previous criminal records.

The arguments dragged on into the afternoon, and the jury was summoned briefly and excused until the following day by Judge Osborne, who then attempted to make some sense out of the various defence motions. On the one hand, he mused, the defence desired to exclude the pictures from the evidence entirely. But on the other hand, some of the defence counsel had indicated they needed the photographs to cross-examine some of the Crown witnesses.

While the selection of such unsavory pictures of the accused for the photo line-up might have been unfortunate, Osborne continued, that had indeed taken place and could not be rectified now. They were, in fact, a crucial part of the whole case for the prosecution—identification evidence. It was midday on Thursday before a compromise was reached: the photo exhibits would be removed from the folders labelled "scmc" or "omc" and placed into new envelopes labelled only by exhibit number. Any reference to police identification numbers and other incriminating markings would be obliterated from the pictures or covered, where possible.

After nearly two full days of waiting for the disposition of the legal arguments, the jury was finally readmitted to the courtroom. It was almost three o'clock when Bruce Affleck rose to begin his cross-examination of Constable Denis.

The witness's sixteen years of experience on the force would doubtless indicate that the constable had considerable experience in the area of photo line-ups? the former Crown Attorney asked mildly.

No, this had been Constable Denis's first such assignment.

But he had received a course or training prior to the assignment?

No.

Well then, had he discussed the matter with another officer experienced in identification procedures?

"Very briefly."

And this other officer, was he an expert in such procedures?

"No, sir."

". . . the only other person to whom you spoke was another officer who as far as you were concerned had perhaps no more experience than you did?"

"That's correct."

Was it true that, after all of the many photo line-ups the constable had shown in Port Hope, some of the viewers had been unable to identify anyone?

"That's correct."

And other people had identified pictures of people who were never charged?

"It's possible."

"You don't recall that?"

"Not offhand."

"Well, do you recall showing the photographs to a gentleman by the name of Rod Stewart? And he identified more than one picture?"

"Yes, sir."

"And I am suggesting to you that none of the persons that he identified are in this courtroom today?"

"That's correct."

And what of the time that elapsed during each viewing session? Wouldn't the witness agree that the finishing times of each witness was important?

"I didn't think it was at the time."

Didn't it matter if someone had taken three hours to make an identification, or had done it immediately?

"It would depend on how long, how much time he has taken to do it. He can be sure when he walks in and takes three hours to do it."

But if the identification had been immediate, wouldn't that be an important factor in the evidence?

"It could make a difference."

"Yes. So therefore the exiting time would be of some significance?"

"Some."

"As a matter of fact if I were to put it to you squarely you don't have the time of exit of many of the witnesses."

"I haven't counted them."

Affleck moved on to the question of the red markings. Wouldn't the constable agree that it would be unfair to make one photograph more outstanding than the rest?

"It wasn't my intention."

"I see. Well, you agree with me that would be unfair?"

"It would be."

"And yet, as I understood your evidence, you marked some of the photographs with a red marking-pen?"

"Yes."

"And you will agree with me that that would make that particular photograph or photographs more distinguishable than the rest?"

"Possible." Denis explained that he had used the marker to indicate a series of pictures when the top photograph was larger than or the same size as the ones underneath.

"And yet there were instances where the red magic marker was used where it was apparent that the top photograph was smaller than the remaining, the underneath photographs?"

"I can't recall that incident."

"Well, we could have perhaps a check on that. You say you can't recall; you are not saying that didn't happen?"

"I am saying I couldn't recall."

"Did you at any time in the exhibition of these photographs have more than one witness at the same time come into the room to look at those pictures?"

"Yes."

"And you would agree with me that it's preferable to have the photographs displayed to one witness at a time?"

"That's correct."

"And did you make any record of the conversation that occurred between those two witnesses?"

"No."

Constable Denis confirmed that Gayle Thompson and Cathy Cotgrave, both of whom were Crown witnesses, had viewed the line-up together on October 28.

When had Gayle Thompson first viewed the line-up?

On either the nineteenth or twentieth of October, the officer couldn't be sure. Nor could he recall who Miss Thompson had identified or whether she had identified a possible gunman—his notes from the session were no longer available. On the twenty-eighth, when Thompson and Cotgrave viewed the array together, they were separated by a table and hadn't said anything at all to one another.

"And obviously the table isn't that far, there wouldn't be that much distance separating the two of them?"

"No, sir."

"And obviously they could communicate with each other either by gesture or by word?"

"Possible." But, Denis had nothing in his notes to that effect.

"Is it possible that could have happened?"

"Yes, sir."

Next Affleck turned to the question of precisely which photographs had been shown to whom in each of the successive showings. It was clear that Denis had no record of which pictures had been shown to which witnesses on any given day, or of how many pictures of each accused had been in the photo array at any one time.

The senior defence counsel then returned to the day when Cotgrave and Thompson had viewed the line-up together. Was the officer certain that the two witnesses had been standing opposite one another at all times?

"Pretty positive."

"When you say 'Pretty positive,' I don't want to mince words with you. Does that indicate there might be some doubt about that?"

"Yes, sir."

But, Affleck reminded the officer, at the preliminary Denis hadn't been able to recall whether or not the witnesses had been side by side when they viewed the line-up.

Judge Osborne interrupted Affleck's cross-examination to brief the jury on the question of prior inconsistent statements, a legal issue destined to recur throughout the trial, usually concerning Crown witnesses. When during cross-examination there appeared to be a difference between what a witness was saying at trial and what he or she may have said earlier—in this case at the preliminary—then that difference was considered to be a prior inconsistent statement, Osborne explained. The evidence to be considered by the jury was the evidence given at this trial, from this witness-box. But the jury could and to a certain degree should take into account any inconsistency demonstrated as a result of what had been said on prior occasions. The previous testimony might bear on the issues of reliability, credibility, and weight of the evidence given by the witness. It was up to the jury to decide whether inconsistency had been demonstrated or not.

Affleck's cross-examination of Denis was concluded on Friday morning. As he returned to his chair at the defence table, Bruce Affleck had every reason to be well pleased. The most cogent evidence against the accused, he knew, was the identification evidence of the eyewitnesses. With surgical precision he had laid bare the woeful inadequacies of the identification procedures followed by the police in the Matiyek murder investigation. Affleck had every hope that, by demonstrating the dubious way this evidence had been obtained, the evidence itself might appear tainted in the eyes of the jury.

Later, reflecting on the Matiyek murder case, Bruce Affleck would confess to harboring misgivings about the lack of a coherent defence strategy. "It was very frustrating to go to court every day for four months and never really know what the defence really is," he'd say. But when he went to lunch on that Friday afternoon in mid-September, Bruce Affleck must have been a happy man. He had left the first major Crown witness in tatters, and the defence strategy of watching the Crown case self-destruct under rigorous cross-examination seemed to be working.

But in hindsight, it is clear that what little strategy the defence actually had also began to fall apart that same afternoon. The session began, innocently enough, with Howard Kerbel's cross-examination of Donald Denis. The police identification officer, so far as Bruce Affleck was concerned, was already in the ground. The rest of the defence counsel needed only to throw a few scoops of dirt on the coffin, and, at the outset, Gary Comeau's lawyer did exactly that.

He noted that there was a total of seven pictures of his client in the photo line-up, the top one marked with a large and very obvious red symbol. Denis agreed.

Some of the pictures also had Comeau's name on the back, which the witnesses might well have seen as they flipped through them?

"Yes, that's possible."

Constable Denis had testified earlier that the red dots were used only when the top picture in a series was larger than or the same size as the photos underneath. "You will also agree with me, will you not, that there are instances in which there are red marks where there are multiple pictures and the top picture is smaller than the pictures beneath?"

"It's possible."

"Just a moment. With respect to Mr. Comeau, it is obvious from just looking—are you saying it is obvious from looking at the pictures of Mr. Comeau that there are other pictures underneath?"

"Yes, sir."

"But yet a red mark appears on Mr. Comeau's picture?"

"Yes, sir."

"Okay. Would it be fair to say that at the time you put the red mark on Mr. Comeau's top picture, one or more of the people who saw the array had already given an indication that Mr. Comeau may have been the gunman?"

"Yes, sir."

"So at the time the red mark was placed there, you already had some suspicion that Mr. Comeau might be the gunman?"

"Yes, sir."

Had Kerbel ended his cross-examination with these damaging admissions, his effort would have been deemed a great success by his co-counsel. Instead, he stayed on his feet, and his cross-examination dragged on and on. He re-tracked Affleck's steps, reestablishing which witnesses had identified which suspects from which line-ups on which dates. Even the other counsel and Judge Osborne, equipped with pen and notepads, had difficulty following Kerbel and Denis through the dense thicket of detail. How the jury was supposed to keep up is impossible to imagine. As it was, the flow of Kerbel's cross was repeatedly interrupted by Judge Osborne, asking the lawyer to clarify, and occasionally to correct, the dates contained in his questions.

Kerbel's rhythm was further disrupted by Chris Meinhardt, who had numerous objections to some of Kerbel's queries. The Crown's objections, while frequently overruled, also led to legal arguments that required the jury to leave the courtroom no fewer than five times in the course of one afternoon.

It was at one such juncture—Meinhardt had risen to object and Terry O'Hara had risen to ask that the jury be removed—that Howard Kerbel uttered an extemporaneous remark that O'Hara would carry with him to his grave. "Perhaps I should make clear," Kerbel blurted out before the jury had left the room, "the point is not necessarily that someone else killed Mr. Matiyek but that there are a great many people who are identified as having been the gunman and that goes to the weight."

O'Hara's memory might not have been entirely fair to Kerbel, taking the remark out of context, but he would always consider it one of the stupidest remarks ever made by a defence lawyer. ". . . the point is not necessarily that *someone else killed Mr. Matiyek. . . .*" "Oh, pardon me, your Honour, members of the jury, I'm not saying that someone other than my client, Gary Joseph Comeau, killed Bill Matiyek . . ." Wasn't that the upshot of Kerbel's remark? O'Hara was flabbergasted.

Kerbel ground away at the beleaguered Denis for the rest of Friday and well into Monday morning, and, little by little, the OPP constable began to rise from the dead. He had by now been on the witness stand for five straight days. It wasn't that his memory had gotten any sharper or that his missing notes had been found, but even some of the defence lawyers were beginning to feel sorry for the poor bastard. How must the jurors feel?

The remaining six defence lawyers kept their own cross-examinations mercifully short, and Chris Meinhardt did what he could to resurrect his witness on re-direct, without particular success. But, behind the scenes, the defence had done itself mortal damage.

Bruce Affleck, in particular, was livid. What, he asked Terry O'Hara privately, had Kerbel been trying to prove? Was he, Bruce Affleck, the senior defence counsel, the point man on Crown evidence, or not? Why should he bust his butt leaving Crown witnesses dead on the highway if Kerbel was going to follow him and restore the witness to the ranks of the walking wounded?

Denis's testimony would prove a turning-point for the entire trial. Imperceptibly at first, the defence team began to come apart at the seams, and by the end of the trial the defence lawyers would be stepping over each other's bodies to win acquittal for their individual clients while the accused looked on in sorrow and shame from the prisoner's box. The brotherhood of the bike would prove far more solid than the brotherhood of the gown.

XXVI

WITH HIS NEXT WITNESS Chris Meinhardt played his highest card—one that he had decided to withhold during the preliminary inquiry. Gayle Thompson was called to the witness stand.

Although she was nervous at first—Judge Osborne had to ask her to speak up—the former Queen's Hotel waitress began to tell her story with growing confidence and conviction, and for the first time the jury really began to enter the dingy confines of the Queen's barroom on the afternoon and evening of October 18, 1978.

She had started work at seven o'clock that night, Thompson began, and it had been a very slow night. Bill Matiyek was drinking there, in the company of Jamie Hanna, Fred Jones, and someone she didn't know named Sonny. But at eleven o'clock "it just seemed that all the doors opened up and people started coming in from every door." The newcomers were all males, and a couple of them—Rick Sauvé and Merv Blaker—she recognized as being members of a local motorcycle gang. She estimated that ten people had entered through the back door alone.

"There was a lot of confusion at first and then they all seemed to pick certain spots and became more or less stationary in those places they had chosen." She recognized one other of the newcomers—his name was Tee Hee, and she had met him some months before through her boyfriend, Randy Koehler. Randy had introduced them, and told Gayle that Tee Hee was his cousin.

Jamie, Fred, and Sonny, who had been sitting with Bill, left his table, "and the next time I noticed Bill's table there were two other people sitting there. . . . One was Rick Sauvé. I don't know who the other person was." Both were sitting to Bill's right, the stranger first, then Rick Sauvé next to him. Thompson correctly identified Sauvé, Blaker, and Hoffman in the prisoner's dock. She also pointed out Larry Hurren and Gary Comeau as people she recognized from the hotel, but whose names she didn't know.

"Now, just going back for the moment to seven o'clock when you arrived on duty, what if anything could you tell us about the condition of Bill Matiyek?"

"He was drunk."

Thompson described the barroom layout and the location of the telephone near the bar. Four or five of the newcomers stayed in the area near the phone. Using a diagram of the room and a marker, she noted the location of Matiyek's table, where Merv Blaker had been sitting, and where she had seen Tee Hee Hoffman standing "at the end of the bar by the telephone."

"And are you able to tell us where the accused Comeau was when you first saw him?"

"When I first saw him he was sitting at the same . . . table that Merv Blaker was sitting at."

"And did you see him leave that table at any time?"

"Just before Bill was shot."

"And did you see what happened to the two people, the accused Sauvé and the dark-haired man, just before, as you put it, Bill Matiyek was shot?"

"No."

"Were you looking in that direction just before Bill Matiyek was shot?"

"I wasn't looking directly at Bill's table, no."

"Now tell us what happened when you saw the accused Comeau leave the table just before Bill Matiyek was shot."

"He walked towards Bill's table."

"And did he—yes, go ahead."

"And shot."

"And what did you do then?"

"After I heard the first shot I saw Bill slump in his chair. I turned and went to the washroom."

"And did you see or hear anything while on your way to the washroom?"

"Two more shots."

She had stayed in the washroom for two or three minutes, Thompson recalled, and had been joined there by Sue Foote, Jamie Hanna, and Cathy Cotgrave. They left the washroom together and saw Bill lying on the floor in the corner by the table where he'd been sitting. Rod Stewart, one of the bar patrons, was trying to help Bill, trying to find a heart-beat or a pulse. She herself got some towels and put them around Bill's neck and over his head.

She hadn't been approached by the police that night, but eventually, Thompson told the jury, she viewed the photo line-up three times. On one occasion, she confirmed, she had looked at the pictures while Cathy Cotgrave was in the room, but they had not spoken to one another and she was unable to see which photos Cathy was identifying. Thompson said she had identified pictures of Sauvé, Blaker, Jones, Bronson, Hurren, Hoffman, and Comeau, though she did not then know the names of the latter two.

"And were you able to at any time while viewing the photographs indicate that you believed that Mr. Comeau shot Bill Matiyek?"

"Not definitely, no."

"Now, after having viewed these photographs did you have an occasion to see a man we know as Gary Comeau?"

"At the preliminary hearings, yes."

"And would you please tell the jury under what circumstances you saw Mr. Comeau?"

"The court had recessed and the lawyers were having some kind of a deliberation and they had all gone downstairs. The witnesses were allowed to come out into what would be the lobby at the top of the stairs and the accused were still in the courtroom but were allowed to move from their, you know, chairs. They were visible from the lobby or the hallway."

"And?"

"And that's when I saw Mr. Comeau standing."

"And when you saw him what was your reaction to yourself?"

"I knew that he was the man that I saw shoot Bill."

She hadn't acted on this sudden flash of recognition right away, Thompson explained to Meinhardt, because she'd thought she would be called to testify at the preliminary hearing and could then identify Comeau from the witness stand. Once she'd realized she wouldn't be called to give evidence at the preliminary, she had spoken to Sam McReelis.

In the wake of the Denis debacle, Bruce Affleck did not lead the cross-examination of Gayle Thompson. The role of chief cross-examiner fell instead to Howard Kerbel, fairly perhaps, since it was his client who had been most damaged by Thompson's testimony, while Affleck's client,

Jeff McLeod, had not been identified at all by the witness. Still, this meant that the most gifted cross-examiner at the defence table would not put a single question to one of the Crown's chief witnesses.

Kerbel opened his cross by putting some back story on the record. Thompson confirmed that there had been a fight at Matiyek's table earlier in the evening, between Fred Jones and Brian Brideau, but she had not heard any threats made by Brideau to Matiyek. She also recounted the argument between Fred and Jamie, after which Jamie had gone to another table.

At Kerbel's request, Thompson marked the location of Hanna's new table on the diagram. Could the witness remember another man sitting with Hanna, an older man who might have had too much to drink?

"There was an older man, yes," but Thompson didn't know who he was and hadn't seen him since.

When the newcomers entered the bar, did the witness see one of them sit down with Hanna and the old man?

"I am not even sure that they actually sat down but there was—I know there was one person present that stopped and conversed with I believe Jamie at that time."

Kerbel knew that this was one more tiny confirmation of Comeau's own account of events. But that was a story the jury was destined never to hear. If his client's story was to be entered in evidence, Kerbel would have to winkle it out of the witnesses, because of the agreement that the accused would not testify.

". . . Did you overhear the conversation that Jamie had?"

"No, I did not."

"At any time while viewing the photo arrays did you select a picture of that man?"

"No, I did not, not to my knowledge. I couldn't begin a description of that person. I don't remember."

But it might be possible that the man at Jamie Hanna's table was in fact Gary Comeau?

"It's possible."

Thompson said her attentions at that point weren't focused on Matiyek's table or on any other, she was just walking back and forth in front of the bar; yet she was certain that it had been Comeau sitting with Merv Blaker.

Having failed to elicit the identification of Comeau at Hanna's table that he wanted, Kerbel now tried to shake Thompson's identification of him as the shooter.

"I take it it would have been possible or there would have been enough time for whoever was seated with Mr. Blaker to get up and someone else sit down?"

"Not and look the same." Gotcha. Gayle Thompson was beginning to match wits with her inquisitor now, and she was plainly enjoying it.

"Well, forget about look the same," Kerbel snapped. "There would have been enough time. Is that correct?"

"There would have been enough time, yes." She also knew when to back off and concede a point, even an unfavourable one, thus underscoring the impression that she was telling the truth. Gayle Thompson was becoming a "star" witness.

"And what was it at that time that you noticed about Mr. Comeau?"

". . . His hair was light, his beard was light."

"So there's no doubt in your mind that you are able to identify Mr. Comeau by his hair and by his beard?"

"Correct."

"No doubt, not even the slightest?"

"No."

"And there's also no doubt in your mind, not the slightest doubt, that Mr. Comeau is the man you saw get up from Mr. Blaker's table, walk towards Mr. Matiyek's table, and shoot Mr. Matiyek?"

"Correct."

Thompson also maintained that she had selected pictures of Comeau on each occasion and told police that he could have been the gunman, but she was not certain. The bar waitress was equally firm and unshakable about the clothing the gunman had been wearing that night. "He had on a green parka coat with a hood that he wasn't wearing. It had fur around the hood and either a black or navy blue or a dark-coloured, I think, woollen or knitted type of toque."

"How was he wearing the hat?"

"Down to about his ears and his hair and his beard all just blended into one."

"So I take it you can't tell us anything about his hair underneath the cap, underneath the toque?"

"Of course not; I didn't see it."

The implication should have been obvious. How could Thompson have identified Comeau as the gunman by the colour of his hair and beard if the gunman's hair had been completely covered by a toque?

From her position in front of the bar, Thompson told the jury, she had a clear view of the gunman as he walked from Blaker's table towards Matiyek's.

"When did you first see the gun?"

"As he was walking towards the table."

". . . and did he have it down by his side?"

"He seemed to have pulled it from a pocket." She pantomimed the motion for the jury, drawing an imaginary gun with her left hand.

"Pulled it from a pocket and you are indicating your left hand?"

"Correct."

"What did he do then?"

"He fired." Nothing more, it had all happened very quickly.

And she was absolutely certain that he had pulled the gun with his left hand?

"It appeared to come out of a pocket. The motion was with his left hand from a pocket or it could have been up his sleeve." The gunman hadn't extended his arm before shooting, he had fired with his arm close to his body.

Kerbel concluded his cross-examination by questioning Thompson closely about discussions she may have had with other eyewitnesses concerning the shooting.

There had been some general discussion of the event, especially on the day after the shooting, Thompson admitted, before the police had instructed them not to discuss Bill's murder among themselves. While the recollections of the others had differed from her own, she could not remember having detailed discussions with the other witnesses.

Lawyers David Newman, Jack Grossman, and Terry O'Hara conducted brief cross-examinations of the witness before formally admitting that their clients, Larry Hurren, Rick Sauvé, and Murray Blaker, had all been on the premises of the Queen's Hotel at the time of the Matiyek shooting. Thompson agreed with Grossman that Sauvé was well known in the Port Hope community and that he had done nothing on the night of the shooting to conceal his identity. After a short re-direct examination by Chris Meinhardt, Gayle Thompson was excused.

It was already the afternoon of Wednesday, September 19, 1979, and the trial of *Regina v. McLeod et al.* had been under way for a full two and a half weeks. Like any lengthy legal proceeding, the trial had begun to assume a rhythm and a routine all its own. It had become a tight little world, hermetically sealed and removed from the greater world and events surrounding Courtroom 21.

For the accused, the routine of trial days was unvarying. They would rise early at the Elgin-Middlesex Detention Centre, eat breakfast, and then don their courtroom apparel. They were seven now—Larry Hurren was held in custody during the trial. Only Tee Hee Hoffman was still on the street. On the advice of their lawyers, all eight of the defendants had cleaned up their appearance. They all wore slacks and at least sports jackets; some wore vests, suit coats, and ties. Merv Blaker had shaved his beard and gotten a haircut. He had also lost considerable weight during his nine months in jail. Gary Comeau had trimmed his beard and hair, although his hair still almost touched his collar. Jeff McLeod's hair had continued to fall out and he was now partially bald. He'd gotten his first haircut in years before the trial, and his long ponytail was gone. McLeod had also slimmed down dramatically, the result of a jail diet and the inaccessibility of junk food.

Much was made in the courtroom and in the press of these changes in appearance. Their booking shots had been widely circulated by the courthouse staff before the trial began, and the secretaries and clerks enjoyed catching glimpses of the bikers whenever they could. How different the eight looked. It occasioned considerable merriment among the staff: where were the glowering hard-nosed desperadoes of the booking shots now?

Once dressed, the seven accused would be manacled and handcuffed and led to a waiting OPP van. As it had been at the preliminary, the van would be escorted by two other OPP vehicles, both bristling with armed guards, for the eight-kilometre drive to the Middlesex County courthouse. Under the watchful eye of their guards, the seven would shuffle to the holding-cells in the bowels of the building, where they would await the beginning of the day's proceedings. The holding-tank was particularly dreary. The cells were tiny and windowless, equipped only with a grey steel bunk, a toilet, and a washstand. When the signal was given, the accused would be led to a private elevator—it had been equipped with bars specially for the trial—to be whisked up the fourteen floors to the courtroom.

Outside the public elevators on the courtroom floor, meanwhile, a line-up formed daily outside the massive wooden double doors through which the public, press, and lawyers entered the courtroom. Security had remained tight, and the novelty of being frisked with metal-detecting wands had long since worn off. It was now regarded as a time-consuming nuisance, performed by two OPP constables wearing apologetic smiles. The ritual would be performed whenever anyone left the courtroom, no matter how briefly.

The courtroom itself was high-ceilinged and spacious, though window-less. Its starkly utilitarian design had been relieved somewhat by a colour scheme that was almost garish. The carpet was purple, as was the fabric that covered the foam padding on the wooden spectators' benches. The walls were papered a sombre brown, broken in places by a fresco of wooden baffles that gave the room, despite its size, excellent acoustics. High over-head, fluorescent lights hidden in square translucent panels buzzed faintly. Despite its modernist fixtures, however, Courtroom 21 remained, like all such spaces, a peculiar place, a cross between a cathedral and a theatre, carefully arranged to impress everyone who entered it with the majesty and mystery of the law, while at the same time affording the public a clear and unobstructed view of the spectacle being played out there.

Symbolism was everywhere. The room was dominated by a massive repro-duction of the Canadian coat-of-arms, a crowned lion on the left, a white unicorn on the right. Just beneath the royal crest sat the presiding judge on a dais raised high above everyone else, like a preacher in a pulpit. To his left, but considerably lower, was the witness-box, to the right a place for a sher-iff's deputy. In front of the bench sat the court reporter and the court clerk. The lawyers for both the Crown and the defence sat at tables on ground level removed some twenty feet from the Judge's perch. Between the tables stood a lectern. Behind the lawyers and also facing the bench was the pris-oner's dock, separated from the audience by a wall of clear Plexiglas. To the right of the lawyers and the defendants the jury sat, their backs to a wall lined with doors. After the Judge, who could look directly into the eyes of anyone in the room, the jury occupied the most favourable seats. Each member could, in profile at least, see the face of every player in the drama—the Judge and his supporting cast, the lawyers, the witness of the day, the audience, and, most especially, the accused, the eight men upon whom they had been summoned to pass judgment.

Nearly half the courtroom was taken up by public seating, rows of wooden pews broken by aisles. In all, there was ample room for upwards of a hundred spectators—the families of the accused and of the deceased, the curious, and the handful of courtroom regulars to be found in any courthouse who appreciate a trial, almost any trial, for what it is—a contest of wits and wills, a microcosm of society, a setting for high, if sometimes boring, true-life drama played out in deadly earnest.

As the hour for the resumption of the trial drew near, the principals were admitted to the courtroom through their various doors in carefully arranged sequence. The accused would be led in first, still in their restraints, and their guards would then take up their stations immediately behind the prisoner's dock. Then, and only then, would the jury be allowed to enter, on the theory that it might be prejudiced by a glimpse of the accused hobbling along like a chain gang. In the eyes of the law, after all, the accused were innocent until proven guilty, even if in the eyes of law-enforcement officials they already had one foot in the yard at Millhaven. This sequential ritual was observed without fail, even though the jurors must certainly have noticed the extraordinary security in the courtroom and the TRU squad members sitting conspicuously behind the accused.

When all was in readiness, a signal would be passed and the Honourable Mr. Justice Coulter Arthur Anthony Osborne would emerge from his chambers through his private entrance, resplendent in his judicial robes. He would climb the steps to his aerie and seat himself in his throne, a high-backed burgundy-leather armchair. With a slight smile or a frown or a preoccupied wave he would nod at the standing multitude, and they would be seated. Mr. Justice Osborne would look down on his court, master of all he surveyed, and the doors at the public entrance to Courtroom 21 would swing silently shut on their heavy, well-oiled hinges. The trial of *Regina v. McLeod et al.* was once again in session.

The designers of Courtroom 21 had thoughtfully provided a special, segregated seating area for members of the press: two short rows of pews near the jury-box, behind and to the right of the prisoner's dock. Most of the reporters covering the Matiyek murder trial would appear in the courtroom only sporadically, hoping to anticipate the most important or sensational testimony. Mac Haig was an exception—he would be present for every hour of every day of testimony—but he had one other constant companion in the press-box, Bill Glaister.

Glaister was a freelance reporter, selling coverage of the trial to a variety of clients including CFPL radio in London, CBC radio news in Toronto, and the *Globe and Mail*. He hoped to spin off stories to a few other media outlets as well. In outlook, appearance, and style it would be hard to imagine two more disparate members of a single occupation than Mac Haig and Bill Glaister. Where Haig was clean-cut, clean-shaven, and quite comfortable in his role as a beat reporter for the *Free Press*, Glaister was bearded, shaggy, and a restless free spirit, always hustling, always with an eye out for the main chance. If Haig tended to be right-of-centre and instinctively pro-police in many of his attitudes, Glaister, who was a few years younger, was inherently sceptical of the justice system in general and the police in particular. Mac had established a good rapport with the police over the years, but Bill, who was often called upon to cover a myriad of assignments in addition to the police and court beats, never had.

That difference was highlighted on the very first day of the trial. Like Haig, Glaister had emphasized the heavy courtroom security in his *Globe* story, since there wasn't much else to write about. But Glaister had noted in passing that some of the courtroom guards appeared to be wearing bullet-proof vests beneath their uniforms. He'd been angrily accosted by a member of the TRU squad the next morning. It's pricks like you that get cops shot in the head all the time, the OPP officer said accusingly. Glaister was taken aback by this sudden attack, and amused. He considered the heavy security a dog-and-pony show, a not very subtle attempt to intimidate the jury, though he couldn't say so in his copy, of course.

By the time the trial had entered its third week, Glaister had also become intrigued by Terry Hall, who was in the audience for much of the testimony, awaiting his own turn on the witness stand. Even in his three-piece suit Hall seemed to play the role of a biker to the hilt. To Glaister the commanding officer of the biker squad looked big, fast, and mean. Of all the bikers in the room, Bill Glaister decided, it was Hall he would least prefer to meet in a dark alley. It was just a feeling, a gut instinct, but Glaister began to suspect that only part of the story was being told in the courtroom, that people and things were not exactly what they seemed. It was a feeling that would deepen into conviction in the weeks and months to come, and it was a conviction that would be confirmed, at least in part, by actual events.

It was Roland Harris, Chris Meinhardt's junior, who called Susan Jean Foote to the stand as the next witness for the Crown. Foote told Harris that she was a lifelong resident of the Port Hope–Cobourg area, and a computer operator at the Ganaraska Credit Union in Port Hope. She also described herself as "a regular" at the Queen's Hotel.

Foote repeated the testimony she'd given earlier at the preliminary, how she'd arrived at the Queen's at about 10:30 on the night of October 18, had gotten herself a beer, and then started watching TV in the shuffleboard room to kill time. She could even remember the name of the show, *McClintock*, with John Wayne. It had been a normal, quiet night in the Queen's Hotel until six to eight Satan's Choice members came in through the back door.

Three or four minutes later Foote had gone to the bar to get herself another beer "and I seen that there was not only the members I seen walk in but others in the front lounge, milling around. . . . It felt tense and heavy in the air and everything and there was more members in the front of the lounge that must have come in different doors." There may have been twenty newcomers in all. "They were milling around the bar as though to make sure everybody knew the Choice were there."

"Just tell us what you saw," Judge Osborne interjected gently.

"They were milling around the bar, in through the chairs and tables."

Yes, she saw some of these persons in court here today, Foote told Harris. She pointed to them in the prisoner's dock: Gary Comeau, Larry Hurren, Jeff McLeod, Tee Hee Hoffman, Merv Blaker, and Rick Sauvé. The latter, she said, had been sitting at Matiyek's table just before the shooting, on Bill's left.

Jeff was distinctive by his very size, and she was sure he'd been wearing a green parka that night in the hotel. She'd last seen him "standing in front of the Matiyek table . . . just before the shooting. . . . There was people mingling around in the bar and just before the shooting it seemed, they started heading toward the table. . . . I seen Jeff and I don't know who else was there."

Perhaps six men in all had converged on Bill's table and then stopped, blocking her view. Thirty seconds or a minute later she had heard, rather than seen, shots fired, and then Bill Matiyek had fallen to the ground. Afterwards everybody had run for the exits.

This time Bruce Affleck once again led the cross-examination. He confronted Foote with her testimony at the preliminary. Wasn't it true that at that time she had made no reference to anyone named Jeff entering the hotel through the back door?

Foote conceded that she had failed to mention Jeff as being part of the group that entered through the back door. She also agreed that she had become familiar with Jeff McLeod's surname only after reading it in the papers.

And hadn't she also testified at the preliminary that she'd been "pretty sure" she'd seen Jeff at a few parties "but I can't say for sure"?

Yes, she remembered giving that answer.

Affleck continued reading from the transcript of Foote's testimony at the preliminary. "'And so you are not sure whether you knew him from previous occasions or not, in all conscience you may or may not have known who he was.' 'Yes.' 'In all fairness then you may have mistaken him for someone else who looked like him?' 'Possible, yes.'"

Yes, Foote agreed, that had been her earlier testimony.

And if Affleck were to suggest that McLeod had not in fact been a member of the Satan's Choice four years before the shooting, when Foote had seen him at parties—would that affect her identification?

"Yes, it would, but I know that I have seen him four or five years ago."

Had the witness spoken to the police since the preliminary hearing?

No.

It was a deft cross-examination, and it may well have given rise to doubts in the jurors' minds as to whether Sue Foote had really seen Jeff McLeod in the hotel at all. Still, the witness stuck stubbornly to her latest story; she was now certain that she had seen Affleck's client—and she was right. Jeff McLeod *had* been in the hotel at the time of the shooting. But that simple fact begged a host of questions, the kind of questions that lawyers and philosophers love. Each eyewitness was reconstructing the events of the shooting from his or her own point of view. Each had, naturally, seen or heard something slightly different from each of the others.

There was the objective reality of what had truly happened in the Queen's Hotel that night. There was the perceived reality, as observed by each of the participants. And there was the remembered reality, which was dependent upon the powers of observation and memory of each witness and which had been further refined through a questionable identification process and then interpreted in a certain way to fit a theoretical (police) construct.

Gayle Thompson had been, in many ways, an excellent eyewitness. In hindsight it appears probable that she had in fact seen what even Gary Comeau and Rick Sauvé, who were closest to the actual event, had not— the shooting of Bill Matiyek. With the exception of Tee Hee Hoffman, she had also been absolutely correct in her identification of the accused. And yet . . . and yet. She had also identified Gary Comeau as the gunman, and in that she was patently mistaken. She, like Sue Foote, had seen Sauvé sitting at the Matiyek table before the shooting, which was true. But Thompson had seen him one chair away on Matiyek's *right*, and Sue Foote had placed him on Bill's immediate *left*. Both of them were correct—Sauvé had been seated at the Matiyek table, but not where either of the witnesses remembered seeing him. At least according to Sauvé and Comeau, he was *across* from Matiyek. And what were they except eyewitnesses to the same event too, albeit witnesses with a very special interest?

Lawyers have a term for this: "the inherent frailty of eyewitness identification." It is an elementary lesson in any law school and in some psychology classes. A group of people might watch any sudden, unexpected event—a hit-and-run car accident, an armed hold-up—and afterwards describe the event, the suspects, in totally different ways. It was this frailty, this internal conflict among eyewitnesses, which the defence team hoped to exploit during the Matiyek murder trial.

So Affleck had done in his cross-examination of Sue Foote. She claimed to be far more certain in her identification of Jeff McLeod at the trial than she had been at the preliminary hearing, which was closer in time to the actual event that she was now describing, from memory, under oath. Jeff McLeod had been there. Sue Foote had seen him. Or she thought she had. But Jeff himself persisted in denying he'd been there to his lawyer. Yet he had, in the last analysis, been in the Queen's Hotel when Bill Matiyek was shot. That much was concrete fact. But it was not a fact in legal terms if Affleck could somehow cast doubt on the identification, as he appeared to have done.

Whittling away a witness's testimony, sentence by sentence, was, in a way, like stripping away layer upon layer of the proverbial onion—eventually nothing was left. Substance could become, at the core, unsubstantial. But it was also incontrovertibly true—and here the sophistries of philosophy and the legal profession jarred against the cold facts of human existence—that Bill Matiyek was dead, the victim of three gunshots fired at point-blank range, and that some specific individual had pulled the trigger.

The cross-examination of Susan Jean Foote continued.

David Newman, questioning Foote about her recollections of the where-abouts of his client, Larry Hurren, before and during the shooting, paced off steps in front of the witness-box to demonstrate the considerable distance that Hurren had been from the Matiyek table—all the way across the bar-room. Foote confirmed that she hadn't seen Hurren move at any time during the evening and that he had not been part of the group that moved towards Matiyek's table in the seconds before the shots were fired.

Each of the defence lawyers hammered away at Foote's apparently inconsistent prior testimony. During the preliminary, Foote had admitted discussing the shooting on several occasions with her roommate, Cathy Cotgrave, yet now she claimed they had barely touched on the subject. Was she saying that her memory had actually improved since February? Yes, she believed that it had.

Helen Ann Mitchell followed Foote on the witness stand. She had been in the hotel on the night of the shooting and remembered seeing Gord van Haarlem, Rick Sauvé, Larry Hurren, and Tee Hee there, although she hadn't known Tee Hee at the time; she hadn't seen any of the other accused members of the Satan's Choice. She did, however, notice that the man she would later identify as Tee Hee Hoffman had been wearing something white on his feet.

In the prisoner's dock the accused seethed at this testimony. They would forever regard Mitchell's jumbled evidence as erroneous and partial. Most of them tended to agree with Sue Foote who had testified at both the pre-liminary and the trial that she could not remember seeing Mitchell, whom she knew, in the hotel.

Mitchell appeared visibly nervous on the witness stand, and her testimony tended to be very vague; she couldn't recall, for example, who had been bar-tending that night. Tee Hee Hoffman's lawyer, Ed Martin, suggested that

Mitchell had been somewhat tardy in reporting her observations to the police. When had she first given them a statement?

"Well, it was after October 18. It had to be, right? It could have been a month after, a week after, I don't know." Martin refreshed her memory by reading from her testimony at the preliminary hearing. She'd said that her first visit to the police had been around Christmas, more than two months after the shooting.

Donald Ebbs questioned Mitchell at length. She was, after all, the only witness who claimed to have seen Gordon van Haarlem in the hotel on the night of the eighteenth. Ebbs reminded Mitchell that she had told the preliminary that the last time she had seen van Haarlem, some time in September, he'd been wearing a striker's patch. In fact, Gordy was already a full-fledged member by then.

"I don't know if it was a striker's patch or a full member's patch because I get Tom, Tom, I don't know what his last name is, him and Gord mixed up. I done that down at the police station."

With the conclusion of Helen Mitchell's evidence the Crown case departed, temporarily at least, from the gloomy confines of the Queen's Hotel. With his next witness Chris Meinhardt planned to introduce the jury to an even more foreign realm—to the world of motorcycle clubs in general, and to the Satan's Choice and the Golden Hawk Riders in particular.

XXVII

THE MATIYEK MURDER TRIAL was now entering its fourth week, and Lawrence Leon had become the object of some sinister goings-on back in Port Hope. The former president of the Golden Hawks had begun to receive threatening phone calls warning him not to testify at the Matiyek trial. Linda Leon had watched the colour drain from her husband's face whenever he took one of these anonymous calls. Once she herself had answered the phone and a male voice had ordered her to "tell your husband he's number one—and he's going to be zero." Another time she had received a threatening letter in the mail. It was addressed to Lawrence, but she had opened it anyway. It was a single sheet of paper with words formed by letters obviously clipped from a newspaper, just like ransom notes she'd seen on TV. "If you're in court," the message read, "you're a dead man." An officer from the Port Hope Police Department had happened to be passing by just as she'd opened the envelope, and she'd turned the hateful object over to him right away.

Then, shortly before Leon was due to appear in court, matters took a more serious turn. Someone shot up Lawrence Leon's car while it was parked in the driveway outside his home. Lawrence himself was away when it happened, and he would say later that the police had been careful not to tell him about it until after he finished giving his evidence.

Suspicion for all of these events focussed, not unnaturally, on members of the Satan's Choice, although no charges were ever laid. One Crown witness, Jamie Hanna, had already testified in open court that she'd been threatened, and the intimidation of witnesses was not an activity unknown to the Choice or to other outlaw motorcycle clubs.

Yet to this day Choice veterans deny with particular vehemence that anyone in the club had knowledge of or involvement in any of the threats against Lawrence Leon, and there are several compelling reasons to believe they are telling the truth. Leon's decision to give Crown evidence on the eve of the trial had been a closely guarded secret, known only to the police, the Crown Attorneys, and Leon himself. So successful had been the secrecy surrounding Leon that when he was called as a witness, on the morning of Monday, September 24, the defence team was taken completely aback. Even Justice Osborne expressed his surprise at the sudden emergence of this unexpected witness, and at the attendant legal arguments that were bound to precede his testimony. "Had I known on Friday that this was going to occur, I would have told you not to come in at all, but unfortunately I did not," Osborne told the jurors apologetically before asking them to leave the courtroom for the umpteenth time. "This witness was not at the preliminary hearing and we were not advised of his existence," Howard Kerbel protested before beginning his own cross-examination of Lawrence Leon. Why, then, would a member of the Satan's Choice have threatened a man who no one in the club knew was going to give evidence?

There was, moreover, the club edict that had been communicated to every member in the wake of the Jamie Hanna fiasco: "Don't threaten anyone, don't try to 'help,' it will only make already serious matters worse for the accused." A member acting on his own, despite this instruction, would have been in grievous violation of club discipline.

In the event, the jury was never told about any of the threats against Lawrence Leon, though the story made the informal rounds of the courtroom and would be widely reported after the jury had rendered its verdict by both Bill Glaister and Mac Haig. Neither reporter would leave his readers with much room to doubt that the Choice had attempted to intimidate Leon. Yet stories about what had really happened to Leon would linger in Port Hope long after both reporters had closed their notebooks on the case, and the whole affair would ultimately, like the alleged removal of a gun from one pocket to another on the clothing of a dead man, remain shrouded in mystery.

Lawrence Leon's testimony was vital to Chris Meinhardt's case. The jury had heard ample evidence, and would hear more, about the behavior of the accused in the Queen's Hotel on the night of the shooting. But to prove planning and deliberation, to demonstrate that Matiyek's death had been "a gangland-style execution," a certain context was necessary to round out the Crown evidence. Leon could provide evidence of enmity between the Satan's Choice and the Golden Hawks. From enmity sprang motive, and from motive, in Meinhardt's view, clear evidence of planning and deliberation.

Only on the morning that he intended to call him as a witness did Chris Meinhardt reveal to the court the substance of Lawrence Leon's testimony, and the disclosure produced a legal furor. Judge Osborne summoned the jury just long enough to dismiss them again before granting the defence team an adjournment to hastily prepare legal arguments as to why Leon's evidence should not be heard or why, at the very least, that evidence should first be subjected to a *voir dire*. (A *voir dire* is a trial within a trial, conducted in the absence of the jury, to determine whether contentious evidence should be admitted. All remarks made during the *voir dire* are expressly banned from publication.)

It was mid-afternoon before Osborne delivered his ruling on the arguments. He began by rejecting the defence motion for a *voir dire* of Leon's evidence. Nor had he found the defence arguments against the admissibility of the evidence itself convincing. "I therefore decline to exclude from the jury the evidence of history [of membership in biker clubs] and do not accept arguments that might have otherwise persuaded me to do so."

With that the jury was recalled, Lawrence Leon was sworn, and the world began to fall apart around the ears of the defence. Welcome to the Life.

Then, as now, Lawrence Leon was a big, slow-moving man, a farmer in heritage and appearance, if not vocation. Chris Meinhardt opened the burly man's testimony by drawing from him a story about an incident that had occurred in the Queen's Hotel at the end of March or early April of 1978.

"Bill and I were sitting in there having a drink and Brian Babcock, Rick Sauvé, and Merv Blaker walked in after we were in there about ten or fifteen minutes. . . . Bill hollered at Brian Babcock [then the president of the Choice Peterborough Chapter] and said he wanted to talk to him. . . . Brian said, 'Come on over to the table.' . . . We walked over to the table. Bill asked Brian what the hell the hassle was about. . . . Brian Babcock proceeded to tell us . . . that the Choice had shut down the Golden Hawk Riders about a year ago and they had a talk between the different chapters and there were no more Hawks and there would be no more Hawks colours. All three of the men there agreed to that thing.

"Bill got mad and hauled off and hit the table and he said that the Hawks weren't shut down and they would never be shut down. . . . There was some arguing back and forth and I can't really recall if it was Rick Sauvé or Merv Blaker but I believe it was Rick said, 'You guys are to shut it down and get out or you will never see the end of this year.' There was some arguing back and forth yet and Bill finally said, 'Listen, you guys make your next move,' he says, 'we'll be waiting.' And then they stormed out."

Leon identified Rick Sauvé in the prisoner's dock, but he was unable to identify Merv Blaker, presumably because of the change in his appearance.

After the altercation in the Queen's, Leon told Meinhardt, Bill Matiyek had begun to carry a handgun, a ".32 revolver automatic" (sic).

Both Rick and Merv flatly denied that the confrontation Leon described had taken place. Indeed. Lawrence's recollection of just when Sauvé or Blaker had threatened Matiyek began to change under Bruce Affleck's cross-examination. Although he had earlier said the incident had occurred "at the end of March or early April," he now decided it had been "the end of February, beginning of March."

"By the way, have you a criminal record?"

Leon admitted having served nine months for possession of a stolen motorcycle in 1971, and a conviction for driving while impaired in 1974.

Affleck questioned Leon in detail about the threats against Matiyek, "and I put to you in all conscience you can't recall which of those three persons said that?"

"I am sure it is Rick Sauvé," Leon answered, even though a few minutes before he had told Chris Meinhardt he wasn't sure if it had been Sauvé or Blaker.

Under cross-examination by Jack Grossman, Leon admitted to another criminal conviction—for assault in 1961 or '62—which he had neglected to mention to Affleck. Leon also told Grossman that the first time he had been questioned by police about the Matiyek murder, in March or April of 1979, he had made no mention of the threats against his friend. And Leon once again seemed uncertain about just who it was that had uttered the threats.

During a brief re-direct, Chris Meinhardt asked Leon why he had not come forward with the information about the threats until two days before the trial began.

"I didn't want to get involved and I was scared. I thought I would be next, and another thing, when you are in a bike club there's a code that you don't give evidence and you don't lay charges against other people. You just look after yourself."

"And on September 2, 1979, what caused you then to come forward with that information?"

"I had given the matter quite a bit of thought and I know if it would have been me instead of Bill, Bill would have come forward, too."

Even as his testimony was concluding in London, it was becoming apparent that Lawrence Leon was not the only subject of strange events back in Port Hope.

Terry O'Hara had still not given up his desire to put Merv Blaker on the witness stand to testify on his own behalf. When court wasn't in session O'Hara spent many hours at the Detention Centre with Blaker, interviewing the veteran biker, probing for the smallest bits of information that could somehow buttress Merv's defence. Occasionally, when one of these sessions produced leads that seemed promising, O'Hara would relay the information by telephone to Joe Bastos, a private investigator, in Kingston. A friend or co-worker of Blaker's in Port Hope would be willing to testify on this or that point, according to Blaker. It was Bastos's job to phone ahead, make an appointment, and then drive to Port Hope to interview the potential witness. It was a routine procedure, one that Bastos had performed dozens of times while working for O'Hara, but in the Blaker case the outcome proved anything but routine.

Again and again, Bastos discovered, the potential informants in Port Hope had undergone a mysterious change of heart from the time he spoke with them on the telephone to the moment he actually arrived on their doorsteps. They were frightened, edgy. Most wouldn't even let Bastos in the door. One, a co-worker of Merv's, said he'd received a visit from a mean-looking guy with a shotgun under his coat. But most of the potential witnesses, who had said they were willing to help only hours before, wouldn't even tell Bastos that much. None were willing to give statements. Bastos would always remember the exact words used by one Port Hope resident: "We've all been told we don't want to get involved."

Years later Bastos would recall that he'd never felt so frustrated in a case, before or since. Merv would say that someone was willing to say or do something for his defence, and by the time Bastos got there it was like talking to a wall. People were scared speechless, and Bastos was certain he knew why.

The young investigator was quick to eliminate members of the Satan's Choice from a list of people who would go around intimidating potential witnesses. It might have been their style to do such a thing, but these were possible defence witnesses, people willing to testify on behalf of a member of the Choice. Also, whoever was doing the terrorizing always seemed to know exactly what Bastos's next move was going to be. Someone, the investigator concluded, was tapping the telephone in Terry O'Hara's Kingston office, and Bastos, now a lawyer himself, minces no words in explaining who he believes that someone was: "The witnesses had been warned off by the cops."

Terry O'Hara came to share the suspicions of his private investigator—he was absolutely convinced that his phones had been tapped. But in the years that followed, he never received official notification that this was so, as required by Canadian law, which meant that the wiretaps, if they ever existed, had been unlawful, had never been authorized by a judge, may not even have been known to the upper reaches in the police chain of command. Neither Bastos nor O'Hara had any proof for his suspicions, then or now. Yet wiretap evidence would come to play a critical role in the fate of one of the men accused of the murder of Bill Matiyek, raising serious questions about the police investigation of Matiyek's death. It would also lend credence, however inferential, to Bastos's and O'Hara's conviction that there was a dark undercurrent to some of the events taking place in Port Hope in the fall of 1979.

Back in Courtroom 21, meanwhile, Chris Meinhardt was continuing to lay the underpinning to the Crown theory that Matiyek's death had been the result of a premeditated gangland slaying. Randy Koehler, a Queen's bouncer and the boyfriend of Gayle Thompson, was called to give further evidence concerning the enmity that had existed between Matiyek and certain members of the Satan's Choice, if not the club as a whole. Dressed in a black T-shirt and blue jeans, Koehler recounted a December 1977 incident involving Matiyek and a number of Choice members, including Merv Blaker, Gord van Haarlem, Tee Hee Hoffman, Rick Sauvé, Gary Comeau, Larry Hurren, Brian Babcock, and Tommy "Retard" Horner. It had been a Saturday night, Koehler recalled, and all eight of the Choice members had arrived together. Three of them—Babcock, Horner, and Hoffman— had been wearing their colours, which they removed after the bouncer asked them to do so.

"The band had just started playing and I was sitting beside the men's washroom door with George Ozak who also worked there at the same time and Horner was walking, sort of walking around and Bill Matiyek come in through the front lounge door. . . . He was by himself. . . . And they had a few words which I couldn't hear and then I heard Matiyek say, 'I am through running. I have had enough of your fucking bullshit.' And he hit Horner in the face. . . . [Horner] came over my lap, a few feet away. . . . The rest of the [Choice] guys jumped up and pinned Matiyek in the inner alcove of the men's washroom and started punching and kicking him. . . . Myself, George Ozak, Rick Galbraith, and a member of the band that was playing, we got it broke up and everything seemed to settle down and Matiyek went over towards the bar and was leaning there and Babcock walked over. There was a couple words said I couldn't hear but then Babcock punched Matiyek in the mouth. . . . And then it was broke up again and when Babcock was walking away he pointed at Matiyek and said, 'We'll settle this later you fat fucker.' . . . The police come in and talked for maybe a minute to Bill and escorted him out the back door and the other guys, they were leaving."

No one in the club ever disputed Koehler's account of this incident, though there was some question as to precisely which members had been present, as Koehler himself would admit shortly under cross-examination. The brawl that erupted after Matiyek had struck Horner with enough force to send him flying through the air was a well-remembered event, just another in the long series of run-ins between the Choice—Horner particularly—and Bill Matiyek. The most serious incidents—Matiyek's shooting at Rick Sauvé's house, and another occasion on which certain Choice members had forcibly removed Matiyek's colours—were never introduced as evidence at the trial.

Almost invariably, even in the Crown's evidence, Bill Matiyek turns out to have been the aggressor. Why anyone in their right mind—even anyone so large as Matiyek—would purposely pick a fight with a member of the Satan's Choice while seven other club members were in close proximity is a mystery, the answer to which has gone with Bill Matiyek to his grave. Certainly Matiyek seems to have had a peculiar love-hate relationship with the Satan's Choice. On the night that he allegedly shot at Rick Sauvé's house, for example, Matiyek had been drinking, without incident, at the Choice clubhouse near Sauvé's home. But, after leaving, Matiyek also took a shot at the Choice clubhouse, according to Brian Babcock, before traveling on to Sauvé's. The next day Matiyek called Babcock to apologize, explaining that he'd been drinking wine and that wine made him do crazy things.

On the other hand, the Choice attitude towards Matiyek seems no less ambivalent. Judge Osborne had earlier ruled inadmissible a particularly intriguing bit of evidence from Lawrence Leon. The Golden Hawks president claimed to have overheard a conversation between Horner and Matiyek in which Horner had invited Matiyek to join the Satan's Choice. Matiyek had supposedly replied that if he wanted to join the Mickey Mouse Club he'd move to Disneyland.

The Crown was attempting to adduce this evidence as further proof of enmity between Matiyek and the Choice, but the conversation, if true, worked two ways. To be invited to strike for any club is a signal honour, a gesture of great respect, and it is not an offer that would be made lightly. That such an invitation should come from Horner, with whom Matiyek was always scrapping, is doubly confounding. But there seems little doubt that Matiyek would be drinking with some of the Peterborough Chapter Choice members one minute and fighting with them the next, drinking with them one day and shooting at them the next.

Under cross-examination, Koehler changed his story slightly—he now testified that neither Merv Blaker nor Rick Sauvé had been in the hotel on the night of the December 1977 brawl.

As he had at the preliminary, junior Crown Attorney Roland Harris conducted the examination-in-chief of Cathy Cotgrave. The former Queen's Hotel waitress repeated her earlier testimony: It had been a quiet evening until about 11 p.m., when fifteen or twenty men had arrived. She saw seven members of that group facing her in the courtroom today, and she pointed to everyone in the prisoner's dock except Gordy van Haarlem.

Rick Sauvé had gone to sit beside Bill and Jamie Hanna. Sauvé had spoken a few words to them which Cotgrave was unable to hear and then Hanna left the table. As she departed, one of the newcomers, dressed in a black-and-green-plaid lumber jacket, sat down in front of Matiyek's table. The man in the plaid jacket had been sitting at Jamie's table. A second man had approached Matiyek's table from the direction of the men's washroom. "He had his hands in his pockets when he was walking over and then he pulled his gun out with his left hand and had his right hand on the door, and then he shot and went right out the door." After that, she had fled to the washroom.

She had had a perfect view of Matiyek's table from her vantage point at the bar, Cotgrave recalled, had watched Sauvé take a seat on Matiyek's left, say something to Bill, whispering in his ear, and then Bill said something to Jamie and Rick said something to Jamie and Jamie left the table.

The man in the plaid lumber jacket was in the courtroom—she pointed to Jeff McLeod. He'd been sitting with Jamie Hanna and an old man before approaching Bill's table. The gunman had reddish, shoulder-length hair, he was about six feet tall, and heavy. Gary Comeau had been wearing a dark-coloured toque and some kind of green parka with the toque pulled down part way over his ears. The gunman had had "not a full beard, just sort of close to his face—and his eyes were pushed back, like, sunk in his head, and he had a big forehead . . . like a receding hairline. . . ."

Cotgrave, who was now convinced that Comeau had been the gunman, was offering a remarkably accurate description of Jeff McLeod as the gunman. Just as she had at the preliminary, Cotgrave had hopelessly confused McLeod with Comeau and Comeau with the gunman. It was Comeau, not McLeod, who had been sitting with Jamie Hanna and then joined Matiyek and Sauvé, except that Nutty had been wearing a black-leather jacket, not a green-and-black-plaid lumber jacket. And it was Jeff McLeod, not Comeau, who had the distinctive receding hairline that Cotgrave was describing with such telling accuracy. It was, indeed, the gunman who'd been wearing a green Hydro parka—she was right there—but he bore only the most general resemblance to either McLeod or Comeau, and his hair was dark brown, not blondish.

As she had watched events unfold, Cotgrave told the jury, "I looked over to [Bill] to sort of say 'get out' or something like that and he just sort of shrugged his shoulders. . . . He was drunk. . . . [The gunman] walked over and pulled a gun out of his pocket and shot Bill three times in the head."

Like Gayle Thompson, Cathy Cotgrave had become convinced that Comeau was the gunman by seeing him in person at the preliminary. "I was certain in my head, but I don't think I said anything about it. I was pretty sure about it, but when I walked into the courtroom and saw him at the preliminary hearing, then I was sure. There was no doubt in my mind at all."

Cotgrave had also picked Armand Sanguigni's picture out of all three of the photo line-ups she'd observed. She was certain she'd seen him in the pinball room with a group of other men, talking to Fred Jones. Jones "was talking to the people in there and he was waving his arms around, like he was in hysterics, or something."

She was also certain she'd seen Larry Hurren and David Hoffman standing beside the bar. "They seemed to be watching the phone—because they were standing by the phone and you can see the phone from where they were standing—like the receiver."

Bruce Affleck opened what was to be a gruelling series of cross-examinations of Cathy Cotgrave by questioning her identification of the gunman. How could she have seen his receding hairline if he'd had a toque pulled down over his ears? Cotgrave conceded that she couldn't have. It must have been an observation she had made later, while looking at the police photographs.

Kerbel questioned Cotgrave about her drug use and she repeated her testimony from the preliminary hearing—that she had shared a joint with Bill on the afternoon of the eighteenth. In all, Cotgrave would spend two full days on the witness stand, almost all of that time under cross-examination. Bernard Cugelman's grilling of the nineteen-year-old barmaid was particularly intense, and at one point it reduced her to tears. Cugelman zeroed in on the minutest of details—the exact description of Armand Sanguigni's moustache, the tiniest of conflicts between Cotgrave's statements at the preliminary hearing and her testimony at the trial. Cotgrave was, after all, the only witness who had identified Cugelman's client, Armand Sanguigni. If his lawyer could shake Cotgrave's identification, Armand Sanguigni would beat yet another murder charge. Cugelman's cross-examination was long and the courtroom atmosphere grew increasingly tense as the Crown Attorneys rose repeatedly to object to Cugelman's questions.

Still, near the end of her ordeal Cotgrave, like Gayle Thompson before her, had begun to rally against her inquisitors. At one point Cotgrave told Terry O'Hara she hadn't understood one of his questions.

"Let me start over."

"If you are trying to confuse me, you are doing a good job," Cotgrave observed.

"I am sorry. I don't want to mislead."

"I bet," Cotgrave answered drily.

As he watched her from the prisoner's dock, Gary Comeau, almost despite himself, had been mightily impressed by the testimony of Cathy Cotgrave. She, along with Gayle Thompson, had now positively identified him as the gunman, and there was no doubt in Nutty's mind that he was now in serious trouble. Cotgrave, especially, struck him as a most convincing witness. For the first time Gary Comeau, ever the bouncing, buoyant optimist, felt a clutch of panic. Only one thing could save him: the missing bullet. And now here it was, Thanksgiving already, the trial had been under way for a full month, and he still hadn't even had an X-ray. He bugged Kerbel about it, but his lawyer told Gary that he'd encountered an unexpected obstacle: he'd been unable to locate a single radiologist in the greater London area willing to X-ray a biker charged with first-degree murder. They just didn't want to get involved, and they didn't want to have to appear in court. Kerbel confided to Comeau that he'd even offered up to two thousand dollars "under the table" to any radiologist willing to do the job, and still no takers. But somehow, some way, they had to get that bullet.

XXVIII

AFTER A THREE-DAY RECESS for the Thanksgiving holiday weekend, court resumed on the morning of Tuesday, October 9, and Jamie Hanna continued the Crown evidence. Bill Matiyek's girlfriend repeated the evidence she'd given at the preliminary, describing a night of heavy drinking, the slap she'd received from Fred Jones, and how she'd moved to another table.

When a group of fifteen or twenty men suddenly entered the hotel, she had told Cathy Cotgrave to call the police, and then gone back over to Bill's table. "I sat on his right side. . . . Rick Sauvé came over to the table and he whispered in Bill's left ear and he then turned to me and said, 'Chick, get the fuck away from the table.' I looked at Bill and Bill agreed with him and said, 'Yes. I think you had better leave,' and he said, 'Good-bye,' and I left."

Rick Sauvé had remained at the table, standing to Bill's left, she recalled. About two or three seconds later she'd heard the first shot.

As he had at the preliminary, Howard Kerbel tried unsuccessfully to get a description from Hanna of the man who'd sat down with her and the old man at her table. She couldn't remember what the newcomer had looked like, what he had said, or whether he had introduced himself. She did remember that the gunman was left-handed, however, and she had had a clear view of him. He was roughly six feet tall with a blond beard and a blond moustache.

Hanna told Jack Grossman that she was certain that Rick Sauvé was not the gunman, and she repeated that she'd last seen Sauvé standing to Bill's left. Grossman doubtless hoped that the jury would pick up on this inconsistency. Sauvé had now been seen in three different places or positions at once, by four major Crown witnesses. Gayle Thompson had put him one chair away to Bill's right during or moments before the shooting, while Cathy Cotgrave and Sue Foote had seen him sitting to Bill's immediate left. Jamie Hanna, too, had seen him on Bill's left, but standing, not sitting.

Roland Harris called David Gillispie to the witness stand. Gillispie repeated his account of going over to speak with Blaker and Sauvé, where he had knelt beside them at their table. "And then one person came to the table, making a statement, which I overheard." Gillispie pointed at Gary Comeau in the prisoner's dock. "He appeared dressed in a parka-type jacket, standing about five foot eight, approximately, weighing about two hundred pounds, fair-haired, facial beard of about one and a half inches." He was about twenty-seven years old and had a slightly receding hairline with "two or three heavy lines in the forehead, wrinkles, like—" Although Gary Comeau had wrinkles in his forehead (as did Jeff McLeod), Gillispie's estimates of Comeau's height and weight were far off the mark. Comeau was six feet tall and weighed at least 250 pounds on the night of the shooting.

The man whom Gillispie had identified as Comeau then directed a question to Blaker and Sauvé: "Are we going to do it to this fat fucker now or what?"

"What did Blaker and Sauvé say?"

"They looked—they glanced at one another, they glanced at me, and they had a look of almost to say with their eyes, 'Why would this man say this in front of myself being there?' "

Gillispie then returned to the shuffleboard room briefly, before re-entering the bar. "I noticed Rick Sauvé sitting at the Matiyek table at this time. . . . Shortly after that, I had noticed persons, as many as eight, accumulating around the Matiyek table. . . . They were facing inwards towards the table. . . . They were standing closely to the table—all seemed to be directing their concentration towards the table area. . . . I couldn't see anything at the table. . . . Moments after I had noted the accumulation 'round the table, I did notice three gunshots and people fled from the hotel." Perhaps ten minutes had elapsed from the arrival of the fifteen people until the time of the shooting.

Howard Kerbel wasted little time in hammering away at the inconsistencies between David Gillispie's various prior statements. Gillispie had made a statement to police within hours of the shooting, early on the morning of October 19. He had given a second sworn statement to the Port Hope police on November 28, 1978, after having, he agreed, discussed the events with Jamie Hanna, Cathy Cotgrave, Gayle Thompson, Rod Stewart, and, indeed, with three or four others. Gillispie couldn't recall the exact dates of the discussions, but he did remember having conversations about the shooting with the other witnesses several times at the Ganaraska Hotel. They had discussed what happened, who they thought had been in the hotel at the time, which members of the Satan's Choice had been present, and who the gunman was.

Then, on December 29, 1978, Gillispie had given yet a third statement to police. He agreed with Kerbel that the December 29 statement had contained "a very substantial change" from what he had told police two months earlier. In the third statement, Gillispie had sworn that the Choice members, including Blaker and Sauvé, entered the hotel after Gillispie, while in his first statement he told police that the bikers were already in the hotel when he had arrived. "In my previous statement it was wrote down wrong." By December 29 another significant addition had been made to Gillispie's recollection for the first time. "In addition there were three or four men standing around Matiyek's table. The next time I looked back is when I heard three shots. I couldn't see Matiyek. . . ." Kerbel read the statement aloud.

And wasn't it true that he hadn't changed his statement until after discussing the shooting with others, and after Sergeant McReelis had told him what Sue Foote had said?

"Yes."

Kerbel returned to the "fat fucker" statement. Again Gillispie said he was certain of the exact wording. Yet in his statement to police on October 19 Gillispie had remembered it somewhat differently. "Are we going to do it with this fat fucker or what?" Then, at the preliminary hearing Gillispie had testified that it was either "Are we going to get on with this fat fucker" or "Are we going to do it to this fat fucker now or what?"

Gillispie insisted that his current recollection was the right one—the remark had been "do it to," not "do it with" or "get on with" as he had earlier stated.

While the strenuous cross-examinations of Gillispie uncovered some inconsistencies in his story, the "fat fucker" statement, in one form or another, remained very much on the record. There was no doubt that Gillispie had told the police about it within hours of the shooting, and it seemed highly incriminating, revealing foreknowledge, criminal intent, perhaps even evidence of planning and deliberation, at least on the part of Sauvé and Blaker, who were alleged to have heard it, and Comeau, or whoever uttered it.

Still more damning testimony was to come in the form of another surprise Crown witness. William Goodwin told the jury that he'd been a resident of Port Hope for eight or nine years, that he knew both Merv Blaker and Rick Sauvé, and Rick's older brother Larry. It was while visiting at Larry Sauvé's in July of 1978 that he'd heard a discussion relating to Bill Matiyek.

He'd gone to Larry's home to borrow a four-wheel-drive truck to pull his boat out of the water. Goodwin happened to mention that Bill Matiyek was having trouble with his bike, a brand-new Harley-Davidson Sportster, and when Matiyek's name came up Rick had replied, "'Oh, he's a goof,' or 'He's a fuckin' goof,' or something like that. . . . I said, 'Well, he could eat youse guys' or something like that. . . . Then Rick returned and said, 'Well, he won't be around very long,' and then a little later on he said, 'I'm going to—' either 'I'm going to blow his brains out' or 'He's going to have his brains blown out' and there about the 'brains blown out' part, I got. . . . He seemed serious about it I guess; Rick's a very soft-spoken guy, and so he seemed serious, you know, but I never thought no more about it at the time."

The defence was at a distinct disadvantage when it came time to cross-examine Goodwin. They had learned of his existence only the night before, and the only thing they had to go on was Goodwin's statement to the police; there had been no time to independently investigate his story.

Rick Sauvé listened to the evidence unfold with growing disgust and disbelief. As far as Sauvé was concerned, the Crown witnesses were flat-out wrong about what he had and hadn't said and heard. He'd never heard the "fat fucker" statement, from Nutty or anyone else. He hadn't been involved in the hassle with Matiyek that Lawrence Leon remembered. What could he do? The hardest thing to fight against was something like that: the harder you fought it, the more it seemed to be true.

Sauvé remembered the day that Goodwin was talking about. He had gone to Larry's to get a piece welded onto the oil tank of his Harley. He'd been in and out of the house, just as Goodwin said, and he might have had one drink. That was it. But he'd never talked about Bill Matiyek, had never even had a discussion of any kind with Goodwin.

He'd known Bill Matiyek for years; their families were related by marriage, and they'd gone on runs together before Rick joined the club. He'd always gotten along well with Matiyek, at least until Bill had taken a shot at his house, with Sharon and Angie inside. Even then he hadn't gone after Bill with a gun, but with a baseball bat, which seemed only fair, since Bill was twice his size. And once he'd caught up with him, Rick had insisted on taking Matiyek on one-on-one, and Bill had backed down, and apologized.

That was just the way Rick was. He believed in certain things. He believed in the club brotherhood, in a certain code of honour. Hell, club standards of trust and respect were higher than anything he'd ever found among citizens. Why couldn't anyone understand that? Just because you were a biker didn't mean you couldn't be a gentleman.

Whether some of the Crown witnesses were lying about them or not, all eight of the accused could now sense that the tide was running heavily against them, and in the days after the Thanksgiving recess the question of the third bullet assumed ever greater urgency. At long last, Gary Comeau was taken out for X-rays, but, for reasons that were never explained to him, the X-rays weren't taken. On a second trip the X-rays were done and everyone's hopes had soared. But the next day when the film had been developed, it revealed no bullet in Nutty's left shoulder or upper back in the area around the entrance wound. The results depressed everybody, especially Nutty, since it was now obvious that he was being set up as the gunman. In the absence of evidence to the contrary, it looked more and more as if Gary Comeau, at least, was going to be convicted of murder. The words he'd spoken that fateful night almost one year ago as they'd sped away from the Queen's Hotel—"Well, at least they can't say *I* did it, I got shot, too"—came back to haunt them now with bitter irony.

Finally, Gordy van Haarlem took matters into his own hands—literally. One night in the Detention Centre he ordered Nutty to lie face down on the floor. "C'mon, Nutty, we gotta find that fuckin' thing." Dogmap began to work Gary over like a masseur, probing every inch of Nutty's back with his fingers. Van Haarlem started high up on Gary's shoulder where the bullet had gone in, and around the scar left by the "operation" in Windsor, then he worked his way down Nutty's back. The probing seemed to take hours, and Gordy was about to resign himself—and all of them—to defeat, when he thought he felt something. He pressed harder.

"Hey, what's this?" He *did* feel something, a small lump, barely noticeable, halfway down Gary's back on the lefthand side. "C'mere," Gordy said to one of the other guys, all of whom were watching and cracking crass jokes despite themselves. "Feel that?" The other guy thought he did feel something, just barely. The others felt it too, the faintest of round little lumps, buried somewhere beneath Nutty's skin.

"That's it! That's gotta be fuckin' it!" Dogmap exclaimed. They eyed Gary's back dubiously while Nutty lay there on the floor, his excitement growing, but feeling incredulous too. The only problem was, the lump was at least a foot away from where the bullet had entered. How could that be? "Ya gotta tell Kerbel, man. Tell him ya gotta get one more X-ray, but of your whole fuckin' back next time."

The next day before court Gary did tell Kerbel about Gordy's discovery. Kerbel agreed to try and arrange one more set of X-rays. Maybe the lump wasn't the bullet, maybe Nutty had a tumor or something. But it was sure worth a try. They were drowning men now, and they knew it.

Meanwhile, in Courtroom 21, Chris Meinhardt and Roland Harris continued to methodically build the case against the accused. If Rod Stewart, contractor, Port Hope town councillor, and eyewitness to murder, wasn't the most important witness against them, he would certainly prove to be the most memorable. As he had at the preliminary, Stewart quickly established himself as an excellent witness. He described how he'd gone to the Queen's to talk with the owner about an impending renovation job, and how he'd been joined by two friends at the bar.

"We were sitting at the bar, talking, and without really noticing that anybody had come in, we realized that there were about fifteen people around us, so they came in together, and they just seemed to be there all of a sudden. . . . [The situation] was very tense and very apprehensive. We immediately identified this group as a motorcycle gang. . . . They congregated in the area behind where I was sitting. . . . Matiyek was called to the phone. . . . I observed him coming in what seemed to be a swaggering way to the phone . . . I think he was drunk. I watched him on the telephone. He appeared to be distraught, nervous. . . . I heard him say, 'It feels very lonely here.' . . . He looked very frightened."

After talking for a minute or two, Matiyek "hung up the telephone. . . .

He walked through this group of people, and he sort of went through the traffic, and the traffic, the group of people, sort of went behind him. Because I know that my feeling of apprehension eased somewhat, when these people left the immediate vicinity of me . . . I saw these people go. I saw them end up—I didn't see them walk across the room, but I saw them end up at Matiyek's table. I saw that by turning around to find out why they weren't behind me. . . .

"I saw the group in what appeared to me to be a horseshoe shape around Matiyek's table. I heard three shots. I didn't identify the first shot or the second shot, but by the third shot I knew it was gunshots. I turned very quickly and I saw the group dismantling and exiting through the archway that leads to what is called the pinball room. I saw one person still facing the general direction of the table, making what appeared to me to be a concealing gesture—that is putting his hand into his belt or under his coat, and that person was wearing a green parka and had dirty blond, browny blond hair. And I saw that person reel to the left and exit through the same door. In fact, while these people were leaving, I was on my way across the room to Matiyek—"

Stewart's voice cracked, and then broke. He began to cry.

"Would you like a glass of water?" asked Roland Harris, who was conducting the direct examination.

"Did you want to sit down?" Coulter Osborne leaned towards the witness from his bench. "They will bring a chair up—just take your time."

Stewart sat down in the chair and buried his head in his hands.

"Do you want to take a break now for lunch, Mr. Stewart? Would that be easier?" Judge Osborne inquired solicitously.

"I would like to get this through," Stewart replied, attempting to regain his composure. "Without thinking about myself, I ran over and found this—this person that I know—and he was all—"

"And it wasn't a very pleasant sight, I take it," interjected Osborne, hoping to avoid some of the more gruesome details.

"No, it was a very unpleasant sight. He had a hole in his face. He wasn't dead. His eyes were open and he was breathing."

"I think you could make life a little easier for this witness, Mr. Harris. There is no need to go into this type of detail."

"Well, I think it may be of some relevance as to whether he was alive."

"He was alive. . . . He had on a kind of like a hunting jacket, and I tried to cover him and eventually somebody brought towels and we had some crazy idea that we could do first aid, and I am sort of halfway trained, in first aid, and so we made that attempt. . . . I couldn't see, but I guess I realized there wasn't very much I was able to do for him."

There had been about a dozen men in the horseshoe in front of the Matiyek table, Stewart recalled. The only one of the accused he could identify was David Hoffman, who had been standing at the bar beside the telephone.

As he had at the preliminary, Bruce Affleck once again decided against cross-examining Rod Stewart, so Howard Kerbel took the lead for the defence. Stewart denied discussing the shooting with any of the other witnesses. He did, however, remember comparing his observations with Peter Murdoch and Peter LaBrash, with whom he'd been drinking that night, and, Stewart conceded, they had discovered substantial differences in what each of them had observed. "It seems to me there were discrepancies . . . and we found that surprising. . . . What we found so surprising was that we all saw different things at the same event."

Stewart also conceded he'd had difficulty identifying any of the men he'd seen in the hotel from the photo line-up. "I found that picture thing extremely frustrating, because I saw familiar faces, but I couldn't say they were at the hotel. . . . I was only able to say that about Mr. Hoffman."

Ed Martin zeroed in on Stewart's identification of his client. Had the witness identified any pictures of David Hoffman during the photo line-up? Stewart said he couldn't remember. (He had, in fact, failed to identify any of the accused, according to OPP constable Denis.) But Stewart stood resolutely by his identification. "Mr. Hoffman stands out like a sore thumb, because he's got that lovely pigtail, and that's why I identified him." Stewart had also not seen Larry Hurren in the area of the telephone beside Hoffman, where a number of other eyewitnesses remembered seeing him, and where, in fact, Hurren had been.

Using the Judge's bench as the bar and a book as the pillar, Terry O'Hara asked Stewart to reconstruct his vantage point for the jury. Stewart agreed that he had turned to his left to avoid the large vertical post, and to talk with his friends Murdoch and LaBrash, and that his back was turned 180 degrees to Matiyek's table. The stool seats did not swivel, so only by turning his whole body could Stewart have possibly seen the "horseshoe," which had not been seen by Gayle Thompson, Cathy Cotgrave, or Jamie Hanna.

"And would you agree that you didn't look in that fashion for very long?"

"I would agree."

But Stewart refused to concede that he had only glanced at the Matiyek table. "It was a purposeful look. . . . It wasn't a glance—a glance is too fast."

That afternoon after the court had adjourned for the day following Stewart's testimony, the lawyers and their clients held a meeting in the deserted courtroom, while the police guards waited outside. For security reasons, all sixteen lawyers and clients were unable to meet at the Detention Centre. The usual client-lawyer conference rooms at the Centre were too small for such a large gathering, and the defendants and their lawyers were suspicious that any such meeting at the jail would be subject to electronic eavesdropping. They felt more secure in the empty courtroom, and the topic under discussion was delicate and highly sensitive—the advisability of entering into a plea bargain.

In addition to his other duties as senior defence counsel, Bruce Affleck had been selected to act as a go-between to arrange a possible deal with the Crown. Affleck had approached Meinhardt about this before the trial began, but the senior Crown Attorney had declined to discuss a deal before trial. But some time after the trial was under way, Meinhardt had had a change of heart, and he approached Affleck with an offer. Sam McReelis, for one, was growing homesick, Meinhardt told Affleck, and Her Majesty's justice would be served if the defence would give up the shooter for second-degree murder, if Comeau and Sauvé would agree to a ten-to-fourteen-year sentence, and all of the others would serve five to seven. Tough terms, to be sure, but then this was the opening gambit in a bargaining process.

The accused discussed all of this at length among themselves. The bulk of the Crown's eyewitness evidence had now been heard, and the plea bargain offer must have appealed strongly to the self-interest of some of the accused. It was now obvious that Gary and Rick were in the most trouble. There was only the scantiest evidence, on the other hand, against Gordy van Haarlem and Armand Sanguigni. Only Helen Mitchell had seen van Haarlem, only Cathy Cotgrave had testified against Sanguigni.

Even here there was a divergence in self-interest: Armand had in fact been in the hotel, Gordy had not. Then there was Tee Hee's position to consider. He had been positively identified by no fewer than five eyewitnesses, including two of the strongest Crown witnesses, Gayle Thompson and Cathy Cotgrave, even though he'd been home in Kitchener at the time of the shooting. Jeff McLeod had been identified by only two eyewitnesses and there'd been no evidence at all that he'd actually done anything. Multiple witnesses had now identified Hurren and Blaker, whose lawyers had already admitted they were there, but, apart from Blaker's having supposedly heard the alleged "fat fucker" statement, there was no evidence that they'd played an active role in the shooting. But Comeau, the alleged gunman, and Sauvé, for his "kiss-of-death" remark, his presence at Matiyek's table at the time of the shooting, and his alleged threats against Matiyek, were the most deeply implicated. Who knew what kind of sentence Gary and Rick might get if the case went to the jury?

It was a question of self-interest versus club bonding and brotherhood, of "truth" versus legal proof of establishing their own destinies, however unpleasant, versus the uncertainty of what the jury might decide. Maybe they'd all be acquitted, there was still that chance.

In the face of all this, the accused demonstrated remarkable solidarity. If it would help Ricky, van Haarlem decided, perhaps remembering the time Sauvé had taken Gordy's own drug beef on himself, then he would, reluctantly, bite it and serve five years in the pen, even though he was totally innocent.

Tee Hee Hoffman was in a similar situation, but with an impressive amount of evidence arrayed against him. The big Kitchener biker now believed he would be convicted despite his innocence. But this deal, which was tantamount to a confession of guilt, bothered him even more. It wasn't doing time that troubled him, but the confession. If the jury convicted him, that was one thing, something over which he had no control. But if he confessed to involvement in a murder with which he'd had nothing to do, what was he doing but compounding a self-corroding lie?

Rick Sauvé was unabashedly in favour of cutting a deal. "After the lying started in court," he recalled, "I said, 'Fuck, guys, let's grab it.'"

But there was also the question of giving up the gunman. It was obvious by now the Crown had nothing on Lorne, and none of the accused were going to rat on him, no matter what. If he'd agree to give himself up, however, that was a different question altogether.

Out of this welter of conflicting hopes and self-interest the defence cobbled a counter-proposal: the shooter would plead guilty to manslaughter, the rest would enter a guilty plea to wounding, and the Crown would cut van Haarlem loose. "Tell 'em to cut Sanguigni loose, too," Armand demanded, almost as an afterthought.

Affleck relayed a counter-offer along these lines to Meinhardt, who was slow in responding. It appeared to defence counsel and the accused alike that Meinhardt couldn't conclude any deal without clearing it with senior officials in the Attorney General's office first. Perhaps Roy McMurtry himself was involved, they speculated. It had been only four months since McMurtry had promised the Ontario public that his office would seek stiffer sentences against bikers, after all.

So far as anyone can remember, Meinhardt never responded to the defence counter-offer, except to add another Crown demand: he wanted the accused to sign some kind of statement along with their guilty pleas. The statement would confirm that Matiyek's killing had been the start of a biker war, likely the Angels-Outlaws war the police officials had been predicting.

That tore it. No one was willing to sign such a bullshit statement, and even Rick and Nutty had to agree.

The plea-bargaining talks sputtered, and then stalled, never to resume, and now there was no turning back. Barring a mistrial or some other major legal miracle, the fates of the eight accused would be decided by the jury.

XXIX

COURT WAS LATE in resuming on the morning of Friday, October 12, the day after the courtroom meeting. Judge Osborne apologized to the jury for the delay, explaining that "there were medical hospital problems this morning." He did not elaborate, but everyone involved in the prosecution and the defence knew what those mysterious "medical problems" were. Gary Comeau had received one last round of X-rays. The results were still unknown and an air of keen anticipation hung over the prisoner's dock. Would the negatives reveal that Gordy really had found the missing third bullet, the object that each of them fervently believed would prove their salvation? And there was a second reason to feel excited this morning. William Goodwin, the witness who had testified briefly for the Crown the day before, was returning for cross-examination and the defence team was about to spring a surprise of its own.

As David Newman rose to cross-examine the witness, the air suddenly became charged. Larry Hurren's lawyer, who had played only a minor role in earlier cross-examinations, quickly became excited and oddly aggressive in his questioning. Newman's attitude drew repeated objections from Chris Meinhardt and several admonitions from Judge Osborne.

The young lawyer suggested that Goodwin had made a number of mistakes in his testimony, "and the reason you are making a number of mistakes is that, for reasons unknown to me, you are biased in giving your evidence here today in court?"

"I have to disagree with you, sir, I am not biased, none whatsoever."

"None whatsoever," Newman repeated, almost mockingly. "You don't feel any personal involvement, other than giving your evidence here in court today, is that correct?"

"The only personal thing I feel is I didn't want to be involved in this."

"You don't feel you are part of a team now or something, do you? . . . I am going to suggest to you that Tuesday night last you were sitting in the coffee shop, which is called The Wooden Spoon."

"Yes, and you were sitting right beside me."

Goodwin remembered seeing Newman, remembered running into a schoolteacher from Port Hope, remembered telling the man from back home that he was in London for a trial.

"And I suggest to you, sir, in discussing the trial you said to him, 'I think we've got all eight of these guys' "—Newman was shouting at Goodwin and Judge Osborne interrupted.

"Mr. Newman—"

"I don't—" Goodwin tried to answer, shouting back at Newman.

"The witness has demonstrated good hearing and he does not need to be yelled at," Osborne said sternly.

"And I didn't say that, neither!" Goodwin insisted.

"Let me finish, sir. I suggest that you said to this gentleman, 'I think we've got all eight of these guys for twenty-five years.' Do you remember saying that?"

"No, I disagree with saying that, too."

"I further suggest to you, sir, that you said, 'My only wish is that these guys, these eight guys, get twenty-five years.' Do you remember saying that?"

"I wouldn't say 'eight' because I didn't realize there was eight involved."

"I further suggest to you, sir, that you laughed and said that you will be—I don't recall the exact age, fifty-four or fifty-five in twenty-five years, 'And by that time, I don't care what happens to me,' and you laughed. Do you remember saying that?"

"I didn't say that to him. . . ."

But Goodwin remembered meeting this man? Yes. Having a conversation with him? Yes. Seeing Newman in the coffee shop? Yes.

"I just know there was a fellow I recognized and three ladies sittin' there."

"With him? That's correct. You remember that?"

"Yes."

"And you don't remember saying, 'I think we've got these guys for twenty-five years.'"

"No, I don't."

"Are you denying that you said that?"

"I am not denying. I said I don't recall."

"I see. You are not denying that, are you?"

"I don't recall. I doubt very much if I said that."

"But you are not denying it, are you?"

"I already said that, didn't I? . . . I can't say if I did say it, but I doubt very much if I did."

The sixth week of the trial closed with the testimony of one Finn Nielsen, a firearms examiner with the Centre of Forensic Sciences in Toronto. After a microscopic examination of the bullet which had earlier been identified as the one extracted from Matiyek's brain, Nielsen had concluded that it was "a jacketed 9 millimetre soft point projectile . . . and it is my opinion that it was fired from a revolver rifled to Colt Rifle manufacturing specifications."

Nielsen had also examined the handgun that had been discovered in Bill Matiyek's clothing. It was a .32-calibre semi-automatic pistol, he reported,

"with a tendency to misfire because of an extremely light firing pin-fall."
He had also received eight unfired cartridges, which were suitable for use in
the pistol.

Chris Meinhardt recounted how each of the three bullets fired had struck
Bill Matiyek and then he asked Nielsen a very strange question: "Does that
assist you at all as to whether there would be one or more persons who
could have inflicted such wounds on the deceased?"

"I don't think I would like to answer that."

Howard Kerbel, who had been busily scribbling notes, snapped suddenly
to attention. "I'm sorry. What was the answer?"

"I would like not to answer that. I don't think I could say."

The significance of Meinhardt's question was not lost upon either Gary
Comeau or his lawyer, and it marked a subtle but substantial shift in the
Crown's case. This was the first public mention of an entirely new police
hypothesis: that Bill Matiyek had been shot not by a single gunman, *but by
more than one*. To Gary, the implications of this single, seemingly innocent
question were enormous. It meant that Meinhardt already knew, or suspected, the result of the most recent X-rays—that they did, indeed, show
a bullet lodged in Gary's back, the missing third bullet. If that were so, and
if the bullet matched the one found in Matiyek's brain, then it would have
been a physical impossibility for Gary to have been the gunman. But if
Comeau hadn't shot Matiyek, who had? There was not a jot of evidence that
any one of the other seven accused had been the gunman. The logical conclusion of this chain of reasoning would have been disastrous to the Crown's
case. After a lengthy investigation, police had accused eight men of killing
Bill Matiyek in cold blood and *the murderer was not among them*. Such a conclusion was unthinkable.

But try it another way: Gary Comeau had been shot. But what if there
had been another gunman? Comeau was the first gunman, the one who had
been so positively identified by Cathy Cotgrave and Gayle Thompson. But
the second shooter had misfired, accidentally shooting Comeau. It would
never stand close scrutiny, but such a theory seemed the only way to salvage
the Crown's case against Comeau.

And, to Gary, Meinhardt's question, his willingness to suggest a second
phantom gunman before the X-rays had even been entered as evidence, was
indicative of something else. It reinforced a suspicion that Comeau had

harbored for months and that he would assert tirelessly in the desperate years that lay ahead: *the police had known all along that he'd been shot, that he could not have killed Matiyek*. And yet they had tried to set him up at the trial. From the night of his arrest, when they'd closely inspected the wound on his arm, to Sam McReelis's remark to his mother during the search of the house (What had he said? *"We think Gary got shot."*), the police had known of his innocence. And then they'd seized and suppressed the only positive evidence Gary'd had to prove the truth: his black-leather jacket. There had been a conspiracy around Bill Matiyek's death all right, Gary Comeau thought grimly, but the brotherhood who'd committed it was not the brotherhood on trial.

Confident now that the information would be of the greatest import later, Howard Kerbel drew from Nielsen specific details about the one bullet that had been found intact. The firearms expert explained that he had not been given the weapon that fired the bullet to examine, but the bullet itself possessed several unique characteristics. It was consistent with Colt-revolver rifling "with six grooves, left-hand twist: that is, there are six lands and grooves in the inside of the barrel, and the projectile, when it leaves the barrel, is spinning to the left." The bullet also revealed "skidmarks," a property peculiar to projectiles fired from revolvers, as opposed to automatic or semi-automatic pistols.

"I take it in your experience you have seen a lot of crazy things that projectiles have done?"

"Yes, I have."

"And I take it you have seen instances in which a projectile has passed through a person's body . . . and has lodged itself in another person's body?"

"Yes, I have."

"We have heard some evidence from a pathologist that one projectile which eventually exited from Mr. Matiyek's body has not been found. . . ."

"Yes."

The bullet had left an apparent burn across the jacket sleeve of the deceased before entering the area under his chin, Kerbel explained. "Would it have been deflected to any great extent by the contact with the arm?"

"It is quite likely that it would have been affected in the way that you described. . . ."

And could the witness determine with any degree of accuracy the direction from which the shots came?

"Well, probably to his [Matiyek's] left side somewhere. . . ."

That concluded Kerbel's cross-examination of the witness for the moment. But "there may be certain other questions that I would want to put to him once I have had an opportunity to look into some other matters. . . ."

There was jubilation when they finally received word about the X-rays—the film clearly showed an entire bullet halfway down Nutty's back, lodged between two ribs. Gordy had been right. Gary was delighted, and amazed that he'd been walking around for almost a year with a whole bullet inside him, and he hadn't felt a thing. He felt frustrated too, though. If only they'd found it sooner. Imagine how they could have used it to cross-examine Cathy Cotgrave and Gayle Thompson! They could have left the credibility of these key, seemingly reliable eyewitnesses in shreds.

The next step, obviously, was to have the bullet surgically removed and compared with the one recovered from Matiyek's body. But that would not prove as easy as it sounded. One might have expected that on simple humanitarian grounds, if no other, the bullet would have been removed at once. Not so. There was no evidence that the object in Gary's back was life-threatening, so there was no immediate medical urgency to perform the requisite surgery. But, furthermore, no evidence had been introduced in court, so far, to prove that Gary himself had been shot on the very night Matiyek was killed. So, legally as well, there was no warrant for operating to remove the bullet. Comeau and his lawyer consequently found themselves in a classic catch-22 situation: In the absence of his jacket, there was no proof Gary had been shot on that particular night, and without evidence he'd been shot that night, they wouldn't remove the bullet. And so Gary Comeau would sit each day in the courtroom for the rest of the Crown evidence, the alleged killer of Bill Matiyek as far as the media, the public, and the jury were concerned, with the irrefutable proof of his innocence inside his own body.

Although it would yet occupy two full weeks of testimony, the Crown case was beginning to wind down. With a couple of exceptions, the remaining witnesses for the prosecution were relatively minor, their evidence-in-chief and cross-examinations brief. The pace of the trial began to quicken perceptibly.

On Monday, October 15, Gary's X-rays were filed as an exhibit. It seemed to Gary that Chris Meinhardt was visibly shaken by this new and wholly unexpected evidence. But the senior Crown Attorney from Lindsay plunged doggedly on with the Crown evidence. The payroll supervisor for General Wire and Cable, Rick Sauvé's former employer, presented time sheets which revealed that Sauvé had been absent from work in the days immediately following the Matiyek shooting. A representative of the United Tire and Rubber Manufacturing company produced documents pertaining to Merv Blaker which showed basically the same thing.

Julie Joncas, bookkeeper, supervisor of waitresses, and girlfriend of Leo Powell, owner of the Queen's Hotel, produced copies of three registered letters that had been sent to the officers of the Peterborough Chapter of the Satan's Choice, informing them in May 1978 that all club members were banned from the hotel. (Rick Sauvé and Merv Blaker would afterwards deny ever receiving such letters.)

Constable Gary Woods of the Port Hope Police Department testified that he had taken part in the arrest of Gary Comeau.

"What items were seized?" asked Kerbel on cross-examination.

"What items were seized?"

"Perhaps just to shorten it up . . . were there any jackets, coats?"

"Not that I am aware of. No."

"I am interested in Mr. Comeau and any clothing that may have been seized in relationship to Mr. Comeau."

Woods checked his notebook. "I have no clothing down here. . . . No, I have no coat noted here."

A second Port Hope Police Department constable, William Wakely (who was exhibits officer for the investigation), followed Constable Woods, and Howard Kerbel continued his search for the one piece of evidence that could get the bullet removed from his client's body.

"Other than the material or the items that you have produced in court today, did you come into possession of any articles of clothing other than these, belonging to Mr. Comeau?"

"No."

"Did you come into possession of any articles of clothing that could not be attributed to any one of the accused?"

"No."

"And did you have any contact with or see any black-leather jackets in the course of your investigation, performing the function of exhibit officer?"

"No, all they had is what was shown here today."

The parade of brief Crown witnesses continued. Mrs. Winnifred Haines, of Bell Canada's security department, presented Chris Meinhardt with a batch of yellow customer record cards which identified a subscriber's name, address, and telephone number. She had brought records for telephones registered to Richard Sauvé, one K. Blaker (Merv's wife), Eugene King (Gary's stepfather), Tom Beckett (the Kitchener Choice clubhouse phone), and David Hoffman, among others. Each card was duly entered as an exhibit.

Mrs. Haines also identified a toll record for long-distance calls made from David Hoffman's home number between September 24, 1978, and the morning of October 19, 1978. Mrs. Haines read the time, date, number called, and charge for each of the long-distance calls. "On the 19th of the tenth month a call to Port Hope, Ontario; number called was 885-2039; a one-minute call; the hour that call was placed was 02, which is 2 a.m. in the morning. Again Code 8 (direct-distance dialling), time of the call 0230 hours, a minimum charge of 25 cents." *Two bits*, thought Tee Hee, the accountant, to himself bitterly. He knew what was coming next. A two-bit phone call was going to be the most expensive long-distance telephone call of his life.

After having the telephone bill marked as an exhibit (number 100), Meinhardt wheeled smoothly around to face the witness. "Now you have indicated, Mrs. Haines, that the fourth call you mentioned that was placed on the nineteenth of October to Port Hope, telephone number 416-885-2039, do you have a card for that number?"

"Yes, I do."

"And would you please tell us to whom that number is registered?"

"It is registered to a Roger, initial K, as in Kenneth, Davey. D-A-V-E-Y."

It is not difficult to imagine Rick Sauvé's feelings as he watched Chris Meinhardt's next witness enter the witness-box and swear to tell the truth, and nothing but the truth. Roger! It had been six years, almost to the day, since Roger had been the best man at his wedding. Who among them then would ever have believed it would come to this? Rick charged with first-degree murder and his best friend testifying against him. And lying! The half-truths that Rick swore Lawrence Leon and David Gillispie and William Goodwin had told against him had hurt. But the testimony that Roger Davey was about to give must have cut Rick Sauvé to the quick.

Roger told Meinhardt that he categorized himself as "a friend" of the accused Rick Sauvé and "more of an acquaintance" of the deceased Bill Matiyek.

"And I understand that in the early morning hours of October 19, 1978, a telephone call came to your residence?"

"Mm-hmm," Davey mumbled. The call had come in about 2 a.m., Davey recounted, and his wife had answered. "She woke me up and I took the message."

"And who was on the other end of the phone?"

"Mr. Sauvé."

"And will you please tell us what the conversation was?"

"He asked me or us, me and my wife, to relay a message to his wife."

"And what was the nature of the message that he wished you to relate to his wife?"

"Simply that he himself and Mr. Blaker would be out of town for a few days and he asked us to ask his wife to phone their employers and tell them that . . . they wouldn't be in town for a few days."

"And did you hear anything in the background as you were speaking with Mr. Sauvé?"

"Well, there was loud music; sounded like a party."

"And did you ask Mr. Sauvé anything as you were speaking with him?"

"Well, I asked him where the party was."

"And did you receive any answer from Mr. Sauvé?"

"Not really, no."

"You asked and you got no answer. Is that what you are saying?"

"That's correct."

Why would Roger lie like this? Rick was positive that it was Diane Davey, not Roger, with whom he'd spoken that night, and he had told his co-accused that. Merv, Tee Hee, and Nutty also knew for a fact that there'd been no "loud music," no "party," on their end of the phone. They'd been as quiet as church mice that morning in Tee Hee's apartment, still frightened, still in a state of shock themselves at what had happened. The last thing any of them would have done was play loud music in Tee Hee's apartment, risking complaints from the neighbors, possibly even a visit from the police. A fuckin' party. You didn't have to be Perry Mason to figure what Chris Meinhardt would make of *that* in his summation to the jury.

Roger Davey was still scared when he got back to Port Hope. Like all the Crown witnesses, an armed police guard had accompanied him whenever he'd ventured out of his hotel down in London. The police had also told him that a guard would meet him in the station in Cobourg, and drive him to his home in Port Hope. But when Roger arrived at the station there was no one there to meet him. He waited for over an hour for the bodyguard to arrive. Shit, it was only a ten-minute drive to his house. Gradually it occurred to Roger Davey that no one was coming, that the police really didn't give a good goddamn what happened to him, now that he'd finished testifying for them. Finally he called Diane and she came and picked him up. Roger Davey felt violated, like he'd been used, and then thrown away.

The testimony of Corporal Terry Hall concluded the trial's sixth week. The big, heavily bearded provincial police officer, looking oddly out of place in a natty, three-piece suit, told the jurors he was the commanding officer of the OPP special intelligence squad: "Our function is to gather intelligence information on various motorcycle clubs for the Province of Ontario; to gather and disseminate it to police departments, other police departments." He had also given lectures on biker activities to police officers and departments across North America and from as far away as Australia.

At Meinhardt's behest Hall lectured the jury on the structure and organization of the Satan's Choice, explaining the position and responsibilities of each club officer at both the chapter and the national levels; he explained the significance and importance of club colours, and how the striking system worked.

Under cross-examination by Ed Martin, Hall confirmed that he had taken part in a raid on the Kitchener clubhouse of the Satan's Choice on the night of October 18. He also confirmed that he had seen David Hoffman at the clubhouse during that raid. Hall said that when he left the clubhouse, some time between 7:15 and 7:30, Hoffman was still there.

Meinhardt, trying to destroy Hoffman's alibi, asked the Corporal whether he'd had occasion to drive from the Satan's Choice clubhouse in downtown Kitchener to the Queen's Hotel in Port Hope. Hall answered affirmatively. "I drove the 195 kilometres in one hour and 23 minutes."

Ed Martin was then permitted a brief bit of further cross-examination on the point. He quickly established that to cover the distance in that time Hall would have been traveling up to 160 km/hr. He did not, however, establish explicitly how long a "normal" trip would take.

Only two Crown witnesses of any significance remained to be called by Chris Meinhardt—Sergeant McReelis and Inspector Cousens. McReelis described his role in the police investigation and read from the first statements that police had taken from the accused. Under cross-examination he denied ever receiving any notes from OPP constable Denis concerning the photo arrays viewed by Sue Foote and Gayle Thompson the day after the shooting. The Port Hope Police sergeant also denied ever having been aware of a wound on the upper left arm of Gary Comeau.

Howard Kerbel asked McReelis if he had exercised a search warrant at Gary Comeau's home on January 10, and the officer confirmed that he had.

"And did you at any time indicate to Mrs. King that her son had been shot, and that perhaps she should go down to the jail in Cobourg to speak to him about it?"

"I don't recall myself saying that, no, sir."

Kerbel next questioned Inspector Cousens closely about any observations the Inspector might have made concerning wounds on Comeau's left arm.

Cousens replied that he had made certain observations of Comeau's left arm at 42 Division Headquarters immediately after the accused's arrest. "I observed that there was an injury noticeable or a scar noticeable to the accused's left arm. . . . I observed what appeared to be an incision on the underpart of the arm, a real rough-looking incision. . . . When I observed this injury I asked Mr. Comeau, 'When did you get this, sir? What's this about?' . . . He was reluctant to talk about it and he declined comment on the cause. . . . He didn't say anything."

Kerbel asked the police veteran to refer to his notes. "I suggest to you that you noted that the wound on the left arm was an entrance wound—is that correct?"

"Referring to my notes, 'injury noticeable to the Accused left arm; appeared to be a small entrance hole,' and I put 'scar' in brackets afterwards."

"Inspector Cousens, did you receive any information with respect to whether or not a person had been, other than Mr. Matiyek, had been wounded or shot in the hotel on the 18th of October, 1978?"

"I received it through a discussion, I believe it was with Corporal Hall and I don't know when it was. I vaguely remember it. There was no names of who may have been injured . . . and I don't know the source of where Hall got it. I didn't note much importance to it at the time."

Like McReelis, Inspector Cousens also denied ever having seen the notes made by Constable Denis after Sue Foote and Gayle Thompson first viewed the photo arrays.

Cousens's candid testimony about the wounds on his arm greatly excited Gary Comeau. Could anyone now seriously doubt that he'd been shot—and that the police had known about it all along? From Hall's intelligence "tip" to Cousens's repeated curiosity about his arm to McReelis's remark to his mother—even though McReelis had denied ever making it—the evidence, surely, was clear.

What Gary theorized was this: the police had assumed, after close examination of his arm, that the bullet had been removed through the jagged incision noted by Cousens, and once he'd been identified as the gunman by Cotgrave and Thompson they'd been content to let the matter ride. The disappearance of his jacket had removed the last shred of evidence to the contrary. The police, even though they knew where the third bullet had gone, and therefore knew that he couldn't possibly have been the gunman, believed that Gary had no way of proving his innocence—a classic frame job.

But to everyone's amazement, the bullet was still in his body, and soon it would be taken out, his innocence finally established, for the whole world to see. Gary was tense with excitement when, on the afternoon of Thursday, October 25, after eight full weeks of evidence against his client, Howard Kerbel finally made a formal motion at the end of the Crown's case.

"With respect to Mr. Comeau, I would ask for an order that steps be taken to remove what appears to be from the X-rays . . . a form of metallic substance in his body, and further, for an order that that substance, if it should be a bullet or a fragment of a bullet, be subjected to whatever forensic tests are required, to compare the projectile with that taken from the body of Mr. Matiyek."

Judge Osborne nodded. "Mr. Meinhardt, what's your position?"

The Crown Attorney's argument was not transcribed, but, judging by Osborne's subsequent ruling, it apparently hinged on the fact that no evidence had yet been adduced that the accused Comeau had indeed been shot in the Queen's Hotel on the night of October 18, 1978.

Judge Osborne surveyed the courtroom. "All right, I will with this now, so that counsel know where they stand: to commence with the conclusion, the application is dismissed, without prejudice to it being renewed upon there being some evidence placed before the court that Mr. Comeau was in fact shot on the evening of October 18. . . . I make that disposition on the initial premise that there is no medical reason requiring the removal of the fragment at this time."

Gary slumped against the hard wooden back of the prisoner's dock. Now he knew, and everyone sitting there beside him knew, it would all come down to Lorne.

XXX

IN THE SAME WAY that Bruce Affleck had been assigned as liaison with Chris Meinhardt in the abortive attempt to reach a satisfactory plea bargain, so Howard Kerbel had been authorized to act as a go-between for the defence team in its dealings with the Satan's Choice. It was understood that Gary Comeau's lawyer had one main task: to get the co-operation of the club member who had gunned down Bill Matiyek.

When word of the plea-bargain attempt had reached Lorne Campbell, he had approved of the deal, agreeing to give himself up for a second-degree murder bit—ten years to life, which usually meant ten years pen time, or even less, if his club brothers accused of Matiyek's death got a break. Then the deal fell through.

As a fall-back position, the defence lawyers asked the club if the real gunman would agree to testify, and Lorne said that he would. With another Toronto Chapter member acting as a go-between (all of the parties involved were now extremely leery of the telephone), it was arranged that Lorne would meet with Kerbel to go over his testimony in advance. These arrangements were handled in an atmosphere of extreme paranoia—no one doubted that the police were eager to arrest still more club members for Matiyek's shooting if they possibly could. On one occasion, when Lorne and two other Choice members drove downtown to Kerbel's office for a meeting, they were certain they were being followed. They cancelled the meeting lest the police see exactly which club members were being interviewed by Kerbel.

Nutty's lawyer recommended that Lorne himself should seek legal counsel, which Campbell did. He would be represented at the trial by veteran Toronto criminal lawyer John Rosen. It was an extraordinary turn of the legal wheel—for a man to testify in open court that he had committed a killing for which eight others had been charged with first-degree murder—and Rosen felt obliged to recommend that his client avail himself of the protection of the Canada Evidence Act.

The Act provides a limited degree of immunity from prosecution, Rosen explained, in that a witness invoking it may not have the testimony he gives in court used against him in subsequent proceedings. This did not mean, Rosen warned Campbell, that the police wouldn't charge Lorne on the spot with the murder of Bill Matiyek, provided there was sufficient *other* evidence.

Lorne prepared himself for the worst. He told his girlfriend before leaving for London that he might be away for two days—or ten years. Campbell was scheduled to appear as the lead witness for the defence. His state of mind before taking the witness stand can well be imagined, and he popped a Valium to steady his nerves, a fact he mentioned to Bruce Affleck. It was a confidence that he would later bitterly regret having shared.

As the senior counsel for the defence, Bruce Affleck made an opening statement to the jury on behalf of the accused. He told the seven men and five women sitting before him that the first witness for the defence would be the gunman who had killed William Matiyek, the testimony of the two waitresses notwithstanding. The gunman would testify that he'd been "on a frolic of his own," Affleck told the jury, and that he had not been encouraged, aided, or abetted by any of the accused.

Lorne Edgar Campbell was then called, sworn, and afforded blanket protection under the Canada Evidence Act at the request of John Rosen. Campbell told Affleck that he was thirty-one years old, a resident of Oshawa, and a six-year veteran of the Satan's Choice Motorcycle Club. Affleck asked him to recap his criminal record and Lorne did so: a ten-dollar fine for carrying a switch knife when he was sixteen, a year's probation for common assault in Scarborough, three years' probation for a 1975 arson conviction in Oshawa, and a year in jail for conspiracy to commit perjury in 1977. "I was convicted for driving under suspension and I lied in court, saying that I wasn't driving the motorcycle, that a guy that was with me was driving the motorcycle and I was a passenger. . . . I was under suspension then, by the way, and following that, I was charged with conspiracy to commit perjury, because of that." Since then, Campbell concluded, he had served an additional six months in jail for assault causing bodily harm.

Affleck walked Campbell through the events of October 18. After work he'd gone home for supper, and then to the Markham Road clubhouse, arriving at around eight-thirty or nine. He'd "just stood at the bar having a beer. . . . There was a phone call from Port Hope saying that there was trouble in Port Hope . . . Gary Comeau took the call. . . . After the phone call he said that there was trouble at the Queen's Hotel . . . and it was mentioned that William Matiyek was down there and a couple of other people from a different motorcycle club . . . Outlaws. I finished my beer, and I went out into my car, and I drove [from] there to the Queen's Hotel in Port Hope."

Larry Hurren had ridden with him, Campbell recalled. Yes, he'd had a weapon, a .38 revolver loaded with six shells that he'd carried "for my own protection" for the past two years. "I bought it in the hotel off a guy in Toronto," but, Campbell insisted, he'd never fired it. No one else at the club knew he was carrying a gun. "We have a ruling—it is an unwritten rule in the club, that nobody carries any kind of weapons on them in the clubhouse. . . . Or you are subject to a thousand-dollar fine by the club." He'd been wearing a green parka coat that night, hood thrown back, no hat. The gun was in the left-hand pocket of the parka.

He and Hurren had left the clubhouse at ten o'clock and arrived at the Queen's Hotel between 10:30 and 10:45. He was left-handed, Campbell told the court, and his facial hair that night was "the same as I have got now": moustache, goatee, and shoulder-length hair.

Lorne said he'd sat down at a table while Hurren went up to the bar. "I observed two guys standing at the bar; they weren't facing me, but I presumed they were Outlaws because of their belts . . . the Outlaw insignia on [them]. . . . I looked over to the other side—there's the wall comes down and then there's a corner . . . I observed Rick Sauvé sitting with Matiyek—with Bill Matiyek, and there was a girl at the table, too. . . . Well, then I noticed that Gary Comeau was sitting between the girl and Rick, on the other side of the table from Bill Matiyek. . . . I heard voices, like it sounded like an argument . . . from Matiyek and Gary Comeau's and Rick Sauvé's table. . . ."

"And what did you do when you heard this argument?"

"I stood up and walked over to the table."

"And prior to this time, did you know anything about Mr. Matiyek?"

"Not too much, only that I knew that he carried a gun . . . I knew he was an ex–Golden Hawk."

"And you walked over to the table, and what, if anything, happened then?"

"Well, Matiyek turned around and as he was turning around, he looked right at me and put his right hand in his coat."

"You are indicating his right hand in his coat, across his chest, towards the left?"

"Yes."

"And what did you do at that time, if anything?"

"I pulled out my gun and shot him . . . for my own protection. I didn't want to get shot."

"And where did you shoot Mr. Matiyek?"

"In the head."

"And how many shots were fired?"

"Three."

After that he left the hotel through the front door and "when I got to my car, Gary Comeau got in my car, after I had it started."

"And what, if anything, was said at that particular time?"

"Only that he was hurt."

"Pardon?"

"Only that he was hurt."

Chris Meinhardt was on his feet, arguing that this, surely, was hearsay.

"Is that not a statement by the accused, your Lordship?" Affleck parried.

Osborne allowed the question.

"Did you make any observations about Mr. Comeau's condition?"

"Not really. He had a coat on."

Affleck tried again. "Anything other than that?"

"Well, he must have had a shirt on."

And again. "Well, other than that, did you make any observations about him?"

"No."

They'd driven to the 401, Lorne said, and then headed west. Somewhere between Port Hope and Courtice Road, a distance of some thirty to forty kilometres, he'd pulled the car over, gotten out, and thrown the gun deep into the bush.

When they'd arrived in Oshawa, Lorne had gone to the Cadillac Hotel and Gary Comeau had taken the car from there.

And why had Mr. Comeau taken the witness's car?

"Well, first of all he said that—"

Chris Meinhardt was once again on his feet, and this time the point was argued in the absence of both the jury and the witness. After a brief discussion Affleck took one more stab at the evidence that the defence team and the accused wanted so badly to hear.

"Mr. Campbell, as you proceeded from Port Hope to Oshawa after the shooting, did Mr. Comeau show you anything?"

"Did he show me anything?"

"Yes?" Hopefully: *That he'd been shot.*

"No."

". . . All right, thank you, Mr. Campbell."

Howard Kerbel fared little better, initially, with his cross-examination. He began by asking Campbell what time he'd left the Queen's.

"It must have been right at eleven o'clock, according to the papers."

"Well, forget about the papers for a moment, from your own recollection, are you able to tell us what time you left?"

"Well, it would have to be eleven o'clock."

"Why would it have to be eleven?"

"Well, from the evidence I read in the paper, this thing happened at eleven o'clock, and so I left right then."

"All right, Mr. Campbell, I want you to tell us from your own knowledge and not from what you have read, but from your own knowledge of what happened that evening: What time did you leave?"

"Eleven o'clock."

Kerbel returned to the car ride Campbell and Comeau had taken to Oshawa after the shooting. There had been conversation? Yes.

"And as a result of that conversation, with Mr. Comeau, did Mr. Comeau show you anything?"

Judge Osborne interrupted. "He's already said he didn't."

"On two occasions, my Lord," Meinhardt agreed. (Actually it was four occasions and counting.)

Kerbel stood his ground. "My Lord, this is cross-examination."

Osborne shook his head in resignation. "Go ahead."

"Well, in the course of that conversation or at any other time while you were in the car with Mr. Comeau, did Mr. Comeau show you anything?"

"He didn't show me anything—like I seen by his coat that he was hurt."

"Well, what did you see? What was it that you saw?"

"Well, his coat had a hole in it and there was blood there."

". . . Can you tell us where the wound was?"

"In his arm."

"Which arm?"

"I think it was his left arm."

"Thank you, sir." It was the standard courtesy from lawyer to witness that signalled the end of an examination. Kerbel had spoken those words thousands of times before, to as many witnesses. But never had he meant them so wholeheartedly as he did on that afternoon. It wasn't much to go on, but with Campbell's testimony and a bit of luck, Howard Kerbel had every reason to believe that his client had just been spared a conviction for first-degree murder.

David Newman asked Campbell whether he had told Larry Hurren that he was carrying a revolver during their drive down to Port Hope. No. Had Hurren seen Campbell carrying it in previous years? "I don't think so, no." Had the witness shown Hurren the revolver during the drive? No.

"You indicated during your examination-in-chief, Mr. Campbell, that you figured there might be a fight down there?"

"Yes."

"What kind of a fight, would that be a fight involving revolvers or guns?"

"No, a fist fight."

"That is what you anticipated?"

"Yes."

"You are certain of that?"

"I am positive."

Campbell told Jack Grossman, in answer to his questioning, that he'd known Rick Sauvé less than two years. He denied having any conversation with Sauvé on October 18 in relation to Matiyek.

"And when—did you agree with anyone to kill Mr. Matiyek?"

"No."

"And did you intend to kill Mr. Matiyek when you arrived at the hotel?"

"I had no such intentions."

"And did anyone suggest to you, sir, that Mr. Matiyek should be killed?"

"No."

Like each of the witnesses before him, Lorne Campbell had, upon stepping into the witness-box, solemnly sworn the oath "to tell the truth, the whole truth, and nothing but the truth, so help me God." Like each of the earlier witnesses he had doubtless, at that moment, intended to tell nothing but the truth. But, unlike many of the earlier witnesses, Lorne Campbell had begun to lie almost from the moment he opened his mouth.

It all seemed so simple, to affirm the oath when the court clerk was reading the words off his sheet of paper. But what was the truth, Lorne Campbell might well have asked. What was the truth about the killing of Bill Matiyek? The police thought they knew the truth. So did Chris Meinhardt. They didn't know bugger-all. And what did it mean "to tell the truth" in a court of law? What was that but a recitation of observations tempered by time and memory, experience and environment? During his own later prison years Lorne Campbell would become fascinated by certain Oriental philosophies and their word for a kind of truth: karma, the consequences of one's actions. If that was a measure of truth, then no one in the courtroom, and certainly no previous witness, carried such a terrible burden onto the witness stand as Lorne Campbell.

He was, above all, an outlaw biker to the very core of his being. To give evidence at any time, in any court, ran deeply counter to his conscience. But for his love of the accused—and Lorne wasn't ashamed to admit this, he loved each of them like the true brothers they were—and but for his remorse at having them held accountable for the consequences of his own actions, he would never have consented to testify in the first place. And, now that he had, he was bound by a myriad of ties, forced to pick his way through a minefield studded with truth and consequences, even under the relatively friendly fire of the defence lawyers. As he waged this awful inner struggle before answering almost every question, it was obvious to everyone in the courtroom that there was something terribly wrong with Lorne Campbell's testimony. But only the accused and perhaps—and perversely—Chris Meinhardt came close to understanding the reasons why.

At one level, Campbell had offered a tissue of omission, half-truths, wishful thinking, and outright lies in his testimony, and, in hindsight, they stick out like neon road-signs.

There was, first of all, the gun. "I bought it in the hotel off a guy in Toronto." That was false. Someone, not one of the accused, had given him the gun before he left Toronto, just in case. But he couldn't say that, because it would mean implicating someone else.

Then there were the Outlaws. "I presumed they were Outlaws because of their belts." Of course he'd recognized Sonny Bronson and Fred Jones. He'd known them from the days before they'd switched patch. But there was no way Lorne was going to start naming names on the witness stand, especially the names of other bikers, even though he did consider them traitors to his club.

"I noticed after that Gary Comeau was sitting between the girl and Rick, on the other side of the table from Matiyek." Here Lorne was guilty of nothing more than a faulty memory. Not one of the eyewitnesses correctly situated Sauvé and Comeau at the Matiyek table. Gary was to Bill's immediate right and Rick more or less directly across from Matiyek.

"I heard voices, like it sounded like an argument. . . ." None of the other witnesses had mentioned an argument, which cast even further doubt upon Lorne's own version of events. He fabricated the argument for a reason.

"I knew that [Bill] carried a gun. . . ." Another falsehood, invented for the same reason. A member of the Satan's Choice, the one who had been warned away from the table by Matiyek while Comeau and Sauvé were sitting there, had told Lorne that Matiyek was armed and was threatening Rick. But if he told the truth on the witness stand, Lorne feared he would be forced to reveal that person's identity (again, not one of the accused), or risk a contempt-of-court citation.

When asked who else had been in the hotel, Lorne had had to think fast.

It was one of the questions he'd dreaded most. "Rick Sauvé and Gary Comeau and Merv Blaker and Larry Hurren and myself." Lawyers for Rick, Merv, and Larry had already admitted their clients were there, so that was safe enough. It was obvious that Nutty had been there (although this was the first formal admission by the defence that Comeau had been in the hotel). Tee Hee and Gordy weren't there. That was true. That Armand Sanguigni wasn't there was an outright lie, but Lorne had heard that Armand was walking and Lorne could never bring himself to testify against a club brother, no matter what.

And then there was the lie that would have the greatest impact of all upon the trial. "I seen by his coat that [Comeau] was hurt. His coat had a hole in it and there was blood there." This was a complete fabrication, he had not, in fact, seen the wound in Nutty's arm, and they had not even ridden together in the same car as they fled the murder scene. And yet it was through this lie that a far greater truth would finally emerge, a truth that the so-called justice system with its gowns and gobbledygook and airs and smug pretensions and solemn vows, as Lorne saw it, and its oh-so-earnest commitment to seeking out the truth might never have seen fit to reveal: that Gary Comeau was not, in fact, the gunman.

So Lorne had told a few lies on the witness stand. More than a few. But at another, higher, level he had basically told the truth about the murder of Bill Matiyek. So that, more than seven years later, when what was done had been done and the only thing left for any of them was the truth, Lorne could fasten his eyes that sometimes appear to see right through a person upon a visitor and say in the soft, soothing tone that Lorne always used to confront peril: "I told the truth, you know, that day in court."

Chris Meinhardt opened his first cross-examination of the trial by asking Campbell about his background in the Satan's Choice. Lorne said he'd originally been a member of the Oshawa Chapter, which had had only five full members before it was amalgamated with the much larger Toronto Chapter, of which he was currently a member. The witness confirmed that he was familiar with the Golden Hawks in Oshawa—there had been about thirty of them.

"And were there any hard feelings developed between the Golden Hawks and Satan's Choice?"

"A lot of fist fights."

"And so I take it then your chapter would be having a bit of a hard time, if there were hard feelings between five of you and thirty of them?"

"No, it wasn't hard feelings."

"Hard times."

"Hard times—most of us take the attitude—like, I am thirty-one years old now and I take the attitude if I am having difficulty with someone from another club, and it happens to develop into a fist fight, it is usually forgotten about and things are smoothed over the next day."

"Did you ever attend at the clubhouse any parties of the Golden Hawks?"

"Yes."

"Do you know Lawrence Leon?"

"Not personally, no."

"You have never spoken to the man?"

"I have spoken to him but I don't know him."

"Do you recall speaking to him and complaining about the Golden Hawks not having enough respect for Satan's Choice?"

"Yes—could I delve on that?"

"If you wish." Chris Meinhardt turned his back on Campbell and began pacing slowly in front of the jury-box.

"Yeah, the Golden Hawks—" What kind of bullshit was this? The guy asks a question and then turns his back. Lorne found it unnerving. "You see, I was living at our clubhouse in Oshawa—"

"Yes, go ahead, witness," Meinhardt said over his shoulder.

"—and they used to come up to our clubhouse periodically and I would entertain them. . . ." With his back turned to Campbell and Judge Osborne, Chris Meinhardt began to mug in front of the jury, rolling his eyes, smiling sardonically as Lorne spoke, as if to say, "Yeah, sure. Right. I believe you, Lorne, though thousands wouldn't." Lorne couldn't see this, but he could sense that some of the jurors were watching Meinhardt and not him. Lorne started to testify again. "I would give them—" he stopped. *Look at me, you smug little prick.*

"Yes, go ahead, I can hear you." Over his shoulder again.

"—I would buy them beer and show them a good time, whatever, and I went down to the Golden Hawk clubhouse one time, and I was told to leave."

"And this is when this argument came about?" He was facing Lorne again now.

"That's about all it was, was an argument."

"And did you come back to the club the next day?"

"Did I come back?"

"Yes?"

"No."

Meinhardt asked who else had been in the Choice clubhouse on the night of the murder and Lorne answered that he couldn't remember.

"And all of you in the chapter, you are good friends?"

"Yes."

"Close friends?"

"Right."

"And as far as the Outlaw Motorcycle Club—it is a club that is known to you?"

"Yes."

"And it is not an unfriendly club to you, is it?"

"No, it is not unfriendly, right. You are using double negatives—why don't you just ask me straight questions?"

Coulter Osborne glowered at Lorne Campbell. "Why don't you just answer the questions, if you can."

"Oh."

Meinhardt asked Campbell to repeat his testimony about the telephone call from Port Hope. He'd been told there was trouble, Campbell explained, and that Bill Matiyek and some Outlaws were there. No, he hadn't felt himself obliged to help Matiyek. But he would have felt obliged to help the Outlaws "if it was against somebody that wasn't in our club."

"I take it, then, that if you felt obliged to assist the Outlaws, you would feel even more obliged to assist a member of your own club?"

"That's right."

"That is something that you are required to do—is to help any member of your own club?"

"No."

"It isn't? . . . Would you explain that, please?"

"If a member is getting himself in trouble—these are not written rules, they are unwritten rules throughout the club, within the club, then it's his fault and he has to look after his own problems and not bring heat onto this club by causing problems."

"How about if a chapter of your club is having troubles with another club—would there be an obligation then?"

"There would be an obligation to smooth things over."

"And if it couldn't be smoothed over and there is trouble, would you feel obliged to assist?"

"What kind of trouble are you talking about?"

"Well, let's say the kind of trouble that you are talking about at the Queen's Hotel with respect to Matiyek and the Outlaws?"

"No, when I went down there I never had any intention of getting into any trouble with Matiyek. I had the intention that the trouble was with the two Outlaws. Matiyek never crossed my mind, because Matiyek to my knowledge wasn't a Golden Hawk and had nothing to do with bike clubs, when I went down there."

"So these two Outlaws you believed at the time were in trouble with God knows who?"

"I thought they were in trouble with guys from my club. I thought they were arguing with guys from my club and I was under the impression that Rick Sauvé was down there by himself . . . I presumed he was having trouble with the Outlaws."

". . . you moved . . . because a brother might be in trouble?"

"That's right."

Meinhardt asked Campbell to describe the route he'd taken to enter the hotel. What did the entrance to the hotel look like? The entrance to the lounge? The bar itself? Campbell fielded each of the questions with relative accuracy. But then he foundered.

"And so you walked in and what did you see and where?"

"First of all, I looked at the bar . . . and the Outlaws were still standing at the bar."

"Who were they?"

"I don't know. I never seen them before."

"Do you know Sonny Bronson?"

"Yes."

"He wasn't one of them?"

"I don't think so. It could have been."

"Well, you know Sonny?"

"Yes."

"You wouldn't have to recognize him by a belt buckle, because you know Sonny's face?"

"I had never had that much to do with Kingston—I know he was in Kingston, but I didn't have that much to do with him."

"Well, you might not have had that much to do with Kingston but surely the members know each other?"

"Well, Sonny hasn't been a Choice since a couple of years after I was in the club, and I never had nothin' to do with him. A couple of them guys changed their patch and went to Outlaws after I was in the club, so I—"

"Did you know Fred Jones?"

"Yes."

"Was Fred Jones one of them?"

"I couldn't say. Jones apparently just got out of jail. After I was in the club for a long time and he went Outlaws after he was out of jail."

"Well, didn't you know Fred Jones well enough on October 18, 1978, to be able to tell [him] by his face rather than by his belt buckle?"

"No."

"All right, now, so you knew these people were Outlaws because of their belt buckles?"

"Yes."

"And although you had seen Sonny Bronson and Fred Jones before, you can't say whether they were Fred Jones and Sonny Bronson?"

"No, I can't say for sure."

"Did you see Fred Jones or Sonny Bronson anywhere in the hotel that evening?"

"Well, if that was them, it was them, but I wouldn't recognize them, unless I started talking to them—if they recognized me, but there was no words—no conversation between me and them guys."

Meinhardt produced a floor-plan of the lounge of the Queen's Hotel, and a marker, and asked him to indicate Matiyek's table on the drawing, the position of Comeau, Sauvé, and the deceased at the table, where Merv Blaker had been sitting and Larry Hurren standing, and where the Outlaws had been at the bar.

Campbell placed the Outlaws on the same bar stools that had been occupied by Rod Stewart and his two friends. He corrected himself a little later: "Oh, wait, these guys weren't sitting on the stools. They were standing up." Even so, none of the other witnesses had seen Jones and Bronson anywhere near Stewart. Such a glaring inconsistency would, Meinhardt hoped, cause the jurors to ask themselves one very obvious question: Had Lorne Campbell really been in the Queen's on the night of the shooting at all?

"And when you were asked by Mr. Kerbel about times, how you could tell times—you said because 'I know when this thing happened' and you said something about having read about it in the papers?"

"Yes, that's why I know it was exactly eleven o'clock. I could give you a guess that it happened between quarter to eleven and eleven o'clock."

"What was exactly at eleven o'clock?"

"That this thing happened."

"What thing?"

"That Bill Matiyek was shot."

"You mean to say when you shot Bill Matiyek?"

"That's right."

"Tell us about it. Tell us exactly what you remember—every detail of what happened as you came up to the Matiyek table?"

"I walked over to the table . . . I was walking, like, right beside it, and towards it, right beside it, and he must have had it in his mind that something was going to happen, and he turned around and put his hand—"

"—turned around where?"

"Turned around and looked at me, I was like right here to him, and he turned around, and when he looked at me, I was only maybe three or four feet away from him."

"And what did he do then?"

"He put his hand in his coat and that's when I reacted."

"Where did he put his hand in his coat?"

"Where in his coat?"

"And are you sure it was his right hand?"

"I am positive."

"No doubt in your mind about it?"

"That's right."

"All right, and where did he put it?"

"Inside his jacket."

"What kind of jacket?"

"I don't remember what kind of jacket. If you asked me what you are wearing tomorrow, I wouldn't remember, because I don't remember things like that, what people are wearing."

"You mean you don't even remember what the guy you shot was wearing?"

"No."

"You indicated he reached across his body with his right hand?"

"Yes."

"And you say he reached inside his jacket?"

"Yes."

"And you don't know what kind of jacket?"

"No. This thing didn't happen in a period of five minutes. It happened in a period of a split second."

"That's true, but you were looking at the table for more than a split second, were you not?"

"Yes."

"Do you recall how Mr. Comeau was dressed at the time?"

"I know he had a leather jacket on."

"You do remember that?"

"Yes."

"And I suppose you do remember the colour?"

"Black."

"And do you remember whether he had his colours on?"

"His colours, no he didn't."

"And you do remember how Mr. Sauvé was dressed?"

"No, I don't."

"Do you remember how Mr. Hurren was dressed?"

"No, I don't."

"So the only person you remember how they were dressed is Mr. Comeau?"

"That's because he's always dressed like that. If he changed, I would notice it."

"And you approached and tell us—he reached across and what happened next?"

"When he reached across, there was no doubt in my mind that he had a gun, so I put my hand in my left pocket and pulled out my gun—"

"I am sorry, how was there no doubt in your mind that he had a gun?"

"Because of the look on his face when he looked at me."

"He looked at you?"

"That's right."

"And from the look on his face you had no doubt that he had a gun?"

"There was no doubt that he was going for a gun."

"And what did you do then?"

"I reached in my pocket and grabbed my gun and shot him, before he had a chance."

"Which pocket?"

"My left pocket, on the bottom here."

". . . So you walked up to the table—you stopped—you saw Matiyek reach?"

"Yes."

"And then you pulled your gun?"

"Yes."

"And you fired?"

"Yes."

"How many times?"

"Three times."

"And where did you hit him?"

"In the head."

"Whereabouts in the head? Did you see?"

"I wasn't thinking too clearly when I shot. I know it was in the general direction of his head."

"And what did he do?"

"Went off his chair."

"Did he make any gesture before he fell off his chair?"

"Gesture, no."

"None at all?"

"No."

"Did he make a sound—try and think?"

"I don't remember him making any sound, no. I remember the girl that was sitting there screamed and that's all I remember and then I turned around and walked out."

Although he had been standing directly in front of the hotel's John Street exit when he shot Matiyek, and even though his car was parked on John Street, Campbell testified that he then left the Queen's through the front door, a far more circuitous route.

"Mr. Campbell, why did you have to walk so far to get out of the hotel?"

"It was the only way I knew to get out of it."

"Didn't you see that there was a door going out on the street where you parked your car?"

"No, no, I didn't notice that. I know there is a door there, but I never noticed it. . . . I may have seen it, but it never clicked in my mind that it was there."

Meinhardt began to review Campbell's criminal record in some detail, dwelling particularly on his perjury conviction.

". . . This was on some driving offence?"

"Yes."

"You said, I think, driving while disqualified?"

"Yes."

"And at that time you were an accused person and you went into the box, right?"

"Yes."

"And you affirmed to tell the truth, as you have today?"

"Yes."

"And then you lied?"

"Yes."

"Now, you were convicted of conspiracy. Did you get somebody else to go in and lie also?"

"Oh, did I talk him into it?"

"No, no, did you have somebody else on the same case go in and also tell a lie?"

"Yes."

"And that some other person, he went or she went in and said that he or she in fact was driving?"

"Yes."

"And this wasn't true?"

"No."

"And so not only did you go into the box and tell a lie, you had somebody else go in for you to tell a lie?"

"Yes."

"And this was over a driving offence?"

"Yes."

The next question hung almost palpably in the air, unasked: *And if you were willing to conspire to lie about something as minor as a driving offence, Mr. Campbell, how many more lies would you be willing to tell over something as important as murder?*

"Now, when you started to give evidence, you heard what your lawyer said about the Canada Evidence Act."

"Yeah."

"What does all that mean?"

For the first time that day, Terry O'Hara was on his feet. "My Lord, I object to that question."

The lawyers argued the point, briefly, in the absence of the jury and the witness. Chris Meinhardt was allowed to repeat the question.

"What do I think the Canada Evidence Act is?"

"No, no, with respect to you giving evidence?"

"Do I think I am going to walk out of here and go free?"

"No, no, I want you to tell me what your understanding—if I can put it in layman's terms, protection of the Canada Evidence Act—what you understand it to mean?"

"Well, I understand it to be when a person does that, what they say can't be used as evidence unless there is evidence off the stand. . . . If I say something on the stand, my understanding is that if somebody confirms it, then . . . I can be charged."

"Is it your understanding then what you say, your evidence, as a statement, cannot be used against you?"

"It can if it's proven as evidence."

"Through some other means?"

"Well, I think even my means—if it's proven that what I say is true."

Meinhardt returned to the shooting one last time. "I take it that you never saw Bill Matiyek actually draw a gun on you, did you?"

"No, I never—if I—if he had of had a chance, I'd be dead right now."

"Are you a good shot with a handgun?"

"I don't know. No, I guess not. I don't go around practising shooting."

"I guess, then, you must have been somewhat surprised when you learned that you shot him three times in the head?"

"Was I surprised?"

"Yes?"

"Then—or—"

"Well, as soon as you learned that you hit him three times in the head?"

"I wasn't surprised, because I was standing right in front of him."

"On top of him—how close were you?"

"Three feet."

"And did your arm extend forward as you were shooting him?"

"Extend forward?"

"Well, did you extend your arm straight out as you were shooting him?"

"I don't know how else you would shoot a guy, yes I did."

"And you were about three feet away from him?"

"Yes."

"Did you get any blood on you—on your hand or on your clothing?"

"No."

"I have no further questions."

At that moment, Lorne Campbell knew he was beaten. He wanted Meinhardt to keep asking questions, to give him a chance to explain things, it was just too important to stop now. He probably didn't realize that his final exchange with Meinhardt had damaged his credibility still further. He'd said he fired standing three feet away from Matiyek, his arm fully extended. But Gayle Thompson remembered seeing the gunman fire from his hip. And firearms expert Finn Nielsen had testified that a revolver fired from a distance of two feet or less would leave powder burns on Matiyek's clothing, and he had found none.

But Bruce Affleck offered his witness one last desperate chance on re-direct, and Lorne grabbed it.

"In response to a question of my friend about the Canada Evidence Act, you made the comment, as I recorded it, 'Now, do you think I am going to walk out of here and go free.' Why did you say that?"

Meinhardt objected to the question, but he was overruled.

"Well, my understanding is that no matter what the Canada Evidence Act provides, there's a chance that I might be charged with first-degree murder too, so I'm not up here, like some people might think, to try to get eight guys from my club off. I did what I did and I'm up here because I did it and they shouldn't go to jail for what I did and that's why I'm here, and it's not like lying on a driving under suspension. I am up here telling the truth and that's why I said that. Maybe I didn't put it right, but that's why—"

"All right, thank you." Affleck returned to his seat.

Although he was entirely within his rights to ask his own questions, Mr. Justice Osborne had, up until now, kept them to an absolute minimum. But he questioned Lorne Campbell closely, and at some length.

"Mr. Campbell, I don't want there to be any misunderstanding as to how far away you were from Mr. Matiyek when you shot him, as you say you did in your evidence, but were you three feet away from him or was the gun three feet away from him?"

"I would be three feet away from him."

"So the gun would be that much closer."

"Yes."

". . . the only persons that were at Matiyek's table that could cause you any concern, would seem to me on your evidence, would be Matiyek himself?"

"Yes."

"And when you went down there you didn't regard him as being a source of concern at all, as I understand your evidence?"

"No, but can I say something right now?"

"Sure."

"When I walked over there, I didn't have no intentions of doing what I did. I never even had intentions of fighting. I went over there to find out what the heck they were arguing about."

"But why—what difference would it make about whether a man you had no concern was saying or what the argument was all about?"

"Just curiosity. I wanted to find out what they were arguing about."

" . . . Now, you mentioned—and this is the last question I have, depending on your answer—you said that you felt obliged to go to the assistance of the Outlaws, if they were under some duress or problem with non-motorcycle-club members?"

"Yes, that's—like—when I say that, it's debatable—if there was a fight in a hotel and they were getting dirt thrown at them, I would naturally help them."

"All right."

"Otherwise I stay out of anybody's problems, but I would naturally help them. . . . But if they had a problem at a hotel and phoned me and said get down here and give me a hand, I would say, 'Phone your own club.'"

"And it perhaps goes without saying, then, that you would also feel obliged to go to the assistance of your own club members under similar circumstances?"

"Yes, it would."

"Your attachment to your own club would be significantly stronger and broader than your attachment to another motorcycle club?"

"Yes, that's right, it sure would."

"Those are all of the questions I have. . . ."

Since he was really little more than a visitor at the trial, John Rosen was able to view his client's testimony with a detached yet professional eye. Years later he would still remember Meinhardt's antics before the jury, remember watching a few of the jurors smile to themselves in appreciation. The Crown Attorney had obviously established a good rapport with them. They already appeared to be, in lawyer's parlance, "a convicting jury." Rosen shuddered inwardly as he left the courtroom. He was glad this trial was not his.

It is still not clear, after reading and rereading the transcript, why virtually no one in the courtroom that day believed, on his evidence, that Lorne Campbell shot Bill Matiyek. Yet his testimony was considered, by everyone who heard it, to be wholly unconvincing. Even Terry O'Hara, who believed then, as he does now, that Campbell was the gunman, found Lorne's testimony to be totally incredible.

"It defies verbal description," Coulter Osborne would say of Campbell's testimony seven years later. In his nearly thirty years of trial experience, the Supreme Court Justice would recall Lorne Campbell "as one of the worst witnesses I've ever seen in terms of his believability."

Howard Kerbel remembers being surprised that Lorne turned out to be a dreadful witness. "He appeared to be stoned, very up, and yet almost blasé . . . he was up, but flat, and he didn't react in the way the jury wanted. They wanted more emotion."

Bruce Affleck believes that Campbell's testimony was discounted because it conflicted, in some ways, with that of the Crown witnesses to whom the jury had been exposed for the previous eight weeks. "Campbell's story didn't dovetail with events. The jury wanted to believe the waitresses, and Lorne Campbell looks nothing like Gary Comeau." If Comeau wasn't the gunman, in other words, then the actual killer should have at least looked like him. "Lorne was also in an intractable position relative to the other witnesses in that their testimony had been honed to a fine edge," either from their appearance at the preliminary hearing or through conversations with the Crown Attorneys.

On this last point Terry O'Hara was highly critical of his co-counsel, and especially of Howard Kerbel. There had been no pretrial preparation of Campbell, because Kerbel refused, until the last moment, to reveal his identity, even to his own defence colleagues. O'Hara is convinced that Kerbel got caught up in the intrigue of clandestine meetings with club members and the air of super-secrecy that surrounded Lorne's court appearance. "His testimony was completely flat, delivered in a monotone, with no humanity and without the slightest emotion. He seemed like an automaton sent to do a job."

And, since no one could ever quite put their finger on exactly why it was that Lorne's testimony proved to be such an unmitigated disaster, they decided it was because he'd been stoned, an accusation Lorne deeply resented. He believes that story got started because of his chance remark to Affleck that he'd taken a Valium—and only one—before entering the witness-box.

Lorne half expected to be arrested the minute he left the witness stand, but nothing happened. Before they parted, John Rosen advised his client that it might be a good idea to get out of town for a while—not to evade a warrant if one were issued, mind you, but just to let any potential heat from Lorne's testimony cool off a bit. Lorne took Rosen's advice.

Court was adjourned for the day after Lorne's testimony, and the mood that night in the paddy wagon was sombre. Each of them knew that it had not gone well. "Anyway, he finished strong," observed Nutty, ever the optimist. "That little speech he made at the end there . . ." his voice trailed off. Even Gary didn't believe it.

Lorne's testimony had salubrious consequences for at least one court-room participant: Mac Haig's story the next day got splendid play. "Biker tells court he, not 8 on trial, killed man" screamed the *Free Press* headline, just below the flag. After eight weeks the Satan's Choice murder trial had at last become front-page news.

Court was unable to resume the next morning owing to the illness of Ed Martin. Judge Osborne sent the jury home and then agreed to entertain a motion from Howard Kerbel. "At this time I would like to continue my application for an order that Mr. Comeau be submitted to whatever surgical procedures are necessary to remove what appears, from the radiological report, to be a foreign metal object lodged in the upper right quadrant of his body."

Judge Osborne made it clear that he took a dim view of the application, and thought even less of Lorne Campbell's testimony. "I kept waiting for the cue cards to appear," Glaister would quote him as saying in *Maclean's* magazine after the trial was over. But, to the surprise of nearly everyone, Chris Meinhardt concurred with Kerbel's motion.

Coulter Osborne grudgingly granted the application. "This is an order releasing the accused, Gary Comeau, from his present place of confinement, to a hospital in this community for what appears to be minor surgery, to remove a projectile that is reasonably clearly evident, from a perusal of X-rays, which were taken some weeks ago."

XXXI

A SCANT TWO HOURS after Osborne made his ruling, Gary Comeau emerged, blinking slightly in the bright sunshine, from a police paddy wagon onto the parking lot outside London's Victoria Hospital. His ankles and wrists were shackled and a chain leash was wrapped around his belly. A policeman held the other end of the leash. Gary was sick of this, he felt like a freak in a carnival sideshow, and suddenly he decided to act that way. He began to bark, howling and growling like a mad dog. His handler didn't say anything, he just tugged on the leash and led Gary into the hospital emergency department.

The operating-room was already crowded. There must have been a dozen people there from the courtroom—Chris Meinhardt and Roland Harris, Howard Kerbel, Colin Cousens, and Sam McReelis, along with a number of the police guards. Somebody told Gary to take his shirt off and to lie face down on the table. He could feel an orderly shave him and then swab disinfectant on a spot on his back. Then he felt the prick of the needle, and after that his back was numb. But it was only a local anesthetic, so he was able to watch, and remember, everything that happened then. A young doctor came in and carefully studied the X-rays before counting the ribs on the film. Then the doctor counted the ribs on his back, made a neat incision through the meat and the muscle on his back, and there, nestled between two ribs, was the bullet, enclosed in a kind of protective cocoon that had been created by his own body.

The doctor extracted the bullet, still in its cocoon, through the incision, and handed it gingerly to one of the cops, who placed it inside a box and everyone gathered around to see. One of the cops whistled softly. "Well, will you look at that." It was a bullet all right, and even after being inside Gary's body for more than a year it appeared to be all in one piece. The doctor sutured the incision closed while someone carefully marked the box and hurried off to have its contents analysed by forensics. Most of the others drifted away then and Gary was finally led, still in chains, back outside.

Alone in the back of the paddy wagon on the way to the Detention Centre, Gary Comeau did something he hadn't done in a long, long time—he broke down and cried.

As the effects of the anesthetic wore off, Gary discovered that the bullet hurt a great deal more coming out than it had going in. The next morning, Thursday, November 1, he was in too much pain to sit through a day in court, and Judge Osborne had no choice but to adjourn the proceedings until Friday. Even then Gary was in obvious discomfort as he sat in the prisoner's dock, trying to minimize the pain with his back up against the hard wooden pew. He sat with his body angled to one side, and Coulter Osborne thought he looked like a hockey player favouring a dislocated shoulder. But the trial continued.

Howard Kerbel called Dr. Warren Thomas Wilkins to the witness stand. The physician confirmed that he had, two days earlier, removed what appeared to be a bullet from the back of the accused Gary Comeau. The bullet had been lodged in fatty tissue, about one and a half inches beneath the surface of the skin on the patient's left side, in the area of the ninth rib. The bullet "had been surrounded by what we call fibrous tissue, which the body had created in an attempt to wall it off as a foreign object."

"So, in fact, it stayed in the body really in a capsule that had been formed by the body?"

"Yes, sir."

"Thank you, doctor, I have no further questions."

Chris Meinhardt asked Wilkins to show the jury exactly where the bullet had been found. He indicated a spot about halfway down his own back and on the left side. Wilkins confirmed, on a brief re-direct by Kerbel, that it was not unusual for a foreign object to migrate inside the body.

Finn Nielsen was recalled to reveal his findings on the bullet that had been removed from Gary Comeau's back. "I compared the projectile microscopically to a projectile which I had previously examined, that was alleged to have been removed from the brain of the deceased person in this case."

"And can you tell us what the results of your examination were?"

"Yes, the projectile which was submitted to me was fired from the same firearm. . . ."

Kerbel paused to let the full impact of Nielsen's words sink in to the jury. "Can you tell us if you observed any other substance or material either attached to or embodied within the bullet?"

"Yes, in the nose of the bullet there was some material embodied which appeared to me to resemble bone."

"Now, with respect to the bullet removed from Mr. Comeau . . . are you able to form any opinion as to whether or not the bullet had, before it entered his body, passed through any other substance?"

"Yes, I think on the basis of the amount of penetration which the projectile made in Mr. Comeau, I think it is possible that it could have passed through something else, so it would not penetrate as far as it normally would have."

"And had it not passed through some other substance before entering Mr. Comeau's body, have you been able to form an opinion as to what the result would have been for Mr. Comeau?"

"Well, if the ammunition employed had been lodged normally, it could certainly have resulted in Mr. Comeau's death."

Chris Meinhardt had noticed something while Nielsen was testifying and turned it to advantage. He established that, while Finn Nielsen wrote with his left hand, he shot with his right hand.

"Is a combination of that very unusual?"

"No, we have one other person in our section who is the same as I. He writes with his left hand and he shoots with his right."

Then Meinhardt returned to his two-gunman theory. If the jury had missed its significance before, they were no doubt fully appreciative of its importance now. Nielsen stated unequivocally that the bullets removed from Matiyek and Comeau had come from the same gun. He could not, however, deny that the third, shattered bullet could conceivably have come from a different gun, a different gunman.

Howard Kerbel called Betty King, Gary's mother, as his next witness for the defence. She testified that her son was right-handed. He had always used right-handed hockey sticks, played tennis right-handed, written letters with his right hand. She'd brought pictures of Gary as a small boy, holding a hockey stick and a baseball bat, to support her testimony.

Kerbel also wanted to get her conversation with Sam McReelis during the January 10 search of her house on the record. Mrs. King confirmed that she'd had a discussion with Sergeant McReelis, and had visited Gary in the Whitby jail as a result of that conversation.

"And can you recall now whether you asked Gary any questions?"

"Yes, I asked him, did he have a bullet wound. . . . He told me that he had it."

David Newman told the court that he planned to call no defence evidence on behalf of the accused, Larry Hurren, and Jack Grossman made a similar declaration with regard to his client, Rick Sauvé. Then, for the first time in nine weeks, the jury finally got to hear testimony from one of the accused. Ed Martin called David Hoffman to the witness stand.

Tee Hee recalled the events of October 18, 1978. He told the jury that he'd finished work at four o'clock, and later gone with Neil Stewart to the Satan's Choice Kitchener clubhouse. They'd arrived shortly before seven. Hoffman had made plans to drive to Stratford with Stewart and Claude Morin, the chapter president, to rent some Halloween costumes from a shop called "Costumes by Colleen." When they arrived at the clubhouse a police search was under way. The last police officers hadn't left the building until some time between eight and eight-thirty.

After the police departed, Stewart had gone to buy a new lock for the clubhouse door, which had been forcibly opened by the police. Hoffman then telephoned Morin and the proprietor of the Stratford costume shop to tell her they wouldn't be coming. Within about fifteen minutes Morin arrived at the clubhouse and he stayed for a short time—fifteen or twenty minutes. As Morin was leaving, another club member arrived. At around nine-fifteen or nine-thirty Stewart returned with the new lock and Hoffman and the others attempted to install it in the clubhouse door. Several other members arrived at the clubhouse around 10 p.m. Hoffman himself had left the clubhouse at around ten-thirty, and Neil Stewart had driven him back to his apartment. After a five-minute telephone conversation with another club member, Hoffman recalled watching the eleven o'clock news and going to bed.

"Did anyone come to your apartment between the time you went to bed on the night of October 18 and the time you got up in the morning of the nineteenth?"

"Yes."

"And who was that?"

"Gary Comeau, Rick Sauvé, and Merv Blaker. . . . They were at my back door, and the banging on the door woke me up and I let them in. . . . They stayed for a while. I am not sure how long they stayed. . . . After I let them in and speaking with them for a short time, I went back to bed and when I woke up in the morning, they were gone. . . . Mr. Comeau told me he had been shot. . . . When he came into my apartment, I noticed him having some difficulty taking off his jacket, and I asked him what was wrong . . . and I helped him to take his jacket off, and I noticed he had sort of a cloth bandage around his arm, and it was bloodstained to some degree, and he removed it, and I saw a wound of some sort, on his arm."

Hoffman identified the copy of his telephone bill that had been entered as an exhibit. He confirmed that the call to Port Hope made in the early morning hours of October 19 had been placed by Rick Sauvé.

Martin produced a copy of the statement that Hoffman had made to the police on November 20.

"Now, in the making of the statement, did you tell the police about the three men who arrived at your apartment after you went to sleep on the night of the eighteenth?"

"No sir. . . ."

"Why not?"

"Well, Gary told me he had been shot. . . . I just felt that if I told the police that, you know, that I would be involved, and you know, tried to get all kinds of information out of me and I just didn't want to become involved or scared, I suppose."

Hoffman denied that there had been any kind of party or loud music on in his apartment when Sauvé placed the call to Port Hope. He confirmed that he owned two pairs of running shoes, one pair red, the other pair blue-and-white.

Had the witness ever seen Cathy Cotgrave on or before October 18? "No, sir." He did, however, remember being introduced to Gayle Thompson in the Queen's Hotel by her boyfriend Randy Koehler in January or February of 1978. Koehler had been an old boyhood friend of Hoffman's, and their fathers were good friends. Hoffman remembered seeing Sue Foote before, but he couldn't recall exactly when or where. He had never seen Rod Stewart in the Queen's Hotel. Nor could he remember ever seeing Helen Mitchell before the preliminary hearing. Hoffman also denied being in the Queen's Hotel in December 1977 during the fight between Bill Matiyek and Tom Horner.

Martin showed Hoffman a telephone bill for the Kitchener clubhouse and noted a call to Stratford on October 18. Hoffman confirmed that was the call he'd made to the costume shop after the police raid, "probably some time around eight-thirty or a little after eight-thirty."

"Have you had any occasion to drive a car from the Queen's Hotel in Port Hope to the location of the Satan's Choice clubhouse in Kitchener, at any time up to the present time?"

"Yes, sir." It usually took him about two hours to drive the 183 kilometres, non-stop.

Chris Meinhardt questioned Hoffman closely about Sauvé's phone call to Port Hope, but Tee Hee maintained he hadn't listened that closely.

"And I understand that on the next day you missed part of the workday?"

"Yes, sir."

"Were you ill?"

"Yes, sir. I wasn't feeling well when I woke up in the morning."

"And when did you get to work?"

"I believe I went to work at noon that day."

"You didn't go and see a doctor or anything?"

"No, sir."

"Just feeling a little rough?"

"Um—no, I don't know—I get headaches periodically. I don't know what the problem was that morning. I just wasn't feeling well, so I didn't go in."

The Crown Attorney turned to Hoffman's club activities. The big biker confirmed that he'd been Kitchener Chapter treasurer from the fall of 1967 until he was arrested in December 1978. Wasn't it also true, Meinhardt continued, that each of the men he claimed to have been with on the evening of October 18 were then current, past, or future members of the Satan's Choice?

"Yes, they would all . . . fall within that category I guess."

The Crown Attorney returned to the late call. "And you say that while Sauvé was making the call, there was no music, no party going on at that time?"

"No, there certainly wasn't."

"And that Roger Davey, when he gave evidence, he must have been mistaken when he said that he heard the signs of a party?"

"I would certainly think so, if he was the man that the call was made to."

"And also, Mr. Koehler was mistaken when he said he saw you at the Queen's Hotel shortly before Christmas of 1977, in an altercation with Bill Matiyek?"

"He certainly is."

"And Sue Foote, who you agree you have seen before October 18, 1978, she is mistaken when she sees you at the Queen's Hotel on October 18, 1978?"

"Yes, she is."

"And Gayle Thompson, when she sees you, she says—is also mistaken?"

"Yes, she is."

"And Miss Mitchell is also mistaken?"

"Yes, she is."

"And Mr. Stewart is also mistaken?"

"Yes, sir."

"Because you were at Kitchener at that time, listening to the late news?"

"Yes, sir."

" . . . Thank you."

It was late Friday afternoon when Hoffman finished testifying and court was adjourned for the weekend. When the courtroom had emptied, some of the others gathered around Tee Hee. They slapped him on the back and pumped his hand. Even a few of the lawyers joined in.

"Congratulations, Tee Hee."

"You were great!"

"You just walked yourself, man."

And indeed, compared with Lorne Campbell, Tee Hee had been a good witness, his answers forthright and to the point. But would the jurors believe him? Tee Hee wasn't so sure. Who knew what the jury was thinking?

As the end of the trial drew near, the jury was very much on everyone's mind. At a courtroom meeting some time earlier Affleck had confessed he was puzzled and deeply worried by the jury's attitude. "They haven't looked our way in six weeks," Affleck told the accused and the other lawyers. "I've never seen anything like it." From his years as a Crown, Affleck knew that it was only normal for the jury to scan the faces of the accused. They might regard them angrily or sympathetically or balefully, but at least they'd study the accused, as if attempting to peer into their souls, in a search for innocence or guilt. But this jury no longer seemed to be doing that.

Terry O'Hara had made his own observation about the jury, though he'd kept it to himself. Coulter Osborne had grown ever more short-tempered with Howard Kerbel, interrupting him, cutting him off, admonishing him the way a teacher would a wayward schoolboy. One day in court, when Kerbel had walked over to the jury-box to hand an exhibit over to the jury, one of the jurors had recoiled visibly. He hadn't wanted to accept the proffered object from Kerbel's hand. The body language made O'Hara wince. The implication of it was too awful to contemplate.

And, indeed, though they sat more or less impassively day in and day out, silent as a dozen Sphinxes, the jurors heard and saw a great deal. They saw Larry Hurren's mother, faithfully attending her son's trial. They noted, not without sympathy, the periodic appearances of other relatives of the accused—mothers and fathers, sisters and brothers and wives, and they had long ago puzzled out who was related to whom. They saw the expensive gold chain that dangled from Howard Kerbel's wrist sometimes, visible below the cuff of his solicitor's gown. One day they had noted the presence of Kerbel's girlfriend—the female jurors especially had noted her immaculate coiffure and expensive clothes, and they discussed it later among themselves. It just didn't seem right that someone should grow rich defending young men like these.

And still Terry O'Hara clung stubbornly to his belief that the accused must take the witness stand. Hoping to convince Affleck that his client would make a good witness, O'Hara and the senior defence counsel drove down to the Detention Centre on the weekend before Lorne Campbell was due to give evidence. The next few days would be Jeff McLeod's last chance to testify on his own behalf. O'Hara had persuaded Affleck to subject McLeod to a mock direct examination and cross-examination, just to see how he'd do in court. The two lawyers spent several hours with the burly biker, Affleck pretending to do a direct examination, O'Hara the toughest cross he could think of. To O'Hara's own surprise, the much-diminished but still massive McLeod proved as light on his feet in the mock witness-box as he had once been on the arena ice of the Scarborough minor hockey leagues. But Affleck remained unconvinced—putting their clients on the stand would be giving Meinhardt just too much, he insisted, as they drove back to downtown London. That day was the first time O'Hara began to suspect that, beneath his hulking exterior, Jeff McLeod was concealing a first-rate mind.

On Monday, November 5, the Satan's Choice murder trial entered its tenth week. It was the final week of evidence, and the proceeding was gaining momentum, gathering speed like a runaway train on an ever-sharper decline. On Monday the jury heard evidence from ten defence witnesses, on Tuesday from seven.

The defendants could feel what little control they still had over their lives slipping from them. Years later, after he had completed his high school equivalency and begun to take university courses, Jeff McLeod read about something called "The Theory of Learned Helplessness." Behavioral psychologists, experimenting with live rats, had made an interesting discovery. They placed the rats inside an electrified cage and allowed them to eat whatever they wanted. But every time the rats fed themselves, the experimenters would jolt them with an electrical shock. After a time the shocks would no longer alter the rat's behavior. They had learned that the punishment was coming, but they would eat their food greedily anyway, helpless to do anything about it. They just braced for the shock. That, Jeff thought, was what it had been like in the final weeks in Courtroom 21 and the years after. Just like those rats, the men in the prisoner's dock knew the shock was coming, but they were powerless now to change anything. They had become conditioned into helplessness.

First thing Monday morning Howard Kerbel called a witness who would lay into place the final piece of the puzzle of the missing third bullet, the one that had now been extracted from Gary Comeau's body. William Philip told the jury that he was an analyst with the biology section of the Centre of Forensic Sciences in Toronto, and that he had examined the Comeau bullet after Finn Nielsen had finished with it.

"On examination of the bullet I found tissue-like debris in the hollow end, and on examining this debris I found five tiny fibres. On examining these fibres I found that four of the five were similar to the checkered surface of the reversible jacket said to be from the deceased in this matter. These similarities consisted of fibre type. All four were acrylic fibres. Also the similarity consisted of the shade of colouring and also physical characteristics such as the presence or absence of delustering agents of the fibres, the size of the fibres, and the presence or absence of striations on the fibres. . . . Certainly the fact that they compared favourably in terms of fibre type, colour, and physical characteristics leads me to conclude that those four fibres are consistent with originating from the one surface of the jacket of the deceased."

As his final witness in Gary Comeau's defence, Kerbel recalled Constable Donald Denis. Mostly, Kerbel had recalled the OPP identification officer to tie up a few minor loose ends in the evidence. But his reappearance afforded Meinhardt, in cross-examination, the opportunity to ask him what had now become an important question.

"With respect to the line-up, did the line-up contain a photograph of Lorne Campbell?"

"Yes sir, it did."

"I show to you Exhibit 52. Is Campbell's picture in that folder?"

"Yes, sir. Number 10-S-4."

"Did any person that was shown the photographic array pick Lorne Campbell as being a person in the hotel on October 18, the day of the killing?"

"No, sir."

"Did anyone even linger at his photograph?"

"No sir."

One photo, compared to Gary's seven or more.

Ed Martin resumed calling evidence for David Hoffman's alibi defence. Seven corroborating witnesses paraded through the witness-box that day, all but two of them associated, in one way or another, with the Satan's Choice. Each recounted his knowledge of Tee Hee's whereabouts on the night of October 18.

Five recalled the events in Kitchener on the night of the shooting: the raid, and installing a new lock. Four of them had actually seen Hoffman as late as 10:45, and the fifth had talked to him on the phone.

Colleen Misener, the owner and operator of Costumes by Colleen, also testified on Tee Hee's behalf. It turned out that, in addition to her business interests, Ms. Misener was also the Chairman of the Stratford Police Commission. A check of her records for 1978 revealed that she had indeed rented Halloween costumes to David Hoffman, Neil Stewart, and Claude Morin. Did the witness recognize any of those three individuals in court? She pointed to Hoffman and said he "looked vaguely familiar." Her records also showed that the costumes rented to the three had been returned on time. (Martin was anxious to establish evidence of good character anywhere he could find it.) The accused got quite a kick out of having someone from the Police Commission saying what nice boys they were.

Meinhardt's cross-examinations, especially of the Choice-associated witnesses, fell into an obvious pattern. He'd linger over the criminal record of each, drawing out as much detail as he could, then establish how each witness was associated with the Satan's Choice.

Meinhardt also elicited admissions from several that they had all met more than once with Hoffman and his lawyer to go over their evidence in advance of the trial.

Gordy van Haarlem took his turn in the witness-box late Monday afternoon. He told Donald Ebbs during his examination-in-chief that he'd been living "here and there . . . I just stayed all over" in October 1978, but whenever he was in Port Hope he would stay at Rick Sauvé's. He had, in fact, slept at Sauvé's on the night of October 17. Late the next afternoon he'd ridden his bike to Peterborough. He'd left his Harley at a friend's and walked downtown, to the Grand Hotel, where he met a couple of friends, including Bobby Cousins, who was then the president of the Choice Peterborough Chapter, of which van Haarlem was a member.

After drinking "a draft or so," the three had then gone to a second hotel, the Trent Inn, and from there to the Queen's Hotel, also in downtown Peterborough. At around eight-thirty they'd arrived at the King George Hotel, where they settled in for the evening. They'd been joined by any number of people throughout the evening, including several guards from the Peterborough jail. It had been an uneventful evening, although van Haarlem had been asked at one point to take his colours off, and he'd remained in the King George until at least 1:30 a.m. He'd left the beer parlor a few times, van Haarlem recalled, going out both the front and the back doors with a couple of people, but he was never out of the hotel for more than fifteen minutes, certainly nowhere near long enough to make the one-hour round trip to Port Hope.

He'd spent the night at his friend's in Peterborough. He'd learned of the Matiyek shooting as soon as he got back to Port Hope the next day. Van Haarlem said that though he had seen Bill Matiyek, he hadn't known him personally. "I never drank with him or anything."

Van Haarlem conceded that several members of the Choice Peterborough Chapter, including Brian Babcock and Tom Horner, had had fights with Matiyek in the past. But he denied that the fights developed into anything more than just personal fights between individual members and Matiyek. "That's all. Just drunk fights." The Peterborough Chapter had had regular meetings in the spring of 1978, van Haarlem added, but there had been no meetings at all in the summer and fall.

"Why was that?"

"Well, there wasn't enough guys on the street to have a meeting, you know. Everybody was in jail, so—"

Don Ebbs cut his client off. "And do you recall how many were on the street at the time?"

"Maybe three. Three or four, maybe."

"Now at any point in time did you ever hear of or know of any plan or scheme to either beat up or kill Mr. Matiyek?"

"No, never."

"Thank you, my Lord. Those are the questions I have at this time."

"Mr. Meinhardt?"

"Mr. van Haarlem, if you had attended a meeting where there was a plan made to kill Bill Matiyek, would you tell us about it?"

"I don't know. There has never been such a meeting, so—"

"Would you tell us about it if you knew?"

"I can't say. I don't know."

Meinhardt then cross-examined van Haarlem on his criminal record. Though he was, at the age of twenty-three, the youngest of the defendants, van Haarlem's record filled a full page of the trial transcript. It included convictions for theft over $200, theft under, possession of a restricted drug, possession of a restricted drug for the purpose of trafficking, failure to attend court, mischief and causing a disturbance, possession of a narcotic a second time, common assault, possession of an unregistered weapon, a third drug conviction, and assault with intent to commit bodily harm.

Meinhardt asked van Haarlem about Helen Mitchell. Was there another member of the club in the Port Hope–Cobourg area that looked like van Haarlem?

"Just Horner . . . he must. The coppers mix us up sometimes."

Van Haarlem said he'd sponsored Horner into the club, and he'd become a full member about three months later.

"And did his becoming a full member depend at all on him hassling Bill Matiyek?"

"What do you mean by that?"

"Was this a job for him as a striker?"

"Oh no. Like he hassled everybody, eh?"

The next morning before court, Terry O'Hara held a meeting with Merv Blaker. Ebbs would complete his evidence that day, O'Hara knew, and then it would be Murray's last chance to take the stand. He urged his client, in the strongest possible terms, to do so. But Merv was reluctant, at this late date, to break ranks with his co-defendants. O'Hara had anticipated Blaker's response and he drew a typewritten document from his briefcase. It was the Kingston lawyer's last, desperate attempt to get his client to give evidence. The paper read:

I, MURRAY LLOYD BLAKER, hereby instruct my Counsel, Terence C. O'Hara, that I do not wish to give evidence at my Trial. I understand that Mr. O'Hara has advised me that it would be in my best interest to give evidence and that if I do not give evidence I will likely be convicted on the charge of First Degree Murder for which I am now being tried. This Direction has been read to me and I understand its contents.

Dated at London this 6th day of November, 1979.

Blaker read the statement again to himself and then asked O'Hara for a pen. The young lawyer watched in silence as, to the bitter and everlasting regret of them both, his client signed the statement.

O'Hara's calculation proved correct—Tuesday, November 6, 1979, was the final day of evidence for the defence. Before the day was through it was obvious that Don Ebbs had more than done his homework on van Haarlem's behalf. The Peterborough lawyer called a total of seven witnesses to corroborate his client's alibi. They included two jail guards and the doorman, the disc jockey, and even the manager of the King George Hotel in downtown Peterborough. Each of them remembered either drinking with or seeing van Haarlem at the King George throughout the night of the shooting. None of them had any connection to the Satan's Choice Motorcycle Club and not one of them had a criminal record.

Meinhardt's cross-examinations of each of the alibi witnesses were rigorous, verging on the tendentious. But, since none of the witnesses had a criminal record or any known criminal association and lacked any apparent reason to lie, the Crown Attorney's questioning proved largely unavailing. It was just as Bruce Affleck had predicted before the trial—his former Crown colleague was devastating when he was "given" something by a witness under cross-examination, be it evidence of bad character or guilt by association. But when the witnesses were squeaky-clean, as van Haarlem's evidently were, he was far less effective.

Ebbs sat down and, shortly after two-thirty in the afternoon, Justice Osborne turned to Terry O'Hara. "Mr. O'Hara?"

The corpulent Kingston lawyer rose with a heavy heart. "My Lord, I don't intend to call any evidence." There was the faintest hint of resignation in his voice.

As the trial neared its end, the relationship between the defendants in custody and their captors had imperceptibly grown friendlier, almost as if the police had decided maybe they weren't really such bad guys after all, once they'd come to know a few bikers personally. Occasionally the coppers would ask them if there was anything special they could do, and the accused decided to ask for some special food. They'd been living on a steady diet of institutional cooking for nearly a year, and they were heartily sick of it. Especially the courthouse lunches. The jurors were given specially catered midday meals prepared in the best hotel kitchens in downtown London. But the accused got only sandwiches, usually just a piece of bologna between two slices of stale white bread.

So, the next time their guards asked them if they needed or wanted anything, they were ready. "Pizza, man." "Burgers and chips with a shake."

The coppers laughed. "All right. Get some money off your lawyers and we'll see if we can't fix you up." Sure enough, they did. They'd pull the paddy wagon into one of the fast-food places along the Wellington Road strip and order a bunch of burgers or pizza or Colonel Sanders "to go," and let the guys pig out in the back of the paddy wagon on the way back to the Detention Centre. They thought they'd died and gone to heaven.

XXXII

THE FINAL JURY SUBMISSIONS of the lawyers took more than a week. They were recorded but never transcribed. The only written record of them that remains is provided by Mac Haig's newspaper accounts, which are reasonably extensive. Bruce Affleck's address, which began Friday morning, was just over an hour in length. Only two Crown witnesses had identified his client Jeff McLeod at all, Affleck reminded the jury—Susan Foote and Cathy Cotgrave. He attempted to exploit Foote's evident confusion of McLeod and Comeau. Cotgrave had testified that she saw McLeod sitting at a table with Jamie Hanna (this was, in fact, Comeau and not McLeod), yet Hanna, who had had the best opportunity to identify McLeod, had not done so. Foote's evidence had been laced with inconsistencies. At the preliminary hearing she had not named Jeff McLeod as being among the group that entered through the back door, and yet at the trial she had. At the preliminary hearing her identification had been doubtful, at best. Yet at the trial she had insisted she was absolutely certain. Had Sue Foote ever really seen Jeff McLeod?

And what of Cathy Cotgrave? She had positively identified Gary Comeau as the gunman. She'd been absolutely positive, Affleck reminded the jury. Absolutely positive. But, because of the bullet that had been removed from Gary Comeau's body "we now know that Gary Comeau, positively identified as the gunman, was not the gunman at all." It has long been known that eyewitness identification evidence is the most unreliable evidence at a trial, Affleck lectured, and the identification of Comeau as the gunman was a case in point.

The former Crown added that there was no evidence whatsoever that Jeff McLeod had participated in a planned and deliberate murder, as the Crown had charged. It would be "inane and foolish" for a group of men to plan to enter a bar where some of them were well known and then kill someone.

"It isn't enough," Affleck concluded, "for you to say, 'Well, I think he was probably there . . . I think he could have been there.' You must be able to say, 'He was there and he is guilty and of that I am morally certain.'"

David Newman followed Affleck on Friday afternoon, and he adopted a totally different strategy. The young lawyer selected the first letter from the last name of each of the jurors and tied that to an issue in the trial—to help the jury remember his submissions on behalf of Hurren, Newman said.

Juror number two, Sandra Johnson, was asked to remember the letter "J," representing the evidence of Julie Joncas. Juror number three, Laura Ann Lippold, should remember the letter "L," which stood for logic the jury should apply to the evidence. Edgar Horace Gudgeon might recall the letter "G" during the deliberations. "G" stood for the gunman who had actually killed Bill Matiyek, and who was still, even after a ten-week trial, unidentified. "K" was the first letter in the surname of Albert Francis Kanters, juror number six. Mr. Kanters should let that stand for knowledge—what knowledge had Hurren possessed that Bill Matiyek was going to be shot? On the evidence, there was no such knowledge. Gloria Hines should bear the letter "H" in mind, which stood for the heavy onus on the Crown to prove beyond a reasonable doubt that Hurren was guilty of murder. And so on, down the list of jurors.

Newman observed that Hurren had already admitted to being in the hotel. But, he argued, "it makes no sense that Larry Hurren would go to a hotel where he knew he would be recognized to commit a murder." There was no evidence that Hurren had been personally involved in the enmity between the Golden Hawk Riders and the Satan's Choice, and "there is no evidence of any animosity between Larry Hurren and Mr. Matiyek." Similarly, there had been no evidence that Hurren had actually done anything in the hotel that night but sit or stand beside the bar.

Hurren's lawyer reminded the jury that Larry Hurren himself was on trial, not the Satan's Choice. Bikers might not be desirable or even "very nice people," but the jurors had promised before the trial that they would not allow prejudice against motorcycle clubs to interfere with an impartial verdict based solely on the evidence.

The club members had gone to the Queen's expecting a fight, "but some fool pulled out a gun and killed Matiyek on a ridiculous impulse" (Haig's wording). But it had not been established that the killer, whoever he was, had any connection with Hurren. Above all else, the jury must not convict Larry Hurren of first-degree murder because of his mere presence in the hotel and his membership in the Satan's Choice Motorcycle Club.

Although it lasted only forty-five minutes, Newman's address to the jury was audacious, and his use of their initials was unprecedented. It certainly was memorable. And it would elicit very shortly yet another rebuke from the Judge.

In the robing-room Terry O'Hara watched in astonishment as the silk gown of a Queen's Counsel flew through the air. "Shiiit!" He and Bruce Affleck were alone, and Affleck was absolutely livid. "And you, Mr. Martin," Affleck mimicked, "your name begins with 'M' and it stands for murder, and we'd hate to see that happen to any of you, wouldn't we, if our clients are convicted. Fuck shit!" A winged collar fluttered to the floor like a wounded butterfly, and O'Hara began to laugh. "And you, Mr. Pearson, your name begins with 'P' and that stands for prick and that's just what you'll find up the cunt of your prettiest daughter if our innocent clients are found guilty. . . ." O'Hara began to howl at Affleck's bitter and ever more scatological invective. Poor Bruce. First his cross of Denis had been undone by

Kerbel and now his jury address had been totally upstaged by Newman.

Affleck liked Newman, not least because the younger lawyer had once referred to him as "The King." But revealing the jurors' identities had been a poorly calculated, theatrical trick. Never again, Affleck resolved, would he work with someone with less experience in criminal law, Terry excepted, of course. ". . . which stands for Harley, and you could find twenty of them on the neat lawn of your suburban London bungalow if you don't acquit our clients. . . ." Affleck stood before O'Hara now, stripped to his skivvies and socks, his body and face florid with rage, but Terry kept laughing, until the tears rolled down his own ruddy cheeks.

Court was resumed at 9:34 a.m. on Monday, November 12, and Judge Osborne turned to David Newman almost at once. ". . . Mr. Newman in his address referred to twelve points which I have noted. They certainly are not objectionable. However, the mechanics of their presentation was wrong and that creates a problem. The difficulty that I find, Mr. Newman, is that your approach, while having significant theatrical merit, is wrong in law, and the jury is going to have to be told that . . . they are not here to give an individual, isolated decision, but they all must consider all of the evidence, and the approach suggested by Mr. Newman was just opposite of that, where the jury was singled out and invited to each consider a given point. They will have to be told that that is wrong and if it happens again I will tell them immediately."

True to his declaration at the preliminary hearing nine months before, that police identification procedures would "form the very core of Mr. Comeau's defence," Howard Kerbel hammered the police in his address to the jury. Kerbel detailed all of the shortcomings in Constable Denis's showing of the photo line-ups before scoring the identifications of the eyewitnesses themselves.

"Cathy Cotgrave and Gayle Thompson stood here in this courtroom and pointed out Mr. Comeau as the man who shot Mr. Matiyek," Kerbel reminded the jury, but it was now clear that Comeau himself had been shot. "So much for courtroom identification. . . . Are you able to convict Mr. Comeau if you don't know who the gunman is? If it isn't Campbell and it isn't Comeau, then there is no evidence that the gunman is one of the men who came in. . . . If Cotgrave and Thompson are wrong about who the gunman was, they could be wrong about other things. . . ."

Kerbel urged the jurors not to let their own prejudices about bike clubs cloud their judgement of the evidence. He also cautioned the jury against letting prejudicial newspaper articles unduly affect their judgement.

Jack Grossman continued in much the same vein. Richard Sauvé, like Larry Hurren, had admitted his presence in the hotel at the time of the shooting. But Sauvé had been easily identified by most of the witnesses. It made no sense for him to take part in a pre-planned killing in a hotel in the middle of his own home town where he knew he would be easily recognized. As for his alleged threats against Bill Matiyek, they were remote in time from the actual shooting. While his client may have had a loose tongue, there was no actual evidence that Richard Sauvé had planned or participated in the shooting of Bill Matiyek in any way. The evidence against Sauvé was ambivalent, and couched in insinuating overtones, Grossman concluded. But suspicion, speculation, conjecture, or probability were not enough to convict an accused at a criminal trial.

Ed Martin explained the conflict between David Hoffman's alibi evidence and that of the five witnesses who claimed to have seen him in the hotel in the only way he could—honest witnesses can sometimes be mistaken. Two of those witnesses, he reminded the jury, also thought they saw Gary Comeau shoot Bill Matiyek, which the jury now knew was impossible. It had been proven beyond a reasonable doubt that Hoffman had been in the company of police officers until at least eight o'clock that night, and David Hoffman had not made up the police raid. "On the other side, the Crown would have you believe that David Hoffman went to Port Hope . . . at speeds up to 100 miles per hour . . . to become involved in something which did not concern him . . . and did not concern the Kitchener Chapter of his club." Martin urged the jury to acquit David Hoffman.

Bernard Cugelman addressed the jury on Tuesday morning. Only a single witness, Cathy Cotgrave, claimed to have seen his client, Armand Sanguigni, in the hotel, the same Cathy Cotgrave who had positively identified Comeau as the gunman. She had not seen him arrive or leave "and she didn't see him again after that glance into the pinball room. . . ." Cotgrave had, in fact, used the same expression, "pretty sure," in identifying both Comeau and Sanguigni. Numerous other persons at the scene had not identified his client at all. It would be extremely dangerous, Cugelman warned the jury, to convict Armand Sanguigni on the strength of a single witness.

Don Ebbs reviewed Gordon van Haarlem's alibi evidence that afternoon. The only witness who had identified his client, Ebbs told the jury, was Helen Mitchell, who had herself admitted occasionally confusing van Haarlem with another member of the Satan's Choice Peterborough Chapter, Tom Horner. All of the other accused had been placed inside the hotel at some specific location, but van Haarlem had been tied to no place, no activity. Mitchell's evidence was vague and extremely frail. "Although there is no onus on the defence, the defence evidence goes much further than the Crown's and establishes beyond a reasonable doubt that van Haarlem was in Peterborough that night." Then Ebbs dropped a bomb in the laps of the accused. Van Haarlem's alibi witnesses, he reminded the jury, were not members of the Satan's Choice, had never been members of the Satan's Choice, had no connection to the club. On the basis of his ironclad alibi, the jury should acquit Gordon van Haarlem.

Ebbs's closing remarks were an obvious reference to David Hoffman's alibi witnesses. Tee Hee glanced at Larry Hurren, who was sitting next to him, and shook his head sadly as soon as the words were out of Ebbs's mouth. Ebbs was stepping over *his* body to win acquittal for his client. They were all saddened and ashamed, especially Gordy. From a lawyer's point of view, Ebbs's desire to represent his client successfully at any cost, even at the expense of a co-accused, was perhaps understandable. But it was a grievous affront to outlaw—and club—mentality, a serious ethical violation. If hang they must, then they would hang together. If they let themselves be split apart, then hang they certainly would, one at a time, separately, and in disgrace.

Some of the lawyers took an equally dim view of Ebbs's behavior. That night several of the defence team argued so angrily that they almost came to blows. So much for the solidarity of the defence team. Now it was every man for himself. But, privately, the accused resolved once again to stick together. They were solid, they told, themselves, and they couldn't help it if their lawyers had no class.

And so, against the bikers' own better instincts, the effect of the summations was to show the jury the difference between a "good" and a "bad" alibi—an advantage which Meinhardt pushed to its limit in pursuit of a conviction for Tee Hee Hoffman.

O'Hara had also detected what he believed to be an oversight in Martin's jury address. Hoffman's lawyer had failed to mention that there was no record of calls having been made by Rick Sauvé either to Hoffman's apartment or to the Kitchener Choice clubhouse on the night of the murder. Meinhardt would obviously argue that Sauvé's phone bill, which revealed calls to the Toronto clubhouse and to the hotels in Peterborough, was evidence that Sauvé had set the assassination plot in motion. But there was no evidence that he had called Kitchener. At lunch O'Hara asked Martin whether he should make that important point in his own submission. Martin said he'd think it over, and let O'Hara know.

O'Hara himself had worked long and hard on his own presentation to the jury, and he would always remember it as one of the best—perhaps *the* best—in his whole career. As O'Hara left the defence table to begin, Ed Martin caught his eye and shook his head slightly as if to say, "Leave the telephone evidence alone."

Murray Blaker had admitted he was in the hotel, O'Hara reminded the jury, but there was no evidence that he shot anyone, no evidence that he said or did anything to encourage the commission of a crime. The evidence of hostility between the Satan's Choice and the Golden Hawks was not sufficient to prove the planning of a murder, O'Hara argued, and Blaker had not been involved in any of the fights with Matiyek, on the evidence. He urged the jury to exercise its common sense, to consider "the way the world works." (Now it was Howard Kerbel's turn to wince. He believed O'Hara was giving something to Meinhardt here, and he was right.) Why would Murray Blaker, who had grown up and lived in the Port Hope area all his life, walk into a bar filled with witnesses who he knew could identify him and be a party to a planned and deliberate murder? It simply defied common sense.

Terry O'Hara had also decided to tackle Lorne Campbell's evidence head on. He was unique among the defence lawyers in this regard. O'Hara believed that Campbell had been telling the truth. It was the *way* he'd told his story, O'Hara sensed, that troubled the jury. And perhaps that was the very point, O'Hara suggested to the jurors. In the flat, emotionless manner with which Campbell had recounted his shooting of Bill Matiyek, the jury might well find confirmation that he was telling the truth. No normal person would describe taking another human life in such a detached, dispassionate way. But then, no normal person would fire three bullets into the head of another human being at point-blank range in the first place. O'Hara had no personal basis for it—he'd never spoken to Campbell—and there was certainly no basis in the evidence, but the Kingston lawyer went on to describe the state of mind of Matiyek's killer as being practically psychopathic. Although he was facing the jury, O'Hara heard the restless rustle of silk and sensed that Meinhardt was about to rise. It was highly unusual for one lawyer to interrupt another's jury submission, and O'Hara knew he had pushed the issue as far as he dared. He moved on, and the rustle subsided.

And what of Campbell's previous perjury conviction? That looked bad, O'Hara conceded, until you thought about it. If the Satan's Choice had decided to send a totally innocent man onto the witness stand in an attempt to win acquittals for the accused, then why select a man with a perjury conviction on his record? That, too, made no sense, unless Campbell was in fact telling the truth. All in all, O'Hara concluded, the jury should find Murray Blaker innocent of first-degree murder. True to Martin's wishes, he hadn't mentioned Sauvé's phone bill.

Chris Meinhardt began his submission for the Crown the next morning. Bill Matiyek's killing had been a planned execution, Meinhardt told the jury, and it was the position of the Crown that "all those who conspired to do it, who helped to do it in any way, are equally guilty of murder." The jury had only to look at the evidence. The quickness of the killing, the three shots to the head, showed that Matiyek's death was an execution. The whole thing had been planned and deliberate, and anyone who assisted in the planning and commission of murder was as guilty as the actual killer. That was the law.

Meinhardt reviewed the evidence. No fewer than seven eyewitnesses had placed Sauvé at the murder scene. Six had identified Blaker, five had identified Comeau and Hoffman, four had seen Hurren, two had ID'd McLeod, and both Sanguigni and van Haarlem had been identified by one witness. All of these men had been banned from the Queen's Hotel since May 1978 on account of their membership in the Satan's Choice, and it was significant that when waitress Cathy Cotgrave told Sauvé the group would not be served he had simply shrugged his shoulders. There was no protest of this announcement, and "from this you may infer that these people did not go there to drink."

One of the bar patrons, David Gillispie, overheard Gary Comeau ask Sauvé and Blaker: "Are we going to do it to this fat fucker now, or what?" That, Meinhardt told the jury, was "a clarion call to action." Almost at once Sauvé moved to Matiyek's table, said something to Jamie Hanna, who moved away from the table, the others approached, "and Matiyek is executed."

Rod Stewart had told the jury about seeing Matiyek on the telephone and recalled seeing a group of men following the deceased back to his table. If the jury accepted Stewart's evidence, these men had formed a horseshoe around Matiyek's table just as the shots were fired. Hoffman and Hurren were part of that horseshoe. Meinhardt then reviewed the evidence of enmity between the Golden Hawk Riders and the Satan's Choice. As recently as July 1978 Rick Sauvé had warned that Matiyek wasn't going to be around very long, that he was going to get his brains blown out, and that was exactly what had happened. Matiyek's murder in so public a place was meant as an example to anyone who dared to defy the Satan's Choice. "I suggest to you this was a public execution. It was meant to be an example to anyone who defied them." Rick Sauvé's words had proved prophetic—"someone was thinking about it and it happened when the time was right on October 18."

And what of the bullet removed from Gary Comeau? That didn't clear Comeau, Meinhardt contended. It proved, in fact, that he had indeed been near Matiyek at the moment he was shot. It was possible there had been more than one gunman in the Queen's Hotel that night, though Meinhardt conceded there was no hard evidence of that.

And then there was the testimony of Lorne Campbell. Meinhardt reminded the jury of Campbell's long criminal record, which included perjury. Campbell's testimony was false, Meinhardt said flatly, because he wasn't even in the hotel. "It is my respectful submission that you should treat him with all the contempt that he deserves." None of the eyewitnesses had picked Campbell's picture from the photo array. "There isn't an iota of evidence except from the lips of a convicted per-jurer that the gunman was a dark-haired man with a goatee and an ear-ring in his left ear. . . . All the evidence points to a blond-haired, blond-bearded gunman."

In any event, the Crown did not have to prove who the actual gunman was. Whoever participated in a planned and deliberate murder was, under the law, just as guilty as the gunman.

Terry O'Hara had urged the jury to consider the evidence in the "way the world works," using common sense. But these men were not like ordinary citizens, living in the ordinary world. They were bikers, members of a motorcycle gang. They may well have believed that none of the eyewitnesses would dare to testify against them after watching such a brazen, terrible act. Bill Matiyek's death was a "planned, deliberate, vicious execution" and there is "abundant evidence for you to conclude that all the accused were parties to the foul and premeditated murder of Bill Matiyek."

Meinhardt's closing remarks lasted a day and a half, and it was the afternoon of Thursday, November 15, when he finally resumed his seat. Judge Osborne turned towards the jury. The final matter to be dealt with, he told the jurors, was his own charge to them, which would be lengthy. He proposed to begin it the following Monday, and when the charge was finished the jury could begin its deliberations. They would be sequestered from that time until they reached a verdict. He mentioned all this now, Osborne explained, so they could make plans ahead of time to be away from home.

XXXIII

AS HE SURVEYED HIS COURTROOM on the morning of Monday, November 19, 1979, Mr. Justice Coulter Osborne faced a formidable legal challenge. The trial at which he was presiding had just entered its twelfth week and this morning it would exceed the Peter Demeter trial in length. It was not the sort of fact that Coulter Osborne would normally concern himself with, but everyone in the Middlesex County Courthouse was aware of it, and a member of his staff had told him that they were about to set "a new indoor record." The Satan's Choice trial was now the longest murder trial in modern Canadian legal history, to be exceeded in length only by the murder trial of Helmuth Buxbaum in the fall of 1985.

The proceeding had turned out to be extraordinary in other ways, too. Barely in the annals of Canadian law had so many individuals been charged with first-degree murder in the death of a single individual. Probably never before had eight people been tried for first-degree murder in a trial that had, in the end, left so little solid Crown evidence standing against any *one* of them as the actual murderer. Judge Osborne was by now personally convinced, as he would make clear shortly, that Gary Comeau had not been the gunman. On the other hand, he believed there was sufficient evidence for the jury to convict some, if not all, of the accused of . . . something.

The jury charge that Osborne was about to begin required a sense of discretion and judicial delicacy that would have challenged the most experienced of senior judges, much less a relatively recent appointee to the bench. The first difficulty was the sheer volume of evidence. The jurors would take with them into their deliberations more than 130 exhibits, plus hundreds of photographs from the police photo line-up. They had heard the testimony of nearly seventy witnesses, had sat through countless cross-examinations. It must surely have taxed the memory, if not the patience, of even the most diligent of jurors. It would be necessary to review all of this evidence as comprehensively and fairly as possible.

Then there were the innumerable points of law upon which Osborne must correctly instruct the jury. In the end, his charge would read like a short course in Canadian criminal law. He had to define the concepts of weight and credibility that the jury must apply to each witness's testimony, the difference between direct and circumstantial evidence, the importance (or lack of it) that might be attached to the prior inconsistent statements of both Crown and defence witnesses, the nature of alibi evidence, and the verdict options open to the jury.

He knew, too, that his charge, no matter what the outcome of the trial, would be scrutinized by whole batteries of lawyers eager to sift through it, weighing every word, every phrase, for a grain of bias or legal error that might provide the basis for an appeal. Osborne had already entertained—and dismissed—a late flurry of defence motions (ranging from severance applications to mistrial motions) that he suspected had been presented for the express purpose of establishing later grounds for appeal. And appeals there were most certainly bound to be. If he erred on the side of leniency in his interpretation of the law and the evidence, and the accused were acquitted, Ontario's Attorney General would order an appeal. But if he was too strict and the accused were unfairly convicted, their verdicts would be quashed by the appellate courts.

Judge Osborne opened his charge by reminding the jury that "those who commit crimes must be fairly but strictly dealt with." But the fact that the accused were all members of the Satan's Choice Motorcycle Club should not, in itself, prejudice the jury against them: ". . . these men [should] obtain the same treatment from you as would men or women from a differently established position in society."

The jury must also base its verdict solely upon the evidence it had heard in court, and not on news stories its members might have read or gossip they might have heard. It was not incumbent upon the accused to prove their innocence, he reminded the jury, but it was absolutely essential that the Crown establish their guilt, "beyond a reasonable doubt." The concept of reasonable doubt was not an abstract, rarefied legal term, but words that connoted "their plain, ordinary, common-sense meaning."

After reviewing the alibi evidence proffered for Hoffman and van Haarlem, Osborne turned to the "pivotal issue" of the identification of the accused by the Crown witnesses. Identification evidence "suffers from an inherent frailty," Osborne cautioned, because "human observation and recollection are somewhat notoriously unreliable in this area."

He then began a careful review of the identification evidence given by each of the Crown witnesses. Cathy Cotgrave and Gayle Thompson were in a somewhat special category as witnesses on the night of October 18, Osborne suggested, because they were both waitresses who "are supposed to know, as part of their undertakings, who is in a hotel, who is sitting where, and what is going on in a hotel."

Both women had identified Gary Comeau as the gunman. But "it turned out later that Comeau, on evidence which seems to me to be pretty conclusive, was shot by the gun that shot Matiyek and it would appear to be a logical conclusion that the bullet that struck Comeau and was made an exhibit here, having been removed from the area behind his ninth rib on the back on the left, was in fact a bullet which had gone through Matiyek and lodged itself in Comeau. The fact that that bullet was located in Comeau is relied upon to support the conclusion that Comeau couldn't have been the gunman on anybody's exercise of common sense."

In their summations, the lawyers for the defence had made much of this fact, Osborne noted, and the jury had been invited to infer that if Cotgrave and Thompson had been wrong in the identification of Comeau, they had been wrong on much else.

That argument had "superficial appeal," the Judge agreed, but the bullet removed from Comeau cut two ways: first, the evidence seemed to indicate that both waitresses had been wrong in their identification of Comeau as the gunman. But it also proved the witnesses had been correct on another point—the bullet conclusively proved that Comeau had been in the Queen's Hotel during the shooting.

Overall, Osborne continued, there had been numerous shortcomings and irregularities in the OPP identification procedures and photo line-ups. He reviewed Constable Denis's lack of training, the disappearance of his notes for October 19, his failure to note many finishing-times, the decision to allow Cotgrave and Thompson to view the photos together, the red dots on the photographs of some of the accused. The constable's approach, "I think largely through his inexperience, was not really correct in the sense that there were a number of inadequacies in the process followed when dealing with the photographs." The jury itself would have to determine how to weigh those inadequacies.

Judge Osborne continued his witness-by-witness summaries of the evidence and even provided descriptions of the key witnesses as they had appeared on the witness stand. Cathy Cotgrave was "the short, I thought attractive, brown-haired girl with short brown hair, rather fair skin. . . . She was the witness who became upset during the course of one cross-examination." She had identified all of the accused except van Haarlem as having been in the hotel that night. She was also the only witness to identify the accused Armand Sanguigni.

Gayle Thompson was "a slight, very well-spoken girl who obviously was possessed of a reasonable degree of intelligence." She had identified Comeau as the gunman, but Comeau "cannot be convicted on the basis of being the person who shot Mr. Matiyek unless you are satisfied beyond a reasonable doubt that he did shoot Mr. Matiyek. In the light of the evidence about the bullet as I say, you may find that conclusion extremely difficult to reach by any standard, let alone beyond a reasonable doubt."

Julie Joncas's testimony, as Osborne described it, conflicted to some degree with that of Rod Stewart. "You will remember Mr. Stewart, I would think, if you remember any witness in this trial. He was a tall, angular person who wore a brown sports coat with leather patches on the sleeves. He was called, I believe, in the afternoon, and gave his evidence somewhat dramatically." Stewart's recollection of a group of men forming around the Matiyek table just before the shooting had not been confirmed by Cotgrave, Foote, or Thompson. (Judge Osborne was in error here. Sue Foote, at the trial at least, did claim to have seen something resembling Stewart's "horse-shoe.") Nor had Stewart been able to identify any of the accused in the photo line-up. The only accused Stewart recognized at all was David Hoffman. "It is for you to assess whether that identification is a reliable one, bearing in mind all the dangers inherent in and frailties of identification evidence."

David Gillispie was "the witness who you will recall was significantly less sure of himself in his demeanour—at least that was my assessment of him—than some of the other identification witnesses. Mr. Stewart, for example, was very positive about what he saw and what he didn't see. Mr. Gillispie was flexible to say the least in his recollection."

Gillispie was the only witness to overhear the "fat fucker" statement, Osborne reminded the jury, and he had identified Comeau as the person who made the remark to Blaker and Sauvé. Osborne seemed to dwell on the inconsistencies of Gillispie's statement to police, his testimony at the preliminary hearing, and his trial testimony during both examination-in-chief and cross-examination. "I remind you again that inconsistencies are matters that bear upon the issue of credibility."

Helen Mitchell was "a somewhat plain-looking young girl who was very nervous in the witness-box." . . . Her evidence was somewhat confusing, perhaps due to the fact that she was nervous. Mitchell's memory also seemed considerably poorer than many of the other witnesses'. She was the only witness who had identified van Haarlem and she was the only witness who remembered seeing any of the accused wearing colours. Mitchell said that she knew van Haarlem personally, that she'd seen him in September 1978. But, Osborne noted, van Haarlem had been in jail at that time. "It is for you to determine whether Miss Mitchell had identified Gordon van Haarlem at all . . . or whether she has identified him to establish beyond a reasonable doubt that he was in the hotel. I frankly think you might have some difficulty in coming to that conclusion."

Next Osborne addressed the twin issues of enmity and motive. The accused belonged to the Satan's Choice, which was not, in itself, a criminal offence. But that membership had become an important issue because of the enmity which had apparently existed between some members of the Choice and Matiyek, and between the Satan's Choice generally and the Golden Hawk Riders.

From enmity stemmed motive. If motive could be proved to exist in the commission of a crime, it might have a bearing on a finding of guilt. If motive was absent, on the other hand, it tended to reinforce a presumption of innocence. But motive alone was neither a necessary nor a sufficient condition for conviction, Osborne noted. If, in the jury's eyes, the accused had committed the crime beyond a reasonable doubt, then motive was irrelevant.

Three witnesses, Randy Koehler, Lawrence Leon, and William Goodwin, had presented enmity evidence. Osborne reminded the jury of Koehler's evidence about the bar fights involving Matiyek and members of the Satan's Choice, Leon's testimony about enmity between the Choice and the Hawks, and Goodwin's conversation with Rick Sauvé about Matiyek. Osborne also recalled Newman's line of questioning of Goodwin's alleged bias.

It was nearly noon on Wednesday when Judge Osborne began to review the Criminal Code of Canada as it related to the case, and the verdict options as spelled out in the law. Among the legal terms requiring careful definition: homicide, culpable homicide, first- and second-degree murder, aiding and abetting, and planning and deliberation.

Murder, the Judge noted, was a fairly straightforward definition under Section 205 of the Code. "A person commits homicide when directly or indirectly by any means he causes the death of a human being."

But the Code breaks homicide into two categories—culpable and non-culpable. Non-culpable homicide is not an offence. If a patient died on the operating-table because of the risks inherent in the surgery, then that was non-culpable homicide. If someone acted in self-defence, as it might be argued Lorne Campbell did, that, too, was non-culpable homicide.

Culpable homicide was also defined in Section 205: "A person commits culpable homicide when he causes the death of a human being by means of an unlawful act. . . ." But the Code broke culpable homicide down into two further categories: murder and manslaughter (i.e., accidental homicide while engaged in a criminal act).

Campbell's evidence aside, there seemed little doubt that Matiyek had died as the result of an unlawful act, and his death was therefore culpable homicide. Culpable homicide became murder under the code when the person causing the death of another "means to cause his death, or means to cause him bodily harm that he knows is likely to cause death and is reckless whether death ensures or not."

Given the nature of Matiyek's slaying, Osborne observed, it seemed difficult not to believe that the gunman, whoever he was, knew he was likely to cause death.

But, the Judge continued, first- or second-degree murder must also be shown to have intent, which could be demonstrated "by the nature of the act, the manner in which it was done and the state of mind of the person committing the act." In terms of the present trial "it seems to me that a person, whoever he was, that proceeds to a table in a bar occupied by another person, and shoots that other person three times in the head at close range, in the absence of evidence to the contrary that person may be inferred to have intended to cause death."

Each of the accused was charged with first-degree murder, which was very carefully defined in the Criminal Code, Osborne cautioned. First-degree murder must be "planned and deliberate," and the Crown must prove that it was planned and deliberate beyond a reasonable doubt.

Both first- and second-degree murder must be proved to have intent, but first-degree murder alone must be shown to be planned and deliberate. Nor did the law intend that it be one or the other, Osborne emphasized. Both planning *and* deliberation must be proved to have occurred to convict someone of first-degree murder. "A planned and deliberate murder does not include a murder that is perpetrated in hot blood, as the saying goes, without any premeditation, or a murder that is perpetrated upon impulse, or at the spur of the moment." In law, the word "planned" carried its plain, ordinary meaning, Osborne told the jury. Something was planned if it had been carefully thought out and when the nature and consequences of an act have been carefully weighed. A plan was also "temporal" in that it was developed over a period of time. The word "deliberate" also carried its common-sense meaning in law, meaning that the act was considered and not impulsive.

In this case, Osborne continued, "it seems to me there is no direct evidence of planning and deliberation." There was nothing in writing, no evidence that the perpetrators had held a meeting to discuss the eventual crime.

On the other hand, the jury might infer a degree of planning from the eyewitness testimony. The accused had all entered the hotel at roughly the same time, though through different doors. They had not seated themselves in a group, but had occupied different positions throughout the room— Hurren and Hoffman at the bar near the telephone, "if you accept the evidence," Sauvé and Comeau at Matiyek's table, still others in the pinball room.

But, the Judge cautioned, if the jury inferred planning and deliberation from this circumstantial evidence, then it must be "the only reasonable inference to be drawn from proven facts" on the part of each of the accused, who must be considered separately.

There had also been considerable argument that the very nature of the crime proved that there was *no* planning and deliberation, Osborne reminded the jury. In their final submissions, the defence lawyers had pointed out again and again the "confusion" referred to by Crown witnesses when the accused entered the bar, the fact that Sauvé and Blaker had telephoned Port Hope to have their absence from work explained. There may also have been "a certain degree of inherent absurdity in the killing of Matiyek," in that several of the accused were well known to the eyewitnesses and would hardly have knowingly committed so serious a crime in front of people who could easily identify them.

Next there was the question of the relationship in law between the gunman and the accused. The jury could draw one of three conclusions from the evidence: first, that Gary Comeau was the gunman, though that now seemed unlikely; or, that Lorne Campbell was the gunman, about which Osborne would have more to say later; or, that the gunman had never been specifically identified.

It was not necessary that the Crown positively establish the gunman's identity to convict the accused, however. Section 21–1 of the Criminal Code specified that "Everyone is a party to an offence who (a.) actually commits it, (b.) does or omits to do anything from the purpose of aiding any person to commit it, or (c.) abets any person in committing it." Osborne read the section twice for emphasis.

To be guilty of aiding and abetting, the accused must be shown to have had some actual—but not necessarily active—participation or to have rendered some assistance in Matiyek's killing. It was not enough to prove that one or other of the accused was in the hotel—a bystander to a crime is neither an aider nor an abettor. No, the accused must have been shown beyond a reasonable doubt to also have had the intent of killing Bill Matiyek, and to have encouraged or assisted his shooting in at least some passive way—perhaps keeping watch, or ensuring that the act was not hindered in some way.

But for any of the accused to be convicted as an aider or abettor of first-degree murder, a number of pre-conditions would have to apply. ". . . It must be established beyond a reasonable doubt that such aider or abettor knew, and I emphasize the word *knew*, *knew* that the person who was the gunman intended to carry out a planned and deliberate killing."

If the jurors concluded that Matiyek's killing was not planned and deliberate, they could convict the accused for aiding and abetting second-degree, but not first-degree, murder.

Osborne then began, for one last time, to summarize the cases for the Crown and the defence. The Crown, he said, had attempted to place Matiyek's killing in a context: the enmity between the Choice and the Hawks; the nature of Satan's Choice as a "brotherhood"; the fact that the Choice had been barred from the Queen's Hotel and therefore had no reason to be there, unless it was to kill Bill Matiyek; the "deployment" of the Choice when they arrived; the relative speed with which things happened—no more than fifteen minutes elapsed between their arrival and Matiyek's shooting. Van Haarlem's and Hoffman's alibi evidence should not be believed, the prosecution argued. Members of all three chapters had been present that night, so the planning ran throughout the entire organization. Even if they hadn't pulled the trigger, each of the eight accused were present for the sole purpose of giving assistance and aid in the planned and deliberate murder of William Matiyek.

The defence had urged the jury to keep in mind the "way the world works" with regard to so public an execution involving such well-known individuals. "Mr. Meinhardt's position, as I assess it, was that when you are assessing the way the world works you should assess the way the world of the accused persons works, not the way the world in general works . . . that these people were inclined to display a show of force and demonstrate their dominance for purposes of future recognition."

After a brief recess, Osborne began his summary of the defence evidence. It was now late Thursday afternoon. He began with the evidence of Lorne Campbell. If accepted at face value, Campbell's evidence meant that none of the accused could be found guilty of aiding and abetting, because he claimed that none of the others even knew he had a gun.

By testifying under the protection of the Canada Evidence Act, Campbell had guaranteed himself immunity from prosecution, at least on the basis of his trial testimony. This Campbell had every right to do under Canadian law, ". . . and you can assess . . . what risk he really ran."

The jury should also assess the witness's demeanour on the stand, as well as his evidence. He said he had never fired his revolver, had never even checked its ammunition, though he had had it for two years; that he knew the Outlaw Bronson, but not the Outlaw Jones; that he wasn't sure if they were in the hotel; that a girl (presumed to be Jamie Hanna) was at the Matiyek table at the time of the shooting.

Then there was Campbell's criminal record. It could be taken into account, Osborne reminded the jury, only in assessing the witness's credibility. "You may conclude that Campbell's criminal record is of a sort that directly bears upon his honesty and integrity. He admitted to having a previous criminal record which included a conviction of conspiracy to commit perjury. . . . That is for you to consider."

Overall, Osborne noted, each defence lawyer had urged the jury to acquit his client. The defence had strongly attacked the inadequacies of the OPP photo ID procedure; had attempted to question the accuracy of the evidence of key Crown witnesses like Cathy Cotgrave and Gayle Thompson because they had clearly mis-identified Comeau as the gunman; had argued that Campbell's testimony proved that there was no planning or deliberation; had contended that some of the accused had been shown to have done no more than enter the bar and then leave it again, while others among the accused were not even present.

While Sauvé's threats against Matiyek may have been "hotheaded and stupid," they were not to be taken seriously or given a sinister connotation. The only witness who had heard the alleged "fat fucker" statement, Gillispie, had clearly made so many inconsistent prior statements that his overall credibility had been left seriously in doubt.

Finally, Osborne turned to the legal issue of self-defence, which, he noted, had been raised only in the evidence of Lorne Campbell. *If* Campbell was to be believed, Osborne repeated, the jury must acquit the accused. If, moreover, Campbell had shot Matiyek in self-defence, there had been no crime committed at all, because self-defence was non-culpable homicide. Therefore, Osborne concluded, "I must somewhat reluctantly but of necessity charge you on the law of self-defence."

After reading the relevant section from the Criminal Code, Osborne noted that it was not necessary to show that Campbell had actually been threatened by Matiyek. If he had had a reasonable apprehension that Matiyek was reaching for his gun and that he could not otherwise preserve himself from death or grievous bodily harm, then Campbell had acted in self-defence.

In addition to verdicts of first-degree murder, second-degree murder, or outright acquittal, the jury must consider another possible verdict: manslaughter. "It can only arise as a possible verdict in this case under very narrow or unusual circumstances. I must tell you I do not find there is much in the way of evidence to support a consideration of manslaughter as a possible verdict. However, I leave it with you for your consideration under the circumstances."

A manslaughter verdict could result only if the jury found that the perpetrator had not had the intent of murder. Such a verdict would be doubly difficult for the jury, because "the gunman . . . may not be and probably isn't, I suggest to you, one of the accused persons before the court." Secondly, it would be difficult to conclude that the gunman had anything but murder in mind when he shot Matiyek.

But if the intent was found to be lacking, the accused could be found guilty of aiding and abetting manslaughter. Furthermore, if the jury found "it proved beyond a reasonable doubt that each accused person formed an intention in common to assault Matiyek and that it has been proved beyond a reasonable doubt that in carrying out that common assault each accused knew or ought to have known that death was the probable consequence, a proper verdict would be guilty of second-degree murder, not guilty of first-degree murder."

Osborne then once again reviewed Campbell's testimony. To say that he did so with acute scepticism would be an understatement. He reminded the jury of Campbell's "physical appearance in the courtroom"; that none of the witnesses had seen him in the hotel; that he never examined the bullets in his gun. "Taking all things into account it is for you to assess the reliability and credibility of Lorne Campbell. Do not be guided by what you conclude I think about his evidence. It is for you to decide whether you believe all of a witness's evidence, part of it, or none of it, and Lorne Campbell is no exception to that principle of law."

Almost as if he was reluctant to let the jury finally begin its deliberations, Osborne summed up the highlights once again. There had been no evidence that Matiyek was threatened or assaulted prior to the shooting. "He was purely and simply shot three times in the head . . . I am referring to the . . . simplicity of his killing. There were no frills attached to it. He was shot and that was it." He touched briefly on the law one last time—the pitfalls of circumstantial evidence, the necessity of proving planning and deliberation, the differences between first- and second-degree murder.

Finally, shortly after noon, Osborne completed his charge. "You have a solemn, perhaps difficult, duty to perform. I know that you will discharge that duty to the state and to the accused persons. . . . You have taken an oath to try this charge against the accused men without fear and without favour. You have also taken an oath at the same time to try these accused men on the evidence and to render a true verdict. All that can be asked of you is that you honour that oath. Once you have, you will have performed your duty as jurors. . . ."

The jury retired at 12:43 p.m., but not before Osborne warned them that he would in all probability have to recall them after hearing the submissions of all counsel on his charge. For that reason, the Supreme Court Judge warned, the jury should go no further in its deliberations than selecting a foreman.

The arguments on Osborne's charge lasted throughout the afternoon. Most of the objections came from the defence on points of law, or, in a few cases, actual misstatements of fact. As a result of the discussions, Osborne agreed to re-charge the jury, which was summoned at 5:45 p.m.

He had, Osborne confessed to the jurors, made several errors in his initial charge.

After correcting his errors, the Judge recapped the four possible verdicts: guilty of first-degree murder; not guilty of first-degree murder but guilty of second-degree murder; not guilty of second-degree murder but guilty of manslaughter; not guilty. He also refined his earlier charge on the subject of aiding and abetting, and clarified several minor points on the evidence.

As it was nearly six o'clock, Osborne concluded, "I propose to exercise my somewhat dictatorial powers and cause the deliberations to end, so that you can get a good night's sleep . . . and then you can resume deliberating tomorrow morning at 9:30." The jury retired at 6:05 p.m.

The jury began its deliberations in earnest on Friday morning. Judge Osborne remained in his chambers, while the people who had been together in the courtroom for nearly three months during the trial—the lawyers, reporters, and court staff—loitered in the courtroom or the hallways, killing the hours with small talk and wisecracks. They started a pool among themselves, betting on how long the jury would stay out.

The six accused in custody were placed in a heavily guarded room by themselves. Somehow they found out about the pool. Such informal betting was a standard feature of almost every important jury trial, although many of the accused didn't know it—this was, after all, the first major jury trial for almost all of them. Rick Sauvé, in particular, found the idea of the pool offensive. It reminded him of the Roman soldiers drawing lots for Jesus' clothing while he was still up there on the cross—not that he thought of himself like Jesus Christ or anything. Even his own lawyer was in on that pool. Didn't they understand that men's lives—his own life—were hanging in the balance here? It seemed to Rick that they had no sense of fair play.

There was a brief flurry of excitement late in the afternoon when somebody reported that the jury was coming back in, but it turned out that they only wanted to get the answer to a single question: was 416-298-2128 the telephone number of the Toronto clubhouse? Court was resumed just long enough for Judge Osborne to answer in the affirmative.

Then the jury sent word that its members were getting tired. They planned to end their deliberations at four o'clock and start afresh in the morning, and court was adjourned for the day.

———

For the accused, Saturday, November 24, began like any other court day—a tasteless bucket breakfast, chains and manacles, the convoy downtown, up Wellington, down Queen to the courthouse.

But for the friends and family of the accused who had gathered for the verdict—Sharon Sauvé, Larry Hurren's mother, Jeff McLeod's father and stepmother, and the others—the Middlesex County Courthouse seemed like a different world on a Saturday. The towering monolith, usually busy with the hundreds of secretaries and receptionists, sheriffs and bailiffs and registrars, lawyers and clients and witnesses who were the living grist for the wheels of the criminal justice system, was deserted. The hundreds of offices were closed, the hallways and elevators silent, save for the remote whisper of the ventilation system. It was eerie, and more than a little foreboding.

Jack Grossman and some of the other lawyers got a special room opened up where the families could sit together, passing the nervous, endless hours. Rick's lawyer seemed to Sharon to be both kind and reassuring. Was there anything else he could do for her? . . . but there was very little. Sharon had her bags packed, firmly convinced that tonight maybe, or tomorrow night at the latest, she and Rick would be together for the first time in almost a year. Somebody said there was champagne waiting at the Toronto club-house, ready to celebrate their acquittal.

Jeff had pinched a die from the Monopoly game at the Detention Centre, and they passed the morning shooting craps. The rules were simple—a six or a five you were guilty, four or three was a maybe, two or one you were innocent. Everybody shot for themselves, and the first number that came up was the one that counted. Rick rolled a six.

"Ah, shit. Hey, best two out of three, okay?"

Everybody hooted at that. "No fuckin' way, man. C'mon, Nutty's turn."

But as the morning dragged on, everybody took many turns playing for best three out of five, six out of ten . . .

The end came swiftly and with little ceremony. Just before noon, word arrived that the jury had reached its verdict. Everyone filed into the court-room, the accused were led in, then the jurors took their places. Judge Osborne merely nodded to the Registrar, who asked that "the jury fore-person please stand. Members of the jury, have you agreed upon a verdict?"

Edward Horace Gudgeon rose to his feet. "We have."

Except for the faint buzz of the fluorescent lights high overhead, the court was deathly still. "What is your verdict with regards to the accused Jeffrey A. McLeod?"

"Guilty, second-degree murder."

"Guilty, second-degree murder," the Registrar repeated. "The accused Gary Joseph Comeau?"

"Guilty, first-degree murder."

Rick knew then that he was getting it, too. *Holy fuck, they're convicting all of us.* He thought about Tee Hee.

". . . the accused Murray Blaker?"

"Guilty, second-degree murder."

". . . the accused Armand J. Sanguigni?"

"Not guilty."

"Accused David C. Hoffman?"

"Guilty, second-degree murder."

"Accused Larry J. Hurren?"

"Guilty, second-degree murder."

"Accused Gordon J. van Haarlem?"

"Not guilty."

"Accused Richard M. Sauvé?"

"Guilty, first-degree murder."

"Guilty, first-degree murder. Members of the jury, hearken to your verdict as the court hath recorded it." The Registrar repeated the verdicts. "So say you all?"

"Yes."

For the first time that morning, Osborne addressed the court. "Mr. Meinhardt, did you have something to say?"

"My Lord, I would like to move for sentencing."

Howard Kerbel rose and requested that the jurors be polled individually with respect to the verdict on Gary Comeau. One by one the jurors said they agreed with the verdict. Jack Grossman, Ed Martin, and Terry O'Hara asked that the jury also be polled for their respective clients. The responses were all the same—the jurors were unanimous in their verdicts, as required by law.

The only one of the accused who showed any emotion was Jeff McLeod, Mac Haig reported in the *Free Press* on Monday. The big biker shook his head repeatedly while the jurors were being polled. *This can't be. It just can't be. This is Canada. I didn't do nothin'.*

Osborne turned to the jury. One of them was crying a little, and some of the women in the spectators' gallery were weeping silently, too. "Members of the jury, I recognize that this been an enormously long and an enormously difficult task for you. There is one further matter with respect to which I must seek your assistance." Osborne watched the crying juror sympathetically. ". . . I am wondering if perhaps before I do that if the foreman might indicate if you would prefer to adjourn for five or ten minutes and deal with it or pursue this now."

"Carry on," Edward Gudgeon answered stoically.

"All right. I will deal with this as incisively and as briefly as I can. . . ." The four accused who had just been found guilty of second-degree murder—McLeod, Blaker, Hoffman, and Hurren—would each be sentenced to imprisonment for life. But it was within the jury's discretion to recommend how many years each of the four must serve before becoming eligible for parole. Each must serve at least ten years, but not more than twenty-five. The jury was not, however, obliged to make any recommendations at all. "Would you mind retiring, members of the jury, just to consider what I have said to you?" The jury retired once more, at 12:20 p.m.

It returned four minutes later. It had no recommendations.

Osborne addressed the jury for the last time. "I do not make a practice of commenting upon juries' verdicts. However, I do wish to say that I have heard it said that genius is the ability to act wisely, without precedent. There is an inherent genius in the jury system in my view, and in my view your role as *the* jury of 1979 has enhanced my view of the jury system." After cautioning the jurors that they must never disclose what they had said during their deliberations, Osborne expressed his gratitude once more, and the jury was discharged.

At 12:28 p.m. on Saturday, November 24, nearly three months after it had been assembled, the jury was disbanded. Its members left the courthouse for the last time and re-entered the now seemingly mundane world of homes and families and jobs.

Shortly after, Judge Osborne wrote each juror a letter, personally praising them for their sacrifice and diligence. Given the length of the trial at which they had just served, he also offered to exempt each of them from jury duty for the next ten years. Remarkably, not one of them accepted his offer.

Back in Courtroom 21 there was still some unfinished business. The lawyers for Hurren, Blaker, Hoffman, and McLeod requested an adjournment to prepare for sentencing submission, and this was granted. Gordon van Haarlem and Armand Sanguigni were asked to stand, and Judge Osborne told them they were free to go.

Then he turned to Gary Comeau. "Mr. Comeau, would you stand up, please? Before I sentence you, Mr. Comeau, do you have anything you wish to say?"

Nutty was in a state of shock.

"I take it, Mr. Kerbel, Mr. Comeau has nothing to say?"

"It is my understanding that he has nothing to say."

"Pursuant to the provisions of the Criminal Code I am required to and do sentence you, Mr. Comeau, to imprisonment for life. You may sit down. Mr. Sauvé?"

Rick stood. His face was ashen.

"My Lord, I understand Mr. Sauvé has nothing to say," said Grossman, standing beside his client.

"Is that correct, Mr. Sauvé?"

"Yes sir."

"Mr. Sauvé, I am required as well on your conviction of first-degree murder to sentence you to imprisonment for life. Is there anything further, gentlemen?"

"No, my Lord," Chris Meinhardt answered for the Crown.

"No, my Lord," Bruce Affleck agreed for the defence.

"All right. Would you remove the accused, please? This trial is ended, subject to the matter of sentencing."

Before he was led from the courtroom Jeff McLeod spoke briefly to his father. Fighting back his tears, Jeff's dad told him not to worry, that he still believed his son was innocent, and they would fight this thing on the appeal. No more of this Legal Aid stuff. Mr. McLeod would personally see that he got the best possible lawyer the next time. He'd hire Eddie Greenspan himself.

The six convicted bikers were returned to the holding-cells in the court-house basement. Their lunch, stale bread and a slice of bologna, was waiting for them. Nobody felt like eating. They were numb. They each felt bad enough for themselves, but it was impossible not to feel especially bad for Tee Hee. The guy was absolutely, totally innocent. At least the rest of them had actually been in the hotel. Tee Hee had told the truth, and no one had believed him.

Gary Comeau took one bite of his sandwich and felt his stomach churn in a wave of nausea and rage. He threw the rest of the sandwich through the bars. "Wait'll I get my hands on the fucker that's been pushin' these fuckin' sandwiches!"

They looked up at Nutty's sudden outburst and the absurdity of it all washed over them. They just had to laugh, and the sound of their manic laughter echoed through the bleak holding-cells of the London courthouse. What else could they do? You had to either laugh or cry, and it was better to cry when you were alone.

Sharon Sauvé asked to see her husband. Rick appeared, finally, looking pale and drawn, on the other side of a thick pane of glass. Jack Grossman had already explained to her what the verdict meant—twenty-five years with no hope of parole. Twenty-five years! She was only twenty-two, Rick just twenty-seven. Grossman had said to just call him if there was anything he could do. He'd been very kind to her after the verdict came down. But there was no way anyone could help or prepare her for something like this.

They tried to talk, about Angie, their daughter, about other people, almost as if nothing had happened, but the glass in front of her began to wave and blur as the tears came to Sharon's eyes, and then she saw that Rick, too, was crying. They both broke down, weeping for Angie, for themselves, for what might have been; and time, Sharon was to find, healed none of it. She could never talk about that terrible day without crying, without reliving it. Even six years later, it still seemed like only yesterday.

Mac Haig had lingered in the empty courtroom; there was something he wanted to check out. He approached the prisoner's dock and the spot that Jeff McLeod had occupied for so many months. He'd noticed McLeod putting something on the railing in front of him just before the jury had returned with its verdict. Yes, it was still there. It was a single white die. Intrigued, Haig picked it up. He noticed that it had been placed so that the number one was face up. Strange. The newspaperman shrugged, and carefully put the die back on the railing, before collecting his notes and leaving the deserted courthouse.

Even their jailers had seemed shocked by the severity of the jury's verdicts. The sympathy of the OPP squad members assigned as their individual guards, which they had sensed before, was clearly evident now. Jeff's guard even shook his hand, told him he was sorry, and offered to appear as a character witness on his behalf at the sentence hearing. It was as if they had crossed over some invisible boundary, a line that divided free men from the condemned, the living from the dead, which, in Rick's and Nutty's case, they pretty well had.

In the paddy wagon on the way back to the Detention Centre they were quiet at first, until Tee Hee looked up and sighed. "This is gonna be a helluva blow to my sex life." That cracked everybody up and they started laughing all over again. The coppers up front looked at one another and then into the back of the van. They must have thought they'd all gone crazy.

Once they'd settled down again, the sergeant riding shotgun turned around. "Hey, Comeau," he shouted back over the noise of the engine. "I got just one question."

"Yeah?" Warily.

"Whaddaya think ever happened to that leather jacket?"

"I dunno," Nutty snarled back without thinking. "You ask McReelis, he'll know."

Terry O'Hara was profoundly depressed as he drove back to Kingston. It didn't help matters at all that he had to detour over to New Dundee, to the Hoffman family farm. David Hoffman had shared O'Hara's hotel room during the last week of the trial, and the lawyer had found himself liking the Kitchener biker quite a lot. He was, O'Hara discovered, intelligent, articulate, and thoughtful. Apart from Murray Blaker, O'Hara hadn't really gotten to know any of the other accused, and Hoffman had turned out to be a pleasant surprise. Before court that morning, O'Hara had promised to take Tee Hee's belongings back to his family if things didn't work out, and the lawyer kept his promise.

O'Hara had a lot of time to think on the long drive between Kitchener and Kingston. He felt terrible about Murray, of course, and really bad about Hoffman, too. After that, he decided, he was really sorry for Gary Comeau.

Shit, they should have been able to win that one by postcard. How could they have lost him for first-degree murder when he had a bullet from the murder weapon in his back all along? What kind of planning and deliberation did that show? An articling student could have won it. But because of the delays in removing the bullet, Comeau had sat there, all through the Crown evidence, with the crucial evidence inside his body. And then, when the bullet was finally extracted, it had been too late. Too late to cross-examine the waitresses on this critical piece of evidence, too late to deflect the jury from the way they'd been thinking of Comeau all those weeks.

Never before had Terry O'Hara been so disgusted with the criminal-justice system. It had just sentenced six innocent men to at least ninety years in prison—and had let the guilty man slip through its fingers, entirely free.

O'Hara drove on into the gathering dusk. Although the day had been sunny, the fields beside the 401 looked cold and barren, and nightfall came early, the outer gloom reflecting his inner despondency.

Lorne Campbell had taken his lawyer's advice. The day after his testimony he'd split from Oshawa and gone up north, up into cottage country, to stay with a friend who owned a lodge. He began to drink heavily—alcool, pure overproof alcohol that the Ontario Liquor Control Board imported from Quebec—and the next four months blurred past in an alcoholic haze. His mood brightened a little when he heard they'd gotten the bullet out of Nutty—at least his testimony had done *some* good—but then his depression had returned.

Someone in London phoned the Toronto clubhouse with the news of the verdicts, and then someone in Toronto relayed the word to Lorne. Lorne's host watched as the biker hung up the telephone and left the lodge without a word. His friend kept watching as Lorne walked down to the lake by himself, and out onto the end of the dock. And he was still watching as Lorne Campbell, who was, outwardly, at least, one of the toughest men he knew, stood there on the end of that dock and began to bawl like a baby.

They put Rick, Nutty, and Larry Hurren into the hole that night at the Detention Centre. Somebody explained that it wasn't any kind of punishment, just special observation in case any one of them might suddenly turn suicidal. It had been known to happen when men learned that they would have to spend the rest of their lives—or a good part of them, anyway—in prison.

Nutty's thoughts returned to the sergeant's remark in the paddy wagon. *Whaddaya think ever happened to that leather jacket?* What had that copper been trying to tell him, anyway? Finally, Nutty thought he knew. *Well, son-of-a-bitch.*

XXXIV

BILL GLAISTER WAS NOT in agreement with the verdicts. He ascribed both the first- and second-degree murder convictions more to the tenor of the times—the anti-biker hysteria that was being whipped up by police through the news media—than to verdicts based upon the evidence—at least the evidence he'd heard, and he'd been in court every day.

Mac Haig, on the other hand, judging by his post-trial pieces, which tended to be hawkish and critical of the rulings that had disallowed parts of the Crown evidence, appeared to feel that the verdicts handed down had not been harsh enough. The two reporters did find themselves in agreement on one point, however. They were both disappointed by Sanguigni's acquittal. Haig and Glaister had heard a great deal of court-house scuttlebutt about Sanguigni and, watching the slender Toronto biker in the courtroom day in and day out, they were both inclined to believe that, more than all of the other accused combined, Sanguigni represented a genuine threat to society. Armand Sanguigni was one scary dude, and it was too bad that he hadn't been locked up.

Glaister had sold a story about the trial to *Maclean's* magazine, and he'd hoped to focus it on Terry Hall, the OPP biker squad, and the anti-biker war they'd been waging in Ontario for so many years. He planned to call his piece "The biggest gang of all."

Glaister's fascination with Terry Hall had remained undiminished by the end of the trial, and the more Crown evidence he heard, the more his reporter's instincts told him that something was not quite right about the testimony of some of the Crown witnesses. It was nothing he could quite put his finger on, but Glaister suspected that the police investigation of

Matiyek's murder had not been entirely on the up and up. Had one of the police forces involved—or individual officers, in any case—threatened or somehow coerced some of the witnesses into giving evidence? Or had some of the evidence been suppressed? Glaister didn't know. But, as part of his research for the *Maclean's* piece, he resolved to do a little investigating on his own. On the morning of Friday, November 16, after Chris Meinhardt had finished his jury submission and before Judge Osborne was due to begin his charge to the jury, Bill Glaister set out, alone, for Port Hope. He planned to spend the weekend in the town, locating and interviewing as many of the witnesses as he could find, and what happened to him in Port Hope did nothing at all to allay his suspicions.

He arrived in Port Hope early that afternoon, and headed straight for the Queen's Hotel. It had, he discovered, been renamed after Matiyek's death. The old Victorian pile at the corner of Walton and John streets was now called the Walton. Despite Rod Stewart's renovations, Glaister found the interior of the bar about which he'd heard so much to be just as Stewart himself had described it: dark, dingy, and a little ominous. He asked around and found a few of the witnesses right there. They seemed edgy at first, reluctant to talk—the jury had not yet rendered its verdict, after all—but eventually people began to open up a little, almost as if, even though the evidence was all in, the real cause of Matiyek's death, the motive, had never been satisfactorily explained at the trial. The Crown's grandiose theory about a gangland slaying didn't sit quite right with some people, and they seemed as curious about Glaister's own opinions as he was about theirs. Why *had* Bill Matiyek been shot? It was all very strange.

Glaister left the Walton for the Ganaraska, the town's only other bar. He met Rod Stewart there, and Glaister downed a few beers with the town councillor and two of his friends. After a while, Stewart began to boast about the dramatic way he had given his testimony. Hadn't he been great? What a performance! He should have been given the Academy Award for that. Glaister listened in amazement, remembering Stewart's testimony, how the tall Port Hope town councillor had choked up in the box while narrating the facts and buried his head in his hands, weeping at the terrible memory of Matiyek's shooting.

The reporter excused himself to make a phone call, and when he returned to the table Stewart was still there, but his two friends—and Glaister's notebook—had disappeared. Where were his notes, Glaister demanded. Stewart said that his friends had taken them to Cobourg to be copied, they'd bring them back. His amazement at Stewart's earlier admissions now turned to anger. What the fuck was this? Those notes were *his*, no one had any right to take them without his permission, much less to make copies. Glaister called the cops. When the police arrived, the reporter told them what had happened, and Stewart insisted the notes would be returned. Glaister agreed to wait, which he did, with growing impatience. Finally, almost two hours later, Stewart's buddies brought Glaister's notebook back. Glaister was by now thoroughly pissed off. By telephone he consulted some of his editors at the *Globe and Mail*, for whom he'd been filing steadily throughout the trial. They were as upset as he was at this unwarranted intrusion upon a reporter's right to seek, and record, the facts.

Glaister went to the Port Hope police station and demanded that Stewart and his friends be charged with theft. The police took statements from Glaister, Stewart, and Stewart's two friends. The officer noted that all four of them appeared to have been drinking. Glaister left for Toronto right after that, abandoning his earlier plans to spend the weekend in Port Hope. The whole place gave him the creeps.

About a week after they'd all been convicted, Rick Sauvé received a letter from one of the jurors, the young woman who had been crying when the verdicts were read. The letter was highly charged, emotional, extraordinary. She wrote:

> How can I tell you how very, very sorry I am. What I wouldn't give if we could have given you a different decision, but we, too, had a duty to follow. The pain in your eyes will haunt me for all years to come and I'll feel that agony of having to agree to it, like selling out a friend.

Reading that letter seemed almost as terrible a blow to Rick as the verdict itself. Why had she written to *him*? What was she trying to say? Had she been so close to voting for acquittal that if they'd just done a little more—like taking the witness stand—she would have voted the other way?

Baffled, Rick showed the letter to the other guys. Nutty, in particular, jumped on it as if it was some kind of vindication. "Ya see? She *knew* we were innocent! Maybe she's sayin' she got heavied by the jury foreman, or some of the other men on the jury! We gotta show this to our lawyers! Maybe they can use it for the appeal!"

Gary Comeau had already embarked on what would prove to be a decade-long struggle to prove his innocence, and he attacked the problem with characteristic energy and enthusiasm. They'd be at this thing on appeal, everybody would see. They couldn't give up hope. They had to fight back against this fuckin' frame job. Most of the others, Rick in particular, found it hard to share Nutty's optimism. It was just Nutty being Nutty.

Rick never wrote back. What was he supposed to say to her?

On the morning of Friday, December 17, 1979, Larry Hurren, Jeff McLeod, Merv Blaker, and David Hoffman made their last courtroom appearance, to hear Judge Osborne impose their sentences for second-degree murder. Both the defence and the Crown called pre-sentencing evidence. Chris Meinhardt's first witness was a newly promoted Detective Sergeant Terry Hall.

Hall repeated his earlier evidence to re-establish his expertise on the subject of outlaw motorcycle clubs and their criminal activities. "Through my experience I found it could be various types of crimes: small-time to big-time, extortions, trafficking and manufacturing of illicit drugs, robbery, assault, rapes, theft of property and of motor vehicles, possession of—"

Bruce Affleck interrupted. "May it please your Honour, I take exception to this evidence, with the greatest deference."

"I will—" Osborne began to reply, but Affleck interrupted him, too.

"You will hear it out?"

"I will hear it out."

"All right. Thank you. I couldn't believe I was in a courtroom there for a moment, I thought it was some kind of an American movie."

"Well, I'm sure my friend's personal views don't assist anyone," Meinhardt snapped.

Hall didn't miss a beat. "—restricted weapons, prohibited weapons, dealing in these weapons, sale, transporting; I would have to say, even to the field of loan-sharking, contract killing, and contract muscle work." Members of Satan's Choice would sometimes work directly with other forms of organized crime on a fee-for-service basis. A majority of the members had criminal records, and a majority of members were involved in some form of criminal activity. "Violence is a way of life with the motorcycle club." Their dress and their names are calculated to instill fear in the public: Hell's Angels, Outlaws, Satan's Choice, Vagabonds, Wild Ones, Chosen Few, Coffin Wheelers, Black Spider.

Bikers were difficult to prosecute, Hall continued, because they were so often successful in intimidating prospective Crown witnesses—up to and including police officers and even lawyers themselves. Clubs were also difficult organizations to penetrate with undercover operatives because strikers were often required to commit criminal acts and "obviously a police officer would not be able to commit a criminal act."

Hall had also found a difference when dealing with bikers individually or in groups. "On a one-to-one basis generally there is a friendly atmosphere—not necessarily friendly, but respectful atmosphere, but when they are together in large numbers, the confidence is gained; the small man becomes big and the weak man becomes strong."

The pre-sentence evidence for the defence was not transcribed. Osborne began his address by noting that the jury had made no recommendation regarding sentencing. "I think it should be stated in a specific way, in view of what I perceive to be a general public misunderstanding as to the effect of a sentence of life imprisonment, that upon conviction of second-degree murder, the mandatory sentence is life imprisonment." The only issue before the court was the number of years that each accused must serve before parole eligibility.

A person convicted of that charge must serve at least ten years in prison, and this could be expanded to twenty-five years. "Increasing the parole-eligibility period, or refusing to do so, is a matter of great significance. The period of discretion is fifteen years of someone's life.

"As I pass sentence in this case, I wish to make two general observations: in the first place, I do not in any way take issue with the evidence led by the Crown as to the characteristics of outlaw motorcycle clubs or their members.

"Secondly, I observe that it is a human tragedy that the lives of seven people have been, to a certain measure, destroyed, as a result of what occurred in Port Hope on October 18 last year. I refer, in that regard, to the deceased, and the six persons that have been convicted of his murder.

"While I do not regard it as reasonable to confer upon these convicted persons any benefit as a result of their being members of an outlaw motorcycle club, at the same time I do not think it is appropriate to impose upon the accused convicted persons the sins of all motorcycle clubs except to the extent that those criminal activities have been connected with the accused convicted persons. Although I have no reason to speak in any way in a manner that would endorse membership in Satan's Choice Motorcycle Club, I cannot bring myself to conclude that its members are, of necessity, sub-human."

Accordingly, Osborne concluded, each of the accused should be eligible for parole after ten years in prison. "It is my hope that your actions while in confinement will, in fact, justify your release at that time."

Did the accused wish to make a statement before sentencing?

None did.

"The sentence which I impose therefore—would you stand please—is one of life imprisonment for Jeffrey McLeod, Larry Hurren, Merv Blaker, and David Hoffman. I make no order extending the period of eligibility for parole beyond that period referred to in Section 671 of the Criminal Code. If you will give me a moment, I will endorse the record. I don't think there is anything further, is there, gentlemen?"

"No, my Lord."

"No, my Lord."

"Would you remove the accused, please? Thank you, gentlemen." Court was adjourned at 12:05 p.m. The trial of Her Majesty the Queen versus Jeffrey McLeod et al. was over.

All six of them were now officially lifers, pending the outcome of their appeals. They had, by law, thirty days from the date of their conviction to either waive their rights to appeal or to file the appropriate motion with the Appeals Division of the Ontario Supreme Court. Each of them appealed, on the advice of their legal counsel, and the Crown filed appeals against the acquittal of Armand Sanguigni and Gordon van Haarlem.

When it was obvious that Comeau, Sauvé, and Hurren were not suicidal, they were released into the general population. They spent their second Christmas together behind bars, and the start of the new year and a new decade found them still at the Detention Centre in London.

Nutty received word that he'd have to appear in court in Cobourg to face the still-outstanding assault/bodily charge against him over the Alderville

Indian Reserve fracas. He was outraged. Christ, he was already doing twenty-five years. He'd be in prison until well into the next century. What the fuck was Meinhardt trying to prove?

"Simple," Howard Kerbel told him. "Meinhardt wants to get one more conviction for violence on your record before the appeal."

Man, these guys just don't know when to quit. Couldn't they just enter a guilty plea, or something? No, he had to appear in court, Kerbel said.

So they made up a special convoy just for Nutty, his own personal paddy wagon following the gun truck. "If we're coming back tomorrow, we'll have a little surprise for you," the guards told Gary, which made him all the more suspicious. The next day they beat the assault beef (he hadn't been anywhere near the fight, in fact), but Gary didn't really give a shit.

On the way back to London the coppers pulled into a Mac's Milk store. One of them went inside and came back to the cab with a malt cup. Then they swung open the back door of the paddy wagon and handed him a full cup of something cold, Nutty figured it was a milk shake. He took a drink from the cup and discovered it was ice-cold beer, the first he'd tasted in well over a year. Aaaaaah. It was heavenly, and they kept that malt cup topped up most of the way back to London. Nutty pigged right out, with inevitable results.

"Uh, I hate to say this, but I gotta piss like a racehorse. . . ."

They stopped at a gas station and backed the van right up to the door of the men's washroom so that Nutty Comeau, convicted first-degree murderer, Satan's Choice and one-percenter all the way, could hobble down the wagon steps in his manacles and go directly into the pisser.

They cut him off, finally, before they reached London, to give him time to sober up a little, and Gary didn't even mind. Coppers.

They were driven to Kingston on January 27, 1980. Destination: the Regional Reception Centre at Kingston Penitentiary, where Ontario's federal prisoners are first admitted into the system. They were to be examined and analysed before being moved into the particular pen where they'd begin doing their time. Word was they'd be shipped to Millhaven, which filled them all with apprehension.

They'd just been told to strip prior to their physical examinations when Rick Sauvé got his first taste of the bureaucracy that is the Canadian correctional system.

"We don't have the correct medical file for this man," a prison official told the guards who'd brought them in. "Without the file, we can't accept him."

"Well, we don't want him." The transport guards were anxious to head back to their homes in London.

"We can't accept this man without the proper file," the federal official repeated firmly.

They told Rick to get dressed and he got back on the bus with his guards. They drove around for a while, trying to figure out what to do with him. They yelled at each other, blaming one another for the foul-up, while Rick listened. He felt like a side of beef that had gone bad and everybody in the butcher shop was blaming everyone else for the smell.

Finally they took him to the bucket in the nearby town of Napanee, where he spent the night. He was put in with the population at first, and there was a kid who wanted to tell him all his troubles. "Oh Jeez," the kid whined, "I just got screwed in court—I got thirty days."

"Look, I don't wanna talk right now, okay?"

It was a relief when they finally locked him in the hole. He lay down on the bunk and turned his face to the wall, that punk kid's words echoing through his brain. "Screwed in court, thirty days, screwed in court, thirty days . . ." Rick Sauvé was afraid his own life had become more than he could bear.

BOOK SEVEN
THE FISH

"Well, six white horses that you did promise were
finally delivered down to the penitentiary,
But to live outside the law you must be honest—
I know you always say that you agree;

All right,
So where are you tonight, Sweet Marie?

—BOB DYLAN, "ABSOLUTELY SWEET MARIE"

XXXV

Solicitor General   Cumulative Summary

Canadian Penitentiary Service   Part One

COMEAU, GARY JOSEPH Inmate Number 5171 Jan. 29, 1980

Institution—R.R.C. (Ont.) [Regional Reception Centre, Kingston Penitentiary]

Brief comment to leisure time activities: Subject states that most of his leisure time has been consumed with the activities of the Satan's Choice motorcycle club of which he has been a member for ten years. . . .

Brief comments re family relationships: He states he still has good family relationships and relies on it heavily. He could not however resolve the obvious conflict between full time commitment to Satan's Choice and any relationship with his family. He did state very emphatically that he was until the time of the offence a full time Satan's Choice member.

Potential problem areas: This individual is serving Life for 1st. Degree Murder and (may be) the gunman in a murder October 18, 1978. It is advisable that this man not be encouraged to associate with others involved in this crime and that of the six he is the most hostile towards the system.

General impression: The subject was somewhat defiant during interview but adamant that he was innocent. Some rapport was established but the subject remained aloof in many areas. The subject's attitude at the present time is very difficult to assess since his whole being seems consumed by his appeal and his statement of innocence. He is also extremely concerned at his being labeled both in the press and by other parties as trigger-man in this offence and is concerned of the consequences.

Offence (official & inmate's versions): Comeau is serving Life for 1st. Degree Murder in result of October 18, 1978 slaying of a motorcycle club member in Port Hope hotel. Subject adamantly insists that he is innocent. . . . [Of all] the individuals involved currently at R.R.C. Comeau seems the most defiant and the most hostile and the most potentially violent of the group. No conclusion can be reached on the scant information, however it is suggested that this individual of the group be most closely watched.

Institutional assessment: Comeau age 28 is serving Life for 1st. Degree Murder, his first penitentiary incarceration. Subject has a brief criminal record but a longstanding relationship with Satan's Choice. This individual denies his guilt and refuses to discuss the offence in any way but is regarded by this writer as potentially aggressive if pushed or cornered. Special attention should be given to this individual especially following the results of his appeal. Initial placement is recommended in Millhaven Institution.

Recommend M.I.

Kingston Pen, it turned out, was a bung-hole, and every story Jeff McLeod had ever heard about the place was true. The normal reception period for new inmates was six weeks, during which time each individual was supposed to be subjected to interviews, physical and psychological examinations, personality inventories, and the processing of the rapidly accumulating paperwork.

Jeff found himself looking for the smallest of hiding-places between the proverbial rock and a hard place. It was obvious that the prison authorities wanted him to dissociate himself from Nutty, Rick, and the others, and for Jeff the time at KP was a time for some serious soul-searching. He didn't need anyone to tell him that it was the biker lifestyle that had landed him in this jackpot. Would his predicament be enough to snap him out of the Life? He began to suspect and fear that the club association would ultimately cause his death. But maybe it would also get him respect and protection in the jungle.

Then, too, his five co-defendants were his friends. They were the only people in here he knew and trusted. Jeff knew one other thing for certain: he did not want to be sent to Millhaven. Anywhere but there.

Rick Sauvé's papers caught up with him the next day, and, after a single night in the Napanee bucket, he was returned to KP. Immediately the authorities were on him, too, to break with the other five guys, and from the club.

"How would you like to be identified with them for the rest of your life?" he was asked. "How would you like to be on the same prison range with them for the rest of your life?"

"Yeah," replied Rick, "can we arrange that?"

On just their third morning at KP the guards didn't unlock their cells, though they opened everyone else's.

"You one of the bikers?" the guard asked Jeff.

Oh no, here it comes. Jeff said he was.

"You're going to Millhaven this afternoon."

Whoa, thought Jeff. What about all the tests they were supposed to get? He asked a prison official about it. Why Millhaven? Why *him*?

"Because you're a member of a criminal organization and you've committed the most serious crime known to man," he was told.

They were transferred that afternoon.

Although it had opened only in 1971, Millhaven maximum-security federal penitentiary, located a few miles west of Kingston, quickly established itself as one of the most hated and feared prisons in Canada. It was, and is, synonymous with brutality—murder, suicide, assaults, gang warfare—and life in its cell blocks bears a close resemblance to Thomas Hobbes's famous description of man's existence in a state of nature—nasty, brutish, violent, and short.

Twentieth-century liberal notions of penology—concepts like reform and rehabilitation—assume a cruelly ironic irrelevance at a place like Millhaven. Or, as a veteran OPP sergeant remarked with a certain note of satisfaction: "Cons only learn how to do two things at Millhaven—pump iron and screw Greek style." The cons themselves call the place Thrillhaven.

They arrived on the afternoon of January 30, 1980, shuffling along in their chains, carrying their suitcases. Since none of them had ever done time in a federal pen, indeed most of them had never done serious jail time until the murder of Bill Matiyek, they were, in prison parlance, "fish"—first-time federal offenders.

Two cons doing life bits for murder, John Dunbar and Kenny Logan from the Lobos Motorcycle Club in Windsor, gave each of them a special "CARE package," a bag full of sundries, the sorts of things the average citizen on the street could buy in two minutes at a drugstore, but in Millhaven, on their first day, it meant a lot. Even a small tube of Crest toothpaste was somehow oddly reassuring—a tangible reminder that there was still a world outside. It was a kindness that none of them ever forgot.

Dunbar and Logan also taught their brother bikers the ropes in the newcomers' first weeks at Millhaven. Above all, they were told, mind your own business. Don't get involved in somebody else's trip. That didn't sound too hard.

Jeff McLeod's father kept his promise to his son and retained Eddie Greenspan to handle Jeff's appeal. Greenspan had juniored the Demeter murder trial with defence lawyer Joe Pomerant and was, by 1980, well on his way to becoming the most renowned criminal lawyer in Canada. Legal Aid assigned appellate counsel for the remaining five, and their reputations would become only slightly less lustrous than Greenspan's. Clayton Ruby, a Toronto criminal lawyer widely known for his civil-libertarian views, would act for Larry Hurren. Another Toronto criminal lawyer, Alan Gold, agreed to represent Rick Sauvé. Gold was a well-respected veteran in appellate cases. Eddie Greenspan's younger brother Brian would serve as Tee Hee's new lawyer, and Ross McKay, who had acted for Armand Sanguigni at the preliminary hearing, would represent Gary Comeau. Taken as a group, they represented a formidable collection of legal talent, the best and the brightest of the Ontario criminal bar.

In the way of all cons, the men convicted of Bill Matiyek's murder had, to varying degrees, a tendency to blame their own lawyers for the jury's verdicts. The lone exception was Merv Blaker. Terry O'Hara had tried to tell him, had warned them all, what would happen if they failed to enter the witness-box. It was obvious now that O'Hara, whose advice they'd scorned and whom they'd tried to get Merv to fire, had been dead right all along. When Merv announced that he'd asked Terry to represent him at the appeal, everyone gave Blaker their blessings. Their association with and respect for O'Hara would grow through the years, long after they'd lost touch with all the other lawyers. Of the nearly two dozen lawyers who would act over the years for the Crown and the defence in the matter of the death of William Matiyek, only O'Hara would see the case through from the preliminary hearing before a provincial court judge in a makeshift courtroom in Port Hope to the Supreme Court of Canada and beyond.

The first classification officer to interview Gary Comeau had been quite right—his pending appeal, his desire to establish his innocence in the death of Bill Matiyek, had become an all-consuming obsession in Nutty's life. Each of his co-defendants would maintain his individual innocence ceaselessly and without question, but none of them attacked the problem or worked so tirelessly to resolve it as Gary Comeau.

As his final act for his former client, Howard Kerbel sent Gary an opinion letter listing a total of forty-eight points upon which an appeal might be argued. He also bequeathed his client something even more valuable—a complete set of trial transcripts. It was an impressive document. Even without the *voir dires* and the jury charges, the seventeen volumes of evidence filled an oversized cardboard carton and weighed nearly thirty-five pounds.

Judging by the sheer weight of the evidence, both literal and figurative, justice certainly appeared to have been done. So why the fuck was he sitting in Millhaven, doing twenty-five years for first-degree murder? Gary read and reread the transcripts. Meticulously, laboriously, he pored over each of its 3,561 pages. He began to write his own critique of the evidence in the hope it might assist his appeal lawyer. He worked at it all through the winter and spring of his first year at Millhaven, exposing every inconsistency, omission, half-truth, and downright lie, as he saw it, in the Crown evidence. The task occupied most of his spare time, and in the end the handwritten critique filled fifty-one pages of foolscap.

It sure was a good thing Canada had abolished the death penalty, Nutty reflected. Otherwise he and Rick might be sitting on Death Row right now.

The names Arthur Lucas and Dwight Turpin meant nothing to Nutty. He knew only that Canada had formally abolished the death penalty for premeditated murder in 1976 and, somewhat more vaguely, that the last hangings in Canada had occurred long before, in 1962. Gary's new lawyer was intimately acquainted with all of these facts, but when Comeau first met Ross McKay at Millhaven in March 1980, he had no idea that the fates of two men hanged eighteen years before would come to have a direct bearing on his own life.

McKay had graduated from Osgoode Hall Law School in 1957, in the same class as Bruce Affleck. McKay had landed a job with one of Toronto's top criminal-law firms and he appeared destined for a brilliant future as a trial lawyer when, in the spring of 1962, a double tragedy befell his career, in the forms of Arthur Lucas and Dwight Turpin. In one disastrous eight-week period that spring, McKay defended both Lucas and Turpin on unrelated charges of capital murder. He lost both trials, and his clients were sentenced to death by hanging. Both verdicts were appealed, but both were upheld. Lucas and Turpin were hanged back-to-back in the Don Jail just before midnight on December 10, 1962.

It was sheer coincidence that McKay had defended both men, but the coincidence became historic when, in 1976, the House of Commons voted to abolish the death penalty. Lucas and Turpin were the last two men to be legally executed in Canada, and Ross McKay would be remembered forever after as the lawyer who had had two clients hanged back-to-back.

The experience left McKay emotionally and professionally traumatized and he began to drink heavily. By 1965 he was deemed unfit to practise by the Law Society of Upper Canada, and he was disbarred. For the next ten years McKay dropped out of sight, but in the mid-seventies he resurfaced. He had joined Alcoholics Anonymous and, though he was no longer a young man, he set out to rebuild his practice and professional standing, after winning readmission to the bar. His efforts met with sympathy and encouragement in the legal community, and Gary Comeau had known nothing of McKay's background when he retained the Toronto lawyer to represent him on his appeal.

He had, McKay assured his new client, already begun to review the trial evidence, and the prospects for a successful appeal looked excellent. McKay even became quite excited during that first interview. Had Gary read the transcript volumes of the judge's charge to the jury in his case? He had? Well he, Ross McKay, considered Volumes 15 and 16 of the transcripts to be the most disgusting volumes he'd ever read. Why, he'd even thrown one of the books right across his law office it had angered him so. It was an outrage.

Gary lapped it all up. Yes, of course, the system had been out to get them all along, the coppers, the judges, even their own lawyers. An excitable person at the best of times, Gary returned to his cell after the interview with McKay brimming with confidence and optimism. He told Rick and the others what McKay had said. Their appeal chances looked good. And even if the Ontario Court turned them down, McKay had promised to argue the case right up to the Supreme Court of Canada. Hey—hadn't Nutty told them? Finally things were starting to go their way.

In 1980, Millhaven Institution was home to about three hundred of Canada's most dangerous offenders in its general population, and an additional seventy-five in its Special Handling Unit, or SHU, a special prison-within-a-prison, one of just two such units in the Canadian federal prison system.

Besides the swift, sudden violence that was apt to break out at any time within its fences, Millhaven was also notorious for its "cliques," tight groups of prisoners who banded together for their own protection. Most of the cliques are organized along racial, ethnic, or even geographic lines. There is a black clique, a Native Brotherhood, an Italian clique, even a rounder clique—cons who grew up together on the streets of west Toronto.

The notion that the six Satan's Choice members convicted of Bill Matiyek's murder would now dissociate themselves from one another and from the club, as the authorities constantly pressured them to do, was absurd. Millhaven was the last place in the world where a man would break his criminal ties. The higher a joint's security rating, Jeff McLeod learned, the more important one's friends became. In Millhaven, at a maximum-security level, belonging to a group or clique was necessary for sheer physical survival, and in Millhaven's general population, survival became a full-time job. The first precept of con ethics—mind your own business—had seemed simple enough to the fish at the beginning. But, in Millhaven, no thing was ever quite that simple, because there was always somebody looking to mind *your* business.

Jeff McLeod called them "boobirds." They came like vultures to prey on the weak. Whenever you were challenged it was imperative to meet the threat, whatever it was, swiftly and decisively. That sent a message—"Don't nobody else try it." Guys who didn't take action were asking for more fights, more trouble. In Millhaven nice guys didn't finish last, they just didn't finish.

Naturally, they formed their own biker clique. Bikers got respect at Millhaven—at least they were given physical respect. Everyone knew they were tight, and they could hurt you. But most cons didn't like bikers. They were all bandits, after all, and at one time or another most of them had had confrontations with bike clubs on the street, and many of them had lost.

Gary described Millhaven as The Dead Zone. Either you kept busy, or you went mad, that was the bottom line at Millhaven. He saw so many men there go crazy. There were so many stabbings, so many shootings, that after so many years it was just The Dead Zone. You just went numb, there was so much going on.

Keep busy. The Choice members formed their own hockey team, the Millhaven Bulldogs. Nutty played goal, Larry Hurren and a friend of the club were defencemen, and Rick, Jeff, and Bernie Guindon, who had been transferred to Millhaven in 1981, were the ace—and only—forward line. Tee Hee was their coach and general manager. Even with natural athletes like Bernie and Jeff, the Bulldogs were in no danger of being mistaken for the Edmonton Oilers—Larry barely knew how to skate. In one game they managed just three shots on the opposing goalie, but they had fun, and the exercise helped to relieve their nervous tensions and anxieties.

Millhaven offered perhaps half a dozen hobbies to help cons pass their time. There was leather-working, copper work, art, and petit point, among others. But leather work cost money for hides and stamps, and Rick never had been any good at drawing. So he took up petit point. He started with small patterns and then moved on to the largest, most intricate designs he could find, some of them involving up to one hundred thousand separate, tiny stitches. It seemed improbable: a member of Canada's most feared bike club, convicted of the most serious crime there was, sitting in his prison cell surrounded by hundreds of hardened convicts, laboring for hours with his needle and thread, but Rick's mastery of the fine art of petit point was his first prison accomplishment. He sent some of his better efforts home, classic patterns like "The Blue Boy" and "The Red Boy." Sharon got them mounted and framed, and they hang on her apartment walls to this day. The best thing about petit point was that it was time-consuming, and that was the one thing Rick and his fellow cons had too much of—time.

XXXVI

LIKE HIS MORE FAMOUS older brother, Brian Greenspan is, in private, a talkative, affable, immensely likeable man. The sons of a Niagara Falls scrap-dealer who died before either of his boys had reached high school, the brothers Greenspan look remarkably alike. Both men have rounded, baby-faced features that make them look considerably younger than they really are, both wear their dark hair combed straight across their foreheads, both are heavy smokers, and both are born raconteurs.

About twenty percent of Brian Greenspan's practice is devoted to appel-late work, much of it steered his way by a carefully nurtured network of friends and former law school classmates in outlying cities who prefer, for want of time, expertise, or experience, to let someone else argue their clients' appeals before the august Justices of the Ontario Supreme Court, Appeals Division, in the rarefied atmosphere of Osgoode Hall.

Brian Greenspan opened his file on David Hoffman in January 1980. There was, at first, nothing particularly memorable about the case—a Kitchener member of the Satan's Choice convicted of second-degree murder, another standard Legal Aid referral, that was all—until an extraor-dinary conversation with a Kitchener colleague took place late in 1980 or early in 1981, about the time that Tee Hee and the others were beginning their second year in Millhaven.

Greenspan had driven to Kitchener for the day and he was lunching with a colleague who happened to mention, in passing, that he was acting for members of the local Satan's Choice chapter on a number of weapons and explosives charges. The main evidence against them, he added, was police wiretaps on the telephones and in the clubhouse. Would Brian mind looking over the authorization for the intercepts?

The Toronto lawyer replied he'd be happy to help when "the bells started ringing." He thought of the Hoffman appeal. It was an amazing coinci-dence, and Greenspan wondered about the wiretaps all the way back to Toronto. He checked the Hoffman file straight-away and noted the date of the murder—October 18, 1978. He immediately dashed off a letter to Doug Hunt, an old friend whom he trusted in the Attorney General's office. He was acting for David Hoffman on appeal, Greenspan explained, and it had just come to his attention that police had lawfully intercepted private communications at the Kitchener clubhouse of the Satan's Choice during the fall and winter of 1978. Had any private communications involving his client been intercepted on the night of October 18, 1978?

Two months later he received a reply. Hunt confirmed that the police had lawfully intercepted private communications made by means of a telephone located at the Kitchener clubhouse. Hoffman had been intercepted on three occasions on the evening of October 18, 1978: at 7:36 p.m., 7:55 p.m., and 8:40 p.m. The last conversation in which Mr. Hoffman was involved occupied eleven feet of tape and lasted approximately four or five minutes.

The telephone calls that Tee Hee had made after the police raid, the conversations that he'd known would corroborate his alibi and extend by a few precious minutes the time he could prove he was in Kitchener, had finally emerged, two and a half years after they were first recorded, a year and a half after he had frantically searched for them among the other wiretaps the police had disclosed on the eve of his trial. Just as Tee Hee suspected, they'd been in the possession of the police all along. He was now entering his sixteenth month of imprisonment for second-degree murder.

COMEAU, Gary Joseph Inmate No. 5171 Millhaven Institution

Parole Eligibility Date December 6, 2003

Progress Summary as of November 11, 1981

Educational/vocational: Has not undertaken any but routine cleaner's duties as the attitude toward his conviction is that on appeal he will be released and therefore has no commitment to the bettering of his skills.

Employment: Seems to perform "J" Cleaner duties adequately.

Personal development: No evidence he has any plan to change as he remains adamant he is innocent. . . . Claims to be innocent and therefore improperly incarcerated when police demanded all involved serve time when guilty party was concealed.

Transfer/release/supervision: After appeal probably in Spring 1982. Seeks to be in trade skill and upgrading institutional programs.

Leisure: Inmate Committee—Christmas bags. Reads, sports, group, hockey, baseball, tennis, cards.

Like the others, Gary Comeau was well settled into Millhaven by the late fall of 1981. He didn't really have a choice. But oddly, many of the very traits that had brought him here in the first place—his manic energy, his aggressiveness, his refusal to obey authority—stood him in good stead in Millhaven. He was elected to the Inmate Committee, which represented all of the prisoners in the joint. The committee met regularly with the prison warden to air grievances, and even occasionally with his superiors—the Regional Director of Correctional Service Canada and the Commissioner of Corrections, the senior bureaucrat in charge of the entire federal penitentiary service. It was a good chance to gain insights into how the system worked and, in a modest way, to struggle to change it.

"We only got what they planned on givin' us," Gary would say of his service on the Inmate Committee, "but the committee helps to get it faster." They fought to improve conditions, usually in a material way. The committee helped to get washing-machines and clothes driers installed on each range, and ice machines in every cell block. Millhaven had been pressed into service before it was fully completed, and, ten years later, power receptacles had still not been wired into individual cells. The Inmate Committee pushed to have the work completed so that every con could have his own radio, TV, or stereo.

Nutty also became involved in a variety of athletic and leisure activities to help pass the time. In the winter there was hockey with the Bulldogs, in the summer baseball and tennis—he played doubles, usually. He became an avid reader, devouring up to five newspapers per day, and dozens of books; non-fiction, most of them: he hated novels.

One night in December 1981, Dr. Carole Clapperton received an emergency call to treat an inmate in the Millhaven infirmary. Clapperton, then thirty-four, had had a remarkable career for someone who received her primary-school education in a two-room schoolhouse in the tiny village of Baltimore, Ontario. She'd begun her medical career as a Registered Nurse before earning an Honours BA from Queen's University and a medical degree from McMaster in 1979. After completing a further two-year course in family medicine at Queen's, she opened her own general, family-oriented practice in Kingston.

To supplement her income, Clapperton also became a contract physician with Correctional Service Canada. Most of her work for the CSC was centred at Kingston's Prison for Women, but she was also on call for Millhaven. She was still relatively new at this prison work, and emergency calls to Millhaven filled her with trepidation. She never knew what she might find—a body, a slasher, an assault victim. She'd already learned to gauge the degree of physical danger by the attitudes and number of the guards assigned to accompany her within the prison. If there were only one or two, the situation wasn't too serious. But if there were five or six, tight-lipped and weapons at the ready, it scared the hell out of her. Tonight didn't seem too bad—there were only two.

She knew little about her patient. They'd said his name was Baker, or something like that, and he was suffering from chest pains. The staff nurses had said he wasn't a complainer, and when he mentioned the chest pains it worried them.

Clapperton waited at the nurse's office for the guards to bring the patient from his hospital cell. As the gate opened she suppressed a gasp of surprise. She recognized Murray instantly as the shy Indian boy with whom she'd shared a classroom for eight years back in Baltimore. But did he recognize her?

"Hello, I'm Dr. Clapperton." She said it officiously, a trifle too loudly perhaps, as they all walked to the examining-room, and Carole saw the flash of recognition in Murray's eyes. She glanced back at the guards. Whatever he was doing in here, her old childhood friend clearly wasn't considered much of a security risk. The guards were chatting quietly to one another, and they hadn't noticed her surprise.

As she examined the prisoner, she said softly, "Well, Murray, I think our lives have taken different paths since we saw each other last." She asked about his family and Murray told her he had a ten-year-old daughter. At that the guards' interest was aroused (clearly these two knew each other, perhaps the meeting was even a set-up), and Clapperton dared not say any more.

Although he was trembling like a leaf, Clapperton diagnosed Blaker's chest pains as nothing more than a muscular disorder, and she gave him a prescription before the guards escorted her out of the prison. Even after she returned home, Carole Clapperton was dumbfounded. Murray Blaker in Millhaven! However could it have happened?

Jeff McLeod was in his cell brushing his teeth one morning when he heard a strange sound somewhere on the range. It sounded like a scuffle, followed by an odd gurgling noise, the likes of which he'd never heard before. Then he heard the footfalls of three or four men running. Jeff looked cautiously out his cell door, and he could see a guy lying on the floor of another cell further down the range.

When he went for breakfast, Jeff saw that the guy was still on the floor. His throat had been slashed from ear to ear, and there was blood everywhere. His eyes were still open.

Jeff, normally a voracious eater, was picking at his breakfast when Rick came up. "Did you hear they found a body on our range? We gotta go back for lock-up."

"Yeah," Jeff grimaced. "I saw him."

The guy was still lying there when they returned to the range, and his eyes were still open. It was the first murder victim that Jeff McLeod had ever seen in his life. (In the melee at the Queen's Hotel, he'd never seen Bill Matiyek after he hit the floor.) Despite himself, Jeff looked into the dull, lifeless eyes of the con on the floor. "Oh God," Jeff thought to himself. "I wanna get outta here. . . ."

Throughout the spring and summer of 1981 Brian Greenspan continued to build the appeal case for David Hoffman. Once the existence of the police tapes of his client's telephone conversations on the night of the murder had been confirmed, Greenspan asked to see the Interception Log from the clubhouse telephone wiretap.

The police summaries of Hoffman's conversation revealed that he'd been overheard talking to three different individuals. In the first call, at 7:36 p.m., Hoffman had spoken to Claude "Gootch" Morin about the raid. He told Morin that the police "took guns also some samples. Asked Gootch to [purchase] a new lock when he comes over."

Twenty minutes later, at 7:55 p.m., police had listened as Hoffman called "an unknown female" concerning an "appointment." At 8:40 p.m., the police noted Hoffman's voice on the line once again, this time talking to "Joe." Hoffman asked Joe if he'd forgotten the appointment; and Joe wondered if the police were looking for anything in particular during the raid.

With mounting excitement Greenspan ordered police transcriptions of the recordings. The Toronto lawyer concluded that he had, through the sheerest coincidence, uncovered important new evidence in Hoffman's case. The tapes provided further proof of Tee Hee's alibi, an alibi that he had, after all, told police about even before his arrest three years ago. He'd told the police, the preliminary hearing, and the trial jury about the conversation with Gootch directly after the raid. The "unknown female" on the second call was obviously Colleen Misener, the owner of Costumes by Colleen, and the unexplained "appointment" referred to Hoffman's planned meeting with her in Stratford to rent Halloween costumes for the Vagabonds' party.

The last call, at 8:40, was the kicker. Suppose it had lasted only five minutes. That would have given Hoffman just two hours to make the 195-kilometre drive from the clubhouse to the hotel in Port Hope, entering the bar, as the witness claimed to have seen him, at about 10:45, when the rest of the Choice had apparently arrived.

That was still physically possible—just possible—if Hoffman had finished his conversation with Joe Ertel, jumped immediately into a car, and gone barrelling off to Port Hope to commit planned and deliberate murder. But why would he do that? The Toronto Chapter members had gone to Port Hope in response to a call from Rick Sauvé. It was now clearer than ever that Sauvé had not called the Kitchener Chapter on the night of the murder. So, unless it had been planned far in advance, how would Hoffman have known that his club brothers planned to kill Bill Matiyek, and *in the Queen's Hotel*? But how could any of them have known that Matiyek would actually be in the hotel that particular night?

The phone conversation with Ertel strengthened Hoffman's alibi in one other way. At the end of the conversation, Ertel had said he'd be seeing Hoffman soon at the clubhouse, and that was exactly what he had done, according to all the alibi witnesses—dropped into the clubhouse briefly to help put the new lock in the door. At that point in the evening, Hoffman simply would not have had the time to get to Port Hope.

The tapes, Brian Greenspan decided, provided fresh evidence that David Hoffman had been unjustly convicted of second-degree murder.

The presentation of fresh evidence at appeals court, while not unprecedented, is highly unusual, not least because of the very strict legal criteria that must be satisfied before new evidence can be heard. First, it must be shown that the evidence was not available at the time of the original trial, and, second, it must be proven that the new evidence is cogent—that is, that a reasonable person might be persuaded that if the evidence had been heard by the jury, the outcome of the trial could have been different.

Greenspan believed that the newly uncovered wiretaps would satisfy both criteria. But he intended to leave unasked a third, and most intriguing, question: *Why* had the wiretaps been unavailable at trial? Why had the police failed to disclose them two years earlier, as they were required by law to do?

It was a sticky legal wicket. Greenspan's first commitment, after all, was to his client, to have David Hoffman's murder conviction overturned. This could be done only if the appellate court judges agreed to hear the fresh evidence. But if it was suggested that the trial lawyers could have known or should have known about the existence of the wiretaps, then the first criterion for fresh evidence might not be met.

And so, when the appellate court judges asked Brian Greenspan whether he was alleging any improprieties against the Crown prosecutors, Hoffman's lawyer replied that he was not, in any way, alleging bad faith on the part of Chris Meinhardt. And when they further asked whether Greenspan was suggesting that the law-enforcement agencies had intentionally withheld evidence, he would also answer, noncommittally. "I have no evidence to that effect, one way or the other."

And, in truth, Greenspan did not have the evidence. Somehow, when Ed Martin, Hoffman's trial lawyer, had forwarded his trial records to Greenspan, he had neglected to include the two thick volumes that comprised the Crown's pre-trial wiretap disclosures. The contents of the volumes, which had so concerned the defence lawyers before the trial began, had never been used as evidence and therefore had had no effect on the trial's outcome. But buried deep within the pages of the wiretap transcripts was the proof that someone, somewhere, had, in fact, reviewed the wiretap evidence before the Satan's Choice murder trial began. The police and the Crown Attorneys had seen fit to disclose conversations recorded on the Kitchener clubhouse telephone both before and after the night of the murder, on October 10 and on October 29. But the recordings from the night of the murder, which would have been so crucial to Hoffman's alibi defence, were omitted, even after the Crown and the police knew that Hoffman's lawyer intended to mount a defence of alibi.

In the end, incredibly, all of these omissions and failures would be seen as proof that the criminal justice system worked. An innocent man had been convicted of murder, true, but that would be caught and corrected at the Court of Appeal—cause for self-congratulations all around.

Just how such a thing had happened in the first place would be conveniently overlooked. No public investigation of why the police had failed to disclose the evidence was ever held. Brian Greenspan, concerned mainly with the narrow question of proving Hoffman's innocence, was not inclined to press the broader point, and Martin's failure to provide him with all of the trial documents deprived Greenspan of the proof, in any event. But the fact is that had Brian Greenspan not gone for lunch in Kitchener with a particular colleague in the winter of 1980, David George Hoffman would be in prison to this day.

Working as a team, the lawyers crafted an appeal strategy based mainly upon Justice Osborne's trial rulings and his jury charge. Although Greenspan found the charge to be "even-handed and fair," Clayton Ruby was particularly incensed that Osborne had admitted the evidence of club membership, club insignia, and the testimony of the police biker experts. He was convinced that such evidence made it simply impossible for bikers to receive a fair trial, owing to the powerful tendency to find guilt by association.

They hoped to persuade the appellate court that Osborne had also erred by underplaying the possibility of a manslaughter verdict in his jury charge; that he had further erred by admitting evidence of the Satan's Choice as a "brotherhood"; that he should not have allowed evidence of the December 1977 brawl, and Sauvé's threats against Matiyek in February or March of 1978, to be heard by the jury "where such acts of hostility had no nexus in time or place to the alleged homicide"; that he had improperly bolstered the eyewitness evidence of Cotgrave and Thompson by his "how wrong were they" presentation concerning the bullet in Comeau's back; that he failed to adequately instruct the jury on the specific shortcomings of the photo array procedure; and that he erred in admitting hearsay evidence concerning Matiyek's utterances on the telephone moments before his death.

The Court of Appeals is a far different place from a trial court, and the game is played under an entirely new set of rules. The appellants have no right to be present to hear the arguments for or against them, so the six men convicted of the murder of Bill Matiyek remained securely locked away at Millhaven while their futures were being decided. A jury composed of twelve of one's peers is also absent. Instead, an appellant's fate is determined by three members of the Ontario Supreme Court, Appeals Division, a trio of the wisest and most learned practitioners the Ontario bar has to offer.

The proceedings are not transcribed, since appeal hearings are concerned with arguments on legal issues and points of law, and almost never with the introduction of actual evidence. Nor is the appeals court a place for the court-room theatrics or the slashing cross-examinations so appreciated by jurors, journalists, and the general public. In theory, at least, appellate sessions should be governed by logic and reason, by a firm grasp of precedent and usage, by measured decorum, as the elite among lawyers and judges assist Lady Justice, blind but serenely balanced, along her ineffable and majestic way.

In theory. In practice, the Appeals Division of the Ontario Supreme Court was, as recently as the 1960s, notorious for the bluntness of its judges and the pertinacity of the solicitors who dared appear before them. The appeals courts that surrounded the inner foyer of Osgoode Hall were not biker clubhouses, but they were no place for the foolish, faint-hearted, or inexperienced members of the Ontario bar, and sometimes the very lack of decorum, the shouting, the rudeness, the epithets that poured down from the benches, were very like a biker club chapter meeting.

"Hey Nutty," one of his fellow cons greeted Gary Comeau one day at Millhaven. "Isn't Ross McKay your lawyer?"

"Yeah. So?"

"Did you hear what happened to him?"

"No."

"They picked him up the other night at the corner of Yonge and Dundas singing 'Amazing Grace' . . ."

"*Whaaat?*"

" . . . and last week he started reciting Hail Marys in the middle of a bail hearing."

"Fuck off!"

A little con humor, Gary decided. And not very funny. McKay was his horse now, and Nutty was sure he was riding a winner. He could just *feel* it.

XXXVII

MR. JUSTICE COULTER OSBORNE had certainly been right about one thing when he pronounced sentence on the six bikers more than two years earlier: the killing of Bill Matiyek had been a tragedy for all seven families involved. For the parents of the six men convicted of Matiyek's murder the sentencing of their sons to life imprisonment was almost as great a loss as that suffered by Doris and Metro Matiyek themselves. In fact, the chances that Gene and Betty King and Pierre and Adeline Sauvé would live long enough to ever again see their sons outside of prison walls were slim indeed.

It was hardly surprising, then, that on the morning of January 19, 1982, the families of all six of the appellants crowded into Courtroom 7 at Osgoode Hall. Sitting before the august Justices of the Ontario Supreme Court that day were, in no particular order, a farmer, the foreman of a sign company, a retired federal civil servant, a hospital cleaner, a switchboard operator, and a retired natural-gas company employee. They were, in a word, decent, hard-working folk who had lived their lives in respect of the Queen's justice and in the good order of Canadian society, and they had attempted, with obviously mixed results, to inculcate these values in their offspring.

But the fate met by their sons at the hands of Canada's criminal-justice system had proved, for each family, to be a deeply corroding experience. To the extent that they had personally witnessed the police search and seizures within their homes, to the extent that they had attended the London trial, to the extent that they had visited their sons in Millhaven, they were forced to confront their unquestioning faith in the legal system. To a man and to a woman they were convinced beyond certainty that their sons were innocent of aiding and abetting a planned and deliberate murder. They believed in the system, yes, but it was the system that had convicted their sons. Murders, trials, prisons, hangings, these were things that happened to *other* families, different families, not decent families like their own. Even Gene King, Gary's stepfather, who had always been his sternest critic, had to admit that twenty-five years in prison seemed a stiff price to pay for joining an outlaw motorcycle club.

There was also a considerable deal of guilt in Courtroom 7 that day as the three wizened judges seated themselves behind their lofty bench. If "if only" is the litany of a thousand convicts—if only I'd been out when the phone rang that night, if only I'd never called Toronto, if only the club- house line had been busy, if only Bill hadn't been so drunk, if only we'd known . . . —then it is also the bitter self-recrimination of two thousand parents—if only we'd raised him differently, if only we'd worked even harder, if only we had money, if only we'd hired the best lawyers, if only we'd known . . . then everything would have been different.

The first day of the appeal was devoted to the legal arguments of the law- yers for the appellants, abstruse and difficult questions of case law and precedent, and of semantics, an endless dialogue between the elite lawyers of the Toronto criminal bar and the even more elite judges of the appeals court. It must have been, to the average onlooker, exceedingly difficult to follow. But Adeline Sauvé, Rick's mother, was not average. She was almost totally deaf. And so she occupied herself by watching the behavior, the body language, the movements, of the lawyers in their long black robes and the three judges sitting, almost immobile, behind their bench.

It was after lunch that first day that she noticed, in disbelief, the judge sitting in the middle. It couldn't be. She looked away and let time pass, and then looked back again. And again. He hadn't moved a muscle, his head was down upon his chest. Not only was he not listening, that man was asleep. And suddenly the truth of the world struck Adeline Sauvé with all the pain of childbirth, with the awesome force of a thunderclap rolling across a scuddy summer sky: *These men don't give a damn what happens to my son!*

Betty King noticed it, too, but with little sense of wonder. She already knew that her son Gary had come to be nothing more than a piece of paper, a file somewhere, a dollar to be made, another human soul to be ware- housed in Millhaven, that most soulless of all places. She had, after all, grown up in Newfoundland, on the Southside Hill of St. John's. Life had always been hard, and there were few illusions. Her Gary. What wouldn't she have done for him? My God, she'd even stolen for him, once, to put clothes on his back. But she would not, could not, lie for him. No, others had done that on the witness stand, but not her. Police who enjoyed violating her home, police who had so little self-respect they would lie under oath, a judge who fell asleep. There was little outrage and even less wonder left in Betty King.

Brian Greenspan would not have said that Mr. Justice Arthur Robert Jessup was asleep that day on the bench, any more than he would accuse the police of purposely suppressing the evidence in favour of Tee Hee Hoffman. Judge Jessup was from the old school, after all. Brian Greenspan, denizen of the criminal-justice system and master of the arcana of the brotherhood of the bench, believed that Justice Jessup was merely expressing his boredom with whatever issue was being argued before him on that particular afternoon. Or maybe he was resting. That was all. You just had to understand how the system worked.

David Hoffman's lawyer presented his arguments that the wiretaps represented "fresh evidence" on the second day of the hearing. He carefully sidestepped the question of whether he believed either the Crown Attorneys or the police had deliberately suppressed the evidence thirty months before, and the judges ruled in Greenspan's favour. They agreed to hear the new evidence, quite literally, and a cassette player was installed in Courtroom 7.

It was a highly effective, even dramatic, moment as the three justices listened intently to telephone conversations that were now three and a half years old. Even Mac Haig, who had been sent to Toronto to cover the appeal hearing for the *London Free Press*, had to admit it certainly put Hoffman's case in a new light. You had to wonder if the five eyewitnesses who had been so positive in their identification of Hoffman had really seen the big Kitchener biker in the Queen's Hotel that night after all.

Greenspan reminded the court that Hoffman had proffered an alibi even before he was arrested for the murder of Bill Matiyek. He argued that the tenor of the recorded conversations clearly showed that his client was in no rush to leave Kitchener on the night of the murder, and that there had been no telephone call to the Kitchener clubhouse from Rick Sauvé on the evening of October 18. Brian Greenspan urged the justices to overturn David Hoffman's conviction on second-degree murder.

Jane Arnup, the daughter of Mr. Justice John Arnup and the partner of Brian Greenspan, slipped into the courtroom that day to watch her colleague make his arguments on the fresh evidence. At the conclusion of the case for the appellants she watched as Mr. Justice Jessup rose, gathered his papers together, and thanked everyone in the court for coming. He and his colleagues would now begin their deliberations and get back to those affected, Jessup explained before turning to leave the bench. That was all very fine, except that the lawyers for the Crown had not yet argued their evidence in reply to the appellants' presentations.

"Arthur, Arthur," Jane Arnup heard her father hiss in a loud stage-whisper, "we haven't heard the reply arguments yet." Totally unruffled, Arthur Jessup resumed his seat on the bench.

The Crown's response to the appellants' arguments filled the third day of the appeal hearing, and the proceeding was then adjourned until mid-April, when two days were set aside for the completion of all the other arguments. When the hearing resumed on Tuesday, April 12, however, Mr. Justices Jessup, Arnup, and Morden surprised everyone by announcing that no further arguments would be necessary, as they had already reached a decision. The Court of Appeals' ruling confirmed all of Brian Greenspan's fears about the prudence and fairness of Coulter Osborne's jury charge.

The trial judge had not misdirected the jury concerning the law on aiding and abetting, the appeals court concluded. Osborne had made it clear that mere passive acquiescence was not enough to constitute aiding and abetting. "'A person may be taken to be aiding and abetting if with the intention of giving assistance he is near enough to provide it should the need arise.'"

Nor had Osborne erred in admitting the evidence of Matiyek's last telephone conversation. "The majority of this Court is satisfied that this evidence was admissible as being relevant to the deceased's state of mind and the inferences that could be drawn from this."

The issues of club membership and enmity, which Clayton Ruby had argued passionately should not have been heard by the jury, were also admissible evidence, the three judges agreed. "The case could not be realistically assessed by the jury without considering the fact that the appellants were members of Satan's Choice and the deceased was a Golden Hawk. In our view the use to which this evidence could be put was adequately dealt with in the charge to the jury with respect to its ultimate potential bearing on the relevant issue of motive. . . ."

Had the trial judge improperly bolstered the identification evidence of Cotgrave and Thompson and failed to adequately instruct the jury concerning the shortcomings of the police identification procedures? Once again the three justices of the appeals court were unanimous in their ruling that he had not.

Only on their final point—Is the fresh evidence admissible and does it necessitate a new trial for Hoffman?—did the justices find in the appellants' favour.

The justices reviewed the eyewitness testimony, and then the substance of Hoffman's alibi—the plan to drive to Stratford to rent costumes, the police raid, the struggle to repair the broken lock. "Since [Hoffman] was convicted by the jury, it is obvious that his alibi evidence was rejected. Mr. Brian Greenspan, counsel for Hoffman, applied to this court to tender fresh evidence of a very unusual nature. Unbeknownst to anyone at the trial, the Kitchener clubhouse of the Satan's Choice Club was on October 18th the subject of an authorized interception in connection with an unrelated investigation, and a telephone wiretap was in place. Three telephone calls having some relevance to this case were extracted from the tape and played in open court."

The justices reviewed the wiretap evidence. "At 8:40 p.m. a call was received for Hoffman, which he answered; the caller was clearly Joe Ertel. Hoffman in the recorded telephone call said to 'Joe': 'I'll see you in a couple of hours.' Hoffman and Tom Ertel had both testified at the trial that Tom and Joe Ertel arrived at the club about 10 p.m.

"[The Crown's] primary submission is that the three telephone calls do not add anything to the evidence at the trial except to place Hoffman in the Kitchener clubhouse fifteen minutes later than was shown at the trial. The Crown submits that Hoffman still had ample time to drive to Port Hope and be there within the time frame given by the Port Hope eyewitnesses. It was the Crown's theory at trial that this is what Hoffman did—leave the clubhouse as soon as the police search party departed, and head for Port Hope as fast as he could, and arrive at the Queen's Hotel bar with the others.

"In our view this is too simplistic a view of the fresh evidence. Hoffman's whole defence was an alibi. His whole story of that evening could have been concocted, except what was corroborated by the police search party. Obviously he had no knowledge that everything he said on the telephone was being recorded. He was not concocting conversations for the benefit of the wiretap.

"That recording, in the circumstances, had a unique authenticity of its own . . . with a credibility far beyond what this jury seems to have attributed to Hoffman's corroborating witnesses. It demonstrates that, at least in those respects, what Hoffman told the police, and repeated at trial, was true, and adds weight to the other parts of his new evidence with which the corroborated parts fit together. It also shows that whoever Sauvé may have called that night, no one called the Kitchener clubhouse about anything connected with Port Hope.

"In such circumstances it appears to us that this new evidence might well have affected the jury's verdict. This is sufficient to set aside the conviction of Hoffman and to direct a new trial.

"In the result the appeal of Hoffman is allowed, his conviction is set aside and a new trial is directed. The appeals of the other appellants are dismissed."

Two days later, on Thursday, April 15, 1982, Tee Hee Hoffman gathered up his personal belongings, bade farewell to Nutty, Rick, Merv, Beaver, and Jeff, and emerged through the gates of Millhaven, subject to his bail restrictions (until the new trial), a free man. He had served two years and five months of hard time.

XXXVIII

THE DISMISSAL OF HIS CASE by the Court of Appeals almost broke Nutty. At last he, too, entered the Millhaven Dead Zone. Plunged into a deep depression that lasted nearly ten months, Gary Comeau became, to his own mind at least, a virtual zombie. His hopes had been built up far too high before the appeal, he knew that now. None of them needed to be told the consequences of the appeals court's unanimous ruling. Had there been one dissenting opinion, their case would have been heard automatically by the Supreme Court of Canada. Now their lawyers would first have to seek leave from the country's highest court before a new appeal would even be heard, and winning the high court's permission to entertain the appeal would be an uphill battle. When Gary had first met him, Ross McKay had likened their position, reassuringly, to that of a hitter in a baseball game. The trial had been only strike one, McKay had assured Gary; they had two more strikes to go. Well, now they'd swung at a second pitch, and missed by a country mile. Because of the Ontario court's unanimous ruling they had one more cut, all right, but now the count was no balls and two strikes, and the odds were weighted heavily, probably overwhelmingly, in the pitcher's favour. They were all good enough ballplayers to understand what that meant. The thought of spending the next twenty years of his life in places like Millhaven filled Gary Comeau with the blackest despair he'd ever known.

Each of them came to terms with it in his own way. Despite his daunting size and appearance when he was on the street, Jeff McLeod had never thought of himself as a particularly tough or violent person. Hell, before he'd put on his patch he couldn't even remember the last time he'd had a fist fight, outside of a hockey game.

More and more Jeff McLeod had come to see the violence that surrounded him at Millhaven as a sea of madness. There was only one island in that unkind ocean, and that was the school. Gradually Jeff began to gravitate towards the teachers and the staff. He became the clerk of the school and a student, and he resolved, at last, to devote himself to serious study. "Hey, you're here," he was forced to admit. "The walls are real. *Do* something." And so Jeff McLeod began to read.

Rick Sauvé had tried not to share Nutty's high expectations, and now he was sure he'd been right. Look what hope had done to Nutty. Rick had a hard time, too, after their cases were dismissed, but he tried not to let on. To Nutty, hope and faith that their innocence would somehow one day be established was like fuel, it was what kept him going. To Rick, hope was a kind of demon, a seductress that must be held at arm's length at all costs. Every time he'd let the demon into his life so far, the bitter disappointment that followed had been almost more than he could bear. Hope, he decided, was a luxury that had brought him only to the abyss. How close he'd actually been to that edge, to losing his sanity, only Rick knew, but he resolved never to let that happen to him again. Hope was a luxury that he could and would learn to live without.

And what about Sharon and Angie? His daughter, who had only just started school the year he was arrested, would be thirty by the time he got out. He'd done what he could—sold his bikes and given all the money to Sharon for Angie's education, sent what little money he could spare from his prison job to Sharon. But it wasn't fair to Angie to grow up without a father. There was one more thing he could do.

When Sharon came down on one of her regular visits, Rick asked her to stop coming, to forget about him. "Get a divorce. Find somebody else. I'll understand. Just make sure he'll be a good father for my daughter, that's all I ask."

Jeff, who lived on the same range as Rick, felt torn apart himself. It was the cruellest, saddest thing that he had ever seen. That was when Jeff began to think of Rick and Nutty as the Living Dead Men, because that was exactly what they had become—the Living Dead.

Their seek-leave hearing was scheduled for September 22, before the Supreme Court in Ottawa, and a few days before it, Ross McKay paid his last visit to Gary. McKay came into the visiting-room all flitty. Gary sat in silence, watching his lawyer, waiting for him to explain what had happened at the Ontario appeal.

"We lost the appeal," Gary said at last, simply.

"What?" McKay seemed surprised, as if he didn't know. "They didn't tell me that."

The lawyer seemed agitated suddenly, and ran out of the room. When he returned, McKay told Gary that he'd been out west during the appeal. At the Supreme Court, McKay promised, things would be different. "I'm going in there Wednesday and I'll get right back to you."

Gary Comeau never spoke with Ross McKay again.

Terry O'Hara drove up to Ottawa on the day before the seek-leave motion, and he dropped in to the Supreme Court building on Wellington Street. Just to kill some time he sat in on a session involving Ross McKay, who was arguing some kind of motion, and O'Hara could see by McKay's performance that something was desperately wrong. Ross wasn't drunk, but he wasn't himself, either. O'Hara suspected that his friend was losing the battle against substance abuse, against the dependencies that had started to dog him after the hangings of Lucas and Turpin twenty years before.

O'Hara's fears were confirmed the next day, when McKay failed to show up for the seek-leave arguments. The Court was forced to proceed without him, and the other four lawyers did the best they could, arguing Comeau's case in McKay's absence.

O'Hara learned later that McKay had stayed in his Ottawa hotel room that day and, as the Kingston lawyer would put it, "Ross jumped into a coke spoon." Still later, O'Hara learned that McKay had been told only a few days before that he was suffering from terminal cancer.

Clay Ruby broke the news to Gary, by telephone.

"Uh, Gary, I've got some good news and some bad news."

"Yeah?"

"The bad news is that your lawyer never showed up for court. The good news is that we all covered for you the best we could. It looks good."

Well, fuck. From his very first conviction, when he'd been driving with a hot ID that just happened to belong to a former cop, to sitting through a murder trial with the proof of his innocence inside his own body, to having gone unrepresented by legal counsel before the highest court in the land, Gary Comeau could certainly have been forgiven his black mood that day at Millhaven. Man, when it came to the fuckin' law, if he hadn't've had such bad luck, he would have had no fuckin' luck at all.

To no one's great surprise, their seek-leave motion was denied. All of the legal avenues available to them were now exhausted.

Strangely, though he felt himself to be little more than a zombie, and though he'd always look back on that period as the most despair-filled time in his entire life, Gary Comeau began to win positive progress reports from the prison staff. In a report dated August 19, 1982, Nutty's classifications officer noted that "subject is doing academic upgrading in Science, Math and English, school reports indicate that subject is doing quite well in these subjects. . . . Subject has completed a couple of courses, school reports positive progress and good conduct in the school area. . . . Conduct and performance have been satisfactory, if subject had been eligible he would have earned all remission."

Perhaps Inmate Comeau was coming to terms with his imprisonment and with his guilt after all.

By the fall of 1982 the different levels of the "Security Matrix" of the Canadian federal prison system began to affect their lives, and the distinctions between lifers doing first-degree and second-degree murder became apparent. Although it is often mistaken by the public as a sign of excessive leniency, the security grid, through a system known as "cascading," is designed to provide maximum public protection while at the same time affording each federal inmate the best possible chance for successful rehabilitation—at least in theory.

The security matrix can best be imagined as a series of screens, placed one atop the other, with the prisoner tumbling or cascading down through the mesh over the term of his incarceration. The top screen, the finest sieve, is maximum security, the one just below it is medium, the next is minimum, followed by halfway house and then parole. The length of time required for a prisoner to complete the cycle and reach the street is determined first by the length of sentence, then by a timetable imposed by the correctional system, and finally by the individual's behavior while in prison.

An offender sentenced to at least ten years for second-degree murder might spend a minimum of three years in a maximum-security joint (S–6), and another two or three years in medium security (S–5.and S–4), before being transferred to minimum security (S–2), where he could become eligible first for guarded passes (Escorted Temporary Absences or ETA's) in the seventh year of his sentence, unescorted passes (Unescorted Temporary Absences or UTA's) in his eighth year, and assignment to a halfway house in his ninth year.

All of this is dependent upon the individual's good behavior at each stage, but for convicted murderers there is no "time off for good behavior": a convict never spends less than the minimum ten years in institutions. A sentence of ten years to life for second-degree murder means exactly that—and a truly bad actor might never be released from prison. As the prisoner cascades down the security matrix the physical controls over his life are relaxed, and the onus for positive behavior is placed more and more on the individual inmate. The discipline imposed by the prison system is, by degrees, replaced by self-discipline.

In the case of a prisoner sentenced to ten or even fifteen years, the cascade security-grid concept is reasonably useful, and relatively successful. But for cons like Rick and Gary, who have been convicted of premeditated murder and sentenced to twenty-five years *no matter what*, the system is totally unavailing. A first-degree murderer might pass through the initial stage from a maximum- to a medium-security institution, but after that there is very little that can be done. There are no walls or fences around an S–2-rated facility, nothing to physically prevent an inmate who wishes to do so from simply walking away. Yet few prisoners, nearing the ends of their sentences and looking forward to halfway house and eventual release, ever succumb to this temptation. But it is clearly impossible to put freedom so tantalizingly close to a man with ten or fifteen years left on his sentence— the urge to run would become irresistible, or it might drive him crazy. UTA's are likewise out of the question, and even ETA's are risky. Despite his prison record and no matter how outstanding his achievements, the convicted first-degree murderer is consigned to languish for fifteen years or more in medium security. The system's hands are, quite simply, tied.

Merv Blaker became the first among them to begin the long trip down through the cascade. In August 1982 he was granted a transfer to Joyceville, a medium-security institution just east of Kingston. The soft-spoken Blaker had completed the maximum-security portion of his sentence in near-record time, and his parting from Rick, Gary, Jeff, and Larry was bitter-sweet. Although they had entered Millhaven together, Merv's transfer was the first concrete indication that their lives would now begin to run radically different courses. Merv, Jeff, and Larry could look forward to transfers down the security matrix, to ETA's and UTA's, to halfway house and, eventually, the street. But for Gary and Rick, both of whom turned thirty in Millhaven that year, the outlook was simple and stark: they faced twenty-one more years in prison.

Christmas of 1982 was particularly difficult, though holidays in prison are never easy. Practically, Christmas is like an ordinary weekend to a con, except that on most weekends, an inmate can at least look forward to family visits. But prison staff need their holidays, too, so federal institutions are closed to visitors on December 25.

Rick always tried to isolate himself from holidays, but there were always the cards and letters to remind him what he was missing. The cliques would gather and exchange small gifts among themselves and everyone kicked in some food from his Christmas bag to put on a little spread. Once back in his cell, though, it was hard not to feel miserable. Rick always felt as if he was cheating his family, and especially Angie, because he was in prison and couldn't help out. And, the previous two Christmases at Millhaven, there had still been a glimmer of hope because of the appeals. Now even that small, flickering flame had been extinguished.

Betty King came to see her son that year, as she always did, on the morning of Christmas Eve, since she wasn't allowed to come on Christmas itself.

It tore her apart to see Gary locked up this way, year after year; saying good-bye to him after a visit was the worst. Normally, though, Betty was able to control her emotions. But on Christmas Eve, 1982, Betty broke down and cried during her visit. Gary felt absolutely horrible, it really hurt. On the one hand he felt so very shitty for putting her and the rest of the family through the nightmare that his life had become. But on the other hand, he shouldn't be doing life for murder in the first place. The whole thing made him angrier, and more determined than ever not to take any of it lying down.

Merv Blaker was spending his first Christmas at Joyceville, and he was surprised when he opened his mail and discovered a Christmas card from Dr. Carole Clapperton. More than a year had passed since their meeting at Millhaven. He decided to write her back.

Although their own legal avenues were now exhausted, Rick and Gary and the others hoped there might still be one last chance, and it was admittedly a long shot—Tee Hee. David Hoffman spent Christmas of 1982 at home with his parents on the farm, his first Christmas on the street in four years. He still faced the charge of second-degree murder, and the prospect of yet another trial. That trial, Nutty and Rick reasoned, might be the only way to get their case reopened. If it happened, they'd definitely take the stand this time, and tell the world what had happened that night in the Queen's Hotel. They were as determined as ever not to implicate the other club members who'd been there, or Lorne, but they no longer had much to fear from a contempt citation for refusing to answer questions. What could anyone do to them now? They were already serving twenty-five years.

But Tee Hee's trial was fated never to take place. After winning a new trial for his client, Brian Greenspan traveled to Kitchener, where he met David Hoffman for the first time. Greenspan was particularly impressed by Hoffman's appearance. The man resembled a human-sized version of a large Mack truck, Greenspan thought, and that augured poorly for his trial.

With Hoffman's blessing, Greenspan began discussions with Cobourg Crown Attorney C. Roland Harris. Neither side, it appeared, really wanted a second trial. Greenspan certainly didn't—there were still five eyewitnesses who would doubtless repeat their testimony that they'd seen Hoffman in the Queen's at the time of the shooting, and this time the trial would likely be held in Cobourg, a venue that Greenspan believed would still be most unfriendly. What worried Greenspan the most, though, was Hoffman's distinctive appearance—the ponytail, the glasses, his very size—all of which would not help Greenspan to persuade a jury that the eyewitnesses had confused David Hoffman with someone else.

A plea bargain was arranged. The Crown would drop the second-degree murder charges and Hoffman would plead to the less serious offence of accessory to murder after the fact. The evidence on the latter charge was, after all, incontrovertible, based on Hoffman's own trial testimony that Comeau, Sauvé, and Blaker had arrived at his Kitchener apartment within hours of the shooting. The only real question was the length of Hoffman's sentence as an accessory. Harris wanted Hoffman sentenced to seven years. Greenspan balked—his client had already served two years and five months in Millhaven on a second-degree murder conviction for which he was probably innocent—and, in the end, the two sides settled on four years. Greenspan felt bad about the deal—he didn't believe Hoffman's involvement after the fact was worth four years—but he also didn't believe they'd do any better.

On March 21, 1983, Chief Justice Gregory Evans of the Ontario Supreme Court sentenced Tee Hee Hoffman to four years for accessory after the fact to the murder of William Matiyek, and, after nearly a year on the street, David Hoffman returned to prison.

Except for Nutty, the five men convicted of the murder of Bill Matiyek came to terms with their imprisonment, each in his own way. Jeff plunged into his studies. He resolved to earn a university degree while in prison, which seemed at the time a hugely ambitious undertaking. Rick, perhaps inspired by Jeff's example, decided to do the same, and he began to upgrade his Grade 10 education. In Joyceville, Merv Blaker, who had only Grade 8, decided to return to school and learn a trade, something he could fall back on when his prison term was over. Larry Hurren seemed to retreat into his own little world.

Only Gary refused to accept the now-overwhelming odds against them. Perhaps it was his mother's emotional breakdown on Christmas Eve, or maybe it was the seeming finality with which the last door had been shut on them when Tee Hee pleaded instead of standing trial, but for some reason, Gary Comeau snapped out of his depression in March 1983. They just couldn't give up. They were all innocent. He vowed to fight on, and that winter he launched a one-man campaign against the justice system. Comeau began to write an endless stream of letters from his prison cell in Millhaven. He started with all the lawyers in their case. In March 1983 he mailed a form letter to each of them:

Dear [lawyer's name],

As you are probably aware the final chapter in our case came to an end with the guilty plea of David Hoffman last week. But as far as we're concerned it is not over. So I have taken it upon myself with my co-accused in agreement to try and bring this injustice to the public via the media.

I will be writing to all the defence lawyers who were involved at the trial and appeals, asking for their permission to mention their names if I do get a response from the media. . . . If you are contacted would you pass on your views on this case as a concerned party?

You may think I am a man grasping at thin air but as long as we breathe we will proclaim our innocence. I personally will not take this frame job lying down. I must try. Thank you for your time and I'm hoping to hear from you soon.

Yours very truly,
Gary Comeau

Clayton Ruby, Ed Martin, and Alan Gold, among others, responded, saying they'd be happy to help any way they could.

Gary had by now been elected Vice-Chairman of Millhaven's Ten-Plus Fellowship (the association of cons with sentences of ten years or more), and he handled most of the group's correspondence. Even while composing letters on behalf of Ten Plus he always found a way to emphasize his innocence, as in this letter to Liberal MP Warren Allmand on March 18, 1983:

Dear Mr. Allmand:

I am an inmate at Millhaven Institution serving 25 years for first degree murder with no hope for parole for 25 years. (I am innocent, but that is another matter) . . .

I belong to a group called Ten Plus in which I am vice-chairman. This group consists of inmates serving 10 or more years for various offences. There are many members serving time for first degree murder. The members of our group cordially invite you to one of our meetings, which are held on a weekly basis. We are hoping that if you or one of your aides could attend we could discuss the difficulties we are having coping with this rather harsh sentence. Our group also has outside members in the community who attend our meetings on a weekly basis, too. These meetings are well supervised and I believe such a visit by you could be arranged here. I personally agree with you that some inmates convicted of first degree murder could straighten out their lives and be useful citizens in society, if given the chance. . . .

Yours very truly,

Gary Comeau

Vice-Chairman

Ten-Plus Fellowship

In June, Comeau made his first appeal to the news media. He'd read a *Toronto Star* article about a woman serving twenty-five years for first-degree murder and it wasn't bad. He decided to write the reporter who'd written the story—but he never received a reply. Undaunted, he carried right on with his letter-writing.

In November, Nutty wrote to Lynn McDonald, the New Democratic justice critic and MP for Broadview-Greenwood:

Firstly, I should introduce myself. My name is Gary Comeau and I met you at the Odyssey meeting at Millhaven. . . . I mentioned to you that in fact I was innocent, too. One of the reasons I am writing you is to seek help from you. To help me in my cause of the injustice done to myself and co-accused by the Ontario Attorney General's department. My case has been described as both shocking (in the way we were persecuted) and bizarre (in the way the evidence unfolded) at the trial held in London, Ontario in 1979. . . . During the trial I was identified as being the gunman by two eyewitnesses. Later in the trial the scientific evidence proved that I was positively not the gunman but in fact I was shot by the gunman. The Crown Attorney at the Ontario appeal finally conceded I was not the gunman. We had our appeal dismissed except for one of my co-accused. He was identified by five eyewitnesses who testified he was in the hotel at the time of the shooting. At the appeal wiretap evidence was introduced and this evidence proved beyond a doubt that this man was not in the hotel at all—in fact he was one hundred and forty miles away at the time of the shooting. I believe (and so do most of the people in the law practice with whom I have talked re my case) that most of the witnesses at the trial were coerced or threatened with criminal charges if they did not make up or change their stories.

Yes, I was a member of a motorcycle gang and no, I wasn't an angel. I also know the public isn't too happy with motorcycle gangs. But I am a human being who was persecuted and framed for a crime I did not commit or anticipate.

We will try not to let the system get away with what they did to us. We will try and will never give up until this injustice is corrected and our innocence proven. Some of the lawyers on the case have agreed to talk to anyone interested in trying to correct this travesty of justice. . . .

Thank you for your time.

Yours very truly,
Gary Comeau

There is an aura, a fixity, about the law that often leaves the mistaken impression that laws are ordained by some mystic higher power, and the trappings and solemn symbolism of the courts do little to disabuse the average citizen of this notion.

But the truth about the law tends to be far more mundane. According to a number of Canadian parliamentarians, the 25-year mandatory sentence for first-degree murder was the product, not of some immutable commitment to justice or some carefully reasoned consideration of right and wrong, but of pure political compromise. There had been, after all, a considerable body of public opinion that strongly supported the retention of the death penalty. As a trade-off for the abolition of hanging, the abolitionists conceded the harshest possible prison sentence for pre-meditated murder, the 25-year mandatory.

But there had also been a second trade-off, one that was little noticed at the time. The parliamentarians had also passed Section 672 of the Criminal Code, which contained a provision known as "judicial review" for all convicted first-degree murderers. After serving fifteen years, a lifer would become eligible to have his sentence reviewed by a judge and jury. If he could convince at least eight of the twelve jurors that he had indeed been rehabilitated during the past fifteen years, the lifer could then apply to the National Parole Board for an earlier release on parole.

It would be some years before the judicial-review decision would come into play and when it did, in April 1987, the newspapers would describe it as an "obscure law." But to men like Rick Sauvé and Gary Comeau, judicial review was anything but obscure—it was literally the only hope that they might avoid spending a full quarter-century behind bars. Of course, they still had eleven and a half years left to serve before becoming eligible for judicial review. But that still beat hell out of twenty-one and a half.

By June of 1983 Larry Hurren and Jeff McLeod had earned transfers to Collins Bay, a medium-security prison on the western outskirts of Kingston. Jeff had been eligible to transfer out of Millhaven somewhat earlier, but he had actually elected to stay in the prison that he'd dreaded so much, in order to complete some of his studies. Only Rick and Gary now remained at Millhaven, but, on July 29, 1983, another club member arrived to keep them company—Lorne Campbell.

Lorne entered Millhaven wary and vigilant. Word on the street had it that someone inside was looking for him. He'd made his share of enemies over the years—collecting bad debts with a baseball bat, that was bound to happen—but so far as he knew, no one he knew from those days was at Millhaven. The only guys he knew in there were Rick and Nutty. Gradually it occurred to Lorne that maybe *they* were the people who were looking for him, and, in keeping with his creed of always confronting trouble before it could confront him, Lorne resolved to seek out Gary and Rick as soon as he finished reception.

The intervening three and a half years had been eventful for Lorne Campbell. He'd gotten part of his life together, eventually, and left his friend's lodge, returning to his wife, to his job as an ironworker—and to the Life. But in the spring of 1983 Lorne was convicted of a string of charges, and sentenced to five and a half years.

Lorne arrived in Millhaven on a Tuesday, and he was released into the population on Friday. On Saturday he got his welcome to Thrillhaven. In the twinkling of an eye one con baseball-batted another inmate and beat him senseless not ten feet away from where Lorne was standing. It happened so swiftly, and so absolutely without warning that even Lorne, who was no stranger to the homicidal properties of the average Louisville Slugger in experienced hands, was shaken.

When he finally did meet up with Rick and Nutty, Lorne discovered they bore him no ill-will. Rick still believed, as did Lorne, that Lorne had saved his life by doing Matiyek. As for the fact that both his brothers were doing murder one for a killing that Lorne himself had committed, well, whose fault was that? Lorne had shot Matiyek before Matiyek could shoot any of them, the coppers had busted all the wrong people, the jury had refused to believe Lorne when he had told them the truth, and Rick and Nutty and the others were solid enough not to rat on Lorne. Lorne had killed to save them, and they were laying down their lives for him. The code of the brotherhood, their finest principles, were upheld. Everybody was solid as hell. And in Millhaven.

As Rick and Nutty neared the end of their time in maximum security at Millhaven in 1984, Rick had learned all that a place like Millhaven has to teach. He had schooled himself at the feet of the older, more experienced lifers, asked them how they'd adjusted to spending the rest of their lives in prison. "Ya gotta keep busy and keep changing," they told him. "Avoid routines. Routines are *bad*."

Rick frowned. "Whaddaya mean by routines?"

"You'll know," they answered. "You'll just know."

Rick had learned not to get too close to someone doing shorter time. Inevitably they'd be gone one day, and he would still be there.

He had learned that in the joint you were always on guard, always on point, like the leader of a combat patrol in some sinister jungle. He had learned to develop a sixth sense about trouble: how to walk into the yard and smell it, like some foul, malignant odor that was in the very air he breathed.

He had learned how to walk down the range, looking neither right nor left, *never* looking into the open doors of other cons, because "privacy is a precious thing in prison."

He had learned that it was the little things, the little changes, that drove an institutionalized man into a frenzy. The big things didn't seem to matter. When he'd first arrived at Millhaven, Rick was amazed to see the cons laughing and joking when somebody was killed on the range. He'd thought them callous, cold-hearted bastards. Yet a change in something like feeding-time or habits could incite a riot.

But Rick graduated from being a fish to a solid con on the day that he saw a man bleed to death on the floor of the range. The dying man was lying there in a steadily growing pool of blood, writhing in agony, pleading to God and the cons present, including Rick, for help. With every atom of his being Rick's instincts had been to help that man. But he, like all the others, had watched, and turned away. *Don't get involved in someone else's trip.* In that moment Rick knew he'd become like the others. He had succeeded in denying all of the best instincts that separated men from other animals. He, too, could watch a man die before him with all the indifference that one cow, chewing its cud, might watch another cow, disembowelled and in mortal agony, die upon a barbed-wire fence. It was strange that civilized society would organize and countenance a place like Millhaven, where even the innocent and the decent were reduced to brutes. Not for the first time in his life, Rick Sauvé found himself wondering who the real outlaws were.

He returned to his cell and laughed like crazy at the crass jokes that followed after the con on the floor had breathed his last.

"Hey, didja hear the one about the queer they buried out at the cemetery yesterday?"

"Naw, what?"

"Cocksucker was dead."

When he'd finished his five years at Millhaven, Rick Sauvé was summoned before an internal review committee, which had the ultimate authority over his application to transfer into medium security.

"We notice, Inmate Sauvé, that you have not a single institutional charge against you in your time here," one of the panel members said. "How do you explain that?"

Rick was taken aback at the question. He smiled and shrugged, "Prob'ly 'cause I didn't do nothin'."

"Oh, no. There are two kinds of inmates here. Those who do things and get caught, and those who do things and are smart enough not to get caught."

Rick marvelled at the logic. He'd had a spotless record, it hadn't been easy, and he was proud of it. But as far as *they* were concerned, that made him *more* guilty. It meant that he was smarter, and therefore a greater risk.

The cons weren't the only people who were brutalized at a place like Millhaven. But they'd approved his transfer.

Gary Comeau left Millhaven for Collins Bay on April 13, 1984. Statistics provided by Correctional Services Canada, the official jailers of the society that had so humanely banned capital punishment, show that Gary and Rick had survived ten murders and five suicides during their years at Millhaven, in a population of 375 men. They had also survived countless unsuccessful suicide attempts, slashings, beatings, assaults, stabbings, shootings. . . .

A man's body might survive an experience like Millhaven. But his spirit would never, ever, be quite the same.

BOOK EIGHT

THE CONS

"Maybe the death penalty is more merciful. To spend your whole life locked up in a cage like a wild animal, never to taste freedom again, to be in the power of jailers, some of whom may be fiends—he can pace only so many steps each way . . . man's inhumanity to man, I'd go mad, I'd go mad. Men who are locked up must go mad in some degree—as beasts do. . . ."

—EARL ROGERS, AMERICAN CRIMINAL LAWYER,
QUOTED BY GARY COMEAU IN A LETTER
TO WARREN ALLMAND, MARCH 18, 1983

XXXIX

COLLINS BAY PEN IS A FIVE-DOLLAR CAB RIDE and a world away from the trendy track lights, brass rails, and grey-and-mauve decor of the college nightspots in downtown Kingston, where freshly scrubbed coeds from Queen's University, dressed in tasteful sweater-and-skirt ensembles, sip their cappuccinos and spritzers. The clothes on the back of each coed, changed daily, no doubt, cost their fathers more than the average Choice dancer, her face no less shining, her body no less firm, can earn in a week of bump-and-grind.

Seen from a distance through the taxi window, the Bay seems at first glance to be some kind of fantastic amusement park, a product of the Disneyland school of Canadian prison architecture. Its Gothic turrets and cathedral-like spires, its gun towers topped by vermilion metal caps, are visible for miles above the pizza parlors, shopping plazas, and used-car lots that sprawl along Bath Road on the southeastern edge of the city.

The entrance is an unprepossessing plate-glass door six storeys below the tip of the tallest of the bizarre red spires. But, once inside that door, any resemblance to Disneyland abruptly ends. A second, identical glass door is locked from the inside, and it is here that prison reality begins. The visitor is forced to stand waiting for someone to open that door. There is no buzzer to push, no intercom, and no door-man. Someone, somewhere, scrutinizes the person standing between the doors. The sensation while waiting is one of eerie surveillance and utter powerlessness. At length the door buzzes softly and the lock clicks open.

The visitor enters a stark institutional waiting-room, furnished with a small wooden table and a single wooden chair. Behind the table sits a guard wearing the two-tone green uniform of Correctional Service Canada. Before him is a legal-size clipboard. The newcomer states his business, signs a form on the clipboard, and names the prisoner he has come to visit, surname preferably prefaced by the prison form of address. "I'm here to see Inmate Sauvé, Inmate Comeau. They're expecting me."

Behind the lone guard is a large one-way glass window. If the visitor's bona fides are in order, unseen fingers behind the glass will throw an invisible switch and a heavy gate made of three-inch steel grillwork will slide open on metal runners. The visitor steps through and the door glides closed behind him, silent save for the low hum of an electrical current. The gate locks with a muted, metallic clash. It is not a pleasant sound.

The disoriented visitor slowly realizes that another panel of one-way glass still faces him on his right, senses instinctively that the confident, scrutinizing faces behind it are still watching him. To the left is a warren of standard, government-issue offices, straight ahead a short hallway, and then a jog to the right. At the end of the hallway another guard sits in his institutional green, another table, another clipboard, and, to the right, yet a third pane of darkened glass. Gradually it dawns on the visitor that the sheets of glass form a rectangular cage: glass above, steel below, a guardpost within a fortress. The steel walls contain small slits resembling the slots on a mailbox. They are gun ports.

Before the visitor, who stands with his back to the steel-and-glass cage, is a long, wide corridor behind another steel grillwork gate. The corridor looks like a hallway in any Canadian secondary school, its neat tilework spotless, gleaming with wax.

Considering that the visitor had at first been denied permission to visit with Inmate Comeau, a decision that had been reversed only after the filing of an institutional grievance, a letter to the Solicitor General, and a personal phone call to the warden, the staff at Collins Bay Institution are surprisingly courteous and accommodating. The visitor is ushered into a private office for the interview and waits, a trifle nervously, for Gary Comeau to arrive. The newcomer has never met a convicted first-degree murderer before.

At last Gary Comeau bounces into the room. He no longer weighs 270, but he is still a big man—tall, barrel-chested, bearded, with a deep voice and an aggressive, nervous energy that seems to fill the small room.

"How long will you be needing?" the secretary who has escorted Comeau asks the visitor.

"Oh, he'll need at least two days to hear everything I've got to say," Comeau answers, before the visitor has a chance to open his mouth.

"Uh, this morning, and maybe a few hours after lunch, thanks."

The secretary nods, and closes the door.

Comeau begins to talk, rapid-fire and pushy. "You won't believe our story, what the system did to us. It'll make Donald Marshall's case look like nothin', believe me. All we need is the truth. If we have the truth we're walkin'. But I wanna get one thing straight. I was in the hotel. Rick Sauvé was in the hotel. Blaker was in the hotel, McLeod was in the hotel, and Hurren was in the hotel"—he pronounces the word with the accent on the first syllable: hotel—"but I ain't givin' ya any more names. There were nine to twelve in all in the hotel. . . .

"Twenty-five witnesses at our trial either lied or thought they saw somethin' that wasn't the case, some unintentionally lied. But there's no doubt in my mind that the police threatened and coerced people. It was a terrifying event. Look, I'm sorry that it happened. I never knew the man, but he put himself in that position. We walked into a situation, that was all. We were in the wrong place at the wrong time."

The visitor, bewildered, is scribbling rapidly, trying to get it all down. It is as if Comeau has been waiting years to make this speech. This moment is the culmination of years of letter-writing, and at last someone has come to listen, to check things out, to write it all down on a piece of paper.

Finally Comeau comes up for air, and the visitor jumps in to regain control of the interview.

"Okay, why don't we start at the beginning. Where were you born, and when?"

"I was born on January 6, 1952, in Toronto."

"Parents' names?"

"My mother is Elizabeth King. She lives at 33 Hexham Drive, in Scarborough. . . ."

By noon the visitor has a severe case of writer's cramp and a sinking feeling in the pit of his stomach. This story is huge. There's no way it could ever be done as a newspaper story, it would take a book. . . . It's like a jigsaw puzzle; all investigative stories are, at the outset. But this is a monster, with thousands of pieces. It could take years to fit them all together. And look who's painting the picture on the top of the box—a con, a biker convicted of first-degree murder. The guy's a greaser, he still acts and talks and thinks like a biker. Can any of what he says be true?

By the end of the first day Comeau has concluded his story, culminating with the shooting of Bill Matiyek. ". . . I didn't see the gunman coming up. The next thing I knew, bang-bang-bang. I didn't discuss it, I didn't aid and abet, I didn't know it was going to happen, and I sure as hell wouldn't have been sitting beside him if I knew a guy was going to come up and start blasting away with a .38. They may call me Nutty, but I'm not stupid. . . . The five of us are in here for nothin'. . . . I was at that table, and you had to be at that table to understand what was going on. . . . Besides, we're different now, we're changed men. . . ."

Yeah, right, the visitor, a sceptic by occupation and experience, thinks to himself. Eight years later, which of us isn't?

Overnight the writer's cramp gradually disappears, the sinking feeling does not. Tomorrow the visitor will meet with Rick Sauvé for the first time. Terry O'Hara has described him as "a lippy biker," whose mouth had gotten him in a lot of trouble, on the evidence. If Sauvé is the lippy biker, what does that make Comeau? Maybe, *depending on what happens tomorrow, the visitor tells himself, he'll just bow out of this one. Send the paper a bill for expenses and eat the time, chalk it up to experience. Aren't prisons full of "innocent" men? Depending on tomorrow . . .*

The next morning the visitor is once again at the steel-and-glass cage, looking down the gleaming corridor. Finally, at the far end, Rick Sauvé emerges. He walks with the easy gait of a natural athlete, his long hair a light brown, almost blond, the toes of his running shoes pointing outward, cool blue eyes fixed on the middle distance, his gaze confident of everything and yet nothing. He approaches the open gate, and what happens next depends on the mood of the gatekeeper. Sometimes Inmate Sauvé is allowed to pass without question through the gate, and sometimes he is waved summarily back, to wait momentarily on some unknown protocol.

Eventually Inmate Sauvé passes out of the corridor and through the gate; he removes the keys and loose change from his pocket, takes off his shoes and wristwatch, and then steps quietly but not meekly through the kind of metal detector found in front of every airport loading-gate; he retrieves his valuables from the guard's table, slips back into his shoes, reclasps his wristwatch. He turns, then, and, with a barely perceptible nod and the slightest of dry, ironic smiles, Rick Sauvé greets his visitor.

Sauvé is a complete and utter shock. He is quiet, handsome, totally self-possessed, articulate. There is something very special about this man. Unlike Comeau, whose restless energy filled the room, Sauvé seems comfortable within his own space, and inviolate in that space.

As Sauvé's story unfolds, it is clear that he fits none of the biker stereotypes. Married and a father, with a long history of holding steady jobs, a union leader, virtually no criminal record before his murder conviction, he had never spent a night in jail before his arrest. He describes the climax of the night that changed his life forever, the call from Brian Brideau, the calls to Toronto, the entrance into the Queen's, the confrontation with Bill Matiyek, the menace in Matiyek's eyes as he pointed a gun at Sauvé through the pocket of his coat.

". . . We're trying to get out of there now. I'm not takin' my eyes off of Bill, I don't wanna get shot. I'll always remember his eyes, he was scared, he was drunk, and he looked serious. The last thing he seen was me. He got shot. I'd never seen anything like that before. You see it on TV, but it's nothing like seeing somebody shot in front of you. You can't describe it. I saw part of his head come out . . . how do you describe watching a man die? It's something you can't take your eyes off of. It happens fast,

but it happens in slow motion. It leaves an indelible mark on your mind. You're glued right there. . . . He had a pained look, he just slumped to the side, to his right. . . ."

The facts are recounted quietly, matter-of-factly, credibly. Sauvé's answers to the visitor's questions are direct and to the point. Only once does he interrupt. "Can I say something?"

"Sure, yeah." Pen poised in mid-air.

"I just wanna say I have no faith at all in what you're trying to do."

"Yeah, well, uh, I'm not sure yet just what I am going to try to do. And, like I told Nutty yesterday, there's no guarantees about any of this. . . ."

Throughout the day there is a tension in the tiny interview room. Sauvé is not aloof, exactly, but he seems to wear an invisible shell around himself. Only once is the armor pierced, when the visitor asks him where he thinks he might be now, if none of this had happened.

He shrugs. "In Cobourg, probably . . . working at some job as a laborer or something. . . ." He pauses and looks away, and the pain over all the lost years is suddenly palpable. "Kids. I'd probably have had four or five more kids. I really like kids." The moment is fleeting, the invisible barrier quickly returns.

At the end of the afternoon Sauvé sums it all up. "To be truthful, the people down there [in Cobourg and Port Hope] don't give a fuck about us—I guess it's an episode they'd just as soon forget about. We were an easy target. There was a man killed, there's no doubt about that. But there was no conspiracy, no prior planning."

The sinking feeling is gone as the visitor watches Sauvé's back disappear down the long corridor. As the visitor turns away, passing through the buzzing gates, the glass doors, and into the freedom of suburban Kingston on a hot July day, his stomach feels just fine. Maybe a few days, and only a few, in Port Hope, poking around, wouldn't hurt. . . .

Within a few weeks of arriving at the Bay, Gary Comeau was assigned to the prison electrical gang that worked throughout the institution repairing wiring, fixing burned-out motors of all sorts, and doing general mainte-nance. One of the group's tasks was to maintain and repair the high-intensity lights used to illuminate the prison yard. The lights were mounted just beneath the top of the high limestone walls that surround the 27-acre enclo-sure that is Collins Bay Pen. One day Gary was given the job of riding the cherry-picker up to the top of the wall, to replace a burned-out bulb and to wipe the reflector and lens. For some reason the guy operating the boom raised Gary a little higher than he really needed to, and before he quite knew what was happening, Gary Comeau found himself *above* the top of the wall. He looked down on Bath Road, at the Frontenac Mall across the street from the joint. The scene blew his lights out. Except for a half-hour car ride from Millhaven, it was the first time Gary had seen the world outside prison walls in six years. He watched the cars streaming past on Bath Road, the shoppers in the Mall parking lot. "Aaaaah," he thought, "civilization." This was much better than a car or a paddy wagon, looking down on everything, fresh air all around; it all looked so bright and new, a real bird's-eye view. It made him feel, for one brief instant, as if he was free.

Back on the ground, that momentary vision of freedom lingered in Gary's mind for weeks.

Jeff McLeod was now well established at the Bay, and he was breaking new ground for them all. Physically and mentally, Jeff bore little resemblance to the hulking, 320-pound biker who, with the others, had drifted into the Queen's Hotel on October 18, 1978. The beard and ponytail were long gone (his hairline, which had begun to recede that first winter in the Cobourg bucket, had continued its steady retreat, and Jeff was now half bald), and, by dint of self-discipline, decent nutrition, and exercise, McLeod now weighed a svelte 190. He had continued his studies in the Queen's University prison education program, and was well on his way to earning a Bachelor of Arts degree in psychology. Almost unbelievably articulate and highly analytical, Jeff McLeod was fast becoming one of the best formally educated inmates in the fifty-year history of Collins Bay.

By the spring of 1984, Jeff had become the Assistant Coordinator of the Collins Bay Exceptional People's Olympiad, a position of senior leadership among the prison population. Held each summer, the Olympiad brought together hundreds of mentally retarded children from across Ontario for a weekend of Olympic-style games in the prison yard. The Bay's five hundred cons organized the games themselves, building all the special equipment needed for the events, decorating the yard, setting up special stages and sound equipment, even handling the public relations.

The Games are a major undertaking, requiring a year-round planning and fund-raising effort by a small committee of volunteers, who have been given their own small office inside the institution. Former and current members of the Satan's Choice have often played a key role in the Olympiad over the years, and the club donated "The Satan's Choice Trophy," a four-foot-high pyramid of wood and metal, which is awarded each year to the outstanding individual competitor of the weekend. The trophy is one of the club's few concessions to positive public relations and, besides, it was always fun to hear some bigshot, like, say, the Solicitor General of Canada, have to read out the club's name before awarding the trophy.

The Olympiad is always a hectic time, one of the high points of the year at Collins Bay, and Lorne Campbell found himself getting into the act. Each con who wants to is paired off with an individual athlete for the whole weekend, serving as host, coach, and guide, all rolled into one. It was an unlikely sight: hardened cons, all tattooed and muscle-bound from years of pumping iron, walking around with retarded children, each guy scream-ing and yelling, urging his "own" kid on during the competitions, but the fact was that the prisoners truly enjoyed themselves. It was such a relief, after prison life, where everyone is always hustling or being hustled for money, drugs, muscle, to spend a few days with a kid who only wanted some love and affection and encouragement. Self-pity is a cheap and common commodity in any prison, but it was hard to feel sorry for oneself after watching those kids, Lorne discovered. For three days he watched the com-petitors challenge and often overcome their natural limitations. Lorne was no whiner about himself, he'd done the crime, he'd do the time, that was the natural order of things. But where did these kids fit into the natural order? Or Rick and Nutty and the others? At least he and Beaver and Jeff and Merv would get back on the street in the not-too-distant future. Even Nutty and Rick would get out of prison some day. But those kids would have those limitations forever. Now that really *was* a life-bit.

Meanwhile Merv Blaker continued his own steady progress at Joyceville, across town from Collins Bay. Still gentle, soft-spoken, and painfully shy, Merv baffled the prison authorities. He appeared to be the most harmless convicted murderer any of them had ever met. It was even said that some-where deep within his prison files lay a report from one of his Classifications Officers which concluded that Merv must be innocent.

Blaker continued to upgrade his education from Grade 8 to Grade 10, and he began to study for his apprentice machinist's licence. He'd always enjoyed tinkering with his Harley, after all, and such a highly skilled trade would, Merv reckoned, stand him in good stead once he made parole.

Dr. Carole Clapperton had answered Merv's letter in response to her Christmas card, and a steady correspondence resulted. She began to visit Merv at least once a week, and the visits quickly blossomed into a deep and abiding friendship. The more Carole heard about Murray's case, about his trial and conviction, the more certain she became that somehow, somewhere, he had become the victim of a dreadful miscarriage of justice.

How *had* it happened? Nearly six years after he was buried, rumors and reverberations continued to swirl around the death of Bill Matiyek, most of them emanating from Port Hope. It was almost as if the big biker was still uneasy in his grave.

It so happened that Merv, after he transferred from Joyceville to Warkworth, wound up doing time with Jules Joncas, the brother of Julie. Once, after returning to the joint from an escorted pass, Jules told Merv he'd talked with his sister about Merv's trial. Julie told her brother that a number of Crown witnesses had been coached by the police, told what to say during their testimony. Jules's escort on the visit, a Living Unit Officer from Warkworth, had overheard the conversation. Jules's story confirmed Merv's long-standing suspicions, and he made a note of the date of their conversation on a calendar. But when Blaker returned to Jules and the Officer later, seeking more information, they both denied that the conversation had ever taken place.

Roger Davey had continued to hang out as an independent rider on Port Hope's biker scene, and he'd confessed one day to a friend of Merv's that he had, in fact, lied on the witness stand. He hadn't taken the call from Rick in the hours after the murder, Davey said, his wife had. He hadn't wanted to give testimony at all, but he'd been coerced into doing so by the police. Word of this conversation, too, reached Merv Blaker.

And then there was the story about Lawrence Leon. Rumors swirled that Lawrence had shot up his own vehicle during the trial, and then phoned the police, to make it appear that the Satan's Choice had done it. The owner of the bowling-alley had immediately phoned Sharon Sauvé's parents with the news. Don and Betty Ashton positively worshipped their son-in-law, and were as convinced of Rick's innocence as his own parents.

This strange tale, too, was relayed to the men serving life for Matiyek's murder.

Nutty continued his letter-writing from Collins Bay, and he decided to try his hand at investigating some of these rumors, which he didn't doubt for one minute were all true. Considering that he was locked up in prison, and that he had few means at his disposal, Gary Comeau did remarkably well.

First, he tried to locate Bill Glaister. The *Maclean's* freelancer had told some of the accused about Rod Stewart's astonishing barroom revelation before the jury returned its verdicts. But, by 1984, no one at Canada's national newsmagazine seemed to remember Glaister at all, much less know where he might be found four years after his story was published.

Gary pondered the story about Roger Davey. He told Terry O'Hara about it one day during a visit, and asked the Kingston lawyer if he'd pursue Davey's admission further if Roger indicated a willingness to talk. O'Hara said that he would. But, Gary wondered, how should he approach Davey? All of his own letters in and out of the prison were censored. Screw it, Comeau decided at last. He'd just write Davey himself, and, late in November, Comeau received a reply, dated November 20. It was just a note, printed in block letters, but it represented the first real breakthrough in Gary's eighteen months of writing letters.

MR. GARY COMEAU:

IN REGARDS TO YOUR LETTER IN THE FACT I WAS A CROWN WITNESS AND FORCED TO MAKE A STATEMENT, FOR ME TO REITERATE *(sic)* MY STORY WOULD INDEED SUGGEST PERJURY HOWEVER INSIGNIFICANT!

I AM WILLING TO TALK TO MR. O'HARA ABOUT THE POSSIBILI-TIES OF HELPING YOU.

OTHER PERSONS INVOLVED WITH THE TRIAL ARE VERY SHY ON THE SUBJECT.

IF AND WHEN MR. O'HARA COMES TO PORT HOPE I WILL MAKE ARRANGEMENTS TO MEET HIM, AS I HAVE NO VEHICLE.

YOURS TRULY,
ROGER DAVEY

Gary was ecstatic. At long last a Crown witness, albeit a minor one, appeared to be on the verge of telling the truth about the police investigation. He was sure that Davey represented only the tip of the iceberg.

Within a few days of receiving Davey's reply, Comeau wrote yet another letter to an organization that he hoped might take up his case, the Church Council on Justice and Corrections, in Ottawa.

My name is Gary Comeau and I am currently serving 25 years for 1st degree murder. I am innocent of this charge but that is not the foremost reason I have written you at this time. . . .

The reason I am writing you is I can offer another case in which another innocent person would have been hung if the death penalty law had been in effect. I feel I must warn you that my case may be very shocking when the whole truthful story is told. As you know my mail is censored so I will briefly give you the information on some of the main facts.

At my trial two witnesses positively identified me as being the gunman who killed William Matiyek. . . . But later in the trial (too late) a bullet was extracted from my body. Mr. Finn Nielsen and Mr. William Phillip are forensic scientists employed by the Centre of Forensic Sciences in Toronto. They both proved through their testimony that it was impossible for me to be the gunman. And at the Ontario appeal the crown prosecutor finally conceded I was not the gunman. My case was dismissed at the hearing for leave to appeal to the Supreme Court of Canada. (My lawyer was mentally and physically incompetent through illness and never showed up at the hearing. That is another matter.)

I am trying to bring this injustice to the forefront hopefully with your help and the help of others. . . . Would you please acknowledge your receipt of this letter. Thank you for your time and I am hoping to hear from you soon.

Yours very truly,
Gary Comeau

The Church Council
on Justice and Corrections
151 Slater St., Ottawa, Ont.

December 14, 1984

Dear Mr. Comeau:

Thank you for your letter of November 29th and please excuse the delay in
our acknowledging it.

As a national Council our mandate, unfortunately, does not allow us to
do individual interventions, however we will bring your concerns before our
Executive Committee when it meets on January 11, 1985. So far it appears
that you are proceeding in the right direction and please rest assured that if
there is anything further we can do, following our Executive Committee's
directives, we will inform you immediately.

Meanwhile we wish you the very best of luck in your quest for justice
and hope you have a very productive 1985.

Sincerely,
(MS) Jean Somers

Gary merely shrugged when he received the Church Council's reply, and
he filed the letter away with dozens of others. It was all very much like fishing. You cast your line hundreds of times before you caught a fish, and even
then you might catch a dozen fish before ending up with one big enough to
keep. Roger Davey's response was one such. There would be others. Comeau
resolved to keep right on fishing after the holidays were over and his seventh
year in prison began. Sooner or later he was bound to land the Big One.

Several months earlier, Gary had mailed what was becoming a more-or-
less-standard letter about his case to Claire Culhane, a British Columbia–
based prison activist, indeed, prison abolitionist. Culhane was a founding
member of the Prisoners' Rights Group, one of the growing number of
Canadian organizations committed to the struggle for prisoners' rights.
Since 1975 Culhane had stumped the country tirelessly on behalf of incarcerated individuals everywhere, attempting to expose prison injustices to
the Canadian public. She had already written two books on the subject and

countless articles, and Culhane, then a 66-year-old grandmother, had probably corresponded with and visited more prisoners than any other private individual in Canada.

She was already well known to prisoners across the country when her efforts on behalf of Norman Fox, a B.C. man convicted of rape, made Culhane's a virtual household name throughout the Canadian prison system. Culhane and a handful of her supporters had launched an independent investigation on behalf of Fox, who had steadfastly maintained his innocence. Months of persistent legwork by Culhane and her supporters uncovered fresh evidence which revealed that Fox could not possibly have committed the crime for which he'd been convicted. After serving eight years in prison, Fox was pardoned and released from jail in a blaze of media publicity. Claire Culhane was there to meet him at the gates.

The cases of Fox and Donald Marshall, a Micmac Indian from Nova Scotia who served eleven years of a life sentence for a murder he did not commit, were living proof that Canada's justice system was not infallible after all.

Tales of unjust conviction are a staple of conversation in any prison (incompetent legal representation, police "framing," mistaken identity, etc.), and the hope that someone like Claire Culhane might come along and prove one's innocence is the fondest hope of many a con. (Jeff McLeod estimates that fully one-half of all prison inmates maintain they were wrongfully convicted for one reason or another, and that anywhere from five to ten percent of them are probably right.)

Culhane's files were already bulging with letters from prisoners hoping she could do for them what she had done for Norman Fox, and Gary Comeau's letter was just one more. But there was one thing that intrigued her about the Comeau case. From what she could puzzle out in Gary's necessarily cryptic letters, Comeau had been convicted of first-degree murder even though he had not, on the evidence, been the gunman, and the actual gunman, on the evidence, had never been charged or convicted. This was in stark contrast to an earlier case in which Culhane had a strong personal interest.

During a June 1975 hostage-taking incident at the B.C. Pen, Mary Steinhauser, a young Classifications Officer, had been killed in a hail of bullets when a tactical squad had stormed the offices where she was being held, along with seven other prison employees. None of the five guards who had actually fired the shots was ever charged, partly, as Culhane understood it, because no one could determine *which one had fired the fatal bullets*. Yet in Comeau's case the exact opposite was true—everyone who had accompanied the gunman into the hotel had been found guilty, even though the triggerman had never been identified. There were, it was true, obvious differences in the two situations—on the one hand a prison guard had killed an innocent person in the course of quelling a prison disturbance. On the other, a group of bikers had clearly been up to no good when another biker was killed. But didn't the same law govern both cases?

Culhane struck up another of her myriad correspondences with the prisoner from Collins Bay.

By the end of April 1985, Gary, Rick, Lorne, and Jeff had been together at the Bay for almost a year. Lorne's admiration for Nutty and Rick, at the way both of them were coping with their sentences, had continued to grow. It hadn't been an easy time for Lorne. Gradually he'd been introduced to Rick's and Gary's and Jeff's families during visits or prison socials, and he couldn't escape the feeling that the parents of the men convicted for the shooting he'd committed had looked at him with something akin to reproach. He felt especially bad about Beaver's folks. Lorne had introduced Larry to the Life, after all, had given him his first ride on a Harley, had sponsored him into the club.

Lorne's role in the killing of Bill Matiyek was by now one of the worst-kept secrets in the Toronto underworld. The whole affair had long since become a part of club lore—and a source of the greatest pride—six members convicted for life on a murder beef, and not one would rat on the real killer to save his own skin. Man, that was solid, and it showed the kind of men the Choice was made of.

Each of the men convicted had felt that he owed his family some sort of explanation about what had really happened in the Queen's the night Matiyek was killed, and each had by now told his family the true story.

By the end of April, Lorne's application for parole to a halfway house had been approved by the Parole Board, and his departure from Collins Bay was imminent. Just before he left, Lorne and Nutty had a heart-to-heart talk while taking yard, away from the prying electronic ears of the prison security system. Suppose his letter-writing eventually did some good, Gary suggested, and their case was reopened, a new investigation held, another trial, whatever. Given the proper circumstances, would Lorne assist an independent investigator? Lorne said that he would. But both men knew that it couldn't end there. If push came to shove, would Lorne do time for the shooting? Again Campbell answered in the affirmative. He was prepared to do up to ten years. But only if it would help Nutty and Rick. There was little point in yet another person doing extra time for the same killing, Lorne and Nutty agreed. The time was not far off when Lorne would have to keep his promise, at least on the first part of the bargain, and Lorne Campbell would prove as good as his word.

XL

ANOTHER VISIT TO COLLINS BAY *after a few days of interviewing in the Port Hope area. This preliminary foray has yielded distinctly mixed results. Roger Davey is willing to swear that he was coerced by police into giving testimony, but also insists (not entirely convincingly) that he took the telephone call from Rick Sauvé and thus did not commit perjury. Linda Leon maintains (not entirely convincingly) that she never made the remark about Lawrence shooting up his own van. But she also describes, entirely convincingly, the terror that Bill Matiyek felt towards the Satan's Choice in the summer before his death, and the fear that her husband felt after. She and Lawrence had separated, Linda explains, and were getting a divorce. Even if she had made the statement in the bowling-alley, what did it prove? Perhaps it was in the nature of a payback against her estranged husband as the result of a domestic dispute. Even Linda knew that Bill Matiyek was carrying a gun that summer. How could Rick Sauvé and the other Choice members who entered the Queen's not have known, as they claimed?*

Both Roger Davey and former bartender Rick Galbraith, experienced, though independent, bikers, found it conceivable that Matiyek was executed for wearing Hawk colours, though both Davey and Galbraith seem to feel that Sauvé and Blaker and the others were wrongfully convicted.

It is time to confront Rick Sauvé.

"Rick, half the people in that town knew that Bill Matiyek carried a gun. Do you really expect me to believe that you didn't know that when you went into that hotel?"

"Do you think I would have sat down across from him if I'd known? Say, what's the point of all this, anyway?"

"Rick, you tell me. What is *the fucking point?* There's no heroes in this story. If you think I'm gonna depict you and bikers in general as some kind of white knights who were just misunderstood, forget it. I'll tell you right now, I have no use for what you guys stand for. You had everything going for you—a beautiful wife, lovely daughter, steady job, supportive family. Why in the world did you join a bike club in the first place?"

"It's, it's . . . brotherhood."

"Brotherhood! You were in a union. Isn't that enough brotherhood?"

A defiant half-grin. "It's not the same thing. . . ."

Sauvé and the visitor part company once again, through their respective electric gates. Sauvé appears coolly defiant to the end, but once he had returned to the range his composure dissolved.

"What'd he say, what'd he say?" Nutty demands, excitedly.

Sauvé explodes. "Fuck, man, he still doesn't believe us. Fuck!"

Terry O'Hara had remained close to the men convicted of Matiyek's murder, and in May 1985 he agreed to write a character reference letter for Merv Blaker. The letter was aimed at the members of the National Parole Board, before whom Blaker would be making his first appearance before the year was out. The letter was an eloquent and densely argued plea on Blaker's behalf, and O'Hara poured out all of his misgivings about Murray's trial and conviction.

O'Hara began by noting that he had represented Blaker at his trial for first-degree murder, which had been "one of the longest murder trials in the annals of Canadian law." After reviewing the particulars surrounding Matiyek's death and the evidence against his co-accused, O'Hara observed that

. . . the specific allegations against Mr. Blaker were somewhat different. There was no evidence of animosity between Mr. Blaker and the victim. The Crown's evidence never suggested that he was part of the group that surrounded the table. The Crown's evidence was unequivocally that Mr. Blaker was seated at another table some distance away from the murder table at the time of the shooting. The case against Mr. Blaker, therefore, rested on the ground that he was there as a party to the intention of aiding and abetting the commission of that murder, essentially by assisting in suppressing resistance by other people at the hotel. It was this theory and this theory alone which was left to the jury with respect to Mr. Blaker. There was no suggestion he took any more active part in the murder than sitting at a table in a hotel some 20 or 30 feet away. Had Mr. Blaker been charged alone on that evidence, in my professional opinion, there is simply no way in the world that he would ever have been convicted. . . .

There is absolutely no question in my own mind, as an experienced criminal lawyer, that Mr. Blaker had no idea what was going to happen at the Queen's Hotel that night, and that had he had the slightest idea that this event was going to take place, he wouldn't have been within 20 miles of the place. Mr. Blaker was a resident of Port Hope at that time. It doesn't seem likely that he would have gone there, where he was known to all of the employees and to most of the patrons. I believe that the conviction of Mr. Blaker was in error and I have a very strong personal belief, having known the man now for some seven years, in his innocence.

Mr. Blaker is, of course, incarcerated in a federal penitentiary. I have kept fairly close contact with him in the years since his conviction. I have been most impressed at the material attitude which he has shown towards his incarceration. He knows that he didn't do it, he knows that he shouldn't be there and yet he understands perfectly well how it happened. I believe he appreciates that if he had not been a member of the Club and lumped in with the club members, even had he been charged, he would not have been convicted. I believe this has completely restructured his thinking and caused him to resolve to stay away from that type of Club and that type of individual in the future.

I believe that Mr. Blaker is a person who will never cause the community the slightest bit of difficulty, and will reintegrate far more quickly than the best ex-inmate.

I've told Mr. Blaker that if there is at any time and any way in which I can assist him upon his release, I would be glad to do so and that offer is maintained. I am quite frankly of the belief that Mr. Blaker is a victim of the system. His conviction was made, it was upheld, and yet, in my judgement, he was wrongly convicted. Having regard to the fact that he has adapted so well to confinement, and made so much of his time in custody, it seems to me that it is very much to his credit and very much indicative of someone who can still make a useful contribution to society despite what has happened to him in the past.

O'Hara's letter was an extraordinary document, a masterpiece of special pleading. A colleague who read it two years later would remark that "It went just about as far as any lawyer can go." Indeed, it was not Murray Blaker alone for whom O'Hara felt admiration. He had by now come to know scores of prisoners in the Kingston-area pens, both as clients and as witnesses, and O'Hara could say emphatically that each of the men convicted of Matiyek's murder were among the top five percent of all federal prison inmates, a development that surprised no one more than O'Hara.

By July 1985 the security matrix was once again affecting their lives differentially. Merv and Jeff had been granted transfers to Frontenac work camp, a minimum-security institution just outside the Collins Bay walls. From a distance, and even to a visitor inside, Frontenac, a low two-storey building, looked like a university dormitory. A con could stand on the front porch and watch the taxis come and go, delivering visitors, picking them up, and almost imagine that he could phone a cab, climb in, and disappear forever. Which was exactly the point. They were on their honour now, and many prisoners freely admit that the very absence of authority, of walls and wire, of guns and guards, made them extremely nervous. But there is little indication that either Merv or Jeff had trouble coping with this invisible pressure.

Increasingly the fates of Jeff and Merv passed, almost imperceptibly, out of the hands of the CSC and into the hands of Canada's National Parole Board. As "model inmates" with pristine records they were granted their first ETA's at their earliest eligibility dates, in 1983. These escorted passes, lasting only four hours, were their first opportunity to see life on the street since their arrest in December 1978. Jeff used his passes to take in a few Kingston Canadians hockey games, Merv to visit with his mother and daughter.

In the case of most prisoners doing second-degree murder, the purpose of the first appearance before the full panel of the National Parole Board is to determine an inmate's suitability for Unescorted Temporary Absences in the seventh year of his incarceration. UTA's are another important step down the correctional cascade. An inmate is allowed to leave his institution, unescorted, for a period of seventy-two hours, and the UTA is yet another check on the prisoner's sense of internal responsibility and self-discipline. He is required to make his own way to his previously approved destination, report to law-enforcement or parole officials while there, and then return to jail before the seventy-two hours have elapsed.

Besides his case-management team, each parole applicant is allowed to select someone to accompany him to the actual hearing, and Jeff selected his girlfriend, while Merv invited Carole Clapperton. Blaker had by now amassed an impressive pile of character references, in addition to Terry O'Hara, and Carole reminded Murray during one of her visits that Terry had also arranged to have Chris Meinhardt write a letter confirming Blaker's minor role in the murder of Bill Matiyek.

Murray's response to this remark startled his friend.

"I don't want his letter," Murray said flatly, as if the Devil himself had just offered him thirty pieces of silver.

In all the years she'd known Murray Blaker, Carole thought, that was as close as she'd ever seen him come to getting angry about what had happened to him.

The hearing was held at Frontenac on November 21, 1985, before a panel composed of four men and one woman. Two of the men were retired chiefs of police, and the woman appeared to be extremely young and inexperienced. Murray Blaker's application was heard first, while Jeff and his sweetheart waited nervously outside. At first the questions were routine enough. The panel inquired where Murray would go if he were granted unescorted passes, and what he would do. To Cobourg, he replied, to visit his family and daughter.

But then, to Carole's astonishment, the panel seemed to want to grill Murray on the crime for which he had been convicted, and for which, innocent or not, he had already spent six years in custody. Exactly how had it happened, they demanded, and who had actually pulled the trigger on Bill Matiyek? The two former police chiefs seemed especially hostile towards Murray, dwelling on his membership in Satan's Choice.

Murray, Carole could see, was beside himself with nervousness, and he turned in a tortured performance, filled with awkward pauses and long silences as he struggled to answer the panel's questions honestly. Murray's hesitations, Carole feared, were being regarded as evasiveness, but his answers, when they finally came, were truthful, even if they were not the responses that the panel wanted to hear. Blaker admitted that, when his prison days were over, he intended to fix up his rusty Harley and use it for transportation, and he flatly refused to tell the panel who had actually killed Bill Matiyek.

Jeff's hearing followed Merv's and, if anything, it was even worse. To say that he had become a "model inmate" would be an understatement. He was more like a shining star within the entire federal prison system. Despite the incessant noise, distractions, and tensions of prison life, Jeff had continued with his university studies. After nearly seven years in custody his prison record was spotless, and he was increasingly regarded as a proud credit to the rehabilitative properties of the Canadian correctional system. Well-spoken but not cocky, agreeable but never servile, Jeff had become the kind of inmate that the system offered up to criminologists, sociologists, and the news media, whenever it was necessary for the world outside to talk to a real live con.

Jeff expected the panel to be thoroughly briefed on his prison record, and his accomplishments, and he anticipated a number of well-informed questions about that. Instead, the former police chiefs began to rant and rave about bike clubs. One of them launched into a story about a gang rape he'd investigated twenty years before. He got so worked up he pounded on the table and stared meaningfully at Jeff's girlfriend as if to say, "Do you know the kind of man you're hanging around with here?" The young woman on the panel kept clearing her throat with a strange clucking sound, as if she was intimidated by the others, or else was reproving Jeff. The whole thing was terribly disappointing, even humiliating, to Jeff and his fiancée.

And then they started in on Matiyek's murder. They didn't seem to know or care about what Jeff had done with his life while in prison, but they seemed very well informed about the crime that had put him there in the first place.

"So who did it?" one of the former coppers demanded.

"I can't tell you that, sir."

"Have you had any visitors or messages here recently?" The ex-cop was leaning across the table, glowering at Jeff as if he was conducting an interrogation. *That man is evil*, Jeff's girlfriend thought to herself.

"What?"

"Come on, admit it, you've been told what to say here today, you've been intimidated."

"What?"

"*Who killed Bill Matiyek?*"

"It's common knowledge. He testified at our trial."

That seemed to take the former police chief aback. He shook his head in disbelief. "Well, this is either the damned finest example of human loyalty that I've ever seen or you're scared stiff."

Jeff tried to regain his composure and steer the discussion, diplomatically, on to the subject of his prison record, but the ex-cops would have none of it.

"In all my time on the Board," one of them said, "I've never seen a biker who wasn't a model inmate."

"And just how long have you been on the Board, sir?" Jeff shot back.

"Well, uh, eleven months," the cop stammered.

"Well, sir, I've been here for the past six years."

To no one's great surprise, Merv and Jeff were granted only the absolute minimum by the Parole Board—six UTA's over the next year, not the twelve that most second-degree lifers with only mediocre records normally received.

Like Merv, Jeff was bitterly disappointed in the Board's decision. Those people didn't seem to care who he was now, or what he had become. All they seemed to know about was who he had been, a member of the Satan's Choice, and what he'd been convicted of doing in the first place. They seemed to have little knowledge or understanding of criminology, psychology, sociology. Jeff, who was now taking second- and third-year-level courses in these subjects through Queen's, began to suspect that he knew more about such things than they did.

Knowing that he would have to face its members several more times before his prison term was ended, Jeff resolved to make his own informal study of the National Parole Board. He discussed the Board with his teachers and case-management team, and kept careful track of the decisions it handed down regarding other prisoners doing second-degree murder.

He discovered that the Board's decisions were completely arbitrary and, apart from an internal appeal process, quite final. Although the Board was nominally under the control of the Solicitor General's department, it had considerable autonomy and was answerable to no one. How had the Board, which had total control over so many men's lives, gotten so much power, Jeff wondered. Even the Prime Minister of Canada had to answer to his

Cabinet, Parliament, and the voters, from time to time. Yet the Board was accountable to no one.

Jeff also learned, to his chagrin, that other convicted second-degree murderers with the same amount of time in were receiving the same number of UTA's as he and Merv, in a few cases even more, no matter what they'd done while in prison. Men who hadn't gone to school, who'd done little or no community work, who'd just sat on the range for six years and watched the paint dry, got the same passes he had. The Board appeared unable, or unwilling, to differentiate between indifferent and exemplary prison records. So where was the incentive for any federal prisoner to improve himself?

Jeff had to admit that what he'd done, all the work on the Olympiad, all the public speaking, the work on his university degree, he'd done at least partly for himself and to impress the system. But he *had* done it. And now it all appeared to count for nothing.

He also learned that many appointments to the Board were made strictly on the basis of patronage, depending on which political party happened to be in power in Ottawa, and his initial suspicions were quite correct—many of the appointees had little or no formal training in penology, sociology, or psychology.

"Their power is arbitrary, their decisions final, their training often nonexistent, and they got their jobs through patronage," Jeff said of the National Parole Board to a visitor early in 1986. The visitor, ever sceptical, was amazed at this description, and wondered to himself how much of it was due to Jeff's own bitterness against the system. The visitor had to apologize to Jeff a few weeks later.

On the morning of March 13, 1986, the *Globe and Mail* published a story on the findings of the Nielsen task force on the justice system that corroborated Jeff's study:

The National Parole Board has received harsh criticism from the Nielsen task force on Government programs for how it makes its decisions, for the calibre of its members, and for having too many staff.

The "unfettered" discretion exercised by board members raises questions about possible disparities and inequities among parole decisions, the task force's report on the justice system says. . . .

It is widely believed that the calibre of the board has decreased in recent years, the report says, because of the appointment of a number of less qualified, less knowledgeable and less educated members. . . . Parole board positions currently are patronage appointments made by the federal government. . . .

But that was just the tip of the iceberg. Beneath the waterline Jeff, Merv, and the other Choice members convicted of Matiyek's murder felt themselves confronted by another obstacle, shadowy and unseen, and this was the *sub rosa* world of police intelligence. As their prison terms dragged on, they came to feel the weight of this mysterious force, pressing down on their lives like an invisible hand.

The clue to the mystery was the remark by the retired police chief at Jeff's first Parole Board hearing that "All bikers are model inmates," a widely held view in police and even certain correctional circles. It was a continuation of the biker-as-myth, biker-as-stereotype figure long popular in the media, where it had been carefully fostered and nurtured by "police sources" in the first place. All bike clubs were "criminal organizations"; therefore all bikers were, by definition, "organized criminals." Even in custody, bikers remained professional criminals, cunningly able to manipulate the correctional system. If a former biker like Jeff earned a university degree, that proved, not that he was diligent and improving himself, but, rather, that he was highly intelligent and manipulative and even more of a danger. Bikers, all bikers, were incapable of reform and rehabilitation.

In a court of law these assertions were one thing. Even the police had to testify under oath, in public, adduce evidence, and face cross-examination, like anyone else. But within the Parole Board or in a correctional context these assertions were something else. The prisoner or parole applicant had no right to examine the evidence against him or to confront its source. The situation was truly Kafka-esque: how could a prisoner refute an accusation when he was unable to learn what the accusation was? And how could he confront his accuser when the accuser's identity remained a closely held secret?

There was no such thing as due process, there were no checks and balances that might critically scrutinize the accuracy of the police intelligence. And so Jeff, Merv, and the others found themselves boxing at shadows, their word as convicted murderers and bikers pitted against unnamed and unknowable "police information." They were completely overmatched and totally powerless.

Jeff used his first unescorted pass to go home for Christmas. That year, 1985, was his first Christmas on the street since 1977. He returned to Frontenac exhausted, having used almost every one of his seventy-two hours to visit with his family, his girlfriend, her family. He hadn't slept for several nights before he left prison, he was so excited, and he barely slept at all while he was on the outside. Every one of those seventy-two hours was precious to him, and it seemed a shame to waste time sleeping. It was almost like starting life all over again.

XLI

BY THE SPRING OF 1986 Merv Blaker was fed up with life at Frontenac Work Camp. He'd finished taking a small-engine course and he'd been assigned to work in the camp barn, shoveling shit for nine dollars a day. He hated the job—it sure wasn't going to lead anywhere—but he had no choice. Cons who refused to work at their job assignments were transferred, against their will if necessary, to Collins Bay. It was, he noted in a letter, "just like a slave camp."

So Merv, who had led them all down the cascade, decided to make an unusual, if not wholly unprecedented, move: he applied to transfer out of minimum security back into medium security at Joyceville. Such a thing had happened before, usually with cons who had difficulty coping with the lack of bars and physical security at camp. But Merv's application was more calculated. At Joyceville he could get his hands on a state-of-the-art computerized lathe and earn more hours towards his apprentice machinist's ticket. At Frontenac he'd only spend another year shoveling shit.

His application was not welcomed by the CSC. The whole point of the exercise, after all, was to earn one's way *down* the cascade, not back up. The prison hierarchy, which is quite comfortable with terms like "security matrix" and "security grid," was not at all comfortable with an inmate who sought to work against the grain.

Blaker's application sat on someone's desk for three months. Only when his family enlisted the aid of their local Member of Parliament in the matter was it finally approved. When he arrived at Joyceville, finally, Merv discovered that the expensive new lathe had sat in the shop for months unused, because even the shop instructor didn't know how to operate it. He located an instruction book and cassette for the machine and taught himself how to use it. He and the instructor learned together. If he was going to serve all this time, Merv reckoned, he might as well make the most of it.

Rick and Jeff continued their university studies. Although he had embarked on his own university education with less formal schooling and several years behind Jeff, Rick was rapidly catching him up. Rick was now a "solid con" in every way, respected by the prison population and authorities alike. There was never any doubt where Rick stood: he was, unabashedly, on the side of his fellow prisoners. He helped to organize National Prison Justice Day, held on August 10 to commemorate the hundreds of prisoners who have died unnatural deaths while incarcerated. Rick spearheaded a national drive to win prisoners the right to vote in federal elections, and the former union leader dreamed grand dreams. What if all prisoners everywhere could put all their cliques and internal divisions and petty rivalries aside, cast votes, form a national lobby to expose the prison system, and fight for better conditions? What a powerful force they would be! They could demand decent jobs for themselves, at living wages, pay their own way, and work to repay the moral as well as the financial debts they owed to the victims of their crimes.

Rick's was an idealistic vision, born behind prison walls with an incomprehension of the reality that Canada had become on the streets. Since 1978, unemployment had soared and Canadian society had proved itself unable to provide jobs to over one million of its citizens. One in every ten willing, able-bodied, and law-abiding Canadians was now out of work. Who, realistically, cared whether the 12,500 federal prisoners convicted of crimes against the innocents of society had a job?

Early in 1986 Rick completed a paper for his course in cross-cultural psychology. The assignment had been to write a grant application to do a study. Rick gave the subject a great deal of thought. He really wanted to do something different, something original. He decided to try and blend his experiences with prison life and his new-found academic knowledge. The finished paper is a remarkable document, both for what it says about Rick Sauvé, and for the insights it affords into the prison system. As he noted in the opening of his paper,

There have been many studies done involving prison systems and their sub-cultures; however, most of these have been done from outside the system. I intend to conduct my study from a perspective differing from other studies, as I will be doing it from within the prison subculture.

Upon entering the prison system for the first time one is stripped of his self and cultural identity. Once inside the institution there is an indoctrination process through which an individual is introduced to a new culture and a new identity. An individual must accept and be accepted in the prison subculture if he hopes to complete his sentence in a relatively safe and expedient manner. Conformity to this culture and identity is an important factor in this acceptance. The new inmate must become accustomed to a new social order, new language, "jail lingo," new values, and in many cases, morals. He may not agree with the new social norms, but he must conform for his own benefit.

Benefits obtained from this acceptance range from choice of jobs, better living quarters and conditions, a safer environment and generally speaking an "easier time" while serving out a sentence. There are no written or formal guidelines to follow and no direction from the administration to assist the new inmate "fish."

The purpose of his study, Sauvé continued, would be to examine how "fish" from different ethnic and cultural backgrounds adapted to the prison subculture, and the different techniques employed by various groups in obtaining acceptance by the mainstream prison culture.

The study would focus on five main groups: The Native Brotherhood, Francophone inmates, Italian-Canadian inmates, the Black Inmates and Friends Association (BIFA), and white, Anglophone inmates. As a control group Sauvé proposed to survey a group of Canadian sailors, serving on a ship at sea. The control group, Sauvé noted, would be comparable in many respects to the prison population. Both groups were isolated from the civilian population, had a similar age bracket, and an informal internal structure as well as a regimented hierarchy. Like a prison, a ship at sea is an institution, with its individual members drawn from a variety of backgrounds and placed in a new environment for an established period of time. Both institutions required conformity among its members, and in both, "socialization is the avenue which builds the new cultural and self identity."

The study would begin with interviews among the members of each represented group to receive their permission and co-operation. An open interview would be conducted, and then a questionnaire would be circulated among incoming fish within one week of their arrival in prison. A similar questionnaire would be filled out by the fish after six months in the institution, and a second interview would be conducted. Certain difficulties might be encountered, he warned, and elaborated on them. In general, Sauvé cautioned, any number of problems might arise "because the prison system is unpredictable on a daily basis."

The paper was a marvel of academic understatement. It implied, doubtless correctly, that a prison was a far more dangerous place to be than a warship at sea, at least in Canada's peacetime navy. Sauvé predicted that the study would find a prison sub-culture that "can best be described as a mosaic structure operating in a melting pot society," in other words, as he knew only too well, that most prison populations are deeply divided along racial and ethnic lines.

Sauvé's university assignment also addressed another of his concerns, the futility of the "cliques" that kept the whole population divided amongst itself. He may well have figured that by studying the phenomenon and coming to understand it, he might be able to help break some of the divisions down.

The paper was a tremendous success among his tutors and teachers, and it was awarded one of the highest marks ever given in the class. Perhaps sensing that Rick was in a unique position to do original research, his teachers urged him to apply for funding and actually carry out his study. Rick said he'd think about it, but to do the study properly would require three years and a return to Millhaven, which was a lot to ask for the advancement of science. It says a great deal about Rick Sauvé, and about the respect he was accorded by the disparate elements of the prison population, that he could realistically even consider conducting such a study.

His paper was significant in one other way, too. Like Jeff McLeod, Rick was acquiring the necessary tools and skills to critically analyse the correctional and criminal justice system. Like Jeff and the others, Rick Sauvé, who had been the "Subject" of countless assessments, inventories, and progress summaries by prison technocrats, was now able to stand the proposition on its head. The system's "subjects" were now increasingly well-qualified to subject the system to a critical evaluation of their own.

And then there was Gary Comeau, now thirty-three. He still looked older than his actual age, even if he still didn't always act it. He remained a prison leader. He was elected Chairman of the Collins Bay Ten-Plus Fellowship, he still worked on the electrical gang, still read his newspapers every day, and he alone still struggled to somehow *prove* his innocence.

Nutty was no jailhouse lawyer, but, as the Chairman of Ten-Plus, he felt obliged to keep up with the latest developments on certain subjects, especially the 25-year mandatory sentence for first-degree murder, current murder trials, and all trials involving bikers. He even followed the progress of the Law Reform Commission of Canada, which had been working for more than a decade to revise and update Canada's Criminal Code. He had ordered and read or skimmed through all forty-six of the Commission's Working Papers, looking for things that might be of interest to other cons, and, while reading the Commission's forty-seventh Working Paper, the one entitled *Electronic Surveillance*, he stumbled across a mention of their own case.

The reference was contained in a section devoted to the legal requirements incumbent on the police to disclose the existence of wiretaps to those under surveillance:

". . . where charges are laid and the Crown does not intend to rely on wiretap evidence, the accused may never get a notice . . . and never learn of the interception. . . . Knowledge of the interception may be important to the accused's ability to make full answer and defence. In the recent case of *R. v. McLeod*, one of the accused on a charge of murder relied on the defence of alibi. He was a member of a motorcycle gang, and unknown to him the gang's clubhouse was wiretapped. It was only after the conviction on appeal and by purely fortuitous circumstances that his counsel learned that tapes existed of his conversation the night of the killing, which tended to support the alibi. As a result, his evidence was set aside and a new trial ordered based on this fresh evidence.

"Further . . . it is important that the accused be aware of the existence of any interceptions. . . ."

The Commission recommended that the rules of disclosure be strengthened so that "where notice has not been given, a person who was the object of an interception shall be given notice of the dates of the interception and a copy of the authorization under which the interception took place," as opposed to the current law which merely requires notice that an interception has taken place. Tee Hee, of course, never received such a notice.

Finally, Nutty noted to his satisfaction, the Commission seemed to take a dim view of police failures to notify the subjects of electronic surveillance. It recommended "that failure of compliance in accordance with the authorization shall be punishable as contempt of court."

Now *that*, thought Gary Comeau, will be the day . . .

By the summer of 1986 both Jeff and Merv had satisfactorily completed their UTA programs, and, in August, Jeff applied to the Parole Board or a limited day parole to allow him to complete his degree program on the campus of Queen's University. The Board granted his request, and Jeff spent the 1986–1987 academic year on campus. It was strange, being a university student, treated like any other undergraduate by day, and being a federal prisoner by night.

He couldn't help being struck by the youth and affluence of his fellow students as he listened to them talking about their spring get-aways to Florida and watched them roar away in their sports cars after class while he sat on a bench, waiting for the bus that would take him back to jail, but Jeff enjoyed the experience, and he got passing marks in all his classes.

On March 3, 1987, the Honourable James Kelleher, Solicitor General of Canada, made a speech to the Queen's University Law School in Kingston. In it, he unveiled the details of a major new initiative against illiteracy in Canada's federal prison population. Roughly half of all federal inmates proved to have less than a Grade 9 level of competency when they entered prison, Kelleher told his audience, and fewer than ten percent of them sought literacy training while incarcerated.

In an effort to improve this situation, Kelleher declared, he was today announcing an ambitious new program of Adult Basic Education throughout the prison system to combat inmate illiteracy. On the same day that Kelleher was speaking at the Law School, Merv Blaker was informed that the National Parole Board would hold another hearing, this time on his application for release to a halfway house.

Upon hearing about his possible release, Merv's friends and family in Baltimore had undertaken an unprecedented task: they decided to circulate a petition on his behalf. It was addressed to the National Parole Board:

> We are friends of Murray Blaker and we think he has paid enough for his minimal involvement in a crime. We support Murray Blaker and want him back in our community soon.

The results of the petition drive were astonishing. In the space of two weekends more than two hundred and thirty residents of Baltimore, Port Hope, Cobourg, and the Alderville Reserve had signed the petition. They were all residents of the same area where, eight years before, feelings against the Satan's Choice had been running so high that the defence lawyers had felt obliged to seek a change of venue.

Still more heart-warming to the Blaker family were people's comments as they signed their names. They told the Blakers of help that Murray had given them before he was sent to jail, recounting acts of kindness that Merv had never told his own family about. "Oh sure, we remember Murray. He wouldn't hurt a fly. Everyone knows he was innocent, but the police had to send someone to jail, so they convicted him," was the reaction of many. "Let him come home."

But despite the petition, the publicity, and Carole Clapperton's personal intervention, the Board rejected Murray's request. In a letter dated May 4, 1987, a Board spokesperson explained that he still had twenty-one months to go before his parole eligibility date, and twenty-one months, the letter concluded, was just too long a period to live suspended between the street and prison. It would take another year and another gruelling interrogation before Merv finally made it to the Peterborough halfway house.

"A Mister Comeau calling. Will you accept the charge?"

"Sure, operator." It is the morning of Friday, February 6, 1987. "Nutty! How ya doin'?"

"Not too good. I'm in the hole."

"Whaaat? What happened?"

There had been an altercation in the prison yard the Saturday before, Gary explains, between three members of Satan's Choice and three Outlaws. The brawl had erupted in a shed where the prison exercise equipment was stored. Details were necessarily sketchy over the prison telephone, but there had been sufficient impromptu batting practice to send at least two of the bikers to the prison infirmary. Gary himself had not been one of the combatants, but he had been in the yard at the time of the incident, and, as a long-time Choice member, he had been charged along with everyone else.

"I didn't have nothin' to do with it, Mick, honest. I was just in the wrong place at the wrong time."

Oh Nutty, where have we heard this song before?

"But that's not the worst part. They may be gonna send me back to Millhaven."

"Oh, no."

"Call my lawyer, Mick, she'll tell ya I had nothin' to do with it . . . I've seen my report. It says I was outside the shack the whole time. I even helped the guards take one of the guys to the hospital. . . ."

"Yeah? One of your guys or one of the Outlaws?"

"Our guys."

"Yeah? Maybe you shoulda helped one of the Outlaws?"

"Call my lawyer, please, Mick? She'll explain everythin'."

The lawyer confirms Gary's story. "He has witnesses, even among the guards, who say he was hundreds of feet away from the shack when it happened. They don't have enough on him to hold him, and certainly not enough to ship him back to Millhaven. If they do, we'll fight it."

A flurry of phone calls to the warden, to Gary's family, to his Classifications Officer, who confirms that he has, reluctantly, recommended that Comeau be shipped back into Millhaven. "It's what we call a 'group scoop,'" he admits candidly. "It's not fair, it's not just, and they're all gonna get smacked with the same brush. We just happened to find eight bikers together outside the shack, three of them lying around all bloody, nobody saw nothin', nobody did nothin', nobody knew nothin'. . . . They were all just in the wrong place at the wrong time. Gary knew better. He's done more than eight years and he knows enough to walk away from trouble and that's what he's done for eight years, but this time he didn't walk away. Gary is still terribly selfish and self-centred, still emotionally immature, and utterly blind when it comes to his club."

Yup, that's our boy.

"Maybe six months back at Millhaven will smarten him up, once and for all."

An internal investigation into the incident determined that Comeau was not involved in the prison brawl and it confirmed his side of the story, but not before Gary spent nearly a week in the hole, or, as it is euphemistically called in prison bureaucratese, "administrative segregation." He graphically described conditions in the hole in a letter shortly after his release:

The cell was so small, it didn't take us long to realize that this situation could become quite volatile, so we decided to make some house rules: Only one man moving around at one time; when you're taking a crap, keep flushing. I think you get my drift.

We were locked up 23 hours a day with one hour exercise in a 35' by 50' pen. It was very cold outside, there was wornout coats, two sets of gloves & one toque for 40 men. Three showers a week in a dirty, scummy, small metal shower stall. The water would run into the other men's cells. The meals were almost always cold and if we got a warm meal it would be all dried up from the mobile food warmer. There was hardly anything to read and if you did find a good book, I spaced it out so as not to read it too fast, to make it last.

The stench of urine and feces was sometimes unbearable. I had to literally wrap my face in a towel to avoid it. It was awful and it was truly amazing, when I look back, how we coped and didn't attack one another. I could go on and on. I was released after thirteen days, on Friday the thirteenth. I had horrible nightmares for five or six nights after. That's the way it was.

Rick Sauvé, meanwhile, had begun to study the question of judicial review, the only hope he and Nutty now had to cut short their twenty-five-year prison sentence. The lawyers he spoke with told him the judicial-review process was still a mystery to them, because the first review had yet to take place (the law had been passed only in 1976). Rick decided to teach himself all there was to learn about judicial review. He discovered that the first case would likely be heard in Quebec, and the province had prepared Rules of Practice concerning judicial review.

The onus was on the prisoner to apply to the Chief Justice of the Quebec Superior Court, who would, in turn, appoint a judge to call a preliminary hearing. The applicant and his lawyer would present evidence on the con's behalf, while someone from the Attorney General's or the Solicitor General's office would, presumably, argue the other side. If the judge believed the prisoner's application had merit, he could order a jury to be empanelled and a full hearing would take place. It was still unclear just what the criteria would be for early release, but they would presumably include the nature of the offence, prison records, psychological assessments, character references, proof of good behavior, rehabilitation, etc. Only three-quarters of the jury, or eight out of twelve, were needed to render a verdict. The jury could either reject the application for early release, or recommend that the National Parole Board convene a hearing for parole.

Judicial review, Rick could see, was not something you began to prepare for two or three months before your fifteenth anniversary date. A good case might take years to build, and even though he was still in only his eighth year, now was the time to start. He mentioned to his CO that it had been a long time since he'd had a psychological assessment. It might be a good idea to get one into his file soon in preparation for the judicial review.

Within a few weeks Rick was called to the infirmary for just such an assessment. After he talked to the psychologist for about an hour, the interviewer told Rick that he appeared to be quite sound in both mind and body.

"The only thing I can't understand," he concluded, "is what you're doing in here for first-degree murder in the first place."

As much as Merv, Nutty, Rick, and Jeff had each grown and gone their separate ways, they yet managed to retain their unity on certain points. The first concerned their innocence. Despite the pressures of the prison system to finally confess their "guilt," express their "remorse," and so embark on their "rehabilitation," not one of the men convicted of aiding and abetting the shooting of Bill Matiyek would ever once admit his guilt.

The second point was Lorne. Even if someone had promised them immediate freedom in return for the name of the real killer of Bill Matiyek, not one of them would have accepted this offer. Call it honour, call it foolishness, they hewed to the code of the brotherhood, even if it meant their lives, which, in Nutty's and Rick's cases, it obviously did. They had not done the crime, but they would, following the dictates of their own individual consciences, nevertheless do the time.

And then there was the system. They were *in* the prison system, but they were not, for a single moment, *of* it. Since the prison service was the only part of society they were now permitted to experience, they naturally regarded it as a metaphor for society as a whole, and they despised what they saw. They were, to a man, unremittingly contemptuous of the hypocrisy of it all. The notion that, by sending a man to a place like Millhaven or even Collins Bay, he would ever become "rehabilitated" was nothing more than a cruel and misguided joke. Whatever their own considerable and undeniable individual accomplishments, they had been achieved *despite* the sprawling Canadian prison bureaucracy, and not *because* of it.

XLII

IT IS DOUBTLESS A TRUISM to observe that the taking of a human life is a drastic act, with inevitably drastic consequences for everyone associated with that act, and the murder of William John Matiyek is certainly no exception. Even nearly a decade after it happened, the consequences of those fatal seconds in the Queen's Hotel at 10:55 p.m. on the night of Wednesday, October 18, 1978, are still reverberating through the lives of many of the secondary characters in our story.

The young jurywoman who had wept uncontrollably when the verdicts were read was irrevocably altered by her service on the Matiyek jury. The experience jarred her out of her complacent life as a housewife and motivated her to resume professional life as a teacher. The Satan's Choice trial and her empathy for the accused gave her career a new emphasis—she became interested in helping young offenders, and she now teaches special education in London.

Gayle Thompson's relationship with bouncer Randy Koehler ended long ago, and the former Queen's Hotel waitress now resides in a small town on Vancouver Island, just about as far from Port Hope as she can get and still remain in Canada. Part of the reason she moved, she says, was to bury the memory of the night that her friend Bill was killed before her eyes.

She still believes that Bill's murder was a show staged to amuse the members of the Satan's Choice. Gayle Thompson is a decent woman, and it still bothers her that her memory and identification of the gunman could have been wrong and that her testimony may have helped to convict an innocent man of first-degree murder. She suggests, quite seriously, that another Satan's Choice might have fired a bullet into Gary Comeau's shoulder after the murder, in order to provide him with an alibi. She obviously was never made aware that the bullet in Comeau's body came within a centimetre of killing him, too, or that fibres from Bill's coat were found imbedded in the bullet in Comeau's back. It has never occurred to her that both she and Cathy Cotgrave might themselves have been made victims by a faulty police photo-identification procedure more concerned with laying charges and winning convictions than with determining the actual truth.

Cathy Cotgrave married Doug Peart, but they have since separated. Cathy still lives in Port Hope, and she still has occasional nightmares about the murder of her friend Bill Matiyek. Like Gayle Thompson, Cathy Cotgrave also has trouble accepting that her positive identification of Gary Comeau was totally wrong and that it may have helped to send an innocent man to prison for twenty-five years.

Like many of the other Crown witnesses, Cathy still hates and fears the Satan's Choice Motorcycle Club, though there is no indication that any of the witnesses have ever been assaulted or intimidated by the club in any way. A few years ago Cathy Cotgrave was in a crowded hotel lounge when she thought she saw Armand Sanguigni across the room. She was petrified when she realized the man she'd testified against was glaring at her, but Cathy Cotgrave is a courageous woman, and she stared right back.

In hindsight, Cathy need not have worried about incurring the wrath of one of the few club members who could legitimately have been described as a cold-blooded killer. On the morning of October 8, 1984, Armand Sanguigni's body was found, along with that of his common-law wife, in their home in Toronto's Davenport Road–Dufferin Street area. A police investigation revealed they had both died as the result of a drug overdose.

Gordon van Haarlem, the other Choice member acquitted of Matiyek's murder, returned to Oshawa following his release from custody in 1979. Although the jury had declared him innocent, the police had other ideas, van Haarlem quickly discovered. The heat was unremitting—he couldn't walk to the store to buy a loaf of bread without being hassled, and he fared little better when he attempted to recover his colours and the other personal belongings the police had seized when they arrested him. It wasn't that he wanted to wear his patch any longer—a year in the bucket simply because he was a Choice had convinced Gordy of that—but he did want to return his crest to the club, as the rules dictated, and resign his membership properly. Repeated attempts by Don Ebbs to regain his former client's property were unsuccessful.

"Fuck it, man," van Haarlem told his lawyer. "They got no right to keep that stuff. I was innocent."

"Forget it," Ebbs advised Gordy. "Innocent or not, you're lucky you're not in jail for life along with everyone else."

In an effort to escape the heat and begin life anew, Gordy moved to a small town just west of Edmonton, where he now lives. But even there van Haarlem's criminal past came back to haunt him. As luck would have it, the police force in his new home town were mainly rookies, fresh graduates of the RCMP training academy in Regina. Gordy was one of only two residents in the small town with any sort of pretensions to a legitimate criminal record, and, as such, he found himself singled out by the local constabulary. Just like a striker or a new club member, the recently graduated coppers had to prove how tough they were, and it wasn't always easy to find the requisite criminals in Stony Plain, Alberta. A few of them were eager to take Gordy on just to prove a point and van Haarlem, though he had put the Life behind him, still hated to back down from a fight. But, apart from a few assault beefs, he has maintained a clean record.

Van Haarlem married Patty and they now have two daughters and own their own home on a one-acre parcel of land with river frontage. Gordy runs his own welding business and, in good times, has several employees operating his welding trucks, which serve the local petroleum drilling and pumping industry.

Today Gordon van Haarlem is in his early thirties. His face has filled out and he is now virtually unrecognizable as the lean, mean biker who once glared into a photographer's camera while being led into a courthouse to stand trial for first-degree murder. He pronounces this post-mortem on his own decision to leave the Life: "The coppers have the upper hand. It wouldn't be so bad if you just got pinched for the things you did. But they can pinch you for anything, any time they want."

With a couple of exceptions, all of the lawyers involved in the Satan's Choice murder trial and appeals are still practising criminal law. Donald Ebbs, the Peterborough lawyer who angered his co-counsel and most of the accused by showing up David Hoffman's alibi to win the acquittal of Gordon van Haarlem, was appointed an Ontario provincial court judge and he is now based in Windsor. Chris Meinhardt and Roland Harris are still Crown Attorneys in Lindsay and Cobourg, respectively. With a single exception, all of the appeal lawyers have continued their distinguished careers. Ross McKay died of cancer on Thanksgiving Day, 1983.

Detective Sergeant Terry Hall transferred out of the OPP biker squad several years ago. He is now an inspector assigned to the London detachment. Hall is contemplating writing a book about his experiences as Canada's foremost anti-biker policeman, a project he has discussed with reporters John Schenk and John Kessel, in the hope that they might serve as ghost-writers.

Superintendent Colin Cousens, the senior investigating officer in the Matiyek case, is now the commanding officer of the OPP's Number Five District, headquartered at Highway 401 and Keele Street in Toronto.

Sam McReelis is still a staff sergeant with the Port Hope Police Department.

The two reporters who provided most of the coverage of the Satan's Choice murder trial are still in the news business. Bill Glaister's interest in crime stories and critical coverage of Canada's police forces continues. In 1986 his investigative efforts uncovered a series of scandals within the Ottawa Police Department which resulted in the laying of criminal charges and the resignation of several constables from the force. Mac Haig is still on the staff of the *London Free Press*, where he alternates between the copy desk and the court beat.

Betty King still lives in Scarborough. In all seasons and all weather, Betty made the four-hour round-trip drive to Collins Bay to visit her son every other Saturday, until his transfer to Warkworth in Campbellford, Ontario, in the fall of 1987. She still goes to see Gary every Christmas Eve morning, and she remains absolutely convinced that her son was wrongfully convicted of first-degree murder.

On January 11, 1980, Rod Stewart was found guilty of mischief in the removal of Bill Glaister's notes from the Ganaraska Hotel in Port Hope, after Crown Attorney Roland Harris elected to reduce the theft charge against Stewart and his two friends to the less serious charge of mischief. All three men were granted absolute discharges by provincial court judge Samuel Murphy. Although he still lives in the Port Hope area, Rod Stewart is no longer a member of the town's municipal council.

David Hoffman was released from Collins Bay Pen in April 1984, after having served forty-two months as an accessory after the fact in the murder of Bill Matiyek. The paranoia of prison life had a lingering impact on his personality, Hoffman believes, making him more cautious, less able to express his feelings and emotions.

Hoffman returned to Kitchener, where he completed his parole uneventfully in March 1987. Although he once dreamed of returning to school and becoming a professional chartered accountant, those ambitions were shattered forever by his criminal conviction. Hoffman's ponytail and horn-rimmed glasses are long gone, replaced by styled hair and trendy aviator glasses, though he still likes running shoes. Apart from his massive club ring, David Hoffman is today virtually indistinguishable from any other young professional. He works as an accountant for a large Kitchener fitness centre.

Tee Hee was married in the spring of 1986, and until recently he refused to have a home telephone—an understandable foible considering the impact the device has had on his life. He finally acceded to pressure from his wife and allowed one to be installed in their apartment, but the number is unlisted.

Tee Hee is once again a member in good standing of the Kitchener-Waterloo Chapter of the Satan's Choice Motorcycle Club.

Bernie Guindon has also completed his prison terms and is back on the street. Now in his mid-forties, Guindon divides his time between his substantial business interests (real-estate speculation and property management) in Oshawa and a camp designed especially for motorcyclists in Northern Ontario.

Bernie peels his shirt away for the visitor and smacks a palm down on a bulging bicep, covering his tattoo of the Satan's Choice devil's head.

"On my patch," swears Bernie, "on my fuckin' patch! It feels so good to be able to say it, this whole thing is totally fuckin' straight!" The youngest of his ten children is named Harley Davidson Guindon.

Sharon Sauvé was unable to maintain the "little house on the prairie" on a waitress's income after Rick was sent to jail. She moved into an apartment in the back of her parents' home in Port Hope, where she still resides with her daughter Angie. She is now the manager of a smoke-shop/news-stand on Walton Street in downtown Port Hope.

To this day, apparently, Sharon is unable to resolve her ambivalent feelings towards her childhood sweetheart. She no longer goes for conjugal visits with Rick, although she still visits him periodically in Collins Bay. On the other hand, she has yet to file for a divorce.

Angie is now twelve, though she seems older. She has survived years of schoolyard taunts of "your dad is a murderer" with a riposte born out of an abiding love and respect for her father that is, on the evidence, unassailably true: "My dad never killed anyone."

Lorne Campbell will remain on parole until December 1988, but, with the exception of a driving-while-impaired charge (sentence: one year suspended licence), he has succeeded in walking the straight and narrow. He has worked at a succession of jobs, including his trade as an ironworker, and he is still with his wife of ten years. They live in Orillia, Ontario.

Now nearing forty, Campbell wants to make something of his life, but there is still something restless and yearning about Lorne Campbell. "I wanna come home, kiss my wife, have my supper, and watch TV," he says, and then pauses. "I'm still looking for something that I'd enjoy doing . . . I'm not sure what it is."

Like Bernie, Lorne is strictly prohibited from associating with any of his club brothers while he remains on parole. The two years he has spent on the street since his release from prison are the longest time without a serious criminal charge in Lorne's adult life.

The Satan's Choice Motorcycle Club was dealt a jarring, though not a fatal, blow by the imprisonment of six of its members for the murder of Bill Matiyek. The Peterborough Chapter, which had already been the weakest before the Matiyek murder, was nearly decimated and continued to exist in name only.

The two American superpower clubs, the Outlaws and the Hell's Angels, became established facts of life on the Canadian outlaw scene. The American giants carved the country up like a Thanksgiving turkey. Quebec and the Maritimes became Angels territory, and Ontario was ceded to the Outlaws. The Angels also established a chapter in Vancouver.

As the years passed, the outlaw cycle of greed, paranoia, and violence wound ever tighter. Murders, bombings, and arson became increasingly commonplace, and every club, it seemed, was fighting battles on two fronts—with police on the one hand, and with rival organizations on the other. Although they are still worn with pride at large club events like funerals and summer runs, it has become a rarity to see an individual biker flying his full colours when traveling alone. There is too much heat, too much paranoia.

The days of long hair, Nazi insignia, and the outrageous "class act" are long gone, and even Gary Comeau admits the club world he knew during the seventies has changed forever. "Things have gotten a lot heavier out there, no doubt about it. The game isn't played by the same rules any more, hell, it isn't even the same ballpark."

Two major events rocked the outlaw club world in the mid-eighties, and produced a re-drawing of the outlaw map in Central Canada.

One was the January 1985 murder of six members of the Hell's Angels Laval, Quebec, Chapter by other club members. The deceased were found in the St. Lawrence River weeks later, their bodies stuffed into sleeping-bags and weighted down with concrete blocks.

Nineteen Angels from the Sorel and Sherbrooke-Lennoxville chapters were arrested and charged with first-degree murder, along with five members of the Halifax Angels Chapter. Eleven more Angels, for whom murder warrants have been issued, went into hiding.

Several of the Angels, including Yves "Apache" Trudeau, turned informer against their erstwhile club brothers. Trudeau also confessed to his own involvement in no fewer than forty-three killings, making him, in the words of the *Globe and Mail*, "the most prolific known killer in Canadian history." In return for his co-operation Trudeau was sentenced to seven years for manslaughter and accorded special prison privileges.

Rick's and Gary's consternation on learning of the deal with Trudeau can well be imagined. A cold-blooded killer who committed forty-three murders, and an informer on top of it, would be on the street in seven years, while they, who never killed anyone and never intended to kill anyone, will do twenty-five, precisely because they have refused to inform.

The Angels organization in Quebec has been severely weakened, at least for the time being. Only time will tell whether it can be rebuilt, whether another club will fill the vacuum, or whether, as seems unlikely, the Life has truly been rubbed out in Quebec.

The second major development, also in January of 1985, dealt a severe blow to Outlaw fortunes in Ontario. On the night of Tuesday, January 22, some five hundred police officers in Ontario and Quebec conducted a series of raids on Outlaw clubhouses and homes in twelve Ontario cities and in Montreal. Code-named Operation Boar, the massive effort was the culmination of surveillance and infiltration of the Outlaws Motorcycle Club and produced 371 charges against 84 club members and club associates.

As they had with the Angels in Quebec, Crown prosecutors found some of the Outlaws only too willing to testify against other club members in return for reduced sentences, police protection, or promises of outright immunity. A few of the Outlaws have already been convicted for large-scale drug-trafficking, and additional trials are expected to last well into 1988.

The rolling-up of the Outlaws' Ontario organization led to resurgence of the Canadian independent outlaw clubs in the province, including the Satan's Choice. In January 1986 the Choice added a new chapter by taking over the Coffin Wheelers club in Sudbury. By the spring of 1987 the Choice had also expanded into a new chapter in west Toronto, and the club had founded a chapter in Thunder Bay. For the first time since the Outlaws split in 1977, Choice membership had risen over the one-hundred mark.

But a student of such matters, able to take the longer view of the ebb and flow of outlaw club politics and fortunes, can't escape the feeling that, when the police act next to bust a club grown too big for its breeches, the Satan's Choice will once again be the most likely target.

And yet, the Life endures. A visitor asks a Choice veteran what motivates a man to volunteer for such a dangerous lifestyle.

"It wasn't like this when I joined in 1969. Clubs were starting all over. Every month there'd be a new club starting up somewhere. Today there are no new clubs. And we'll never have thirteen chapters again. If I was twenty-one today would I join, knowing what I know now? I don't know. But I'm thirty-five, I don't have a family, I missed that boat. This is my life. I'd be lost without it."

XLIII

THE VISITOR RETURNS ONCE more to Collins Bay. It is a brilliantly sunny summer day, and his visit is as special as the weather: he has been accorded a rare privilege, the chance to join Gary Comeau and his family during a trailer visit. Trailer visits, or Extended Family Visits as they are known in institutional parlance, must surely be among the most humane reforms made by the Canadian prison system in recent years. They offer a prisoner the chance to live privately with his wife, children, or immediate family three or four times a year, for a four-day period.

Such visits are a privilege and not a right for Canadian prisoners; they must have maintained a clean institutional record for at least the preceding six months to be eligible, and in this way the trailers are doubtless a further means of exerting "good institutional order" on the part of prison authorities. But these visits are also a welcome respite for prisoners, a chance for physical intimacy with a wife, for renewing family ties, an opportunity to put aside the pressures of prison life for a few precious hours, to enjoy genuine privacy, eat home cooking, and live like a normal human being. It is the only such opportunity that lifers like Gary Comeau and Rick Sauvé are apt to have for a long, long time.

There are two trailers at Collins Bay, each surrounded by their own yards, complete with shrubbery. Except for the high chainlink fence, topped by razor-sharp concertina wire, that surrounds each trailer, and the view of the even higher whitewashed wall that encloses the prison yard, the setting is almost suburban.

Gary Comeau greets the visitor proudly on "his" front porch, and, with a proprietary air, guides him through the trailer. Three bedrooms, a living-room complete with VCR, wall-to-wall carpeting, and colour television, a kitchen with all the modern conveniences and a fridge stuffed with food (visitors pay a nominal daily fee for their groceries): it is a side of Canadian prison life that outsiders seldom see. It is the first time that a journalist has been allowed to join a prisoner and his family on such a visit.

Still, it *is* a prison, and no one doubts that each of the rooms in the trailers are wired for sound. Gary and his visitor retire to the yard outside the trailer, and carefully manoeuvre a picnic table into a corner of the yard-within-a-yard, placing it beneath a tree that obscures the sight-lines from the nearest watchtower. There is, at last, the illusion of privacy, but even so, Gary and the visitor speak in low, guarded tones. In prison, paranoia is a highly contagious disease.

It is the most intimate opportunity the visitor has ever had to speak with Gary Comeau, to talk to him about his life, and the interview lasts for many hours.

Now that he has literally given up his life to protect another member of his club, are there any regrets? Has he ever considered turning informer and ending this extraordinary sacrifice?

"If someone approached me with a deal and said, 'Look, we know so-and-so did it, you confirm it and you're walkin',' I just couldn't do it. It's bred into me. I just wouldn't do it."

What should society do to men who persist in flouting its social conventions and violating its laws, like motorcycle club members? What would be the most effective means of suppression?

Gary hesitates. "If people are breakin' the laws, then pop them fairly and squarely like anyone else. But framing guys just makes them more bitter and hostile towards the system."

Where does he think he would be today had he missed that fatal confrontation in the Queen's Hotel?

"The last three to four months before my arrest, quite frankly, it was gettin' to be the same thing over and over, hangin' around the clubhouse, goin' to the hotel, lookin' for a steady girl. I was feelin' a little empty. I was still interested in the club and everything, but I was lookin' for something else. Maybe I would have met the right girl, maybe I woulda quit the club, maybe I'd still be there. I don't know. I don't regret, ever, being in the club. Even after all this. It wasn't the club that got me here. It was the police. . . . One other thing that's been bothering me a lot for years now is I want the Matiyek family, especially the mom and dad, to know we didn't intend to kill their son that night. I guess you can say he was in the wrong place at the wrong time, as I was. Coming back into the courtroom one time I looked Mr. Matiyek straight in the eyes and tried to show him by expression that I was sorry that this whole mess happened, but we didn't have anything to do with it, do you understand what I mean? I was trying to convey my thoughts with my eyes and expression. I don't know if he read me right or at all."

The visiting-room at Joyceville is a large, high-ceilinged space that resembles an old railway station waiting-room. On a Sunday the cavernous hall is packed with cons and families and children. At every other chair, it seems, a torrid love scene is under way as prisoners and their old ladies make out, shutting out the busy scene around them.

"The unwritten rule is you're not supposed to see them," says a veteran prison visitor. "But it's hard not to, isn't it?"

A less experienced visitor murmurs assent, and his eyes drift upwards, towards the high, vaulted ceiling of the visiting-room. It is about the only place he can be sure he won't see a passionate, petting couple.

At last Merv Blaker appears through the heavy steel door. He looks thin, but healthy, and there are strands of silver in Merv's black hair now. He is still quiet and soft-spoken, and it is sometimes hard to hear him over the babble of voices that echo throughout the hall. At least, the visitor thinks, they can't bug our conversations here, in all this noise.

"I'm doing good," Merv says, adding he's recovered from the depression that followed his handling at the hands of the Parole Board. He failed his examination for a machinist's licence, Merv tells his visitors, but he seems unperturbed. (He will write a second test in a few months, and will pass this one as well as a welding licence.)

At least one good thing has happened in Merv's life over the last few years—he applied for, and was granted, restoration of his Indian status. He and his daughter, Alisa, who is now fourteen years old, have recovered the birthright that Merv's father had signed away nearly half a century before.

How important is Merv's Indianness to him?

The answer, as always, is understated, elliptical. "Well, uh, Mick, it's pretty important, I'd say. Yeah, pretty important. To know who you are and what you came from. I like the way the Indians did things, the way they related to the earth. Yeah, it's important to me."

Where would Merv be now if none of this had happened?

"I think I'd be living in Port Hope still. I'd probably be out of the club, I was just starting to get a little ahead there when this happened. I owned a house, we had a brand-new car, I only drove it three times before we got arrested. I was getting older, more interested in my family, I was into spending more time with them. I had a good job at United Tire, I think I'd still be working there. I was a tire-builder, and a member of the United Rubber Workers' Union."

Visiting-hours are over suddenly, and the visitor rises to shake hands with Merv. His handshake is light, almost tentative, as if the act is somehow foreign.

Merv Blaker returns through the heavy steel door, and is gone.

The visitor's last face-to-face interview with Rick Sauvé is in an office at Collins Bay. He seems more relaxed this time, less distant, and the visitor feels close enough to him now to be able to ask some difficult questions, like how a young man goes about doing twenty-five years in prison.

Rick harks back to the lessons he learned seven years ago, from other lifers, at Millhaven. You don't get involved in other people's trips, you build an emotional shell around you to get through the day, you keep busy.

The shell, he concedes, is especially difficult when his family is around, or in the trailer. It becomes a kind of second nature to keep one's distance, and the guard does not come down overnight. During his first few trailer visits, Rick recalls, something kept nagging at him when he returned to the range. He slept different, somehow. At first he thought it was the relative silence of the trailers (the blocks are tremendously noisy, even at night), but finally it hit him: his dreams were different. In the trailer he dreamed in colour, in the joint he dreamed in black-and-white.

Keeping busy has always been one of Rick's strong points. In addition to his university course load he has taken up meditation in a deeply serious way, learned to box, worked out regularly, jogged, learned photography, and become the Deputy Coordinator of the Disabled Olympiad, the job once held by Jeff McLeod. And then there is the organizing: he has helped to organize the Infinity group, a committee of lifers in Collins Bay, Prison Justice Day, and the right-to-vote drive. The authorities told him that prisoners had not lost the right to vote merely because they were prisoners, but because there was no way to enumerate them under the Elections Act. It sounded like a lot of bullshit to Rick. He discovered that cons in halfway houses were allowed to vote. Weren't they still serving time? "So tell me the truth," he demands. "If we've lost our right to vote and we've lost our citizenship, then we should have the right to apply for citizenship to another country." A smile plays at the corner of his mouth. "Maybe Libya would take me."

How does he spend a typical day?

"It's kind of hard to explain, but how you handle your free time, the time that you aren't distracted by work, exercise, or schoolwork, that's a big part of the day. My friend Rick wakes me up for work at about eight. I put my shell on to face the day. I head down to the gym to check in for work, and then I head over to the Olympiad office to share a couple of cups of coffee with Rick. Usually we talk about anything from sports to world politics. Often we rehash old stories—we've known each other since we were kids.

"Then I go outside to the sports shack, I work in the yard, if something needs doing, I do it. In summer it could be getting the ball diamonds ready, weight repair, or something. In winter there isn't much to do, snow to shovel or something. Then I do about one hour of weight training. At noon there's count, so I go to my cell for count. We eat dinner, and after one we head back to work. Usually I do pretty much the same as in the morning, except instead of weights I usually go for a half-hour run. At three-thirty I come back to my cell from work and read till supper. We get counted again at four. Supper's at five o'clock.

"At six-twenty they call gym up and I head down to the gym to train on the boxing skills. At seven-thirty I come back, stop in the Photo office for an hour and watch a little TV, and bull with the guys. I head to my cell and do schoolwork for the rest of the night until about eleven. Every hour they unlock the cells for a twenty-minute change-over. That twenty minutes I usually head over to Nutty's and we bull. Sometimes I sit in with him for a couple hours if I don't have schoolwork.

"At eleven is lock-up. I do yoga for about an hour to relax both mentally and physically. It helps to get rid of the mask I put on in the morning. Sometimes I watch some late-night TV or I just drop off to sleep. You try not to think about the street too much, it helps the time go easier. At the same time, it's good to think about the special people, it's reassuring to know you have people that care, and that, although you might be isolated, you are not shut away. . . ."

In the summer of 1986, Rick's case-management team suggested that he apply for his first escorted pass outside the prison walls. It was unusual for a lifer to be granted an ETA with only seven and a half years in, but his team obviously felt that Rick was ready. It would be a giant step for Rick, too, to spend even four hours in a private home or walking through the streets of downtown Kingston after so many years of serving hard time. Rick told them he'd think about it.

It wasn't that Rick didn't believe himself ready to venture beyond the walls, even with an escort, but he dreaded his own reaction should his ETA application be refused. He just didn't want to get his hopes up. He bided his time, waiting for the right special occasion to mark his first ETA.

As fall turned to winter it became increasingly apparent that just such an occasion would occur in Rick's life in the spring of 1987. If he passed his two remaining courses, Rick would receive his Bachelor of Arts degree from Queen's at the end of May, and so would Jeff. They would become the first male cons to graduate from the Queen's prison education program, and Rick would become the first inmate in the fifty-year history of Collins Bay to earn his BA while behind bars.

Rick finally applied for the ETA, and throughout the winter of 1986–87 there was at least a passing reference to the application in every one of his letters. He had applied to attend the convocation, he was waiting, he was still waiting, it was looking good, the authorities told him. But after every reference a cautious disclaimer was appended: "of course, I'm not getting my hopes up."

By April 1987 he wrote that his case-management team had assured him that they were "98 percent sure" that the application would be approved, but he still wasn't getting his hopes up.

But how could they refuse? What a public relations coup for the prison service, what an opportunity to trumpet another successful reform. The prison education program, like the trailer visits and Kelleher's literacy program, was among the most impressive reforms in the Canadian prison system in the past decade.

Rick's call on the morning of April 28 came as a complete shock.

"I just wanted you to know, my ETA was denied."

"*What?* You mean they're not even going to let you attend your own graduation ceremony?"

"Right." There is no trace of bitterness in his voice, no indication of the tremendous disappointment he must feel. The mask at work.

"But why?"

"They say security reasons."

"But *what* security reasons?"

"They don't have to tell me."

"Okay, but did they give you any kind of hint?"

"They say they're worried about another club."

"You mean the Outlaws."

"They're concerned there might be some kind of disruption of the ceremony if I'm there."

"Shit, man, your and Jeff's graduations were going to be the last scene in my book."

"I guess you'll just have to find a different ending," Rick says evenly.

It is a widespread belief among cons who have done time there that the wardens and deputy wardens do not in fact run Collins Bay prison. The institution's security apparatus really call the shots there, they aver, and not the genial, liberal, humanistic types who are in nominal command.

This may or may not be true, but it is a fact that at 1:30 p.m. on Saturday, May 30, 1987, the security guards of Collins Bay are not smiling as they escort Rick Sauvé to a car in front of the prison gate. It has taken a front-page story in the *Globe and Mail* ("Prisoner denied leave for graduation ceremony—Murderer won his BA at Collins Bay"), the personal intervention of the Solicitor General of Canada, and a hasty, shame-faced overriding of the invisible hand of the police security apparatus to get Rick through the gate.

It is a steamy, sunny day for a Queen's convocation, but Sauvé's escorts, all seven of them, wear suits and ties in the stifling heat, even the two long-haired and bearded members of the OPP biker squad. There are all sorts of suspicious bulges beneath their suits, and most of the security-force members wear walkie-talkie earpieces.

Rick Sauvé stands in the middle of the escort, his graduation gown draped over his arm. He is not a tall man, but on this day he seems to tower over the beefy guards, his long gold hair, newly washed, flowing down his shoulders, shining in the sunlight. He looks straight ahead, head held high, alert but expressionless.

Sauvé's two-car convoy arrives at the rear entrance to the Jock Harty Arena, the scene of the convocation, and a bevy of photographers and reporters at once encircle Rick and his escort. The guards glower, and physically interpose themselves between Sauvé and any photographer or reporter who dares approach. Rick Sauvé will graduate this day, but only just.

It is a combined operation of the OPP, the Kingston Police, CSC security, and Queen's security. A visitor counts at least a dozen cops inside the arena, two at each entrance, and he knows there are at least that many armed guards stationed at strategic points, unseen, across the campus.

Pierre and Adeline Sauvé are here, and Angie and Sharon, along with half a dozen of Rick's brothers and sisters and assorted in-laws. There can be no prouder father inside the packed arena than Pierre, his chest out-thrust, the buttons on is finest suit practically bursting, and why not? Rick is the first one of his eleven sons and daughters to graduate from university.

His guards maintain a discreet distance, and Rick Sauvé sits erect in his seat, still expressionless, drinking in what must seem a fantastic scene: the pomp of the bagpipers piping in the other graduates in majestic splendor, the pomposity of the commencement speakers, their addresses made interminable by the heat inside the crowded arena.

At last the name of Richard Michael Anthony Sauvé is read out, and Rick kneels before Queen's University Chancellor Agnes Benidickson, who pronounces him a Baccalaureate of Arts. A red-and-black ribbon is placed around his shoulders and a smattering of applause and cheers, louder than for any other graduate, ripples through the heavy air. Half a dozen photographers and television cameramen capture the moment.

What has Rick thought of it all, a visitor wonders. He has noticed, not without approbation, that Rick has not made even a perfunctory attempt to join in the singing of "God Save the Queen" or the opening hymn, "O God Our Help in Ages Past." What must he be thinking of the pageantry, the pretty Queen's coeds in their caps and gowns, the crowd? This is without doubt the largest gathering Rick has attended in eight years, since that night, so long ago, when he and Sharon heard Bob Seger sing "We've Got Tonight" for the first time, in Maple Leaf Gardens.

What must he be thinking? No one will ever know, for as soon as Rick leaves the stage he is surrounded by his escort and hustled out of the arena, the photographers running behind to catch up. One of them does, and just as Rick has left the gloom of the arena she snaps a picture, which moves over the photo wire within hours. It shows Rick in his shirt and tie, gown open at the chest, his diploma clutched securely in both hands. He is, at last, smiling.

Jeff McLeod graduates on this day, too, as he wished, with no fanfare, no attention. It is of course, a one-in-a-thousand shot: two bikers, both serving life for the same murder, which neither of them actually committed, becoming the first male prisoner-graduates of Queen's University. But Jeff has resolutely shunned all media queries, all interview requests. All but one.

Not a week has gone by in months, Jeff tells the visitor, that some media outlet hasn't called for an interview. As the death-penalty debate has heated up, even CSC officials have referred reporters to Jeff, one of the most articulate convicted murderers they've got.

Even though his last request for day parole to Toronto has been rejected by the NPB, Jeff can smell his freedom now. It is only a matter of months, and he wants to put all of it—the club, the prison, even his "model inmate" status—behind him.

He wants to resume his life, the secure anonymity of any other citizen, his "debt" to society paid. His family has suffered enough because of him, Jeff explains, and any more publicity, no matter how favourable, would only prolong the suffering.

He has made this lone exception, Jeff tells the visitor, "because of Ricky and Nutty. I could never have done the time they're doing, I could never have handled it the way they have. I think I would have killed myself by now. How they've done it, I'll never know. But I do know this—the way our trial went, I could just as easily be doing first-degree murder now, instead of them."

Where does Jeff think he would be today, if not for The Night?

"I might be in jail, on another charge. Or, I might have met a woman and settled down, I might have been a successful individual." He pauses. "I sure wouldn't have a degree from Queen's, I know that much," and then he laughs. "I probably wouldn't have lost the weight, either.

"It was a fluke, it was fate that night, what happened," Jeff continues. "It could have happened a thousand times before, and it didn't. It could have happened a thousand times since, and it hasn't. . . ."

The visitor can only nod.

"The only reason I'm talkin' to ya now," Jeff says, his eyes flashing, "is because of Rick and Nutty. . . ."

The visitor knows that, too. It is brotherhood, after the fact. It is the only conspiracy there ever really was.

The Knoxville Cemetery is at the intersection of two lost gravel roads, north of Port Hope. It is a pretty, peaceful place, bordered by ancient, over-arching hardwood trees in early leaf. It is not, one suspects, the kind of place that Bill Matiyek much appreciated while he was alive. It is June.

Lawrence Leon approaches the grave of his friend and, with a great dignity that is both sombre and touching, he doffs his red tractor cap.

Bill Matiyek has been well and truly mourned by his family and friends since his death. Each year they have gathered on October 18 for a private ceremony of remembrance, and each year the family has purchased a memorial advertisement in the personals column of the Cobourg newspaper to commemorate his passing.

As we talk, Lawrence bends down, with surprising grace for a man his size, and pulls a few offending weeds from around the tombstone bearing the inscription: "Taken from us suddenly, October 18, 1978" . . .

But this is also a martyr's grave, for, buried deep in the ground before the headstone, there is another, smaller stone. It is engraved with a Golden

Hawk, with its wings outstretched. "GHRs" is inscribed on one wing, the word "Heavy" on the other.

Lawrence Leon gazes at both stones for a while, in reverential silence. He turns, at last, and walks away. He puts his cap back on and climbs into his truck. Sometimes, after he has visited Bill's grave, Lawrence drives on down the road to the Matiyek place, a scant two kilometres away, to visit Bill's mother and father. But today, he does not do so.

The visitor remains, and contemplates the ultimate outlaw irony: in the end, Bill Matiyek did not escape the farm, after all.

AFTERWORD

In the nearly three years that I have been working on this story the question I have been asked most often is, "How did you find out about this subject in the first place?"

In April, 1985, I was assigned by the *Globe and Mail*, one of my long-time clients as a freelance writer, to cover the trial of a group of Millhaven prisoners on a charge of first-degree murder. Although the trial was preempted by a plea bargain, I was nonetheless fascinated by the glimpses the affair offered into life at Millhaven. Before completing my wrap-up story for the *Globe*, I telephoned my friend Claire Culhane in Vancouver for a few quotes.

A week later I received a thick letter from her. "If you're interested in prison stories," she wrote, "have a look at this." The package contained several letters to her from a convicted first-degree murderer named Gary Comeau. He claimed to be innocent, and the letter contained several xeroxed documents pertaining to his trial.

My editors at the *Globe and Mail* consented to send me to Kingston to check out the stories of Comeau and his co-accused. As generous as the *Globe* often is when it comes to long-shot, money-eating investigative stories, it was clear after only half a day with Gary that the parameters of this story were far too large to be adequately covered in any daily newspaper, and so began a fourteen month period of independent investigation: traveling, interviewing, and digging through court documents, police wiretap transcripts, and moldering newspaper clippings in biker scrapbooks.

I knew little of the Canadian criminal justice system when I began my research and even less about outlaw bikers. The portrait that gradually emerged of the three brotherhoods, the bikers, the police, and the lawyers is not, as the reader will now know, greatly reassuring.

I do not know what expectations the Canadian public holds of its outlaw bikers, but I believe the public desires a criminal justice system that is as impartial and as infallible as we can humanly make it. In other words, if, after exhausting all legal avenues, a group of men are sentenced to long prison terms for first- and second-degree murder, we should be able to assume that they are guilty beyond a reasonable doubt of the crime for which they are being punished.

I believe we can make no such assumption in this case. I believe Rick, Gary, and the others were guilty of something, but that Jeff McLeod has got it about right: "I was a member of the Satan's Choice, we went into the hotel that night as a group, a man was killed and he shouldn't have been, and that makes me guilty of something—manslaughter, maybe. But there was never any intent to shoot Bill Matiyek, so don't tell me I'm guilty of second-degree murder."

I can, admittedly, offer no new hard, physical evidence that what Jeff, Rick, and the others say is true, but then there was, as we have seen, no abundance of direct physical evidence of a conspiracy either throughout the trial. The Crown's case of intent was almost entirely inferential. I have, in fact, in the interest of brevity spared the reader some of the more elaborate trappings of the Crown's conspiracy case. They were patently absurd, they went nowhere, and they did not, I suspect, greatly influence the jury's decision.

I can, however, offer certain new insights into the murder of Bill Matiyek. Chief among them is an ancient and time-honoured philosophical concept known as "Occam's Razor." Simply put, Occam's Razor posits that when offered two conflicting theories about a given phenomenon, one exceedingly complex and the other much simpler, the observer may reasonably conclude that the simpler explanation is, on the balance of probability, more apt to be true.

I am inclined to believe Rick and Gary's (and Lorne's) reconstruction of events because I find it simpler and therefore more credible than any other explanation. It is also supported by the physical evidence.

A word about sources—and about evidence. Book One, the re-creation of the murder itself, is based largely on interviews with Rick, Gary, Merv, Jeff, and other key eyewitnesses. The events preceding the arrival of the Satan's Choice in the Queen's Hotel are derived from the preliminary and trial evidence of Cathy Cotgrave and Gayle Thompson, as well as interviews with them.

The recreation of events from the bikers' points of view is based on interviews where certain details were mentioned, sometimes almost casually. The confrontation with Matiyek at his table in the crucial moments before his death are based on Rick and Gary's recollections, and they are among the very few examples of "creative dialogue" employed anywhere in this book. I have kept this semi-journalistic technique to an absolute but essential minimum throughout, using trial transcripts wherever possible.

Here, again, their "side of the story" is borne out by objectively verifiable physical evidence: the presence of a handgun on Bill Matiyek's body, Jamie Hanna's recollection of a conversation with a member of the Satan's Choice, the "kiss of death" statement, and the entry wound on Gary's left side. Each detail is verified by both the Crown witnesses *and* the accused, though the "kiss of death" was subject to widely varying interpretations. The bullet entry wound must, surely, at last clarify the seating arrangement at Bill's table that so confounded each of the Crown witnesses; Gary was seated at the table, to Bill's immediate right, and Rick was sitting roughly across the circular table from Bill.

But then there is the matter of timing: Gary, Rick, Lorne, and the others had time (six weeks) to concoct their side of the story before the arrests were made; they subsequently had years to invent a story based on the trial evidence during their time together in prison. But it is also clear from a careful reading of the preliminary transcript that Gary Comeau had given Howard Kerbel the same basic account of events that he recounts to this day, an account that helped Kerbel elicit a number of vital points, key among them the fact that Bill Matiyek was indeed in possession of a gun. That fact, at least, was not invented from whole cloth.

Timing: clearly, this is a book that could only have been written in hindsight. What might the jury have made, with the benefit of hindsight, of the curious tale of David Hoffman? We now know that he gave the same story to police (the Vagabonds' Halloween Party, the costume rental, the telephone calls immediately after the Kitchener clubhouse raid), that he gave, under oath, on the witness stand. The proof of his story was in the possession of the police all the time; only sheer coincidence ever brought the proof of Hoffman's testimony to light.

Timing: the one key Crown witness who refused to be interviewed for this book was David Gillispie whose "fat fucker" testimony stands out oddly as one of the few things that the accused (Rick, Gary, and Merv) flatly deny ever took place. Although the "fat fucker" remark entered the record of the police investigation within hours of the shooting (on the morning of October 19th, 1978), a full month elapsed until Gillispie was shown the photo array on November 18th. Why would police investigators allow a month to pass before showing their first, best witness the pictures of the suspects?

Timing: if Lorne Campbell had been a "put-up job," whose testimony was concocted with the protection of the Canada Evidence Act to discredit the police investigation and the Crown case, why would he call this writer seven years later of his own accord and volunteer to help in the preparation of this book?

Timing: and the last, greatest proof of a miscarriage of justice, a proof that has taken the sweep of many years. The jury could not have known that two of the men they sentenced to life would be the first men to graduate from Queen's University from a prison cell; could not have known that each of them would steadfastly maintain his innocence despite tremendous pressure, from his first day of imprisonment to his last; could not have known that each would, in his own way, make some kind of positive contribution to prison or general society despite his conviction that he was wrongfully imprisoned. Proof of innocence? Perhaps not. But proof of the right to be taken seriously, surely.

So the compass needle begins to veer sharply, away from the accused and towards a conspiracy of quite a different brotherhood. There is, I submit, stronger evidence of a police conspiracy in this case than there is of a biker conspiracy.

Among the salient points:

- The failure to disclose the tapes regarding David Hoffman;
- The intimidation of Roger Davey to give testimony against his will, testimony that was almost certainly perjured;
- The willingness to prosecute Comeau as the gunman even though there are strong indications (McReelis's discussions with Comeau's mother, Cousens' close inspection of Gary's arm on the night of his arrest) that police knew or suspected that Comeau had in fact been shot;
- The disappearance of Gary Comeau's black leather jacket immediately following the police clubhouse raid.

Book Two is based on the preliminary and trial testimony of the officers involved, on interviews with now Superintendent Colin Cousens and Inspector Terry Hall, and on the recollections of Rick and Sharon Sauvé and Gary Comeau.

Books Three and Four are based on extensive interviews with Bernie

Guindon and Bill Lavoie, along with newspaper clippings from the 1960s and '70s.

Books Five and Six are based, of course, on the transcripts of the court proceedings, as well as the memories of Terry O'Hara, Bruce Affleck, and Howard Kerbel. I have attempted to re-create both legal hearings as fully and fairly as possible, so that the reader may draw her or his own conclusions from the evidence.

Book Seven draws heavily on the recollections of Brian Greenspan and Terry O'Hara, on the extensive documentation that was prepared prior to the hearing before the Ontario Court of Appeal, and on Gary Comeau's own correspondence. Book Eight is based on Gary Comeau's actual prison records and, obviously, on my own observations.

In writing my own book I have found myself down in the books of many, many others, and I wish to acknowledge them here.

I am, first of all, indebted to the Satan's Choice Motorcycle Club, without whose co-operation, at least by many individual members, this book truly could not have been written. They were at least as wary of a lone scribbler from Sudbury as he was of them, and they lent their efforts, not out of any desire for publicity about their club and its activities, so much as out of a genuine conviction that their brothers in this case were totally innocent of the crime for which they are convicted. The following current or former club members and their wives opened their homes, and often their hearts, to a greenhorn reporter: Lorne and Charmaine Campbell, Bernie and Angelique Guindon, and most especially, Bill and Dawn Lavoie. I am also indebted to these current or former members of the club: Ron Losier, Claude Morin, Larry Vallentyne, Brian Babcock, Gordy van Haarlem, and of course, David Hoffman.

The men convicted of the murder of Bill Matiyek are exceedingly fortunate to have around them a network of truly steadfast friends and family. Without the hospitality, encouragement, and unflagging support of the following, I could never have finished this book: Betty and Gene King, Mitch and Carol Crosby, Rolly and Tammy Sauvé, Pierre and Adeline Sauvé, Dr. Carole Clapperton and George Bailey, Beth (McLean) McLeod, Sharon and Angie Sauvé, and Claire Culhane.

A number of lawyers helped me to understand their own particular brotherhood, including Terry O'Hara, Bruce Affleck, Howard Kerbel, Brian

Greenspan, Joe Bastos, and, closer to home, Phillip Zylberberg. Special thanks to Mr. Justice Coulter Osborne and his Osgoode Hall secretary, Mrs. Norma Pullen.

I am also grateful to Superintendent Cousens and Inspector Hall of the OPP for their co-operation, as well as to Sheriff's Officer Ernie Baxter of the County of Middlesex (London, Ontario) Sheriff's office.

Various Correctional Service Canada officials helped to accommodate my necessary habit of strange and inconvenient prison visiting hours, and I wish to thank the staffs of Collins Bay, Joyceville, and Frontenac Institutions, particularly Kenneth Payne, the former warden at CBI, Yvonne Latta, the former warden at Joyceville, and Classifications Officers Harley Smith, Donna Froats, and Sue Sinclair. Special thanks, too, to CSC public affairs officers Dennis Curtis, Dennis Findlay, and John Vandoremalen, and to Alice Gay at CBI.

A good number of Port Hope area residents agreed to be interviewed on what is still, for them, an extremely painful subject, and I thank especially Cathy Cotgrave Peart, Roger and Diane Davey, Lawrence Leon, Linda Leon, Rick and Gary Galbraith, and Larry Sauvé, along with former Port Hope resident Gayle Thompson.

I'm also indebted to Laura Ann Lippold and Mac Haig of London, to Bill Glaister of Ottawa, and to my friend Rich Orlandini. Besides Mac and Bill, a number of other journalists helped me along the way: Colin MacKenzie, the former City Editor of the Toronto Globe and Mail, Globe reporter Kirk Makin, and my long-time editor at the Globe Don Hendry, as well as my old friend Bob Sarti at the Vancouver Sun.

Like all books, this one has been a truly collective effort involving the labor and support of a number of people at Macmillan of Canada. I must especially thank Doug Gibson, Macmillan's former publisher, who saw the potential in an extremely rough two-chapter draft, and to his successor, Linda McKnight, who followed through on Doug's commitments. Thanks too to Maggie MacDonald, Pat Kennedy, and especially to my editor, Sheldon Fischer.

Besides Macmillan, a number of people and institutions provided financial support for this project. Among them: the Ontario Arts Council, Doug Yeo and Eija Hodge of the Sudbury Regional Credit Union, and friends Sherry Drysdale, and Mike Atkins.

Family and friends made life bearable through some lean and hungry times during this project even if, as I fear, I was not always able to reciprocate. Thanks to Terry Pender, Harvey Wyers, Selina Saumur, and Diane McDonald, and always and forever to my wife Ruth Reyno and my daughters Julia and Melanie for their forebearance and sacrifice.

It is my most fervent hope that this story will not end here. I believe that the case of Bill Matiyek must be reopened, and that the police must regard it as what it truly is: an unsolved murder. I further believe that an independent investigator should be appointed to closely examine the police investigation that followed Bill Matiyek's death. Finally, I hope that all of the people who know the true facts in this case will now have the courage to step forward and speak out.

The myriad of unanswered questions that still linger, nearly a decade later, must be resolved. Gary Comeau, Rick Sauvé, Merv Blaker, and Jeff McLeod ask nothing more, and the family and friends of Bill Matiyek deserve nothing less.

M.E.L.

December, 1987

Onwatin Lake Road

AFTERWORD TO THE 2013 EDITION

In the spring of 1988 when *Conspiracy of Brothers* was first published, I was sent on a nationwide publicity tour to promote the book, a task I greeted with apprehension on two fronts.

The first was when the publisher's national publicity rep sent me on my merry way with a figurative pat on the head and a warning: "Mick, don't expect any of the media people who will be interviewing you to have actually read the book." Instead, I found a remarkably opposite outcome— not only had my radio/television/newspaper interviewers actually read *Conspiracy* in its entirety—but they showed up eagerly clutching their copy, anxious to pursue a particular, often obscure, detail or character or theory. Clearly, the story of *Conspiracy* captured the imaginations of these scores of early readers, as it eventually would many thousands more in the years to come. Needless to say, I was, and am, immensely gratified by this reception.

My second concern was how I would be received on the many open-line radio shows I was booked into across the country. As a former American, born and bred, from a country where outlaw mythology was celebrated in song and legend, I feared the public reaction to this story in a country that— and this, too, has changed in the twenty-five years since—fairly worshipped its police, especially the once-hallowed Royal Canadian Mounted Police.

But this on-air clash of national sensibilities never developed.

Oh, there were skeptical callers who accused me of being "pro-biker." But there were also, to my surprise, an equal number of callers who'd been well treated by their local bike club, or who had witnessed police harass-ment of the club firsthand.

In the months that followed its release, *Conspiracy*, much to my amaze-ment, took on a life of its own—becoming a textbook in college courses ranging from Criminal Justice to Social Welfare, and the subject for a ballad, "Justice in Ontario," by American outlaw country rocker Steve Earle. The book has even, I've been told, served as a training manual for police recruits and newly hired prison guards.

From left: Rick Sauvé, Jeff McLeod, Steve Earle, and Lorne Campbell (Michele Sauvé).

THE RISE—AND DECLINE—OF THE PORT HOPE EIGHT

WHEN RICK SAUVÉ FINALLY called, he chose his words carefully. After *Conspiracy* was published, I'd kept in touch with the book's key figures intermittently at best, and close to a decade had elapsed since I'd last spoken to any of them.

"Rick! How ya doin', man?"

"I'm back inside, Mick."

"*What?* But how—?" My heart sank at the news that Sauvé, of all people, would wind up back in prison.

"I'm *working* inside. I'm working with lifers. I go back inside now almost every day."

I felt a flood of relief, but not surprise.

Of course, Rick Sauvé, of all people, would be back behind bars. Of all the young men I'd met during that extraordinary period of research (1984–86) on *Conspiracy,* of course it would be Rick Sauvé, even after serving over a decade behind the gray walls of the Canadian prison system for a crime he never committed, who could not simply walk away upon his release, happy, even eager, to put the entire nightmarish experience behind him.

None of us are young men now. We are all, in fact, in our sixties, and some of us (Rick, David "Tee Hee" Hoffman, Lorne Campbell) are even grandfathers.

Twenty-five years have elapsed since *Conspiracy* was first published in 1988. That's a long time to know someone, and a person's character arc is well and truly revealed over such a span. During those years I have been asked time and again, "Where are Gary and Rick? *How* are Gary and Rick? Are they still in jail?"

The short answer is no, they are not still in jail.

Both Rick Sauvé and Gary "Nutty" Comeau successfully sought their early release under the so-called faint hope clause that allowed convicted murderers sentenced to "life to 25" to apply for early release after serving fifteen years of their sentence. Both of them, to this day, steadfastly maintain their innocence of the crime, and both, to this day, steadfastly refuse to name the man who pulled the trigger.

The publication of *Conspiracy* stirred things up. A grassroots organization using a variety of rallying cries—"Free the Port Hope Eight," "Justice for Nutty and Rick"—was formed, spearheaded by Gary's sister, the irrepressible Carol Crosby, and Betty King, his mother. They were joined by a handful of total strangers—mostly female and mostly from Ontario—who had read the book and wanted to do their bit as Canadian citizens to right this apparent wrong. The committee published a newsletter that was circulated widely, eventually reaching subscribers in the United States, Great Britain, Sweden, and even Japan.

Conspiracy even stirred up interest on Parliament Hill, with then–Burnaby NDP MP Svend Robinson and Liberal Montreal-area (and former Trudeau-era Cabinet member) MP Warren Allmand calling for a review of the case of the Port Hope Eight. They were joined by then–Liberal MP Christine Stewart, who represented the Port Hope–Cobourg area, where so many of the events in the book took place. Their pleas were largely ignored by the Progressive Conservative government of Brian Mulroney, and eventually the grassroots organizations withered away.

Among those who were stirred to action by *Conspiracy* and by the teachings of prisoners' rights advocate Claire Culhane was a young coed at the University of Ottawa, a graduate student in criminal justice (and one of Canada's most fervent Bruce Springsteen fans). Her name was Michele Bradley. Like many of her classmates, Bradley was fired with an idealistic fervor to reform the Canadian prison system, or, at the very least, to improve the lot of prisoners by visiting them regularly, as a living reminder that they were not alone, not forgotten.

In 1989 Bradley's name was added to Rick Sauvé's visitors' list.

THIS MOVIE IS NOT OVER

IN THE WAKE of the success of *Conspiracy*, I was invited to Toronto to speak before the founding convention of an organization that would focus on, and fight to overturn, the convictions of individuals who had been wrongfully convicted by the Canadian criminal justice system. Donald Marshall, then the poster boy for wrongly convicted Canadians, would be in attendance. So would David Milgaard, who had spent twenty-three years in prison for a murder he never committed. Rubin "Hurricane" Carter, subject of Bob Dylan's famous song "Hurricane," would be there. The new organization, the brain child of a Toronto criminal defense lawyer named James Lockyer, was called the Association in Defence of the Wrongly Convicted, and would later become better known by its less unwieldy acronym AIDWYC (pronounce AID-*wick*.)

The convention, in a downtown Toronto hotel in early 1995, quickly became a rallying point for supporters of the Port Hope Eight. Betty King and Gary's sister Carol were there, as was Larry Hurren, and even Lorne Campbell. We huddled quickly the afternoon before I was due to give my morning presentation.

At the end of our impromptu meeting Lorne took me aside and asked, in his quiet way, "Mick, what can I do to help?"

The question took me aback.

I thanked Lorne, and assured him I could make the presentation on my own, that everything was under control. He nodded, but I could see this was something that Lorne, in his ineffable way, was pondering very seriously indeed.

The following morning the hotel ballroom was packed with hundreds of distinguished members of the Canadian criminal bar, the *crème de la crème* of the Toronto legal profession, and even a smattering of judges. It was an august, well-heeled assemblage if ever there was one—and, in its very midst, I spotted Lorne Campbell, wearing his full Satan's Choice colours, grinning at me expectantly.

I quickly outlined the salient facts of the case of the Port Hope Eight for the multitude before fastening my gaze on Lorne. "Even now," I concluded, "two members of the Port Hope Eight, Rick Sauvé and Gary Comeau, continue to languish behind bars, and the other six have served nearly seventy years collectively for a murder none of them committed, while the actual killer, who confessed to the crime but has never been charged or convicted, sits among you this very day! I'd like to introduce Mr. Lorne Campbell!"

Lorne stood up right on cue, in his full Choice regalia, not taking a bow, exactly, but representing, nevertheless. I can honestly report the audience did not know whether to shit or go blind. What does one do, on a fine Sunday morning in downtown Toronto, when it is revealed that one has a killer sitting in one's midst, a killer who has managed to elude, despite his own best efforts, the eagle eye and long arm of Canadian law enforcement *through the guileful ploy of confessing repeatedly to the crime?*

The crowd broke into polite, if timorous, applause.

Due in no small measure to Lorne Campbell, the story of the Port Hope Eight lives stubbornly on. What is arguably the most egregious case of wrongful conviction in the annals of Canadian jurisprudence stubbornly refuses to be swept under the judicial rug. The fact you are reading this is further evidence of ongoing interest in the long train of events that have followed that fateful October night in a Port Hope, Ontario, bar nearly forty years ago.

No, clearly this movie is not over.

To be fair, the Canadian criminal justice system did respond, after a fashion, to the disclosures of *Conspiracy*, and to the protests it inspired. Within months of the book's appearance, then–Justice Minister (and soon-to-be Prime Minister) Kim Campbell appointed a special investigator, a junior Crown attorney in her department named Don Avison, to re-examine the case. Avison interviewed everyone involved, however tangentially. He spoke to Bernie Guindon. He spoke with Lorne Campbell. I was even summoned to Ottawa for a sit-down with a youthful and earnest-seeming minion of Kim Campbell's justice department apparatus. The episode kindled my own hopes that the justice system might see the error of its ways and learn from its own mistakes. Those hopes were dashed when, in December 1990, Minister Campbell released her formal written conclusions regarding the case of *Regina v. McLeod et al.* She insisted that the convictions were warranted on the evidence and that the guilty parties had received justice. No further action was contemplated or indeed warranted. Implicit in her findings was disbelief in Lorne Campbell's confession of guilt.

Campbell's decision made national news, in a minor sort of way. The *Globe and Mail's* crime beat writer Timothy Appleby filed on the story. His account contained, in the clearest possible terms, a public confession of guilt from Lorne Campbell. Here was no protection of the Canada Evidence Act. Here once again, but this time on the news pages of "Canada's National Newspaper," in the cold light of day, was Lorne Campbell's confession of guilt, clear and unequivocal.

Lorne Campbell says he killed Bill Matiyek because he feared if he didn't, Bill Matiyek would have killed Rick Sauvé. Whether Matiyek himself would have pulled the trigger on that tension-filled night we will never know, but Lorne has continued to accept accountability in the Matiyek slaying, most recently, and notably, in the newly published account of his life, *Unrepentant*. None of the Port Hope Eight is still in prison, so it can no longer be argued that Lorne has manufactured his confession to somehow exonerate his Club brothers.

I know Lorne Campbell. I personally believe his honour (and yes, even outlaw bikers can be honourable men) has been deeply affronted by the justice system's stubborn, even willful, refusal to credit his confession, not least because such acceptance would be a tacit admission that a terrible miscarriage of justice took place.

So who's the liar now?

"SLOW DOWN AND ENJOY LIFE"

MICHELE BRADLEY'S VISITS to Rick Sauvé soon blossomed into romance, and on January 5, 1990, they married. She was waiting at the gate when, on the morning of March 1, 1995, he was finally released from prison. And she was by his side when, only moments later, Sauvé had his first brush with the law "on the outside." The two were, quite literally, speeding away from the prison when they unwittingly tripped a remote-controlled speed-trap radar gun. The citation arrived in the mail days later, and Michele snapped a digital photo of it, which remains on her computer's hard drive to this day.

"We just couldn't get away from that prison fast enough," she laughs.

Rick still laughs out loud when he sees the generic, computer-generated admonition that accompanied the speeding ticket: "Slow down and enjoy life," it cautioned.

In the summer of 2004 I finally reciprocated several visits Rick had made to my home in Sudbury during the late 1990s. I found Rick and Michele living deep in farm country on the very distant outskirts of Lindsay, Ontario. Theirs is a modernized old farmhouse with high ceilings, gorgeous millwork, and hardwood floors. Michele tends a sizable herb garden in the backyard. Lavender is a particular favourite, to be dried, crushed and folded into the soaps Michele makes by hand in her basement workshop.

The place is filled with cats, including the innumerable strays, many of them arriving starving and sickly, that the couple have taken in and nursed back to health over the years.

Michele was still a lot like the idealistic coed I'd met years before— vivacious, energetic, charismatic, and still a huge Springsteen fan. And her idealism had not wavered.

Twice daily she was making the ninety-minute drive between her home and Toronto's notorious Jane-Finch area, where she worked mostly with troubled youth, overseeing a restorative justice program that offered an alternative to incarceration as a real-life approach to criminal justice. A primary feature of restorative justice is that it affords the victims of crime the opportunity to directly and publicly confront the perpetrator of the crime that affected them. "Did you find this approach a useful alternative to incarceration?" I recently asked Michele.

Michele and Rick Sauvé, summer 2004 (Mick Lowe).

"I would go way beyond—I can't think of a word that would go way beyond 'useful' . . . I think it's an absolutely necessary option that should be available to people . . . I never say it's the best way to go because it's not for everybody, but in the traditional system victims and offenders alike are left isolated for a long, long time . . . I can't tell you what a powerful, powerful, process that is—remarkable, remarkable things happen when people are given a safe say and are supported to say what they need to say, so that other people can hear it, and it's just remarkable what people are capable of doing, and the understanding and compassion they can bring to those processes."

The funding for Michele's program was slashed by the federal government in 2012, and she now subsists through a number of part-time pastimes—her soap enterprise, called Gridley's, her weekly shift at a local animal shelter. She has decided to abandon her criminal justice–reform work, at least temporarily.

By the time you read this, Rick and Michele will have been married for more than twenty-three years.

THE LOST TRIBE OF BEAVER CREEK

RICK SAUVÉ DID NOT take lightly his decision in 1998 to return to prison. Only after discussing the matter with Michele and sleeping on it for several nights did he accept the job offered by Lifeline, a tripartite organization co-sponsored by the St. Leonard's Society of Canada, Correctional Service, and the Parole Board of Canada.

Lifeline was premised on the belief that everyone—the Canadian public, the correctional system, and the prisoners themselves—would benefit by helping inmates doing "life bits" for first- and second-degree murder ease back into society through in-prison counselling and practical, post-release support, including the system of Society-operated halfway houses scattered across Canada.

Rick's job was to provide counselling to lifers at Fenbrook Institution, a medium-security federal prison outside Gravenhurst. The prison complex includes a minimum-security institution, Beaver Creek. He would also drive newly released prisoners to halfway houses throughout Ontario. Sometimes those prisoners were headed for Sudbury, which is how Rick and I enjoyed occasional visits during the late 1990s.

"This was such a worthwhile program," Rick says of Lifeline, which also was cancelled by the Harper government in the fall of 2012. But the work took a tremendous personal toll. "It was really, really, really hard, because I started having prison dreams, you know, sometimes I'd wake up and I wasn't sure if I was back inside, or on the outside. It put me back in prison. . . . If I didn't believe it was such a worthwhile program I think I'd've quit doing it.

"But I believe that program was the best program we have—or had—not just for the prisoners, but for the prisons—for everybody. We were a resource for the community. We still get calls from guys we've worked with nearly every week. The first thing we say is 'Are you okay?' and then we'll talk about, you know, life on the outside.

"It was a really, really great program—it was cost effective—it changed lives. We saved taxpayers money, we made the community a safer place— not just for the guys coming out, but for the community, and I just have *no idea* why they cancelled it."

In the fall of 2012 a couple of the individual St. Leonard's Society operations (Windsor and Peterborough) managed to cobble together funding to keep Lifeline on life support until the end of March 2013, but after that the outlook is bleak, as it is, in Rick's view, for much of the prison system. Since his release, I notice, Rick has begun to see prison and prison-related issues within the overall context of public safety. "It's just not good public safety policy to release guys back into the community without any support," he warns. "What we were doing at Lifeline was walking with them back into the community, making sure they were safe and settled in. For us, it was always about the safety of the community, and about the health of the people we were bringing back into the community."

Even long after his release, Rick continued to confront the Canadian criminal justice system and the prison system itself. The denial of the right to vote to Canadian prisoners, referenced in the closing chapters of *Conspiracy*, continued to rankle, and in 1988 Rick took the first step in a process that would make him semi-famous: he hired a lawyer and charged the federal government with violating the Canadian Charter of Rights and Freedoms by denying federal prisoners the right to vote in federal elections.

Convicted felons sentenced to prison are, without question, stripped of their physical freedom through incarceration. But they remain Canadian citizens, nonetheless. Eventually they will all return to society. Even incarcerated Canadian citizens, argued Rick's lawyer, retain the fundamental right to the franchise vouchsafed to all citizens by the Charter. Surely it is in the best interest of society to maintain this slender thread of decency, of interest on the part of convicts in the commonweal of which they will, inevitably and eventually, once again become a part. The government, of course, contested Rick's case, and the lawsuit spent years ricocheting through the courts, being rejected at one level, only to be appealed to, and upheld by, another level. Eventually *Sauvé v. Canada*, which was beginning to garner international attention, made it all the way to the Supreme Court of Canada, which upheld Rick's argument in a unanimous decision in 1993.

The Harper era has, for the most part, been a time of mean-spirited and misguided policy in Canadian corrections, Rick Sauvé maintains, not least because the architects of that policy are so out of touch with prison reality. As a result, initiatives intended to make the average Canadian "safe from crime" endanger us further.

One example is the so-called zero tolerance policy regarding drug use in Canadian prisons. Not only is it doomed to fail, Rick predicts, but it will eventually endanger the health of the Canadian public, including many individuals who are not, and never have been, behind bars.

"When it comes to sanctions," Rick explains, "the policy makes no distinction between the kinds of drugs used. Marijuana stays in the system longest, making it easier to detect, so guys [in prison] are turning more to drugs like heroin and cocaine, which are metabolized more quickly and are therefore harder to test for."

This transition to hard drugs and intravenous use means more exposure to HIV/AIDS and hepatitis C, "and so guys are more likely to infect their loved ones when they come out," Rick concludes.

The "get tough on crime" policies, wrapped into the draconian "anti-crime omnibus bill" passed in the Commons in early 2012, have targeted the work and livelihoods of enlightened prison activists such as Rick and Michele like heat-seeking missiles. These measures, intended to make Canada a safer place, instead jeopardize public safety over the long term, Rick predicts. He is greatly alarmed by the mandated policy of longer sentences, which will lead to prison overcrowding and double-bunking.

Increasingly now when he visits Fenbrook, Rick sees inmates who have aged in place—canes, walkers, and wheelchairs are now everyday sights—"and I wonder *why are they even here?*" The prison system is ill-equipped to cope with this tidal wave of aging inmates—cells are already so small that accommodating a wheelchair-bound prisoner in a double-bunking situation is a practical impossibility, for example.

And then there is the Lost Tribe of Beaver Creek or, as Rick prefers to call it, "The Ethnic Cleansing of the North."

He noticed early on that one particular group of prisoners never participated in "socials" at Beaver Creek—events where the loved ones of prisoners are allowed into the institution to hang out with their imprisoned husbands, sons or brothers. The excluded group are Inuit prisoners from the Canadian Arctic. Many thousands of miles from home, they rarely see their families, for whom the airfare for a prison visit is prohibitively expensive. The full enormity of what he was witnessing didn't fully hit Rick until the day he was driving an Inuk prisoner to a halfway house in Ottawa.

"I asked him what he did for a living back home," Rick recalls. "He said he was a hunter and a soapstone carver. Then I saw a deer, and I pointed it out, and he didn't see it. I saw a great horned owl up in a tree, and he didn't see that, either. I said to him 'I thought you were a hunter! How come you can't see any of these animals?' He said "'Cause all the trees are in the way.' That's when it dawned on me that they were from an environment where there were no trees, that they were brought into this foreign environment. It was just total isolation, and I felt so sad. . . ."

Removing men from their families as an individual punishment for a crime is a penalty Rick understood well. But removing an offender from his natural environment, his culture and language, and even from his accustomed food, was a form of total isolation that verged not only on cruel and unusual punishment of the individual, but also, by tearing families apart for prolonged periods, constituted in Rick's mind a form of government-imposed ethnocide.

RIP: SCMC, TERRENCE GORDON "TERRY" O'HARA, WILLIAM "MR. BILL" LAVOIE, LARRY "BEAVER" HURREN, CLAIRE CULHANE

THE SATAN'S CHOICE MOTORCYCLE CLUB would survive into the new millennium, but only just.

In 2000 the club founded by Bernie Guindon nearly half a century earlier became part of a major "patch-over" that saw many of the independent Ontario outlaw clubs join the mighty, American-based Hells Angels MC. It was a move that played to mixed reviews among many of the old Choice hands.

David "Tee Hee" Hoffman declined to make the switch. He had his hands full at home in Waterloo—his wife was very ill with the cancer that would claim her life in 2001, leaving Tee Hee alone to raise their two daughters, aged ten and eight, which he has done. The former outlaw biker also developed himself into one of Ontario's preeminent weightlifters, and he soon became an early, and outspoken, opponent of the widespread drug use he saw in his sport. The consumption of steroids and other performance-enhancing drugs in all levels of competitive weightlifting is commonplace, and widely accepted by many, but not Tee Hee. Today he even inveighs against the consumption of so-called energy drinks, because they may contain traces of banned substances that can cause an athlete to fail doping tests.

Tee Hee's eldest daughter entered Wilfrid Laurier University in the fall of 2012, a fact of which he is very proud. She still lives at home. He is currently the president of the Ontario Powerlifting Association. Even though an arthritic hip makes it difficult for him to climb aboard his Harley, Tee Hee still rides, and every fall he and a group of fellow Harley owners organize a "run" to raise funds to support cancer research in the Kingston-Waterloo area. Over the years, Tee Hee estimates, they have raised well over one hundred thousand dollars for the cause. The brotherhood of the bike remains, even if the brotherhood of the patch does not.

So, too, with Lorne Campbell. Like Tee Hee, Lorne, who at sixty-four suffers from spinal stenosis and now often walks with a cane, sometimes needs help to climb onto his bike. "It's embarrassing," he admits. But the love of the Harley outweighs vanity, and Lorne, too, is a frequent participant in charity runs, even if it means long rides in bad weather that will leave him laid up for days afterward.

Merv Blaker has remained pretty much the Merv Blaker I met in prison—soft-spoken, kindly, imperturbable. He now lives on a small farm in the Rice Lake area south of Peterborough, where he keeps a small herd of cattle and a few horses.

Lost prison years have left him—outwardly at least—with few scars, one of which was a bum knee he had to have replaced in 2011. Blaker is convinced this painful infirmity stemmed from his years as a near-manic prison jogger, a form of physical exertion that provided some release from the tension, depravity, and sudden violence he was exposed to in prison, all of which was fundamentally at odds with his own easygoing, peaceful nature. I remember visiting Merv when he was at Joyceville, which had at the time one of the highest security classifications of all the Kingston-area prisons, and exuded an especially mean and nasty vibe.

He has found peace now tending to his livestock, raising his ten-year-old son, Joe, and tinkering incessantly with the motors of cars, trucks, and motorcycles in need of repair. The latter includes a now-vintage Harley-Davidson Sportster he purchased in 1975, before his arrest. It is no small tribute to Merv's skill as a mechanic that the bike still runs, carrying him to the odd charity run and biker funeral.

Terry O'Hara, the Falstaff-like figure who represented Merv Blaker at trial, was appointed to the provincial bench in 1995. Clearly the Kingston lawyer had distinguished himself during his brief career at the criminal bar. But after a short stint on the bench O'Hara succumbed to congestive heart disease in 2004. I have no doubt that one of his greatest regrets at the end of his brilliant, too-brief career was the performance of the defence team at *Regina v. McLeod et al.*

Terry O'Hara was fifty-five.

William "Mr. Bill" Lavoie, early Choice member, and true Club believer to the bitter end, was killed in a motorcycle accident. Bill's oral history and photo collection were invaluable to the narrative of *Conspiracy*. I owe him much. Wherever you are, brother . . .

(If you're wondering about Jeff McLeod, I am too: I was not able to track him down.)

Like Mr. Bill, Larry "Beaver" Hurren, a member of the Port Hope Eight, was killed on his Harley in the late 1990s. For reasons of his own, Larry opted to take himself out of the picture when I was researching *Conspiracy*, and thus he remained a minor character. He is survived by a daughter, Shona.

Claire Culhane, prisoners' rights activist, anti-war crusader, and life-long social justice warrior, died peacefully at her home in Vancouver in 1996, at the age of seventy-eight. Many a Canadian prison cell has been just that much darker, the outlook that much bleaker, without her tireless efforts to shine light on conditions inside our nation's prisons.

LIFE LESSONS

SHORTLY AFTER THE PUBLICATION of *Conspiracy*, Claire Culhane's family asked me to write her authorized biography. I jumped at the chance. *One Woman Army: The Life of Claire Culhane* was published in 1992. It says a great deal about this extraordinary matriarch, who was then in her seventies, that her biography is actually more action-packed than *Conspiracy*.

Never one for repeating myself, whether in subject or even in genre, I went on to tell another once-in-a-lifetime true story, about the dramatic struggle over the development of the rich Voisey's Bay nickel deposit in northern Labrador, in my third book, *Premature Bonanza: Stand-off at Voisey's Bay*. I am currently at work on a novel set in Sudbury in 1963. The working title is *The Raids: A Novel of the Cold War*.

I am not, however, who I would have expected to be, writing this coda to *Conspiracy of Brothers*—an old man on a riverbank. On the morning of May 1, 2008, I was struck by a major ischemic stroke caused by a sudden, nearly lethal, near-total blockage of my right carotid artery; as a consequence, my left side is paralyzed, my left arm and left leg nearly useless. Fortunately, I was, and am, right dominant and my speech and my cognition were largely unaffected.

Still more fortunately, my life post-stroke has been blessed by the presence of an extraordinary woman, my beautiful wife Anita. Part muse, part fixer, part guardian angel, part warrior, she has been my constant, ever-dependable companion. Despite my doddering, ungainly gait (I walk now with a quad cane, swinging my left leg from my hip), she walks confidently by my side, head held high, shortening her own stride to match my own—the very embodiment of courage and natural grace.

In these gray, foreshortened days of November, I often feel I'm living one of Rick Sauve's "prison dreams"—dreams, it turns out, that Gary Comeau still has, too—dark, drab affairs where everything is lived in black-and-white. But then Anita walks in and the world opens before me once again, full of life and colour. She is at once the most competent and sweetly generous person I've ever known. But despite her Herculean efforts, caregiver burnout forced us to realize, sadly, that my post-strike condition was more than even Anita could handle, and I was forced to leave the home on my beloved Vermillion River where all my books were written, in October 2010. I have lived ever since in a nursing home in Sudbury.

Despite everything, I find myself in close agreement with the life lessons propounded by Tee Hee and Rick, who have, in the end, concluded that, despite the lost years in prison for a crime they did not commit, and despite the encroaching infirmities of old age, we are blessed to be loved, and to be alive. Amen to that.

But I also agree with Michele Sauvé, whom I overhear speaking to a visitor just as I am about to leave their place, and who reminds me once again that this movie is not—and cannot be—over.

"People think, 'Oh, there's no one left in jail, so it's okay,'" she says of the case of the Port Hope Eight. And then, suddenly, her brown eyes well with tears. "But it's not okay."

"LET RIGHT PREVAIL"

EVEN AFTER ALL THESE YEARS Gary Comeau, who has returned to Scarborough where he works as a freelance courier, continues his tireless quest for exoneration of the conviction that he in any way planned and carried out the death of Bill Matiyek. He now has an AIDWYC-appointed lawyer who is helping in this quest. And Gary Comeau is almost as rah rah as ever, still Nutty after all these years. ·

His manic nature has been tempered somewhat by his own brush with mortality—a mild heart attack in December 2008, which resulted in the surgical implant of two stents to bypass two blocked arteries and, later, a pacemaker. But this infirmity, from which he is now fully recovered, has only made him a more seasoned and patient campaigner on his own behalf. He socializes often with a number of individuals whom AIDWYC has already exonerated. As a self-declared "wrongly convicted person" himself, Gary identifies strongly with people like Romeo Phillion and Tammy Marquardt, who have, with the help of AIDWYC, been released from prison and won judicial recognition that theirs were cases of wrongful conviction. They have received, or are awaiting, financial compensation for the lost years. Gary, of course, has won no such recognition, and so he lives a kind of existentially surreal double life. But he soldiers resolutely on with "The Case."

At the very least, Gary and AIDWYC's efforts have so far yielded what reporters call a "document dump"—a new Crown disclosure of a rich trove of heretofore unreleased documents pertaining to the Matiyek murder investigation. Just what is in the documents is all very hush-hush, Gary confides.

Oh, there are whispers—suggestions the new disclosure contains the raw, working notes of the police investigators handling the Matiyek case, conclusive new evidence that proves what Gary and his mother have known all along—that the police knew Gary was shot that night, even as they were presenting sworn evidence that he was the gunman.

In the end, it is more than a little ironic that Gary "Nutty" Comeau, the once-chatty, manic, hyper man-child Nutty, full-patch member of the Satan's Choice Motorcycle Club, should be the Last Man Standing on the case, the last person attempting to unravel the impossibly complicated skein of events that flowed from the night of October 18, 1978.

But it is so.

In the course of my own inquiries, I happened across the motto of the Law Society of Upper Canada: "Let Right Prevail." It is a principle, presumably, that every lawyer, every judge, every Crown prosecutor, every distinguished "officer of the court" who touched the Matiyek case has sworn, on his sacred honour, to uphold.

But it is Gary Comeau who, against all odds, best embodies this oath when it comes to the death of Bill Matiyek.

Other members of the Port Hope Eight are not sanguine about Nutty's quest. "I really don't think they care," Rick Sauvé says evenly of the legal professionals who have accepted the flame, on the public's behalf, to "Let Right Prevail."

And he may be right. But personally I am loath to ever entirely dismiss the efforts of Gary Comeau. It was Gary, after all, who solved the mystery of the missing third bullet. And it was Gary who, in a prison visit with Claire

Culhane, managed to kite his own stranger-than-fiction story out over the prison walls and into the hands of an obscure but ambitious wannabe author in Sudbury, Ontario, of all places.

Say what you will of Nutty Comeau, the man has been right before.

Let Right Prevail.

THE VISITOR
October 2012
Pioneer Manor, Sudbury, Ontario

INDEX

MICK LOWE was born in Omaha, Nebraska, and immigrated to Canada in 1970. Lowe's journalism has appeared in a range of publications such as *Maclean's, Canadian Business, Canadian Lawyer,* the *Globe and Mail,* and on CBC Radio. He followed his first non-fiction book, *Conspiracy of Brothers,* which was a national bestseller and winner of the Arthur Ellis Award for Best Non-Fiction Crime Book, with a biography of prisoner rights advocate Claire Culhane and then a book on the rush to exploit the Voisey's Bay nickel deposit, *Premature Bonanza: Standoff at Voisey's Bay.* In 2008 he suffered a stroke that interrupted his writing life, among other things. In early 2012, he restarted his writing career with this twenty-fifth-anniversary edition of *Conspiracy of Brothers.* He lives in Sudbury, where he is at work on a novel set in the region in the early 1960s.